Morphological Investigations

Editors: Jim Blevins, Petar Milin, Michael Ramscar

In this series:

The semantic transparency of English compound nouns

Martin Schäfer

language
science
press

Martin Schäfer. 2018. *The semantic transparency of English compound nouns* (Morphological Investigations 3). Berlin: Language Science Press.

This book is the revised version of the author's habilitation, Friedrich-Schiller-Universität Jena, 2017

DOI:10.5281/zenodo.1134595
Source code available from www.github.com/langsci/153
Collaborative reading: paperhive.org/documents/remote?type=langsci&id=153

Cover and concept of design: Ulrike Harbort
Typesetting: Martin Schäfer
Proofreading: Plinio A. Barbosa, Jose Poblete Bravo, Merlijn Breunesse, Stefan Hartmann, Martin Hilpert, Gianina Iordachioaia, Timm Lichte, Ahmet Bilal Özdemir, Steve Pepper, Katja Politt, Valeria Quochi, Edalat Shekari, Andrew Spencer, Carola Trips, Jeroen van de Weijer, Amr Zawawy
Fonts: Linux Libertine, Arimo, DejaVu Sans Mono
Typesetting software: XƎLATEX

Language Science Press
Unter den Linden 6
10099 Berlin, Germany
langsci-press.org

Storage and cataloguing done by FU Berlin

Freie Universität Berlin

Dedicated to the next generation (in order of appearance):
Charlotte, Henriette, Anton, Magdalena, Moritz, Henrike,
Emma, Lene, Mathilde, Marie, Simon, Anne, Theo, Ole,
Jakob

Contents

Contents

Acknowledgments

My first thanks go to Barbara Schlücker. She initiated my work on compounds by suggesting, quite insistently, that I should submit an abstract to her and Matthias Hüning's Naming Strategies workshop in 2008. Likewise, it was her initiative which brought me to a workshop on Meaning and Lexicalization of Word Formation at the 14th International Morphology Meeting, Budapest, where I first met Sabine Arndt-Lappe. Both have been the best of colleagues, providing not only linguistic feedback, but also all-purpose advice and motivation.

In 2011 I first met Melanie Bell when we both gave talks on English compounds at the 4th International Conference on the Linguistics of Contemporary English at the Universität Osnabrück. That was the starting point of a still ongoing collaboration between the two of us, and our discussions and work together crucially shaped my thinking about semantic transparency and compounds. Apart from that, it was also a lot of fun, and overall a surprisingly and overwhelmingly fulfilling experience in a world of academia that I had almost come to see exclusively as a cynical caricature of its original purpose. Thank you Melanie!

Preliminary versions of the material in this book were presented at numerous conferences and talks, and I thank all the audiences for their feedback. Special thanks go to Ingo Plag, Carla Umbach, and Thomas Weskott.

Turning to my actual place of work, the English department of the University Jena, I would like to thank all my colleagues there, especially Volker Gast, Florian Haas, Karsten Schmidtke-Bode and Holger Dießel, who witnessed the whole developmental progress of this work and provided feedback and encouragment throughout. Very special thanks go to my office mate Christoph Rzymski. He was my main statistics and R advisor, and also carefully read and helpfully commented on the manuscript before I submitted it. Quite over and above that, he also provided the office with much-needed Supertee, and generally made office life most enjoyable.

This work is the revised version of my Habilitationsschrift, which was accepted in 2017 by the Philosophische Fakultät of the Friedrich-Schiller-Universität Jena. I thank the original reviewers of the Habilitationsschrift, Sabine Arnd-Lappe, Holger Dießel, and Volker Gast as well as the anonymous referee for Language Science Press for their many helpful comments and suggestions.

Acknowledgments

Speaking of Language Science Press: many thanks to Sebastian Nordhoff, who made working with them a very pleasant experience.

The work by Melanie Bell and me presented in this book was partially supported by three short visit grants from the European Science Foundation through NetWordS—The European Network on Word Structure (grants 4677, 6520 and 7027). The corpus frequencies for our analyses presented in Chapter 7 were gratefully provided by Cyrus Shaoul and Gero Kunter.

Abbreviations

The following conventions were used to reference examples taken from corpora and online dictionaries:

BNC   Example sentence from the British National Corpus. All BNC examples are followed by their unique BNC identifier.

COCA   Example sentence from the Corpus of Contemporary American English. The exact references are given in Appendix D.

DeReKo   Example sentence from the Deutsche Referenzkorpus. The exact references are given in Appendix D.

OED   Example from the online edition of the Oxford English Dictionary. The exact references are given in Appendix D.

WEB   Example from the internet. The exact references are given in Appendix D.

1 Introduction

This work is concerned with the notion of semantic transparency and its relation to the semantics of compound nouns. On the one hand, my aim is to give a comprehensive overview of the phenomenon of semantic transparency in compound nouns, discussing its role in models of morphological processing, giving an overview of existing theories of compound semantics and discussing previous models of the semantic transparency of compounds. On the other hand, I will discuss in detail new empirical investigations into the nature of semantic transparency and the factors that make compounds appear more or less transparent. This part focuses on English noun noun combinations.

1.1 A first notion of semantic transparency

Semantic transparency is a measure of the degree to which the meaning of a multimorphemic combination can be synchronically related to the meaning of its constituents and the typical way of combining the constituent meanings. Semantic transparency is a scalar notion. At the top end of the scale are combinations whose meaning is fully transparent, that is, combinations whose meaning is predictable. Conversely, at the bottom end are combinations whose meaning is opaque. Their meaning cannot be predicted, and a link between the meaning of the constituents and the meaning of the resulting combination can hardly be established. In between, there are combinations with varying degrees of relatedness between the constituents' meaning and the meaning of the whole, and with varying degrees of predictability based on typical ways of combining these constituents.[1]

Examples of English compounds with different degrees of semantic transparency are given in (1).

---

[1] Note that this view combines 2 lines of thinking about semantic transparency. In particular, Plag (2003: 46), in discussing derivations, links semantic transparency to meaning predictability, whereas Zwitserlood (1994: 344) understands the semantic transparency of compounds in terms of the synchronic relatedness between the meaning of their constituents and the compound meaning.

(1)   a.   For example, in the letters between Lady Sabine Winn and her milliner, Ann Charlton, sets of samples were sent, divided between gauzes, ribbons and **silk fabrics**. COCA

      b.   The **bronze lion** was placed in the palace's foundations to please the gods. COCA

      c.   His dad worked for John Deere, his mother was a **school teacher**. COCA

      d.   I am the proud son of a hardworking **milkman**. COCA

      e.   The creeping **buttercup** and Virginia creeper weren't as plentiful as she'd thought. COCA

      f.   But experts call the hypothesis **hogwash**. COCA

      g.   To stay on postcoital **cloud nine**, stick to no-brainer subjects that won't make him think that this one night of passion has changed everything. COCA

The meaning of *silk fabric* in (1-a) appears to be predictable based on the meaning of its parts and the typical, or standard way of combining the modifier *silk* with the head *fabric*. This standard way can in this case either be seen as simple set intersection (a silk fabric is a fabric and is silk) or as an instantiation of some relation between the 2 constituents, here the MADE OF-relation (a fabric made of silk). The meanings of the following 3 items, *bronze lion*, *school teacher*, and *milk man*, are somewhat less predictable: a *bronze lion* might have the corresponding color, or might be made out of bronze. In the latter case, he would not be a real lion, but the image of one. *School* and *teacher* can be linked by a local relation (teacher at a school), but both are not restricted in their combinatorics to a local relation, cf. the occurrences of the 2 constituents in other compounds: *geography teacher* or *school finances*. Likewise, neither *milk* nor *man* seem to suggest an interpretation along the lines of 'HEAD who goes from house to house delivering MODIFIER', cf. *milkmaid*, *milk-soup*, *woodman*, *sandman*, *snowman*, and *garbage-man*. For *buttercup*, some people might see a synchronic relatedness between its constituents and the whole compound, pointing to the resemblance of the color of a buttercup's petals to the color of butter and the resemblance of the petals' arrangement to the shape of a cup. Only the 2 final items in (1), *hogwash* and *cloud nine*, show no synchronic relation between their constituents and the respective compound meanings.

     Note that for combinations like *hogwash* the qualification that the meanings of the compound and its constituents must be synchronically related becomes important. Thus, it is not a coincidence that *hogwash* means nonsense, and neither of its 2 constituents are arbitrarily chosen terms. Rather, the 'nonsense' meaning is etymologically well motivated: According to the OED, it was originally used to refer to kitchen refuse that was used as food for pigs, as illustrated by the following quote.

(2)   Cooks who were not thrifty put all the kitchen leavings into a bucket. The content was called 'wash', and the washman visited regularly to buy it: he then sold it as '**hog-wash**', or pigswill.
        J. Flanders Victorian House (2004) iii. 87 OED

Probably via the intermediate step of the second meaning reported in the OED, 'Any liquid for drinking that is of very poor quality, as cheap beer, wine, etc.', *hogwash* then came to be used with its now most frequent meaning, 'nonsense'. Both of these 2 last steps, that is, from liquid waste for pigs to cheap alcohol and again from cheap alcohol to nonsense are metaphorical extensions that are easy to follow; its current meaning is therefore quite well motivated on the basis of its historical origin.

For *cloud nine*, not even a good etymological explanation is available. In addition, it is more restricted in typically appearing following the preposition *on*, and, perhaps bearing witness to its unclear etymology, an alternative, *on cloud seven*, is available, apparently with exactly the same meaning, compare the 2 earliest quotes from the OED in (3).

(3)   a.   Oh, she's off on **Cloud Seven**—doesn't even know we exist.
               1956 O. Duke Sideman ix. 120 OED
        b.   I don't like strange music, I'm not on **Cloud Nine**.
               1959 Down Beat 14 May 20 OED

Even though neither *cloud nine* nor *cloud seven* have been attested for long, their etymology remains unclear; the best one can find are statements like the following attempt for *cloud nine*: "the number nine is said by some to come from a meteorologist's classification of a very high type of cloud" (Walter 2014).

1.2 Compounds and complex nominals

Compounds share many properties with other complex constructions having a nominal head. The term 'complex nominal' is used in this work to refer to constructions of the general format MODIFIER HEAD, with the head always being a noun and the resulting construction likewise being substitutable in noun contexts. It is a cover term that subsumes constructions that are traditionally called compounds (e.g. *blackbird, railway,* and *volcano ash*) as well as constructions that are traditionally considered as phrases (e.g. *superconducting cable* and *brown hair*), extending on the usage of the term in Levi (1978: 1–2), where it was used to encompass nominal compounds as well as combinations of nonpredicating adjectives with nouns (e.g. *electric clock* or *musical talent*).[2]

For English, with no binding elements nor specific word forms as formal markers of compoundhood, stress placement is often accepted as the only fail-safe criterion for compoundhood: if an X-N construction is stressed on the first constituent, then it is a compound (this has been most famously formalized by Chomsky & Halle 1968: 17–18, who distinguish between a nuclear stress rule and a compound stress rule). However, as Plag et al. (2008: 761) point out after listing the many authors stating exceptions to this rule, there is a considerable number of constructions that are typically regarded as compounds but that do not show fore-stress, compare the examples in (4), drawn from (1) in Plag et al. (2008).

(4)   apple píe, Michigan hóspital, summer níght, aluminum fóil, spring bréak, silk tíe
       (the acute accent marks the vowel of the most prominent syllable)

In this work, all these constructions are complex nominals and the term *compound* is also used with the wider, more general usage in mind. In the discussion of other criteria that have been introduced to diagnose compoundhood the main focus has been on noun noun constructions. Bauer (1998) shows that none of the criteria traditionally employed to distinguish between 2 constructions (listedness, orthography, stress, syntactic isolation of the first constituent, constituent coordination, *one*-substitution) yields strong evidence for a distinction between 2 types of noun noun constructions. Bell (2011) follows Bauer (1998) in that the criteria do not allow to distinguish between 2 different categories and argues for the analysis of all noun noun constructions as compounds. In a similar vein, Bauer, Lieber & Plag (2013: 434) acknowledge that "there seems to be no established set of trustworthy procedures that could tell us reliably and theory-neutrally for a given NN construction whether it is a noun or a phrase", arguing for a maximally inclusive approach in assigning compound status.

Note that the 2 major academic reference grammars of English both maintain a distinction between 2 different categorical types of noun noun combinations:

---

[2]Levi (1978: 1–2) specifically mentions a third group of constructions where the head noun is a deverbal nominalization (e.g. *presidential refusal* or *metal detection*). However, as far as I can tell these constructions are always a subset of either of the first 2 constructions.

Quirk et al. (1985: 1332) distinguish between phrasal and compound noun noun (N + N) constructions (they explicitly name stress and *one*-substitution as indicating compound- and phrasehood respectively), Huddleston, Pullum, et al. (2002: 448–451) distinguish and discuss the difference between 'composite nominals' and 'compound nouns'.

1.3 Aims and Goals

This work has 2 main goals. Firstly, I want to show why the semantic transpareny of complex nominals, and more specifically, of compounds, is an important topic in current linguistic research. Secondly, I want to explore to what extent a more fine-grained analysis of the factors involved in establishing semantic transparency allows one to predict the semantic transparency of compounds.

As far as the data coverage is concerned, I will be mainly concerned with English noun noun constructions.

1.4 Structure

Chapter 2 discusses the role and nature of semantic transparency in psycholinguistics. Chapter 3 discusses the role of semantic transparency in so far as it pertains to phenomena of interest to theoretical linguistics. In addition, it situates semantic transparency with respect to related terms. Chapter 4 is concerned with the semantics of compounds and complex nominals. Chapter 5 discusses 3 previous attempts at modelling semantic transparency.

The following 2 chapters are concerned with 2 new empirical investigations into semantic transparency. Both chapters introduce statistical models for semantic tranparency ratings on both compounds and their constituents that make use of the semantic structure of the compounds. Chapter 6 discusses models that use properties derived from just the set of compounds for which the models predict the ratings. In contrast, Chapter 7 introduces models in which the semantic predictors take the distribution of the semantic structure across a compound's constituent families into account.

Chapter 8 summarizes the main points and gives an outlook to further research.

The webpage for this book is http://www.martinschaefer.info/publications/ semTranBook.html.

2 Semantic transparency in psycholinguistics

Semantic transparency plays an important role in psycholinguistics, in particular in research on word access and word recognition. Many models of language processing are specifically designed to account for effects related to semantic transparency, and many studies have used semantic transparency as an independent variable in their study design. Since these studies usually test properties of specific models and work with different operationalizations of semantic transparency, Section 2.1 starts with an overview of different models of the mental lexicon. In Section 2.2, I review the different ways in which semantic transparency is operationalized in the literature. Finally, the results of studies involving semantic transparency are summarized in Section 2.3, before Section 2.4 concludes this chapter.

2.1 Models of morphological processing

Bybee (1995) writes: "A long-standing debate in the linguistic and psychological literature centres around the representation of morphologically complex words in the grammar and lexicon. It seems as if every conceivable position on this issue has been argued for seriously and debated vigorously at some time in the last 30 years." Twenty years later, this debate is still not settled, with an abundance of models not only differing in their architecture, but also in their focus on different core questions. A central question in early model-building was whether complex words are routinely decomposed into their constituent morphemes or not. Central questions in later approaches are which levels are involved in morphological processing, and how frequency information is best integrated into psychologically realistic models. Finally, in particular in research on English and German inflectional morphology, the question of whether morphology needs symbolic rules was discussed intensely. Because the discussion centers on inflection, this issue will be largely ignored here (but see the discussion of amorphous models in Section 2.1.2; McClelland & Patterson 2002b, McClelland & Patterson 2002a,

Pinker & Ullman 2002a, and Pinker & Ullman 2002b are good starting points for the specific question of symbolic rules in inflectional morphology).

The aim of this section cannot be to retrace all the models proposed and the debates and shifts in focus coming with the different models; instead, it will focus on a representative selection of models which are needed to understand the current state of the debate with regard to semantic transparency. In particular, I will first present morpheme-based models, secondly, amorphous models, and finally, present 2 models from the area of conceptual combination.

2.1.1 Morpheme-based models

The simplest model of the mental lexicon is arguably a model with only whole-word look-up and no morphological decomposition. A famous early model with morphological decomposition was proposed by Taft & Forster (1975), who investigated the behavior of prefixed words. Building on the results from lexical decision experiments, they developed the model for word recognition shown in Figure 2.1, reproducing their Figure 1.

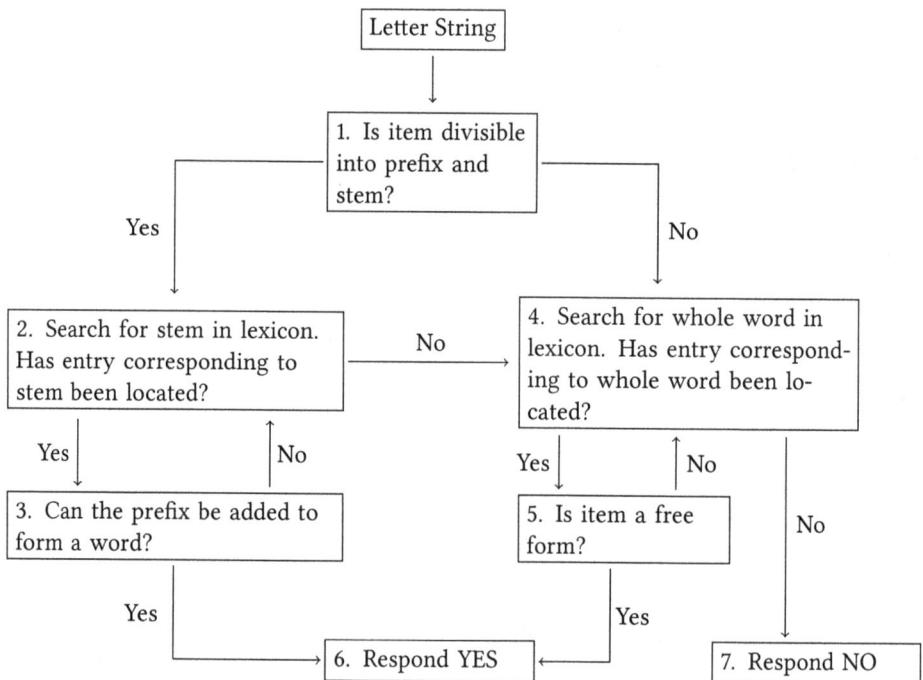

Figure 2.1: Model for word recognition (Taft & Forster 1975)

This model comes with 2 important features. First, it assumes that morphological decomposition takes place in word recognition, the relevant unit for the decomposition being the morpheme-level. Second, it assumes that, for a specific string, only one specific route is taken. That is, if a word is morphologically complex, it takes the decompositional route, but if it is a simplex word, it takes the whole-word route. While there have been many different responses to their model, including e.g. Manelis & Tharp (1977), who rejected the very idea of morphological decomposition in favor of whole-word look-up, the general trend was soon towards mixed models, that is, models that allow morphological decomposition and whole-word look-up for the same items. An early example is the mixed model proposed in Stanners et al. (1979), where one and the same form can not only be stored in memory as a whole but can also at least partially be activated via a decompositional pathway.

A hugely influential and widely-cited model is the meta model for morphological processing introduced in Schreuder & Baayen (1995). This model is of additional interest, as it explicitly addresses problems relating to semantic transparency. A schematic outline of this model, their Figure 1, is reproduced in Figure 2.2.

Schreuder & Baayen (1995) distinguish 3 stages: segmentation, licensing, and combination. At the segmentation stage, the speech input is mapped to access representations which are form-based representations of the speech signal. This is a 2-step process, involving an intermediate access representation and, after segmentation, an access representation proper. An intermediate access representation might still contain more than one word, whereas the access representation proper can at most correspond to one complex word: "Such 'lexical' access representations may be present for full complex forms, for stems, whether bound or free, for affixes, and for clitics. They contain modality-specific form information that is normalized both with respect to the inherent variability in the speech signal and with respect to the variability caused by phonological processes such as vowel harmony and various kinds of assimilation processes" (Schreuder & Baayen 1995: 133–134). The next 2 stages, licensing and computation, both take place at the level of lexical representations. Lexical representations constitute the final output of the lexicon. A lexical representation consists of a concept node, which in turn is connected with syntactic and semantic representations. The interplay between the concept nodes and these syntactic and semantic representations constitutes one of the most interesting aspects of the model. The concept node itself can be understood as a bundling of links to specific syntactic and semantic representations; concept nodes exist only for those concepts

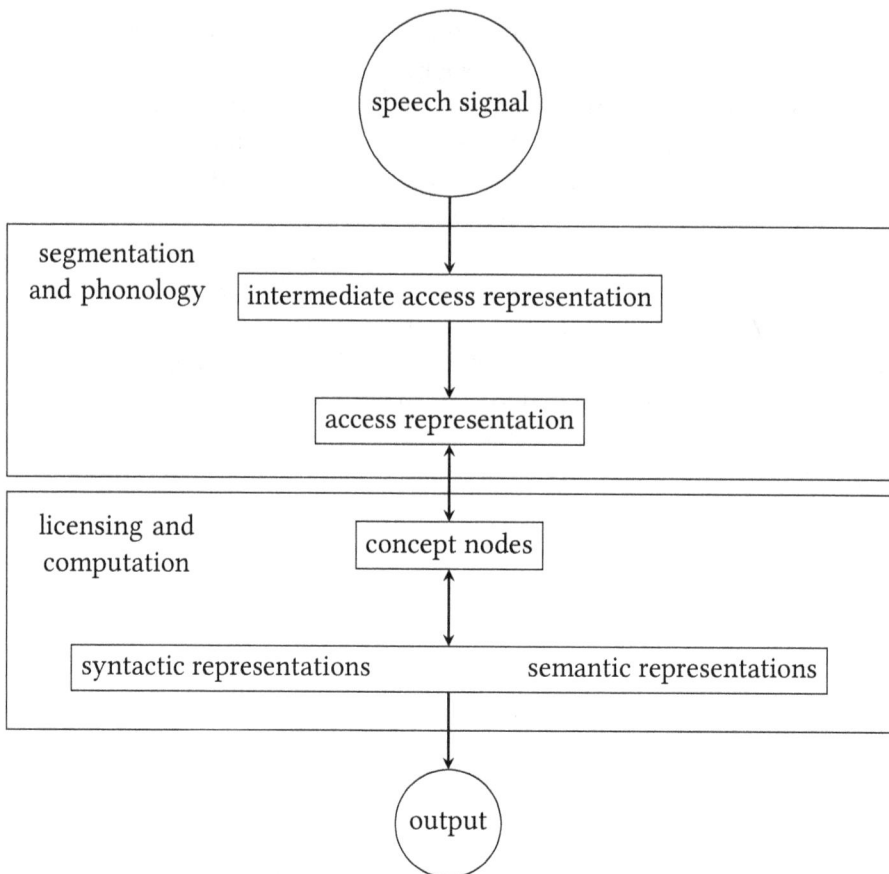

Figure 2.2: Meta model for morphological processing (Schreuder & Baayen 1995)

that "receive verbal expression in the language at the form level" (Schreuder & Baayen 1995: 136). That is, in this account, lexical gaps like the missing liquid related counterpart to German *satt* 'full with respect to food' don't have a concept node, though expressing a concept. Syntactic representations contain information on, among others, subcategorization, word class, and argument structure. Schreuder & Baayen (1995: 136) remain vague with respect to the semantic representation ("specify various meaning aspects"). However, in their figures and discussion it becomes clear that these various meaning aspects are essentially what is responsible for the meaning of and meaning differentiations between concept nodes. Semantic information is only stored once, "the links with the

concept nodes serving as the means for distinguishing and addressing concepts"
(Schreuder & Baayen 1995: 140). Thus, the difference between Dutch *ruim* 'spa-
cious' and *ruim-te* 'space' is a difference in the corresponding links to the syntactic and semantic representations, which for *ruim-te* include links to the syntactic
node NOUN, and to the semantic nodes ABSTRACT PROPERTY and SPACIOUS-
NESS, cf. Schreuder & Baayen (1995: 138). The link structure in this model can be
used to represent different degrees of semantic transparency. This will become
clearer when looking at how a novel complex form leads to the generation of
new lexical representations.

How does the model deal with new complex combinations? Initially, at least 2
different access representations are activated, in turn leading to the activation of
the corresponding concept nodes. At this point, a licensing mechanism checks
whether the associated syntactic presentations allow the system to proceed with
meaning computation. In particular, Schreuder & Baayen (1995: 137) distinguish
3 scenarios:

1. No new concept node is added if the meaning of a complex word can be
   obtained by the union of the relevant sets of representations. They exemplify this via Dutch plural formation by the regular plural -*en* (e.g. *boek*
   'book' → *boek-en* 'books').

2. A new concept node is created in any other case that involves computation.

3. Not fully semantically transparent forms also receive their own concept
   node.

Note that word forms such as Dutch *boek-en* 'books', being transparent and
computable via set union, might nevertheless develop their own access representations. Whether or not this happens is solely frequency driven. However, even
with their own access representation, they will not develop a concept node as
long as their semantics remains unchanged, that is, transparent.

The Schreuder/Baayen model uses spreading activation; as indicated in Figure 2.2 by the double-headed arrows, all levels except the intermediate access
representations can receive activation feedback from higher levels. As Schreuder
& Baayen point out, this architecture can account for a number of well-known
frequency effects. Word-frequency effects, for example, lead to higher activation
levels of the access representations, while the cumulative stem frequency effect
is best viewed as being due to heightened activation levels of the concept node
corresponding to the stem (Schreuder & Baayen 1995: 147).

With regard to semantic transparency, Schreuder & Baayen (1995: 140) assume that "a semantically transparent relation between a complex word and its constituents can be modeled as a substantial overlap between the set of (semantic) representations of the complex word and the sets of representations of its constituents". In particular, empirical effects of semantic transparency can be modeled via the flow of activation (1) between the concept nodes and the syntactic and semantic nodes and (2) from the concept nodes to the access representations.

Schreuder & Baayen illustrate the feedback to the concept nodes with the help of the semi-transparent derivation *groen-te* 'vegetable' from *groen* 'green' and the abstract-noun forming suffix *te* and the fully transparent derivation *trots-heid* 'pride', from *trots* 'proud/pride' and *-heid*. For the former, Schreuder & Baayen (1995: 142) assume that there is hardly any activation from the semantic node of *groente* to that of *groen*, since there are hardly any links between the concept node of *groente* and the semantic and syntactic nodes linked to *groen*. In contrast, for the latter, *trotsheid*, both the concept node for *trots* as well as the one for *-heid* will receive activation feedback via the semantic representations shared with the concept node of *trotsheid*.

The activation feedback from concept nodes to access representations is proportional to the activation level of the concept nodes involved (Schreuder & Baayen 1995: 142). That is, while for a semantically transparent formation the highest extent of activation feedback will flow from the concept node of the complex form itself to its access representation, there will also be feedback from the co-activated concept nodes to their respective access representations. In contrast, for semantically opaque formations, there will be little if any feedback to the individual constituents' access representations, as the corresponding concept nodes are not highly activated.

In addition, semantic transparency is hypothesized by Schreuder & Baayen (1995: 146) to also play a role in the development of concept nodes for derivational affixes. They predict an earlier acquisition of transparent affixes, and they predict the development of representations for bound stems only if these participate in word formations that are compositional.

While Schreuder & Baayen (1995) are mainly concerned with inflection and derivation, we can easily apply the model's general logic to compounds. Thus, using *bank barn* as an example of a novel compound, the intermediate access representation [ˌbæŋkbɑːn] leads to the activation of the access representations for *bank* and *barn*. These, in turn, lead to the activation of at least the concepts BANK1 'institution that lends money etc.' and BANK2 'raised mass of earth', and BARN 'farm outbuilding'. Based on the syntactic representations associated with the concept nodes, meaning computation is licensed, since noun noun compounding is a valid morphological operation in English. While it is partly the aim of this work to find out how or to what extent one can compute a meaning for these 2 items, it is clear that the computation involved will be more than a simple set union. In fact, it seems a fair claim that all compound formation surpasses a regular plural affix in complexity and is typically more than just set union (recall that even the most straightforward noun noun combination given in the introduction, *silk fabric*, already allows a construal with the MADE OF relation). In consequence, this means that after meaning computation, a new concept node BANK BARN will have come into existence.

Libben (1998) introduces a model explicitly designed for compounds, which in many aspects can be seen as building on the Schreuder/Baayen model. Libben (1998) distinguishes 3 levels: the stimulus level, the lexical level, and the conceptual level.

The stimulus level is the level where morphological parsing takes place. A left to right recursive parsing procedure checks both constituents for lexical status and thus avoids wrongly identifying a simplex word as a compound, e.g. dividing *boycott* into *boy* + *cott*, while correctly identifying novel compounds, e.g. Libben's example *redberry* (cf. Libben 1994, where he discusses a parser with these properties in detail).

Word forms, that is, stored representations of actual words, are represented at the lexical level. Libben illustrates this level with the help of the existing compounds *strawberry* and *blueberry*, the novel compound *redberry*, and the surname *Thornberry*. *Strawberry*, *blueberry* and *Thornberry* have representations at the lexical level. In addition, the representations of *strawberry* and *blueberry* have a structured representation indicating their constituent structure. In both cases, their 2 constituents are linked to their respective lexical representations. In contrast, *Thornberry* does not have a structured representation and, consequentially, does not contain links from *thorn* and *berry* to the respective lexical entries. *Redberry* does not have a representation at this level, as it is a new compound.

The meanings are represented at the conceptual level. The links between the lexical level and the conceptual level are used to model constituent transparency. These links allow one to differentiate between the *straw* in *strawberry* and the *blue* in *blueberry*, both of which are linked to the respective constituents at the lexical level, while only *blue* is linked to the corresponding entry at the conceptual level, too. Libben distinguishes 8 different possible configurations, with the first major distinction between componential and noncomponential compounds. Componential compounds are endocentric compounds. They can be paraphrased with the help of the pattern 'compound (noun 1 and noun 2/N1N2) is noun 2/N2', e.g. 'a blueberry is a berry'. Noncomponential compounds do not allow this paraphrase (capturing the exocentric/bahuvrihi types in other classifications, cf. Libben 1998: Footnote 1). Within both classes, Libben assumes a four-fold differentiation driven by constituent transparency: In the first configuration, transparent-transparent (TT), both constituents are transparently related to the compound meaning. In the second configuration, transparent-opaque (TO), only the first constituent is transparent, whereas the second constituent is opaque. The third configuration, opaque-transparent (OT), shows the exact opposite arrangement: the first constituent is opaque and the second constituent is transparent. Finally, in the fourth configuration, both constituents are opaque, yielding opaque-opaque (OO) combinations. Libben's example for a componential TT compound is *blueberry*. The componential TO and OT types are exemplified by *shoehorn* and *strawberry* respectively: The meaning of *shoehorn*, 'implement to be inserted at the heel of the shoe to ease the foot in', is not related to the meaning of *horn*. Likewise, the meaning of *strawberry* is not related to the meaning of *straw*. Libben exemplifies the same 3 types for the noncomponential class, i.e., the non-endocentric compounds, with *bighorn*, *jailbird*, and *yellow belly*, respectively. A *bighorn* is not a kind of horn, but a species of sheep with big horns. It is therefore noncomponential, but it is TT as the horns that are metonymically used to refer to the whole species are horns and are big. A *jailbird* is no bird, but a person who is often or has been often in jail, therefore the first element is transparent. And a *yellowbelly* is a coward, if, as Libben assumes, it is a noncomponential type OT, then he must have a paraphrase along the lines of 'somebody with a bad or unsecure feeling in her belly' in his mind.

Libben (1998) does not give any examples for OO types in this article. Libben et al. (2003) uses *hogwash* 'nonsense' to exemplify the OO category. Conceptually, it is hard to see how one would distinguish between componential and noncomponential types of OO compounds from a synchronic vantage point: if semantically neither constituent is related to the compound meaning, the differentiation between componential and noncomponential compounds becomes useless, even though historically one could perhaps argue for componential vs. noncomponential pathways of meaning development.

Figures 2.3–2.8 reproduce his representation for the 3 non-OO types in the noncomponential and componential versions, containing the links between and within levels, cf. Figure 3, Libben (1998: 38).

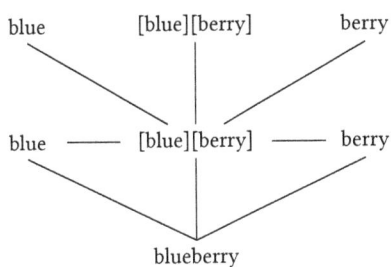

Figure 2.3: TT componential

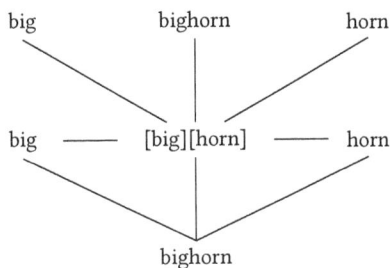

Figure 2.4: TT noncomponential

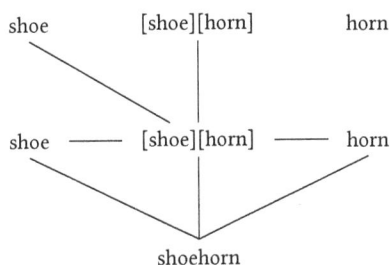

Figure 2.5: TO componential

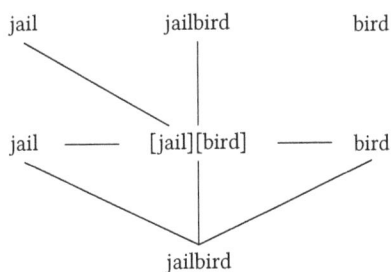

Figure 2.6: TO noncomponential

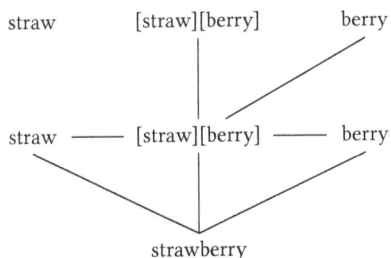

Figure 2.7: OT componential

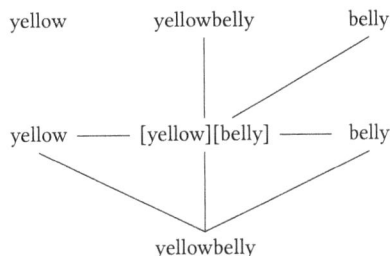

Figure 2.8: OT noncomponential

The links within a level and between levels are always facillatory. The absence of links creates competition, leading to the eventual inhibition of non-targets.

Libben (1998: 33) appears to endorse the operationalization of semantic transparency proposed in Schreuder & Baayen (1995: 140) (see above), that is, that semantic transparency can be modeled as overlap between the semantic representations of a complex word and the semantic representations of its constituents. Furthermore, his stimulus level corresponds to the level of access representations in the Schreuder/Baayen model. It is in the higher levels that the 2 models diverge, with Libben contending that the Schreuder/Baayen model does not "easily handle asymmetries in this overlap" (Libben 1998: 33). He does not clarify which asymmetries exactly he views as problematic. If one considers his 3 examples for the componential types, *blueberry*, *shoehorn*, and *strawberry*, the core difference between the 3 types of compounds lies in the links between lexical and conceptual level, with *blueberry* linking to both constituents' conceptual representation, whereas the other 2 compounds only link to the respective transparent constituent's representation. On the lexical level, they are alike insofar as their structured representation is linked to the representations of the corresponding constituents, in contrast to Libben's assumption for *Thornberry*. In the Schreuder/Baayen model, the 3 types can be distinguished via their different connection strength to semantic representations shared with the concept nodes of the constituents, while their constituent structure is discernable due to the interplay between access representations and concept nodes. It is not clear to me how to best represent *Thornberry* in the Schreuder/Baayen model. However, as far as I can see, there is also no empirical evidence to show that it behaves differently from, e.g., OO compounds. All in all, while Libben's discussion is a helpful clarification of the different types of compounds one can find, it seems that his remark with regard to the observed asymmetry is of greater relevance in distinguishing compound semantics from the patterns found in derivation and inflection, but does not pose any specific problem for the general structure of the Schreuder/Baayen model.

2.1.2 Models without morphemes

From the 1980s onward, alternative models of morphological processing have been developed that differ radically from the models discussed so far. Technically, the most important difference is that morphemes are not represented as distinct representational entities anywhere in these models. As far as their empirical coverage is concerned, many models, especially if they are actually implemented, model only very specific aspects of morphological processing. Most of the models do not target compounds in particular. Here, I present the main ideas behind the very influential models of Rumelhart & McClelland (1986) and Bybee (1995) and then discuss in detail the amorphous model proposed in Baayen et al. (2011), which addresses compound processing as well as the issue of semantic transparency.

2.1.2.1 Rumelhart and McClelland

Rumelhart & McClelland (1986) proposed a connectionist model in order to model the time course of learning the past tense forms of English irregular and regular verbs. Their model is a response to views on inflection in English that assume that part of acquiring morphology is acquiring, or inducing, rules (they point to Pinker 1984 as an example of a model based on this view). English past tense formation is of particular interest in this respect, because the regular past tense formation via the addition of -ed to the end of a verb can be seen as a typical example of word form formation by rule. In consequence, the language learner will at one point have learned this specific rule. In contrast, in their model, such a rule is never explicitly stated anywhere, but the same behavior falls out from properties of the model. The model is very restricted in its domain, since its goal is only to produce the phonological representation of the past tense from the phonological representations of the root form. However, this allows one to clearly see which core aspects are important for this and similar models. Figure 2.9, their Figure 1, shows the basic structure of their model.

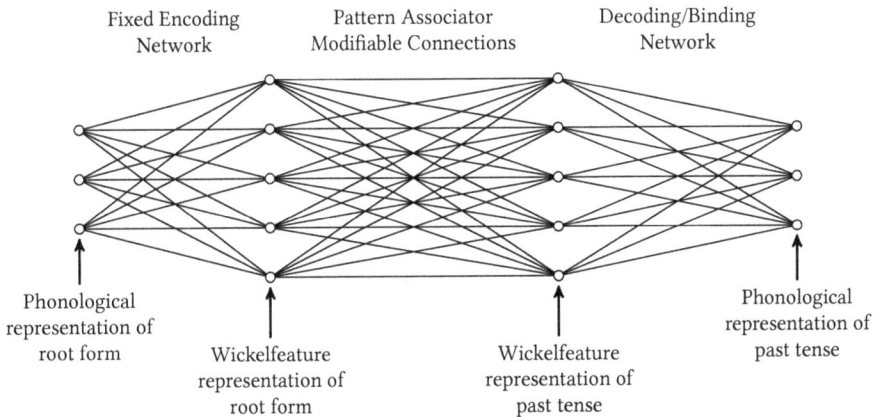

Figure 2.9: A connectionist model for the English past tense (Rumelhart & McClelland 1986: 222). The LaTeX code for the reproduction of their figure was written by Robert Felty and is available at http://www.texample.net.

Of particular interest are the levels of representation they assume, the mechanism that links the levels, and the way the model learns. Rumelhart & McClelland (1986) distinguish 4 different levels, 2 for the phonological representations and 2 for so-called Wickelfeature representations. These representations are paired, that is, there is a phonological representation and a Wickelfeature representation of the root form of an English verb, and a phonological representation and a Wickelfeature representation of the past tense of an English verb. The Wickelfeature representations are feature-based representations of 3-phone sequences, the Wickelphones, named by Rumelhart & McClelland (1986) after the proposal in Wickelgren (1969). The decoding and encoding networks are fixed, that is, there is no variation in how the input phonemic representations are translated into Wickelfeatures, nor is there variation in how the output Wickelfeature representations are mapped on the output phonemic representations.

The core of this model is the pattern associator which contains modifiable connections between the input units, that is, the Wickelfeature representations of the root forms, and the output units, the Wickelfeature representations of the output forms. Whether a unit is turned on or not depends on a probability function which in turn depends on threshold values of the units and the input they receive. Importantly, the units on the same level have no interconnections and there is also no feedback in this model. With this rather simple model architecture, many core characteristics of learning the English past tense could be correctly modeled.

2.1.2.2 Bybee's network model

Bybee's network model was originally proposed in Bybee (1985) and Bybee (1988) (as Bybee 1995: 428 points out, a model with the same properties was proposed in Langacker 1987 and Langacker 1988). Here, I follow her overview in Bybee (1995: 428–431).

The network model is word-based, it can thus be seen as a lexicon organized as a network. In this lexicon, words have varying degrees of lexical strength. The prime factor determining lexical strength is a word's token frequency. Words are related to other words via sets of lexical connections between identical and similar phonological and semantic features. While the words are not broken up into their constituent morphemes, a morphological structure emerges due to the intra-lexical connections. The lexical connections vary in strength. Factors that influence connection strength are the type and the number of shared features, and the token frequency of a specific word. Bybee argues that high frequency words have greater lexical autonomy, which is reflected in weaker connections to other words. This idea is "based on the common-sense observation that items that are of high frequency in the input can be learned on their own terms, while lower-frequency items are better learned in relation to existing items" (Bybee 1995: 429). She further argues that phenomena such as suppletion and the known resistance of high frequency irregulars to change are both linked to lexical autonomy.

Sets of words with similar patterns of semantic and phonological connections reinforce each other, leading to emergent generalizations, which are also refered to as schemata. Whether or not a schema is extended to other words depends on the defining properties of the schema, e.g. whether it is very general or very specific, and the strength of the schema, which is derivable from the number of items that reinforce the schema. Bybee (1995) distinguishes 2 types of schemas. Source-oriented schemas generalize over pairs of basic and derived forms. "These correspond roughly to generative rules, since they can be thought of as instructions for how to modify one form in order to derive another" (Bybee 1995: 430). The regular past tense formation in English with the suffix *-ed* is captured by such a schema.

Product-oriented schemas, in contrast, are generalizations over sets of complex/derived forms. Bybee exemplifies this type of schema with the help of sub-regularities in English past tense irregulars, e.g. the subclass containing *strung, stung, flung, hung* etc. Membership in these schemas, so Bybee, is based on family resemblance.

Bybee herself has not implemented her model; however, she states: "Connectionist simulations could be thought of as testing some of the properties of the network model and Langacker's cognitive grammar, but the model itself is more complex and accounts for more phenomena than any existing connectionist model" (Bybee 1995: 428). Besides connectionist models, analogical models come to mind as candidates for the implementation of the product oriented schemas. Analogical models have been successfully used for some morphological phenomena (e.g. Arndt-Lappe 2011 for stress assignments in English noun noun compounds or Arndt-Lappe 2014 for the affix rivalry between English *-ity* and *-ness*).

2.1.2.3 Baayen et al. (2011)

Baayen et al. (2011) present a very ambitious implemented morphological model, the naive discriminative reader. It is of particular interest for my work, because in some of the simulations run with the model, the issue of semantic transparency is explicitly addressed. In contrast, the triangle model of Harm & Seidenberg (2004), aspects of which the naive discriminative reader follows (cf. Baayen et al. 2011: 439–440), does not address this issue. Here, I aim at explaining its general structure, while focusing on the place of semantic transparency in this model.

The modeling target of Baayen et al's (2011) model are morphological effects in visual comprehension, which they assess by using lexical decision data. It is a 2-layered symbolic network model, with unigrams and bigrams as cues, and meanings as outcomes. Key to the model is the learning algorithm of Wagner

& Rescorla (1972). In Baayen et al. (2011), the modeling focuses on the end stage of the lexical learning process: the cues, unigrams and bigrams, are already associated with the outcomes, the meanings. These meanings range from word meanings to inflectional and affixal meanings, that is, nominative case as well as whatever a suffix such as *-ness* stands for are meanings. Since the model has been trained, it is in a state of equilibrium.

Following Baayen et al.'s (2011: 450) representation, the association strength V_i^{t+1} from a cue C_i at time $t + 1$ results from its previous association strength V_i^t plus the change in association strength ΔV_i^t. The change in association strength is calculated according to the equation in (1), cf. Baayen et al. (2011: 450).[1]

(1) $\qquad \Delta V_i^t = \begin{cases} 0 & \text{if ABSENT}(C_i, t) \\ \alpha_i \beta_1 (\lambda - \Sigma_{\text{PRESENT}(C_j, t)} V_j) & \text{if PRESENT}(C_j, t) \,\&\, \text{PRESENT}(O, t) \\ \alpha_i, \beta_2 (0 - \Sigma_{\text{PRESENT}(C_j, t)} V_j) & \text{if PRESENT}(C_j, t) \,\&\, \text{ABSENT}(O, t) \end{cases}$

ABSENT/PRESENT: cue/outcome is absent or present;
standard settings for the parameters: $\lambda = 1$, all α's equal, $\beta_1 = \beta_2$

The first condition states that there is no change in association strength from a cue C_i to an outcome if the cue is absent. The second and third conditions handle the changes in association strength from cue C_i to an outcome when the cue is present. If the cue co-occurs with the outcome, the change in association strength is positive and the cue's activation strength increases. If the cue occurs, but the outcome is absent, its association strength decreases.

Both changes in activation strength depend on the number and activation strength of other cues that are present. In particular, the higher the summed activation levels of other cues present, the lower the change in activation strength for cue C_i if the outcome is present; if the outcome is absent, the higher the summed activation levels of other cues present, the higher the negative change in activation strength for cue C_i.

Baayen et al. (2011: 450) point out that at the end of its learning, "[t]he Rescorla-Wagner algorithm provides the maximum-likelihood estimates of the weights on the connections between letter unigrams and bigrams and word meanings." To derive the association weights in the system in a stable state, reaching an equilibrium, Baayen et al. (2011) use a method developed in Danks (2003), who

---

[1]Note that I adjusted the index in the first if-statement to the index of the cue under discussion, C_i. This seems to be a mistake in the equation in Baayen et al. (2011: 450), cf. also equation (2) in Baayen (2011: 299), where the index is set to the cue under discussion.

showed that solving the equation in (2), reproducing (9) in Baayen et al. (2011), allows one to derive the association strengths of the individual cues.

(2) $Pr(O|C_j) - \sum_{j=0}^{n} Pr(C_j|C_i)V_j = 0$

   $Pr(O|C_j)$ represents the conditional probability of the outcome given cue C_i, and $Pr(C_j|C_i)$ the conditional probability of cue C_j given cue C_i.

In order to solve this equation, Baayen et al. (2011) for simplicity's sake assume that the association strengths from letter uni- and bigrams to meanings are modeled independently from all other outcomes. They therefore refer to their model as a naive model, in reference to the similarly simplifying assumption of conditional independence for naive Bayes classifiers.

   In order to create a model in equilibrium, the authors proceeded as follows:

1. They created a lexicon of 24,710 word types by selecting lexical items from CELEX (cf. Baayen, Piepenbrock & Gulikers 1995) and from a number of individual psycholinguistic studies. All inflectional forms were also included.

2. The selected words were inserted into 13 different contexts and the resulting search patterns were used to extract a phrasal lexicon from the BNC, consisting of 11,172,554 phrase tokens.

3. The connection weights for the Rescorla-Wagner network were calculated on the basis of this lexicon and the equilibrium equations.

   Baayen et al. (2011) used the trained network to run a number of simulations investigating simple words, inflected words, derived words, pseudo-derived words, compounds, and some phrasal effects. The general procedure is always the same:

1. Selecting the empirical target and modeling it with regression models. They first select reaction times from published lexical decision experiments and from the English Lexicon Project (cf. Balota et al. 2007). This empirical data is modeled using regression models, taking established predictors from the literature.

2. Simulating the empirical target and modeling the simulated data. They select a stand-in for the empirical reaction times (derived from the activation levels of the network output). Then, they use the same regressors in regression models for the simulated data and compare the resulting models with the models for the empirical data.

Thus, Baayen et al. (2011) never use the properties of their Rescorla-Wagner model to directly build regression models for empirical data but always only use properties of the model to simulate the empirical dependent variable. As far as I understand it, the logic behind this approach is that it allows for better comparison of the behavior of the variables of interest in the Rescorla-Wagner model and in the actual cognitive processes. The Rescorla-Wagner model built by Baayen et al. (2011) is intended to realistically model human cognitive processes and should therefore allow one to find a correlate of lexical decision times in activation levels of the relevant outcome strings in the model, and once such a correlate is found, modeling of this correlate is actually more informative than modeling the real empirical data, as there can be no doubt that the empirical data will contain aspects not derivable from the Rescorla-Wagner model due to the latter model being trained only on a very specific dataset.

Here, I am presenting the core results involving semantic transparency, discussing their investigations on derivations and compounds.

Baayen et al. (2011) compared a regression model for the lexical decision times of 3,003 derived words with a regression model with the same predictors for the simulated lexical decision times of the same words. The simulated lexical decision times were calculated in 2 steps: First, the the probability of identification of a word in the set of its most highly activated competitors, the word's *Pid*, was determined, cf. (3).

(3) $Pid = \dfrac{w_{\text{affix}} a_{\text{affix}} + a_{\text{base}}}{w_{\text{affix}} a_{\text{affix}} + a_{\text{base}} + w_c \sum_{i=1}^{n} a_i}$

In (3), the a's stand for the activation levels of the respective items, the w's for weights, and n for the number of the item's highest competitors. After the *Pid* has been determined, it is used to calculate the simulated response time as shown in (4).

(4)   simulated RT $= log\left(\dfrac{1}{Pid} + \phi I_{[l>5]}\right)$

In (4), the second summand in the formula for the simulated RT adjusts the values for longer strings (in order to simulate effects of multiple fixations), ϕ is another weight, and I is set to 1 if the letter length is greater than 5.

In the 2 models, Baayen et al. (2011) point out an imbalance between the coefficients for word frequency and base frequency: for the observed latencies, the coefficient for word frequency is higher than the one for base frequency, while for the simulated latencies, the coefficient for word frequency was lower than the one for base frequency. This is where Baayen et al. (2011) see semantic transparency effects at work: "This is due to the model being a fully decompositional model that does not do justice to the loss of transparency of many derived words (e.g. [...]). We expect more balanced results once opaque derived words are assigned separate meaning representations, distinct from those of their base words" (Baayen et al. 2011: 463). In contrast, similar effects for derived words independent of their transparency reported by Rastle, Davis & New (2004) lead to no such discrepancies between the models for the observed and the simulated data.

For compounds, Baayen et al. (2011) selected 921 compounds for which lexical decision latencies are available in the ELP. The regression modeling follows Baayen (2010), where a generalized additive model is used. The equation for calculating the simulated response times is given in (5).

(5)   simulated RT $= log \left(\dfrac{1}{a_{\text{mod}} + w_h \, a_{\text{head}}} + \phi l_{[l>8]} \right)$
        a = activation, w = weight(expected < 1)

By comparing the 2 regression models for the empirical and the simulated data, Baayen et al. (2011) again note an imbalance they attribute to semantic transparency: "The magnitudes of the effects of compound frequency and modifier frequency are out of balance in the model, which overestimates the effect size of modifier frequency and underestimates the effect size of compound frequency. As with the simulation of derived words, this is due to information about semantic opacity being withheld from the model. Nevertheless, even though the model assumes full transparency, whole-word frequency effects do emerge, indicating that semantic opacity is not the only force underlying whole-word frequency effects" (Baayen et al. 2011: 470). However, closer examination of their data shows that there is in fact no imbalance between the 2 coefficients in the 2 models. Rather, for both coefficients the effect size is higher in the model for the simulated response latencies. This means, in effect, that, at least as far as the comparison between these 2 models is concerned, we cannot conclude that any predictor variable relating to semantic transparency behaves vastly differently in the empirical data as opposed to its role in the model.

2.1.3 Models of conceptual combination

Conceptual combination refers to the process and result of combining 2 concepts to express a new concept. Research on conceptual combination is therefore, naturally, mainly interested in investigating processes at the conceptual level. Compounds offer themselves as a testing ground for theories of conceptual combination, since they appear to be what comes closest to a bare-bones implementation of conceptual combination in language: intuitively, when combining 2 lexical items to form a new compound, e.g. *aquarium* and *computer* to form *aquarium computer*, the new concept thus expressed should result from the conceptual combination of the 2 concepts linked to the 2 constituents. A number of recent studies on compounds have started to exploit differences in semantic transparency to investigate the mechanism of conceptual combination. As the reference models for these studies are either the Competition Among Relations In Nominals (CARIN) model or a later development out of this model, the Relational Interpretation Competitive Evaluation (RICE) theory of conceptual combination, these 2 models will be presented here. Note that both models are relation-based, that is, they assume that the concepts that are associated with modifier and head in a construction are combined with the help of a thematic relation. Gagné & Shoben (1997) contrast relation-based approaches with a second general class of approaches, the dimension-based approaches. In this class of approaches, the head noun is assumed to provide a richer conceptual structure and the modifier fills or specifies a slot in this structure (see Smith et al. 1988 for such an approach. Compare also the discussion of Pustejovsky's generative lexicon in Chapter 4, Section 4.5.1.1). Since these types of models play no role in the studies to be discussed, they are not discussed here.

2.1.3.1 The Competition Among Relations In Nominals (CARIN) model

The core idea behind the CARIN model is " that [...] the difficulty of any particular combination is a function neither of its frequency in the language nor of the complexity of the relation. Instead, we contend that the difficulty is a function of the likelihood of the thematic relation for the particular constituents" (Gagné & Shoben 1997: 73).

In order to assess the likelihood of a particular thematic relation, they used the the number of occurrences of specific relations within the constituent families of the respective compounds. Each binary compound has 2 constituent families: the set of compounds that share the modifier with the target compound, and the set of compounds that share the head with the target compound. That is, for the compound *research project*, the first constituent family is based on the shared modifier and consists of all the compounds that start with *research*, e.g. *research problem, research team, research vist*, and so forth, and the second constituent family is based on the shared head, e.g. *course project, history project, conversation project* etc. These frequencies were drawn from their own artificial corpus, being derived from combinations in the appendix of Levi (1978) and permissible permutations thereof (see Chapter 7, Section 7.1.1 for a detailed discussion).

The relations used in coding essentially resemble the set proposed in Levi (1978) (cf. Chapter 4, Section 4.3.2, for discussion of Levi's set of relation predicates). To Levi's original set, Gagné & Shoben (1997) add 3 further predicates. The first 2 are counterparts to the IN and USE relations reversing the role of modifier and head. The third category, NOUN DURING MODIFIER, is a new category that can be seen as a sub-classification of Levi's IN predicate, picking out only the temporal usage. All but the final relation were already used in work by Shoben and Medin, reported in Shoben (1991). Table 2.1 gives an overview of the relations used, each illustrated with one example, cf. Table 1 in Gagné & Shoben (1997: 72) for the 14 categories from Shoben (1991) and Gagné & Shoben (1997: 74) for the additional NOUN DURING MODIFIER relation.

Gagné & Shoben (1997) tested the influence of constituent-family based relational information with a sense/nonsense judgment. Subjects had to indicate whether a given word pair makes sense, either within a sentence frame (Experiment 1), or when presented in isolation (Experiment 3). In Experiment 1, they found that frequency of the the relation for the modifier family facilitated response times, whereas the number of high frequency competitors increased response times. The results of Experiment 3 confirmed these findings. In both experiments, properties of the head noun did not play an important role. Gagné & Shoben (1997) account for this observed asymmetry between modifier and head by the Competition Among Relations In Nominals (CARIN) model, which holds that relational information is already stored with the modifiers and claims that "the ease with which the appropriate relation can be found depends on both the strength of the to-be-selected relation and on the strength of the alternatives" (Gagné & Shoben 1997: 81).

In their formal implementation of the CARIN model, Gagné & Shoben introduce the *strength ratio*: the frequency of the correct relation, expressed as its proportion in the constituent family, divided by the sum of the frequencies of the correct relation plus the frequencies of the 3 most likely alternatives, that is, those 3 relations occurring most often in the constituent family (where limiting the alternatives to 3 is an arbitrary choice). Again, all frequencies were expressed

Table 2.1: Categories used for relational coding and examples illustrating the application of the coding scheme from Gagné & Shoben (1997)

	relation	example
1	noun causes modifier	*flu virus*
2	modifier causes noun	*college headache*
3	noun has modifier	*picture book*
4	modifier has noun	*lemon peel*
5	noun makes modifier	*milk cow*
6	noun made of modifier	*chocolate bird*
7	noun for modifier	*cooking toy*
8	modifier is noun	*dessert food*
9	noun uses modifier	*gas antiques*
10	noun about modifier	*mountain magazine*
11	noun located modifier	*mountain cloud*
12	noun used modifier	*servant language*
13	modifier located noun	*murder town*
14	noun derived from modifier	*oil money*
15	noun during modifier	*summer cloud*

as proportions in the constituent family. As Gagné & Shoben (1997: 81) point out, this strength ratio corresponds to Luce's 1959 choice rule: the strength of the first choice is weighed against the strength of other competing choices (Luce 1959). Following other applications of the choice rule, they use an exponential decay function in their implementation, cf. (6).

$$(6) \quad \text{strength} = \frac{e^{-a p_{\text{selected}}}}{e^{-a p_{\text{selected}}} + e^{-a p_1} + e^{-a p_2} + e^{-a p_3}}$$

In this equation, a is a free parameter, and p_{relation} stands for the proportion of a specific relation for a specific item in the item's constituent family in the corpus, with p_1 standing for the proportion of the most frequent relation, and p_2 and p_3 standing for the second and third most frequent relation, again within the item's constituent family. Gagné & Shoben (1997: 81) report "about" 0.36 as the optimum value for weight a.

Note that the effect of the exponential decay function is to make large numbers smaller, resulting in a number of non-trivial changes with regard to the final result, compare the 2 plots given in Figure 2.10.

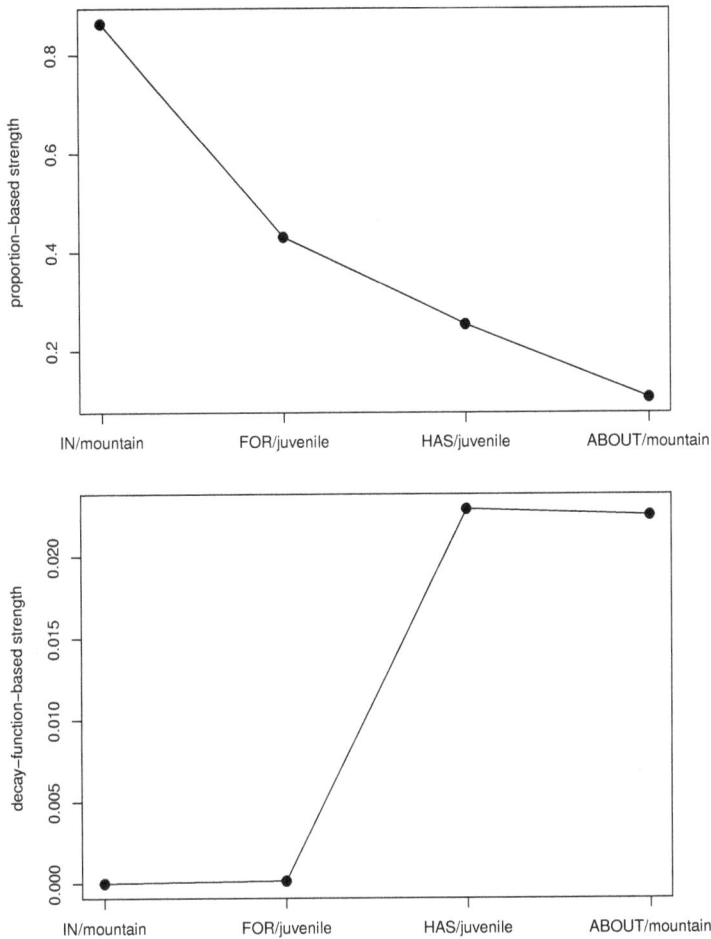

Figure 2.10: Comparison of the relation proportion and the strength ratio for the 4 examples from Gagné & Shoben (1997): IN and ABOUT in the constituent family of *mountain*, FOR and HAS in the constituent family of *juvenile*.

Both plots are for the modifiers of the 4 compounds *mountain stream, mountain magazine, juvenile food*, and *juvenile instincts*, with the relations categorized as IN, ABOUT, FOR, and HAS respectively. The proportions are given in Gagné & Shoben (1997: 81–82). The plot on top, calculated by just using the proportions, shows that the modifier *mountain* in *mountain stream* has the highest proportion-based strength (the strength measure C in Pham & Baayen (2013) is also purely proportion based, see (31) in Chapter 5, Section 5.3.2). Using the exponential decay function, it has the lowest strength. In Spalding & Gagné (2008), this strength ratio is renamed "competition", a reasonable choice considering the results of the exponential transformation. Note that the use of this function does not simply reverse the order, as can be seen by comparing the 2 last entries, *juvenile* in *juvenile instincts* and *mountain* in *mountain magazine* respectively.

While the equation as it stands can be used to calculate the strength ratios of modifier and head alike, Gagné & Shoben (1997) discuss it only in the context of the modifiers, in line with their results and the CARIN theory.

2.1.3.2 The Relational Interpretation Competitive Evaluation (RICE) theory of conceptual combination

The main difference between the RICE theory and the CARIN theory concerns the role of the head noun. While the experiments reported in Gagné & Shoben (1997) showed that the frequencies of the thematic relation of the head's constituent family played only a negligible role, Spalding et al. (2010), using a verification task, found relational priming for the head. In their relation verification task, a verification frame of the general form XY = Y RELATION X is presented, e.g. *knitting blog = blog about knitting*. The subjects had to judge the acceptability of the interpretation given in the verification frame. Spalding et al. (2010) report 3 experiments using variations of this task. In Experiments 2 and 3, the relations were primed, with either both the prime as well as the target embedded in a verification frame or the prime occurring in a sentential frame making clear the intended conceptual relation. In both experiments, they found robust relational priming effects for the head. In Experiment 4, they used the relation verification task without priming to re-run one of the experiments reported in Gagné & Shoben (1997). They found effects due to the relational structure of the head as well as due to the relational structure of the modifier. Spalding et al. (2010: 286–287) argue that the design of the experiments reported in Gagné & Shoben (1997) is prone to hide any relational effects due to the head. Thus, the modifiers typically suggest multiple relations, but the the head's relational frequency was determined independent of any specific interpretation, being based on the frequencies of the relations in the constituent family. For the verification task, they argue that the "effect of the modifier should be decreased relative to the sense/nonsense task, as it is not required to suggest a set of relations. In contrast, the head should be highly involved in determining whether the suggested relation is acceptable, and because no other relations have been suggested, relational effects associated with the head should be evident" (Spalding et al. 2010: 288).

The model that Spalding et al. (2010) propose, the Relational Interpretation Competitive Evaluation (RICE) theory of conceptual combination, assumes a suggest-evaluate framework: First, a number of different relations is suggested by the modifier. Secondly, these relations are evaluated by the head. Finally, the specific nature of the relations needs to be elaborated with the help of pragmatics and world knowledge.

In the development of the 2 models, semantic transparency did not play any role; the studies where semantic transparency is used as an independent variable to investigate conceptual combination are discussed in Section 2.3.3.

2.1.4 Conclusion: the different models

This section gave an introduction to 3 large classes of models that play a role in the discussion of semantic transparency: as an example for a morpheme-based model, I discussed the Schreuder/Baayen meta model and, in addition, the model for compounds proposed in Libben (1998). Both models explicitly discuss semantic transparency as an important factor motivating within and across level linking. In contrast, the amorphous models did not focus explicitly on semantic transparency, but in the discussion of their models especially for derivation, Baayen et al. (2011) hypothesize that semantic transparency could explain discrepancies between the models for the empirical and the simulated data. Finally, I presented 2 models of conceptual combination. The role of semantic transparency within these models will be discussed in detail in Section 2.3.3.

2.2 Measuring semantic transparency

Complex words with different degrees of semantic transparency have been widely used in the literature (see especially Section 2.3). However, measuring semantic transparency is not a very straightforward matter. In different studies, compounds have either been classified into different categories of semantic transparency by the authors themselves, or scales have been used in order to get human subjects to rate word formations for semantic transparency, with the ratings in some cases then being used to establish different categories. I first survey the tasks that are mentioned in the literature in order to elicit semantic transparency ratings. Section 2.2.2 gives an overview of the methods.

2.2.1 Establishing semantic transparency

The first experiment that involved semantic transparency in compounds is described in Monsell (1985: 186–190), reporting an experiment by him and Conrad. They only looked at "relatively well-lexicalized" compounds, "loosely define[d ...] as consisting of constituents which it is no longer appropriate to separate even by a hyphen" (Monsell 1985: 186). They used a binary distinction transparent vs. opaque compound, working with the following definition: "For 'transparent' compounds, the derivational relation between the primed constituent noun and the compound is obvious (e.g. *rope* in *tightrope*). For the 'opaque' compounds, the relation is non-obvious, lost in the mists of etymological history (e.g. *butter* in *butterfly*)" (Monsell 1985: 186). They also used pseudocompounds as a control, which are described as "polysyllabic, monomorphemic words comparable in length and frequency to the compounds, and whose initial or final syllable(s) is an unrelated 'accidentally' embedded noun (e.g. *fur* in *furlong*, *bone* in *trombone*" (Monsell 1985: 186). He points out that the residual syllable sometimes also formed a word, a case in point being *furlong* with its second syllable *long*. Note, though, that this is etymologically a compound, according to the OED derived from the precursors of today's *furrow* and *long*. Monsell does not give any explanation of how these types were assigned to specific lexemes. In contrast, in the following studies, the classification of the complex words is often established in pretests.

Sandra (1990) adopts Monsell's binary classification. His target language was Dutch. In a pilot study, Sandra established a number of opaque compounds. This pilot study yielded 2 sets of compounds where either the first or the second constituent was opaque relative to the whole compound. Groups of 10 to 12 subjects were given lists of compounds and then asked to write an accurate definition for each of them. The more frequently a constituent was used in the definitions, the more transparent the compound was considered to be. It is not entirely clear which cut-off points he used, but he reports that in most cases for the opaque compounds the constituents either did not occur in the definitions or occurred only once. None of the constituents occurred more than 3 times (Sandra 1990: 537). As this pilot study and the resulting materials show, Sandra was fully aware of different types of opaque compounds; however, semantic transparency was treated as a 2-level variable in the experiments (opaque vs. transparent compounds). The transparent compounds were then constructed from the opaque ones. An example from his data is *koplamp* 'head-light', a compound where the first element did not occur in the definitions obtained in the pilot study, and *kopbal* 'header', constructed by replacing the second element of *koplamp*, *lamp*, with *bal* 'ball', in order to have a transparent compound (cf. Sandra 1990: 543,562).

In contrast to Sandra, Zwitserlood (1994), also working on Dutch compounds, used a different method to establish her compound classes; in addition, the classification she used is not binary but ternary. She used a pretest to establish semantic relatedness: First, 84 pairs of Dutch compounds sharing their second constituent were selected from the CELEX database (Baayen, Piepenbrock & Gulikers 1995). For all pairs, the semantic transparency of the relation of the second constituent to the whole compound differed. In the pretest, 14 subjects rated one compound of the pairs with regard to the degree to which the first word, the compound, was related to the following word, the second constituent of the compound. The ratings used a 5-point Likert scale, ranging from 1, 'very unrelated', to 5, 'very related'. The results were then used to classify those compounds with a median score higher than 4 as transparent, while those with a score lower than 2 were classified as opaque. In addition, within the pairs of compounds a difference of at least 2.5 in median scores was required, leaving her with 49 compound pairs and a binary distinction. Apparently via inspection of the data it became apparent that it actually made sense to add a further distinction between truly opaque and partially opaque compounds. For truly opaque compounds, no semantic relationship to either constituent could be established. In contrast, for partially opaque compounds a semantic relationship to the first constituent could be established. This observation was empirically validated by having 8 subjects give definitions. For the truly opaque compounds, the first part was not referred to in the definition of the compound. For the partially opaque ones, the first part was always referred to in the compound's definition. Examples for her 3 categories are given in (7), taken from her Table 4, cf. Zwitserlood (1994: 358).

(7) a. fully transparent: *kerkorgel* church:organ 'church organ'
     b. partially transparent: *drankorgel* drink:organ 'drunkard'
     c. truly opaque: *klokhuis* clock:house 'core (of an apple)'

Libben et al. (2003) come to a 4-fold categorization of 2 constituent compounds with regard to transparency, splitting the partially opaque category introduced in Zwitserlood (1994) into 2 distinct categories depending on the locus of the opaque constituent, yielding the four categories illustrated in (8), cf. Libben et al. (2003: 53).

(8) a. transparent–transparent/TT   *car-wash*
     b. opaque–transparent/OT   *strawberry*
     c. transparent–opaque/TO   *jailbird*
     d. opaque–opaque/OO   *hogwash*

In addition, Libben et al. (2003) used a sophisticated selection procedure to arrive at their experimental items. Their categorization procedure proceeded through 3 distinct stages:

1. They selected 116 bi-syllabic adjective noun and noun noun compounds (except the trisyllabic *strawberry*), balanced across the 4 categories for constituent frequency, compound frequency, and length.

2. The same set of 91 undergraduate students performed 2 rating tasks. In Task 1, the students rated the 116 compounds on a 4-point Likert scale in terms of the extent to which its meaning was predictable from the meaning of its parts, with the scale ranging from "very predictable" to "very unpredictable". In Task 2, the same list of 116 compounds was used, but this time with one constituent underlined. "Again, a four-point scale was employed and participants rated the extent to which the constituent retained its individual meaning in the whole word on a four-point scale with alternatives ranging from 'retains all of its meaning in the whole word' to 'loses all of its meaning in the whole word' " (Libben et al. 2003: 54).

3. Based on the results of the 2 rating tasks, a set of 40 compounds, 10 of each category, was selected. The actual classification employed the following criteria: In order to be classified as a transparent-transparent compound, the compound needed to be in the group of compounds with the highest overall transparency ratings in Task 1 and the greatest balance between the ratings for the first and the second constituent in Task 2. In contrast, the opaque-opaque compounds were the most balanced with lowest overall transparency ratings. Finally, transparent-opaque and opaque-transparent compounds showed mid-range overall transparency and the greatest imbalance in transparency ratings for their first and second constituents.

Libben et al. (2003) report a tendency to rate more frequent compounds as transparent. All 40 examples used by Libben et al. (2003) are given in their Table 1. It is noticeable that only very few of their 40 compounds are adjective noun combinations. The class of TT compounds does not contain any adjective noun combinations, while the OT class contains *shortcake*, the TO class contains *oddball*, *slowpoke*, *sourpuss*, and the OO class contains *deadline* and *stalemate*.

Jarema et al. (1999) use the same classification (citing a precursor of the Libben et al. (2003) paper)[2] in order to investigate French and Bulgarian compound

---

[2]Cf. below, Footnote 3.

words; however, the study does not mention how the classification was arrived at.

Pollatsek & Hyönä (2005), working on Finnish, distinguished between transparent compounds and opaque compounds. The opaque compounds had either an opaque first constituent, e.g. *verivihollinen* 'blood enemy' (*veri* 'blood', *vihollinen* 'enemy') or had overall an opaque meaning, e.g. *kompastuskivi* 'stumbling block' (*kompastus* 'trip, stumble', *kivi* 'stone'). For the latter, Pollatsek & Hyönä (2005) write that they were often metaphorical, *kompastuskivi* being a case in point. As a result, there were no words that were opaque only in their second constituent. This selection was done by intuition and backed up by having 8 subjects rate the compounds on a 7-point Likert scale ranging from 1, 'totally transparent', to 7, 'totally opaque'. Pollatsek & Hyönä (2005) do not discuss how these 2 concepts were explained to the subjects.

Juhasz (2007) started with 40 transparent and 40 opaque English bilexemic compounds words, chosen based on her own intuitions, "with transparent compounds classified as those where both lexemes in the compound contribute to the overall meaning of the compound (e.g., *dollhouse*) and opaque compounds classified as compounds where the meaning of the compound word was not easily computable from the meaning of the 2 lexemes (e.g., *pineapple*)" (Juhasz 2007: 379). This classification was then validated via a rating study employing a 7-point Likert scale and 8 subjects.

Frisson, Niswander-Klement & Pollatsek (2008), also working on English, use the same 4-fold distinction as Libben et al. (2003), but their rating task in establishing this distinction is not as explicitly described. They had 40 subject who "rated the transparency of 182 compounds [...] [and] were asked to indicate, for each constituent separately, whether its meaning was transparently related to the meaning of the compound as a whole or not" (Frisson, Niswander-Klement & Pollatsek 2008: 92). However, it is not clear from their account whether the rating for each constituent was binary or on a scale, nor whether they had any fixed criteria for how exactly the ratings were then used in establishing the 4 sets.

Wong & Rotello (2010), working on English as well, collected transparency ratings for 80 compounds from 40 undergraduate students. All of the compounds occur as unhyphenated single words in the online Merriam-Webster dictionary. The subjects gave ratings on a 7-point Likert scale, ranging from 'the word is very opaque' to 'the word is very transparent'. Thus, the task required the subjects to understand the concept of semantic transparency. Wong & Rotello (2010: 48) write that "[t]ransparency was described as the degree of semantic relationship between the two lexemes of the compound and the whole word; examples were provided for both transparent and opaque compounds." All compounds with an average transparency rating greater than 4.50 were classified as transparent, and all compounds with a rating below 4.50 were classified as opaque. In addition to the transparency ratings, Wong & Rotello (2010) also collected judgements for familiarity and concreteness on 7-point Likert scales. The resulting 2 sets of compounds differed significantly with regard to both measures, with the transparent compounds being judged as more familiar and more concrete. The compounds and their constituents that were actually used in the experiments were also matched for the mean number of letters and of syllables, and, if listed in Kučera & Francis (1967), for frequency. However, it seems that the matching did not form the basis of the original selection of 80 compounds.

The study by Reddy, McCarthy & Manandhar (2011) on English differs from the papers discussed so far in that it does not explicitly use the term *semantic transparency*, but discusses the phenomenon under the heading of *compositionality*. However, their understanding of the notion of compositionality amounts to the same as the understanding of semantic transparency as meaning predictability (see Chapter 5, Section 5.2 for more details). Subjects were asked to give a score ranging from 0 to 5 for how literal the phrase AB is, with a score of 5 indicating 'to be understood very literally' and a score of 0 indicating 'not to be understood literally at all'. In addition, they also asked for judgements on how literal the individual constituents are in the compounds, likewise on a 6-point scale (again, cf. the discussion in Section 5.2 in Chapter 5 for more details).

Ji, Gagné & Spalding (2011) used 2 different ways to establish the semantic transparency of English compounds. For the material used in Experiment 3, Hongbo Ji first classified 30 items each as either transparent or opaque, with all items selected from the CELEX database. Ji, Gagné & Spalding (2011: 412) write that the classification "was guided by linguistic criteria", using *pullover* as an illustration of the opaque class ("because it is a type of sweater, rather than a type of over"). Of the 30 opaque compounds, 15 were fully opaque, 8 were of type TO and the remaining 7 of type OT. On this set, ratings of overall transparency were collected from 9 undergraduate participants, using 7-point Likert scales ranging from 1 'totally opaque' to 7, 'totally transparent'. No information on how the concept of transparency was explained to the participants is given. For the material used in Experiments 4 to 6, thirtyseven participants rated the semantic transparency of 135 CELEX compounds, again on a scale form 1 to 7. A set of 36 pairs of transparent and opaque compounds was selected. Among the opaque ones, 17 were fully opaque, 10 were TO and 9 were OT. The description of the compounds in terms of TT, OT and TO seems again to be based on the first author's own judgements, as there is no indication as to otherwise. However, for the actual analyses, the opacity types were ignored.

El-Bialy, Gagné & Spalding (2013) distinguished between OT, TO, and TT compounds in English, but do not say how they arrived at their classification.

Marelli & Luzzatti (2012), with Italian as the target language, worked with 2 different semantic transparency measures. Twentyfive undergraduate students rated compounds on a 4-point scale, ranging from 'very unpredictable' to 'very predictable'. The subjects were asked to base their predictability rating on the extent to which the compound meanings could be predicted from the constituents' meanings. In addition, they separately let 20 students rate the individual constituents with regard to the extent to which their meaning contributed to the whole compound meaning, again using a 4-point scale.

The transparency measure for the first constituent correlated with the compound transparency measure, and the transparency measure used was "the residuals of the first-constituent transparency regressed on the compound transparency, following Kuperman et al. (2008) [Kuperman, Bertram & Baayen (2008) employ the left-constituent residuals for a number of measures, though not actually semantic transparency, M.S.]" (Marelli & Luzzatti 2012: 648).

Marelli et al. (2015), again a study on Italian, use 2 different distributional semantics based measures. In addition, to validate their measures, subjects rated pairs of compound constituents and one of their nearest neighbors for the relatedness between the meanings of the 2 words, using a 5-point rating scale ranging from 1, 'completely unrelated', to 5, 'almost the same meaning'. Their approach will be discussed in more detail in Chapter 5, Section 5.4.

In Pham & Baayen (2013), the first author rated English compounds as transparent, partially opaque, or fully opaque, with no further criteria for his decisions given. Furthermore, for the transparency ratings in their Study 3, subjects were asked to rate the transparency of a compound "specifically with respect to whether the constituents of a compound help to understand its meaning" (Pham & Baayen 2013: 467). They employed a 7-point Likert scale ranging from 'not at all' to 'fully'. Their approach will be discussed in more detail in Chapter 5, Section 5.3.

2.2.2 Summary: measuring semantic transparency

Setting aside authors classifying compounds based on their linguistically guided intuitions, Table 2.2 summarizes the 3 methods that have been used to measure the semantic transparency of compounds.

Table 2.2: Overview of ways to measure semantic transparency

1. **Evaluating constituent occurrence in definitions of compounds**
   Sandra (1990) and Zwitserlood (1994) used the criterion of whether or not
   a constituent occurred in the definitions given by subjects for a given compound.

2. **Likert scale ratings**
   A number of studies employed Likert scales in rating semantic transparency.
   Below, they are ordered by the wording of the questions for the subjects.
   2.1 Zwitserlood (1994):
       To which degree is the AB related to the B?
   2.2 Libben et al. (2003) (cf. also Marelli & Luzzatti 2012):
       a) *To which extent is the meaning of AB predictable from the mean-
          ings of A and B?*
       b) *To which extent does A/B retain its individual meaning in AB?*
   2.3 Juhasz (2007) (cf. also Pollatsek & Hyönä 2005, Ji, Gagné & Spalding
       2011, Wong & Rotello 2010, Pham & Baayen 2013):
       How transparent are the meanings of the ABs?
   2.4 Reddy, McCarthy & Manandhar (2011):
       a) *How literal is the use of A/B in the phrase AB?*
       b) *How literal is the phrase AB?*

3. **Mixed and other methods**
   This category collects those methods that are not based on the author's intuition but more complex than a categorization based on a single Likert scale
   rating.
   3.1 Libben et al. (2003): classification into 4 categories based on a combina-
       tion of the rating results for the whole compounds and the individual
       constituents.
   3.2 Marelli & Luzzatti (2012: 648): residuals of the transparency of A re-
       gressed on transparency of AB used as a measures for first constituent
       transparency.
   3.3 Marelli et al. (2015): distributional semantic measures as stand-in for
       semantic transparency.

A further point worth mentioning is the heavy reliance of many studies on
CELEX as a source for the compounds. Since CELEX is a dictionary-based
database, a consequence of this approach is a predominance of lexicalized compounds in the datasets (for more on CELEX, cf. the comments in Chapter 7, Section 7.3.2).

2.3 Psycholinguistic studies involving semantic transparency and compounds

In the studies reported in this section, semantic transparency is invariably used as an independent variable. Section 2.3.1 discusses studies using priming paradigms and Section 2.3.2 discusses studies measuring eye movement. Finally, Section 2.3.3 discusses 3 studies that specifically aim to test aspects of the conceptual combination approach discussed in Section 2.1.3. These studies use both priming paradigms and eye movement measurements.

The studies reported in Pham & Baayen (2013) and Marelli et al. (2015) are discussed in detail in Chapter 5. Although both report studies where semantic transparency occurs as an independent variable, they also discuss models with semantic transparency as the dependent variable.

2.3.1 Priming paradigms

2.3.1.1 Sandra (1990) on Dutch compounds

Sandra (1990), working on Dutch compounds and combining constituent priming with a lexical decision task, reports 3 experiments.

His first experiment was designed to test the hypothesis of automatic morphological decomposition of opaque compounds (e.g. *melkweg* milk:way 'milky way' or *vleermuis* vleer:mouse 'bat') and pseudocompounds (e.g. *zonde* 'sin', containing the string *zon* 'sun'). The primes were either associatively related or unrelated to the initial or final constituent of the targets, and these primed target constituents were in turn "never obviously related to the compound meaning" (Sandra 1990: 536–537). An example of a pairing of prime and initial constituent is the pair *melk* 'milk' - *melkweg* 'milky way', an example for a pairing of prime and final constituent is *rat* 'rat' - *vleermuis* 'bat'. The subjects had to perform a lexical decision on the target words, which were presented in single trials with lexical decisions on the prime as well as the target items. Instead of a stimulus onset asynchrony between prime and target, Sandra used a fixed short *response to stimulus interval* (RSI) of 240 ms. That is, after the subjects had made their lexical decision on the prime, the target was presented after an additional 240 ms. The time between the presentation of the prime and the target therefore varied depending on the subjects' response latencies for the first lexical decision. No significant facilitation effects for pseudocompounds and opaque compounds, primed on their initial or final constituents, could be observed, though there was a facilitation of 25 ms for the opaque compounds in the related condition for pairings of prime and final constituent. His second experiment asked whether transparent compounds (e.g. *melkfles* milk:bottle 'milk-bottle') are morphologically decomposed in their recognition process. Here, the procedure and the primes where similar to the ones in Experiment 1, but the targets where exclusively transparent compounds. For transparent compounds, related primes led to faster lexical decision latencies, with no significant difference with respect to which constituent was primed, although priming of the initial constituent lead to larger facilitation. His third experiment was a replication of the condition 'prime related to word-final constituent', using opaque and transparent compounds. Examples of the prime-targets pairs of interests are *rente* 'interest' – *zandbank* sand:bank 'sand-bank' vs. *brood* 'bread' – *hoeveboter* farm:butter 'farm butter'. Only facilitation for the transparent compounds was found. Thus, Sandra (1990) finds reliable priming effects for both the first and second constituent of transparent compounds, but no effects for opaque and pseudocompounds. He takes his results as evidence against across the board automatic decomposition.

Sandra did not distinguish between fully and partially opaque compounds (see above, Section 2.2.2), but, as pointed out by Zwitserlood (1994: 363), his data contains many partially opaque compounds. I will come back to this point after presenting Zwitserlood's experiments.

2.3.1.2 Zwitserlood (1994) on Dutch compounds

Zwitserlood (1994), also on Dutch compounds, reports 2 experiments, again using a lexical decision task, combined with immediate partial repetition (Experiment 1), and semantic priming (Experiment 2). She distinguished between transparent, partially opaque, and fully opaque compounds. In the study employing immediate partial repetition, the compounds were the primes and either the first or the second constituent served as targets on which the subject had to perform a lexical decision. For example, *kerkorgel* kerk:orgel 'church organ' and *drunkorgel* drunk:orgel 'drunkard' both served as primes for *orgel* 'organ', and, additionally, as primes for *kerk* 'church', and *drunk* 'drink'. Zwitserlood found facilitatory effects for all 3 compound types. This, so Zwitserlood (1994: 364), suggests that information about the morphological make-up of a word is available at some non-semantic level of lexical representation. In the second experiment, the targets where semantically related to either the first or the second constituent of the compound that served as the prime. To illustrate, targets for the primes *kerk-orgel* and *drankorgel* were either *muziek* 'music' or *priester* 'priest' or *bier* 'beer' respectively. This time, a facilitatory effect was only found for transparent and partially transparent compounds but not for truly opaque compounds.

In interpreting the results of the 2 experiments, Zwitserlood (1994: 365) comes to the following 2 conclusions with regard to Dutch compounds: (1) "[C]ompounds are represented as morphologically complex, either in terms of an absence of inhibitory links between morphological relatives at the level of lexical form, or in terms of facilitatory between-level links connecting form-level and morphological representations". (2) At the semantic level, all compounds have their own representation. In addition, transparent and partially opaque compounds are linked to the semantic representations of their constituents, but fully opaque compounds are not.

The results from her second experiment require further discussion, since, as mentioned above, according to Zwitserlood (1994: 363), most of Sandra's opaque compounds were also partially opaque. If this assessment is correct, it is in fact surprising that Sandra did not find any facilitation for them.

Zwitserlood (1994: 363) points to Sandra's usage of single trial presentations and his usage of response to stimulus intervals (RSIs) instead of stimulus onset asynchronies, which in effect means that the time between initial prime presentation and target presentation was longer than the SOA of 300 ms between primes and targets used by Zwitserlood, with the semantic activation possibly already decayed. Sandra's own views on the difference between SOA and RSI priming cannot explain the results. Sandra (1990: 534) speculates that the RSI in combination with lexical decisions on both prime and target makes subjects less likely to suspect that there should be a relationship between prime and target. In contrast, so Sandra, the fact that primes in a standard set-up, that is, the prime is followed by the target of the lexical decision task after a fixed SOA intervall, do not call for a response might reinforce the suggestion made by the paired list of primes and targets that there must be some kind of relation between the two. This, in turn, can lead to subjects using attentional strategies distorting the results, leading to inhibition effects for unrelated prime-target pairs (see Sandra 1990: 534 for more discussion and references to earlier literature). Accordingly, if Sandra's prime target pairs are in fact in many cases related, both methods are expected to lead to facilitatory effects.

Another noteworthy difference between the 2 studies is that in Sandra's study the compounds were the target, not the primes, whereas in Zwitserlood's study, the compounds were the primes and the targets were simplex words. If all compound types are automatically decomposed, one can assume at least some activation of the concepts relating to the constituents. In contrast, the step from the individual constituents' concepts to the conceptual representation of the partially opaque compounds could, in comparison, require more activation.

2.3.1.3 The Sandra and Zwitserlood results and the Libben model

Libben's (1998) model draws heavily on the results from the 2 experiments described above. In particular, he takes the asymmetric results of Zwitserlood's partial repetition priming, where facilitation for all compound types was found, and the results from the semantic priming paradigms, where only facilitatory effect for transparent (Sandra) or transparent and partially transparent compounds (Zwitserlood) were found, to support the existence of a lexical level: "It seems necessary to postulate a purely morphological and not semantic level of constituent structure to account for the observations that native speakers seem to know that a compound such as STRAWBERRY contains the lexical unit STRAW but not the meaning STRAW" (Libben 1998: 36). That is, the facilitatory link between [straw][berry] and [straw] at the lexical level explains the repetition priming, and the missing link between [straw][berry] and [straw] at the conceptual level the missing semantic priming (compare Figure 2.7 on page 15). However, note that this data, as Zwitserlood already mentions, can also be accounted for via facilitatory within-level links, that is, in the Schreuder-Baayen model, via links between the access representation of BERRY and STRAWBERRY.

2.3.1.4 Libben et al. (2003) on English compounds

Libben et al. (2003) used a 4-way distinction between fully transparent (TT), fully opaque (OO), and partially transparent, with the latter being divided into transparent modifier - opaque head (TO) and vice versa (OT). Libben et al. (2003) report 2 experiments.

In the first experiment, the subjects performed a word recognition task, having to answer whether they had ever seen the word before, cf. Libben et al. (2003: 55). The targets were pairs of the same compound written as one word or written with its 2 constituents separated by 2 whitespaces, e.g. *deadline* vs. *dead line*, with all subjects seeing both versions of the same compound. Libben et al. (2003: 58) state the following 4 "dominant results" for the first experiment: (1) a split form leads to longer recognition latencies for all compound types, (2) compounds with an opaque head take longer to be recognized than those with transparent heads, (3) all opaque compounds pattern together in the split condition, and (4) compounds with transparent head are less effected by prior presentation as intact stimuli, that is, written as one word. As their results show, TO and OO compounds are indistinguishable across the 2 conditions, and thus, taken (4) into consideration, behave overall quite similarly.

The second experiment combined lexical decision with constituent priming. The primes where either the first or the second constituent of the targets, the compounds, or some neutral prime. Every subject saw the same compound twice, each time with a different prime. *Jailbird*, e.g., was primed with either one of the 2 related constituents *jail* or *bird*, or the neutral *table*. Constituent priming lead to reduced recognition latencies for all compound types, regardless of whether the first or the second constituent served as the prime. Libben et al. (2003: 60) write that "OT compounds showed RT patterns that were nondistinct from TT patterns". Descriptively, the response times for TT, OT, and TO are shorter when primed on the first constituent than when primed on the second constituent, but the difference between TT and OT across the 2 conditions is bigger than for the TO compounds. In addition, there is a considerable gap between TT and OT response times on the one hand and TO and OO response times on the other hand. Just as in Experiment 1, there was a repetition effect due to the fact that every subject saw every compound twice. TO and OO compounds benefited from this repetition effect, in contrast to the TT and OT compounds.

> In conclusion, then, our findings suggest that semantic transparency plays a critical role in the processing of compounds. The semantic transparency of a compound as a whole is related to the transparency of its individual morphemes, and whether or not they are in the morphological head or non-head position. If semantic transparency were simply a property of a whole word, then OO, TO, and OT should have been indistinguishable (which is not what occurred). If it were only the number of opaque elements that influences constituent priming results, then TO and OT compounds should have patterned together (which they did not). Thus, the results force us to a complex view in which we must consider the opacity of individual morphemes in a construction, their position in the string, and their morphological and semantic roles in the meaning of the word.
> (Libben et al. 2003: 63).

Again, the results partially contradict the results of Sandra (1990), who only found facilitation for fully transparent compounds. As an explanation, Libben et al. (2003: 63) point to the difference between using semantic priming, targeting association lines in the lexicon, vs. the paradigmata they used, targeting the activation component of the word recognition process. One other reason for this discrepancy might be the different ways that were used to establish the differences in transparency in the first place, cf. the presentation of the different transparency measures in Section 2.2.2. In addition, they did not use the same methods, Libben et al. using SOAs and a decision on the target, while Sandra used RSIs and decisions on primes and targets, cf. the discussion in the section on Zwitserlood (1994) (the order of presentation, that is, constituents as primes and compounds as targets, is, however, the same in both studies).

The results can be seen as partial support for the hypotheses put forward by Libben (1998), who argues that the 4 configurations, TT, TO, OT, and OO, are associated with different profiles and time paths in word recognition. However, as noted before, the same results can also be explained in the Schreuder/Baayen model.

2.3.1.5 Jarema et al. (1999) on French and Bulgarian compounds

Jarema et al. (1999), using an earlier incarnation of Libben et al. (2003) as a point of departure and also employing a constituent-based classification system,[3] report 2 experiments, one on French and one on Bulgarian. Whereas Bulgarian has right-headed compounds just as English, French also has left-headed compounds, allowing to disentangle linear position and headedness. Both experiments combined a lexical decision task with constituent repetition priming. This corresponds to the task in Experiment 2 in Libben et al. (2003): the targets were the compounds and, in the critical conditions, either their left or their right constituent served as prime. For the experiment in French, they used left-headed TT, TO, and OO compounds, e.g. *haricot vert* bean green 'green bean', TT, *argent liquide* money liquid 'cash', TO, and *éléphant blanc* elephant white 'white elephant, i.e., something whose cost exceed its benefits', OO. In addition, they used left-headed and right-headed opaque compounds of type OT, e.g. *garçon manqué* boy failed 'tomboy' (= 'a girl who likes rough, noisy games and play'), OT$_L$, and *grasse matinée* fat morning 'sleep-in/lie-in', OT$_R$. It remains unclear from their presentation whether all right-headed compounds in French fall into the OT class or whether there are other reasons for not including other right-headed compounds. Priming effects were found for all positions and all compound types. For the left-headed compounds, there were significantly stronger priming effects for the initial constituents, while there was no significant difference between the 2 constituents for the OT$_R$ compounds. For the left-headed compounds, no differences in priming effects due to transparency status were found. In the second experiment on the Bulgarian data, they worked with the 4 Libben-categories. They report that "significant main effects of compound type

---

[3]This precursor is unavailable to me. The exact citation is: Libben, Gary, Martha Gibson, Yeo Bom Yoon and Dominiek Sandra. 1997. Semantic transparency and compound fracture. CLAS-NET Working Papers, 9, 1–13.

and prime type were found in both the subject and item analyses [...]" Jarema et al. (1999: 367). However, the actual numbers they report indicate that F_{item} for compound type did not reach significance, cf. Jarema et al. (1999: 367). For TO compounds, the second constituent was a significantly weaker prime. No constituent priming effects were found for OO compounds. Jarema et al. (1999: 367) conclude that OO compounds in Bulgarian are processed and accessed as monomorphemic units. As Jarema et al. (1999) point out, their results for Bulgarian pattern with the results from Libben et al. (2003) for English, who also found that the second constituent was a weaker prime for TO compounds. The French data is interpreted by Jarema et al. (1999: 367) as evidence for a combined effect of headedness and position for the head initial cases. Since for the French TT, TO, OO, and OT_L compounds linear position and headedness go together, their first constituent yields stronger priming effects. In line with this, the non-existence of a stronger priming effect of the first constituent for French OT_R compounds is argued to result from the leveling out of the effects of linear order on the one hand and the effects of headedness on the other hand. Both constituents facilitate compound recognition, but the first constituent does so in virtue of its position, the second constituent in virtue of its status as the head.

2.3.2 Eye movement studies

2.3.2.1 Pollatsek & Hyönä (2005) on Finnish

Pollatsek & Hyönä (2005) report 3 experiments on Finnish compounds, investigating eye fixation patterns in silent reading. In the first 2 experiments, sentences were presented on screen and the subjects were asked to silently read them. Besides semantic transparency, the frequency of the first constituent (occurring as a separate word) was manipulated, while whole-word frequency was matched. Target words where presented in sentence frames, positioned near the beginning of the sentences. The sentence frames were matched for compounds with either a high or a low frequency first constituent up to the word following the target word. However, the sentence frames differed for opaque and transparent compounds. In the second experiment, the sentence frames were matched for pairs of transparent and opaque compounds, with pairs always having either a high or a low frequency first constituent. In the first experiment, the frequency of the first constituent influenced the gaze duration, but no effect on gaze duration was found for semantic transparency. There was a main effect of semantic transparency for the duration of the initial fixation. Pollatsek & Hyönä (2005) also report 2 effects occurring after the processing of the compound which involve semantic transparency but go in opposite directions: (1) After opaque compounds, there were more regressions to prior words. (2) After opaque compounds, the following word was skipped more often than after transparent compounds. For all 3 effects, Pollatsek & Hyönä (2005) are careful to point out the possibility that the different sentence frames are responsible for the effects, and in Experiment 2, a replication with pairwise controlled frame sentences, these effects disappeared. However, an interaction between transparency and word frequency in the duration of the second and third fixation was close to significance, with smaller frequency effects for opaque compounds. Experiment 3 employed an eye movement contingent display change technique. More specifically, in the critical condition, only the first 2 letters of the second compound constituent where shown, with the other letters being replaced by similar letters. After fixation (or rather, in the saccade leading to fixation) of the second constituent, the similar letters where replaced by the correct letters. Materials were otherwise similar to the materials in Experiment 2. No reliable effects of semantic transparency were found.

2.3.2.2 Frisson, Niswander-Klement & Pollatsek (2008) on English compounds

Frisson, Niswander-Klement & Pollatsek (2008) report 2 experiments on English compounds. The first experiment is a close replication of the second experiment in Pollatsek & Hyönä (2005). However, in contrast to Pollatsek & Hyönä (2005) they distinguished between TT, OT, TO, and OO compounds, and the frequencies of the first constituents were not manipulated but kept as close as possible. The 3 types of opaque compounds were paired sentence-wise with TT compounds. In the first experiment, compounds were presented unspaced. They did not find a transparency effect, but wondered whether or not there is a power problem in their analysis, given that their sets were comparatively small (14 OT, 10 TO and 10 OO compounds) and their rater agreement was not "that" high (cf. Frisson, Niswander-Klement & Pollatsek 2008: 96; see also my discussion of their rating in Section 2.2.2). Experiment 2 used the same materials as Experiment 1, except that this time the compounds were spaced. In the spaced condition, they found a significant effect of transparency, but not on the compounds themselves but only in their spillover region, defined by them as either the word following the target or the 2 words following the target (depending on whether the first word had 5 or less than 5 characters, cf. Frisson, Niswander-Klement & Pollatsek 2008: 94). Gazes in the spillover regions of opaque compounds were longer. They take this as evidence that spaced presentation of compounds that are usually written as one word forces a decompositional route.

Thus, as far as the compounds themselves are concerned, their results mirror the results of Pollatsek & Hyönä (2005) in that no transparency effects are found. Speculating on reasons for this absence of an effect in view of the presence of an effect in the experiments of Sandra (1990), Zwitserlood (1994) and Libben et al. (2003), Frisson, Niswander-Klement & Pollatsek (2008: 102) entertain 2 hypotheses: (1) The studies might tap into processing levels not captured by eye-movement measurements; eye movement taps into other, possibly lower-level processing levels than the above-mentioned priming studies. (2) The effects due to semantic priming in the above-mentioned studies might be partially task-induced. The high proportion of compounds in the corresponding lexical decision tasks might lead to subjects using strategies not used in normal reading.

2.3.2.3 Juhasz (2007) on English compounds

Juhasz (2007) reports another experiment on English compounds, working with a binary contrast between opaque and transparent compounds. The compounds were embedded in sentences, and eye movement was investigated. For each compound, there was an individual sentence frame. She finds a main effect of transparency for gaze durations, with transparent compounds leading to shorter gaze durations. However, she argues to treat this effect with caution, as it goes against the results by Pollatsek & Hyönä (2005) and Frisson, Niswander-Klement & Pollatsek (2008) (see above), who used more uniform sentence embeddings. In contrast, she argues that her finding that the frequency of both lexemes influences gaze durations but does not interact with the transparency of the compound is of more interest, pointing to similar decomposition of transparent and opaque compounds. Another finding she singles out as important is a main effect of transparency in go-past durations (defined by her as "the sum of all fixations on the compound plus the duration of any regressions back to the beginning of the sentence before the reader moves their eyes to the right of the compound" Juhasz 2007: 382). Opaque compounds lead to longer go-past durations. Go-past durations also show an interaction between transparency and beginning lexeme frequency by participants: for transparent compounds, there was a significant effect leading to shorter durations, whereas no significant effect emerged for the opaque compounds. Juhasz (2007: 385–386) hypothesizes that this interaction can be linked to the ease of sentence integration for semantically activated highly frequent concepts: Following Libben's (1998) model, one can assume that the transparent compounds are linked to the lexemes of their constituents at the conceptual level. The frequency of these concepts, in turn, will influence their semantic integration into the sentence.

2.3.3 Experiments targeting conceptual combination

2.3.3.1 Ji, Gagné & Spalding (2011) on English compounds

Ji, Gagné & Spalding (2011) report 6 experiments. The first and the second experiment were lexical decision experiments testing monomorphemic words against
compounds, without at this point controlling for transparency. For frequency-
matched compounds and monomorphemic words, the authors found that the
compounds were processed faster. In Experiment 3, different types of compounds
were compared against monomorphemic words, again using a lexical decision
task. Transparent as well as opaque compounds both were faster than monomorphemic words. As far as frequency is concerned, high frequency of the first constituent was beneficial for both types of compounds. One the one hand, this
experiment suggests that not only transparent compounds are decomposed. On
the other hand, so Ji, Gagné & Spalding (2011), the frequency effects for both
types of compounds suggest that the results in this experimental setting most
strongly reflect activation at the lexical level (as opposed to the semantic or the
conceptual level), as otherwise high frequency constituents should have been
problematic for opaque compounds. The aim of the following 3 experiments was
to test whether the results so far are compatible with the assumption that all compound processing requires conceptual combination (as argued first in in Gagné &
Spalding 2004). If conceptual combination is obligatory, one would assume that
integration costs for opaque compounds are higher than for transparent compounds, since the meaning of opaque compounds cannot be successfully computed by the compositional system. In Experiment 4, the stimuli where divided
by a white space in order to speed up semantic access (Juhasz, Inhoff & Rayner
2005 reported faster lexical decision times for spaced versions of normally concatenated compounds). This manipulation removes the processing advantage for
the opaque compounds which now, in contrast to Experiment 3, pattern with
the monomorphemic words. In addition, the frequency of the first constituent
interacts with the compound's semantic transparency: high frequency first constituents were associated with faster responses to transparent compounds but
slower responses to opaque compounds. In Experiment 5, the compounds were
not separated by spaces, but the constituents were represented in different col-
ors, leading to the same results as Experiment 4. Finally, in Experiment 6, the
results were replicated without spacing and color marking, showing that the
type of non-word fillers used in the experiments was responsible for the different patterns in Experiment 3 in comparison to Experiments 4–6. In Experiment 3
(as in Experiment 1), the nonword fillers mimicking compound format were con-

structed by combining a real word and a nonword (e.g. *rostpepper* and *chivesonse*, with the first and second constituent being nonwords respectively), while in Experiments 4–6 the nonword fillers aimed to mimic compounds were constructed from 2 real words (e.g. *word wine* for the spaced version, cf. Ji, Gagné & Spalding 2011: 414; technically, these nonword fillers are perhaps better described as novel but implausible compounds). Ji, Gagné & Spalding (2011) argue that this data is best explained by a meaning construction account (again, note that the fact that nonword fillers were partially in compound format probably facilitated meaning construction).

2.3.3.2 Marelli & Luzzatti (2012) on Italian compounds

Marelli & Luzzatti (2012) report 2 experiments, a lexical decision study and an eye tracking study. Their target language is Italian, allowing them to manipulate the headedness of the compounds. Besides headedness and semantic transparency, they also considered frequency effects. In contrast to previous studies, 3 separate semantic transparency measures were used (one for whole compound transparency and 2 for the transparency of each constituent), and they were left as continuous variables, converted to ratio measures ranging between zero and one and mean-centered. In practice, this should mean that they proceeded as follows: assuming a given compound has an average transparency rating of 3.75 on a 4-point scale ranging from 1 to 4, this can be converted to a ratio measure in the zero to one range as in (9).

(9) $\quad \frac{3.75-1}{3} = 0.9167$

If the overall mean for the compound transparency judgements is 2.7, then the centered value for the above ratio measure is calculated by by subtracting the corresponding ratio measure, 0.5667, yielding a centered value of 0.35. Marelli & Luzzatti (2012: 648) mean-center all their predictors to "ensure a more reliable estimation of parameters in the subsequent analyses", refering to Kraemer & Blasey (2004). Kraemer & Blasey (2004: 141) quote a dictum ascribed to Lee Cronbach: "In regression analysis, always center!" Costs of unnecessarily centering are minor, and centering might prevent irrelevant and misleading regression coefficients as well as problems with multicollinearity, so Cronbach according to Kraemer & Blasey (2004: 141).

   Both experiments investigated the same set of 48 endocentric compounds (34 noun-noun compounds, 7 adjective-noun compounds, and 7 noun-adjective compounds), equally divided in head-initial and head-final stimuli. Marelli & Luzzatti (2012: 647) exemplify the head-initial category with *pescespada* pesce-spada fish-sword 'swordfish' and *camposanto* campo-santo field-holy 'graveyard', the head-final category with *astronave* astro-nave 'starship' and *altoforno* alto-forno high-oven 'blast-furnace'. For both their experiments, the authors report complex interactions.

The lexical decision study did not use any priming, that is, subjects simply had to decide whether a string was a real word or not. The response times of the lexical decision study were analyzed via a regression analysis. While constituent transparency did not yield significant effects, whole compound semantic transparency participated in two 3-way interactions, one with compound headedness and frequency of the first constituent, one with compound headedness and frequency of the second constituent. For head-initial compounds, higher compound transparency lead to inhibitory effects of constituent frequencies. In contrast, for head-final compounds, constituent frequency was the more facilitatory the more transparent the compound was. Marelli & Luzzatti (2012) argue that the whole-compound-transparency measure is actually the same latent variable that conceptual combination accounts are after, i.e., "how well the combination of the constituents represents the compound meaning (e.g., the degree to which 'a fish with something shaped like a sword' is considered a good circumlocution for a *swordfish*)" (Marelli & Luzzatti 2012: 653). To explain the 3-way interaction, they make 2 assumptions: (1) There is a dedicated processing route for the semantic combination of constituent meanings, access to which in turn is mediated via constituent frequencies. (2) For Italian, head-final structures are the default structures. Again, whether a structure is head-final or not clearly influences how its constituents are combined, Marelli & Luzzatti (2012: 653) illustrate this with their example from above, *astronave*, which, if head-initial, would have to mean 'the star of the ship'. As they point out, this issue would have to be resolved by using shared knowledge. They explain the 3-way interaction as follows: Integration of the 2 constituent meanings is always attempted, and the individual constituents will be the more involved in meaning composition the greater the whole-compound transparency is. Further, the integration process assumes the first constituent to be the modifier. For the default head-final structures, constituent frequency is therefore the more facilitating the greater the semantic transparency. This holds across the board for the frequency of the second, head, constituent, and for the modifier frequencies for the compounds with high semantic transparency. In contrast, for the head-initial compounds, the second constituent has an inhibitory effect in the high transparency range, explained by Marelli & Luzzatti (2012) by time-intensive conflict resolution.

For the second experiment, the eye tracking study, the compounds were embedded into sentences. As in Experiment 1, there were no main effects of semantic transparency, but compound semantic transparency participated in a number of two and 3-way interactions. Constituent transparency, as in Experiment 1, did not emerge as significant.

For first fixation duration, considered by them to be a measure of very early processes, Marelli & Luzzatti (2012) report a 2-way interaction between first constituent frequency and compound semantic transparency. In particular, the more transparent the compound, the more facilitatory the first constituent frequency becomes in reducing the first gaze duration.

Marelli & Luzzatti (2012) argue that this points to information about a compound's compositionality being available very early in processing. Assuming that higher frequency eases the access to a constituent's meaning, this easier access is beneficial for compound recognition when the compounds are compositional, leading to shorter first fixation durations. However, for opaque compounds, this ease of access is not beneficial, since, so Marelli & Luzzatti (2012: 658), "when the compound meaning is more opaque, the constituent enters into competition with it". As they point out, headedness does not play a significant role (recall that in Experiment 1 headedness was involved in the two 3-way interactions).

For gaze duration, first-constituent frequency and semantic transparency also interact: for more transparent compounds, frequency is facilitatory, for less transparent ones, inhibitory. Note that again headedness plays no role here. However, there was a 3-way interaction between second-constituent frequency, headedness and semantic transparency. For head-final compounds, the frequency effect of the second constituent, that is, the head, is small and facilitatory. In contrast, for head-initial compounds, second constituent frequency inhibits transparent compounds and facilitates opaque compounds. Marelli & Luzzatti (2012) argue that this can be explained by assuming right headed compounds to be the default structures. On identifying a compound as compositional, this route is first taken for semantic processing, while no attempt at semantic combination is made for compounds evaluated as opaque early on.

Finally, Marelli & Luzzatti (2012: 661) model total fixation duration, that is, gaze durations plus any further regressive fixations. Total fixation duration is "assumed to reflect the processing load required to semantically integrate a word in its sentence frame" (Marelli & Luzzatti 2012: 661). They report a 3-way interaction between headedness, second constituent frequency, and whole-compound semantic transparency. For head-final compounds, the frequency of the second constituent is the more facilitatory the more transparent the compound is, whereas for head-initial compounds, the effect of second constituent frequency is inhibitory for transparent compounds. This finding fits in with the finding for gaze duration.

Marelli & Luzzatti (2012) argue that their data does not fit well with neither Schreuder/Baayen nor the Libben model; I will come back to their alternative suggestion in the conclusion to this chapter.

One aspect that they do not discuss further but that should be kept in mind when considering their results is the fact that, as Marelli & Luzzatti (2012: 647) point out, noun noun compounding is not as productive in Italian as in Germanic languages (so much less productive, in fact, that they needed to include adjective noun compounds in their dataset to arrive at their 48 compounds). This might well have consequences for the role of constituent frequencies but perhaps also constituent transparencies in accessing compound meaning. If there are overall not very many noun noun compounds, the judgements on constituent transparency might reflect a variety of factors in a rather unsystematic way.

2.3.3.3 El-Bialy, Gagné & Spalding (2013) on English compounds

El-Bialy, Gagné & Spalding (2013) report 3 experiments, all combining a lexical decision task with semantic priming. All 3 experiments investigate the influence of the first constituent on the ease of compound processing while first and second constituent transparency are manipulated. In Experiment 1, fully transparent TT compounds and partially opaque OT compounds were preceded by primes that were either semantically related or unrelated to the compounds first constituent. Forty pairs of OT and TT compounds were selected, with all pairs sharing the first constituent (e.g. *eyetooth*, 'a canine tooth, esp. of the upper jaw', OT, and *eyesight*, 'the power/faculty of seeing', TT). These pairs were matched with one semantically related prime and one semantically unrelated prime, with the semantically related prime being selected from the Florida Word Association norms database (Nelson, McEvoy & Schreiber 1998) and the unrelated prime a length and frequency match for the first compound selected from the CELEX database. For *eye*, the corresponding primes were *ear* and *king*. The data was analyzed using linear mixed effects models and separate models were fitted for each compound type. Prime relatedness was a valid predictor of response time only for the TT compounds, but not for the OT compounds. The second experiment investigated TO and TT compounds in order to see whether the facilitation resulting from semantically priming the transparent first constituent in Experiment 1 was stable regardless of the status of the compound's head. Again, the paired compounds shared the same first constituent, e.g. *sugarcane*, 'a type of plant from which sugar is manufactured', TO, and *sugarcube*, TT. Prime selection and general procedure was parallel to the procedure used in Experiment 1. The results of fitting one model per compound type again showed prime relatedness to be a valid predictor of response time only for the TT compounds.

The results of the first experiment are predicted by conjunctive activation based approaches (this label is used by El-Bialy, Gagné & Spalding 2013 for the general idea behind the models discussed among others in Sandra 1990, Zwitserlood 1994, Schreuder & Baayen 1995 and Libben 1998), because semantically unrelated primes are not predicted to lead to facilitation effects. Similarly, the results are consistent with their own meaning construction approach, because priming should increase the conflict in computing the meaning of opaque compounds. The result of the second experiment is unexpected from the viewpoint of the conjunctive activation based account, where one would expect an effect for every transparent constituent. El-Bialy, Gagné & Spalding (2013: 86) argue that these results "support the meaning computation approach's idea that the meanings of constituents conjointly influence compound processing, although not to the extent that the TO condition would result in negative priming". The third experiment compared TO and OO compounds, exemplified by them with *catnip*, a plant name (motivated by the fact that the plant contains a feline attractant), OO, and *catwalk*, TO (note here that it is not very clear why this would be a TO compound, since lexicalized it stands for a narrow footway or platform, which is only metaphorically related to a walkway that cats can or even tend to use). Prime relatedness was a valid predictor for OO response time, but not for TO response time, a result predicted by neither the conjunctive activation nor the meaning computation approach. In the general discussion, El-Bialy, Gagné & Spalding (2013: 90) hypothesize that "perhaps in every type of compound, having a semantically related prime provides a boost to compound processing through this lexical mechanism". They further hypothesize that "[t]hose effects, by themselves, are not strong enough to create a significant semantic priming effect for TO or OT compounds because the benefit of faster access to the primed constituent is offset by a disadvantage that arises due to the construction of additional, conflicting meanings" (2013: 90). El-Bialy, Gagné & Spalding (2013: 92) also isolate 2 possible sources to explain why they but neither Sandra (1990) nor Zwitserlood (1994) found semantic priming effects for OO compounds (but see also Section 2.3.1, pages 38 and 39 for Zwitserlood's comments on Sandra, who did not distinguish different classes of opaque compounds): On the one hand, their study was the only study with perfectly matched primed constituents across conditions. On the other hand, their experiment used 32 OO compounds, while the numbers of fully opaque compounds in the 2 other studies was much smaller (Sandra 1990 used 2 sets of 16 different opaque compounds in Experiment 1, and 18 opaque compounds in Experiment 3; Zwitserlood 1994 used 13 OO compounds in Experiment 1 and 12 OO compounds in Experiment 2).

2.3.4 Overview: experimental traces of semantic transparency

Tables 2.3 and 2.4 give an overview of the experimental traces of semantic transparency discussed in the previous section. Both are organized by year of publication, the first table collecting the experiments on English compounds, the second table the experiments on compounds in other languages.

2.3.5 Conclusion: experimental traces of semantic transparency

As the discussion of the studies investigating semantic transparency has shown, the results taken together do not yield a uniform picture. In addition, several factors make a comparison of the results difficult: (1) There is not a single true replication of any of the experiments, although some experiments are attempts at a replication in a different language (cf. Experiment 2 by Jarema et al. 1999, which partially replicates Experiment 2 in Libben et al. 2003, and Experiment 1 by Frisson, Niswander-Klement & Pollatsek 2008, which largely replicates Experiment 2 by Pollatsek & Hyönä 2005). (2) As outlined in Section 2.2.2, the way semantic transparency was established was usually not exactly the same. Note that this even holds for approaches that use the same ratings to begin with. Thus, Libben et al. (2003) and Marelli & Luzzatti (2012) both start with ratings for compound semantic transparency and constituent transparency, but in the former these ratings are then used to establish a 4-fold categorization while in the latter the 3 ratings are retained as continuous variables. (3) Different kinds of tasks or slightly differing variations of tasks are used.

These 3 factors make a comparison of the results difficult. For now, we will ignore the problem of missing true replications, neglect that the transparency measures themselves are not the same across the experiments, and instead focus on the picture that presents itself when considering the results of the different experiments in light of the different tasks.

The main difference between lexical decision and eye movement measures is that the former involves a conscious judgement whereas the latter is measuring unconscious processes. Precisely because of this metalinguistic nature, some researchers (for example Baayen 2014) advise to move away from the lexical

Table 2.3: Semantic transparency effects for English compounds

source	exp.	paradigm	findings
Libben 2003	1	word recognition (split/nonsplit condition)	transparent head facilitates; all opaque compounds pattern together in split condition
	2	constituent priming (first/second constituent on compound) + lexical decision	facilitation for all types; OT and TT pattern together
Frisson et al. 2008	1	eye movement (silent reading)	no effect for semantic transparency
	2	eye movement/spaced representation (silent reading)	longer gazes in spillover region for opaque compounds
Juhasz 2007	1	eye movement (silent reading)	shorter gaze and go-past durations for transparent compounds; interaction between go-past duration and transparency
Ji et al. 2011	3	lexical decision, compounds vs. monomorphemic words	all compound types faster than monomorphemic words
	4–6	lexical decision, compounds vs. monomorphemic words (exp. 4: compounds spaced, exp. 5: constituents colored)	facilitation for transparent compounds only; interaction between first constituent frequency and semantic transparency: high frequency facilitates transparent compounds and inhibits opaque compounds
El Bialy et al. 2013	1	semantic priming + lexical decision (prime related to first constituent on OT and TT compounds)	primes valid predictors for TT compounds only
	2	semantic priming + lexical decision (prime related to first constituent on TO and TT compounds)	primes valid predictors for TT compounds only
	3	semantic priming + lexical decision (prime related to first constituent on TO and OO compounds)	primes valid predictors for OO compounds only

Table 2.4: Semantic transparency effects for compounds in other languages

source	exp.	paradigm	findings
Sandra 1990	1–3; Dutch	sem. priming (const. to compound) + lex. dec.	facilitation for transparent compounds
Zwitserlood 1994	1; Dutch	immediate partial repetition + lexical decision	facilitation for all compound types
	2; Dutch	semantic priming (compound to const.) + lexical decision	facilitation for transparent and partially transparent compounds
Jarema et al. 1999	1; French	constituent priming (first/second constituent to compound) + lexical decision	facilitation for all types; left-headed compounds: more facilitation for first constituent, no transparency effect; right-headed compounds: no difference between first and second const. priming
	2; Bulg.	const. priming (first/second to compound) + lex. dec.	effects for all types except OO; stronger effects for initial constituents
Pollatsek and Hyöna 2005	1; Finn.	eye tracking/silent reading	main effect of semantic transparency for duration of first fixation; effect of sem. transparency on regressions and skips
	2; Finn.	eye tracking/silent reading	no replication of previous findings; non-significant interaction transparency/word frequency
	3; Finn.	eye tracking/contingent display change	no reliable effects of semantic transparency
Marelli and Luzatti 2013	1; Italian	lexical decision	no constituent transparency effects; 3-way interactions compound transparency and (1) headedness and first const. frequency and (2) headedness and second const. freq.
	2; Italian	eye tracking/silent reading	only compound transparency effects: 2-way interactions with (1) first const. freq. for first fixation duration, and (2) first const. freq. for gaze duration. 3-way interactions with (1) second const. freq. and headedness for gaze duration, and (2) headedness and second const. freq. for total fixation duration

decision task altogether if the goal is to study actual language processing. For lexical decision in connection with semantic priming, Bueno & Frenck-Mestre (2008) show that lexical decision is less sensitive to early semantic processing than, in their case, a semantic categorization task. Thus, if one takes semantic priming to reflect a (relatively) late process, and, in contrast, assumes that repetition priming reflects an early process, one can align these findings with the eye tracking data from Pollatsek & Hyönä (2005) and Frisson, Niswander-Klement & Pollatsek (2008) in so far as the zero findings in the eye tracking studies likewise might indicate early processes, and the only significant finding with regard to semantic transparency, the longer gazes in the spillover region reported by Frisson, Niswander-Klement & Pollatsek (2008) being likewise a delayed effect. Across the 2 different tasks, it seems that if an effect of semantic transparency is found, then it is always a delayed effect. However, this does not go together with the findings by Marelli & Luzzatti (2012), where there were in fact effects of semantic transparency for non-delayed eye tracking measures (e.g. first gaze duration). Marelli & Luzzatti (2012: 662–663) argue that the model that fits their data best is the multi-route model proposed in Kuperman, Bertram & Baayen (2008) and Kuperman et al. (2009), complemented by a route dedicated to conceptual combination. The Kuperman et al. model as presented in Kuperman et al. (2009) is perhaps closest in spirit to the Baayen et al. (2011) model discussed in Section 2.1.2.3 above, except that it is not based on the Rescorla-Wagner equations but makes use of more traditional information-theoretic approach:

> A fundamental assumption of our model is that the time spent by the eye on a constituent or word is proportional to the total amount of lexical information available in long-term memory for identification of that constituent or word at that timepoint [...] Events with small probability and hence a large information load require more processing resources and more processing time [...]. (Kuperman et al. 2009: 1112)

In particular, Kuperman et al. consider 7 lexical probabilities to be fundamental, the 4 final ones being conditional probabilities (cf. Kuperman et al. 2009: 1112–1116): (1) the probability of the compound, (2) the probability of the first constituent, (3) the probability of the second constituent, (4) the probability of the second constituent given the first, (5) the probability of the first constituent given the second, (6) the probability of the second constituent given the set of all strings that can occur in word-initial position, and (7) the probability of the first constituent given the set of all strings that can occur in word-final position. The weighted information based on these probabilities is then used to estimate the time expected to be spent on the corresponding items. Since all these probabilities are based on frequencies, Marelli & Luzzatti (2012) suggest complementing this model with a semantic route, as they find semantic transparency effects over and above the frequency effects.

As far as I can tell, such a model would find the full support of the proponents of conceptual combination, since there is a dedicated route especially reserved for conceptual combination, and there is no doubt that the frequency effects, whether they are lower level effects or not, are real and independent of conceptual combination.

However, it is not clear to me whether the data with respect to semantic transparency excludes all other models. Marelli & Luzzatti (2012: 662) argue that the Libben model cannot explain the early effects of semantic transparency, since it accounts only for semantic effects at late stages. Libben (1998) is not very explicit on whether his model allows feedback from higher levels to lower levels; if it doesn't, then there is no mechanism to explain the early transparency effects. Marelli & Luzzatti (2012: 662) discuss the Schreuder/Baayen model together with other "strictly parallel (i.e., horse-race) dual-route models" and argue that these kind of models only partially fit the data, since "in the first place, the 2 routes do not seem to be independent, since compound and constituent properties influence each other during compound access, and in the second place, the relative weight of the 2 routes seems to be modulated by semantic transparency (see the third-level interactions) rather than by whole-word frequency (e.g., Schreuder & Baayen, 1995) [...]" (Marelli & Luzzatti 2012: 662). As far as I can ascertain, Marelli & Luzzatti (2012: 662) are talking about models like the Morphological Race Model (cf. Frauenfelder & Schreuder 1992), which is a dual route model with strictly parallel processing. The Schreuder/Baayen model, in contrast, features feedback and spreading activation across all levels, so it is hard to see to what extent the data is principally problematic for this kind of model. At this point, and given the available data, I do not think that a principled choice between models is possible. However, I think it is a fruitful idea to follow Marelli & Luzzatti (2012) in assuming that the conceptual combination approach is not incompatible with other approaches, but can be seen as a complement, or, in the case of the Schreuder/Baayen model, perhaps as a way to further spell-out what happens at the level of licensing and computation and how the interplay between concept nodes and semantic representations could work.

2.4 Conclusion

This chapter discussed the place, operationalization, and effects of semantic transparency in psycholinguistics. Section 2.1 introduced 3 classes of psycholinguistic models of morphological processing: morpheme-based models, amorphous models, and models of conceptual combination. Section 2.2 introduced the different operationalizations of semantic transparency used in the psycholinguistic literature. Finally, Section 2.3 presented the experimental results pertaining to semantic transparency. Section 2.2 has shown that the operationalizations of semantic transparency are never exactly the same. Section 2.3 has shown that experiments have not been replicated, but instead a wide variety of sometimes only slightly, but often considerably different paradigms has been used. These 2 factors are partly responsible for results that all in all fail to give a very clear picture of the role of semantic transparency for language processing– results which also at this point do not permit a clear decision in favor of one of the 3 classes of models discussed in Section 2.1. In addition, and this was the point which ended the previous section, at least the models of conceptual combinations should rather be seen as complements to the other models than as competitors. Using semantic transparency not as an independent variable, but instead trying to understand the factors that determine semantic transparency itself, as done in the work to be discussed in Chapter 5 and the new empirical work discussed in Chapter 6 and 7, might in the long run lead to better operationalizations and more comparable experiments. However, before I turn to this issue, Chapter 3 discusses the place of semantic transparency in theoretical linguistics and sets it apart from related notions, and Chapter 4 looks at the semantics of complex nominals in general.

3 Semantic transparency: related phenomena and notions

Outside of psycholinguistics, semantic transparency has only played a negligible role in the discussion of specific linguistic phenomena, e.g. derivational morphology. Two areas where semantic transparency has received some attention as a possible explanation are the phenomenon of outbound anaphora and the factors determining stress assignment in English noun noun compounds. Both are discussed in the first part of this chapter. In the second part of this chapter, I briefly discuss a number of other notions that describe phenomena that are closely related to semantic transparency or even partially or fully overlapping with semantic transparency. At the end of the chapter, I briefly discuss the notions of phonological and orthographical transparency.

3.1 Semantic transparency reflected in other linguistic phenomena

Semantic transparency is traditionally mentioned in introductions to morphology, but how it is assessed or what sort of linguistic patterns it is connected with is rarely discussed. Whether coincidental or not, the 2 areas where semantic transparency has been discussed in more detail both involve English compounds: the possibility of anaphoric reference to parts of a compound, and the factors driving stress assignment. Both will be discussed in turn.

3.1.1 Semantic transparency and outbound anaphora

Semantic transparency has been discussed as a factor influencing whether parts of words are accessible as targets for anaphoric reference, or whether they constitute so-called anaphoric islands. The term *anaphoric island* was introduced in Postal (1969) in the discussion of the behavior of the constituents of complex words and of entities contained in the meaning of words with respect to anaphora, whether as targets of anaphoric references or as anaphorically referring expressions. Postal (1969) argued that words, whether monomorphemic or derived, are anaphoric islands. Being an anaphoric island means that neither internal constituents of morphologically complex words nor entities contained in the meaning of a word can serve as antecedents to a following anaphoric element nor can they themselves refer anaphorically to other elements. The property of serving as an antecedent for an anaphoric element is discussed under the term outbound anaphora, the property of refering anaphorically under the term of inbound anaphora. Outbound anaphora has been linked to semantic transparency in Coulmas (1988), Ward, Sproat & McKoon (1991) and Schäfer (2013).

A classic set of data that led Postal to introduce the notion of anaphoric islands is (1), reproducing (53) from Postal (1969).

(1)　　a.　　Harry was looking for a rack for **books**$_i$ but he only found racks for very small **ones**$_i$.

　　　　b.　　*Harry was looking for a **book**$_i$rack but he only found racks for very small **ones**$_i$.

While anaphora from *ones* to *books* is easily possible in (1-a), it is not possible to refer back to *book* via *ones* in (1-b). In Postal's terminology, *books* within the phrase *a rack for books* allows outbound anaphora, but *book* within the compound *bookrack* does not allow outbound anaphora.

Soon after the publication of Postal's paper, it was observed that his claim does not hold for all morphologically complex words. Rather, it was pointed out that there is data that shows different degrees of acceptability. Lakoff & Ross (1972) illustrated this cline in acceptability with the data and judgments reproduced in (2), their (2b) and (3a-b), where *one* in (2-a) and *it* in (2-b) and (2-c) are intended to refer to the guitar, which is contained in the derivation *guitarist*.

(2)　　a.　　*A **guitar**$_i$ist bought **one**$_i$ yesterday

　　　　b.　　?*The **guitar**$_i$ist thought that **it**$_i$ was a beautiful instrument.

　　　　c.　　?John became a **guitar**$_i$ist because he thought that **it**$_i$ was a beautiful instrument.

This cline cannot be explained by Postal's original proposal, which makes a categoric difference between islands and non-islands. Other authors offering counterexamples to Postal's strong claim include Tic Douloureux (1971), Corum (1973), Browne (1974) and Watt (1975), whose main claims and accounts are discussed in Ward, Sproat & McKoon (1991), as well as Levi (1977). A representative set of counterexamples involving English compounds is presented below, first with anaphoric references to the first element of the compound, cf. (3), secondly with anaphoric reference to the second part of the compound, cf. (4).

(3)   a.   Although casual **cocaine**$_i$ use is down, the number of people using **it**$_i$ routinely has increased.

       b.   Patty is a definite **Kal Kan**$_i$ cat. Every day she waits for **it**$_i$.

       c.   I was an **IRS**$_i$-agent for about 24 years. … I stopped working for **them**$_i$.

The examples in (3) are from the appendix of Ward, Sproat & McKoon (1991). *Cocaine use* in (3-a) is a synthetic compound which should disallow anaphoric reference to its 2 constituents. However, the following *it* refers back to the denotation of *cocaine* and not to the denotation of *cocaine use*. Similarly, *it* in (3-b) refers back to the denotation of *Kal Kan*, that is, to a specific brand of catfood, where *Kal Kan* is embedded in a standard endocentric compound, and finally, in (3-c), *them* refers back to the IRS, the US Internal Revenue Service. Another notable feature of these 3 examples is that in 2 of the 3 compounds the actual anchors for the anaphors are proper names (*Kal Kan* and *IRS*). This corresponds to the distribution of cases involving pronominal reference to non-heads in the corpus investigated by Ward, Sproat & McKoon (1991): two-thirds of them are proper names (cf. ten Hacken 1994: 76).

    The data discussed by Ward, Sproat & McKoon (1991) is restricted to anaphoric reference to the first element of the compound, whereas Levi (1977) presents data showing that reference to the second element is also possible, cf. (4), her (17b), (18b), and (19a).

(4)   a.   State **taxes**$_i$ were higher than municipal **ones**$_i$.

       b.   Steam **irons**$_i$ need more maintenance than **those**$_i$ that iron dry.

       c.   Student **power**$_i$ is insignificant compared to **that**$_i$ of the Dean.

In (4-a), *ones* refers back to the denotation of *taxes* and not to the denotation of *state taxes*. *Those* in (4-b) refers to the denotation of *irons* and not to the denotation of *steam irons*. Finally, *that* in (4-c) refers back to the denotation of *power* and not to the denotation of *student power*.

    Coulmas (1988) discusses sets of German data that either allow or do not allow anaphoric reference, cf. (5) and (6), his (3–4) and (5–6).

(5)   a.   *Atomwaffen$_i$gegner   haben gegen ihre$_i$ Lagerung in
            nuclear:weapons:opponents have   against their storage   in
            Europa protestiert.
            Europe protested
            Intended: Opponents of nuclear weapons protested against their storage in Europe.

    b.   *Der **Fuß**$_i$gänger hat sich   in **ihn**$_i$ geschossen.
           the pedestrian has himself in it   shot
           Intended: The pedestrian has shot himself in his own foot.

(6)   a.   **Atom**$_i$waffengegner   haben immer wieder dagegen
           nuclear:weapons:opponents have always again against
           protestiert, daß **solche**$_i$ Waffen in Europa gelagert werden.
           protested, that such   weapons in Europe stored will
           'Time and again, opponents of nuclear weapons have protested
           against storing such weapons in Europe.'

    b.   Die **Diamanten**$_i$suche war noch nicht lange unterwegs, da   hatten
           the diamond:hunt   was yet   not   long underway, then have
           sie **ihn**$_i$ schon.
           they it   already
           'The diamond hunt had not been on for long when they already found
           it.'

Coulmas also gives some acceptable English examples, for example (7), his (12) and (15b).

(7)   a.   The **rocket**$_i$ launch had to be delayed because of some unexpected problems with **its**$_i$ fuel tanks.
    b.   The **river**$_i$bank was damaged when **it**$_i$ overflowed after three days of heavy rain.

It is not the rocket launch but the rocket that has problems, likewise, it is not the riverbank but the river that overflows. Coulmas hypothesizes that the ability of outbound anaphora is proportional to the compositionality of words and to the correspondence between formal and semantic compositionality (1988: 321).

    Ward, Sproat & McKoon (1991) take semantic transparency to be a key factor in the facilitation of outbound anaphora. They argue that anaphoric reference to parts of a word is only possible if the individual constituents invoke individual discourse entities. Whether or not the individual constituents of a compound invoke individual discourse entities does, in turn, depend on whether they are semantically transparent or not. In case of semantic opacity, they assume that "[morphologically complex words] can no longer be straightforwardly interpreted on the basis of their component parts" Ward, Sproat & McKoon (1991: 454). Once a word is semantically opaque, so they argue, outbound anaphora is inhibited, as their example in (8) shows, where # marks pragmatic deviance.

(8)   Fritz is a **cow**$_i$boy. #He says **they**$_i$ can be difficult to look after.

While Ward, Sproat & McKoon (1991: 455) assume that the distinction between transparent and opaque words is gradient, they provide no measure for this gradience.

Considering the above-mentioned preponderance of proper names as anchors for anaphora in the corpus used by Ward, Sproat & McKoon (1991) and their own analysis that anaphoric reference requires the constituents to invoke individual discourse entities, one could also argue that the very fact that reference to individual entities is the core function of proper names makes them more likely to actually lead to the activation of the corresponding referents, even when embedded in compounds.

In Schäfer (2013), I discuss German adjective noun constructions and attempt to provide a measure for different degrees of semantic transparency. Adapting paraphrase tests proposed in Fahim (1977), I distinguish between 5 different classes of AN compounds that I hold to be semantically transparent to a decreasing degree. The 5 classes are briefly illustrated in (9), ranked from most to least transparent.

(9)   a.   Endocentric pattern A: $[AN_N]$ = $[AN]_{NP}$:
              Rotwein = roter Wein 'red wine'
       b.   Endocentric pattern B: $[AN_N]$ ≈ $[AN]_{NP}$:
              Großstadt ≈ große Stadt 'big city'
       c.   Endocentric pattern C : $[AN_N]$ ≠ $[AN]_{NP}$:
              Grünspecht ≠ grüner Specht 'Green woodpecker'
       d.   Exocentric pattern A: $[AN_N](x)$ → $[A](x)$:
              Ein Dummkopf ist dumm. 'A stupid.head is stupid.'
       e.   Exocentric pattern B: $[AN_N](x)$ ↛ $[A](x)$:
              Ein Rotkelchen ist nicht rot. 'A red.throat (a robin) is not red.'

While the patterns as presented here are dependent on the semantics of the corresponding phrases, the proposed 5-fold distinction is more or less a mixture of criteria involving institutionalization, internal semantic structure and metonymic shifts.

In Schäfer (2013), I also tried to provide empirical support for my classification by doing a small corpus study. However, I only found attested examples of patterns involving outbound anaphora for the first 2 endocentric classes.

3.1.2 Semantic transparency and compound stress

Semantic properties of compounds correlate with the stress patterns found in English compounds. Plag et al. (2008) show that the categories of compound constituents as well as the semantic relations between compound constituents are highly predictive of compound stress. Bell (2012) also finds certain semantic relations to be highly predictive of noun noun stress patterns, in particular, of right prominence. Bell (2012: 49–51) hypothesizes that the factor semantic transparency might be a higher order feature that unites this group of relations (cf. also the generalization in Giegerich 2009: 6 that "end-stress favours transparent over non-transparent semantics"). How does Bell (2012) operationalize semantic transparency? In a first step, Bell (2012) equates semantic transparency with semantic compositionality. In the context of her work, which focuses exclusively on noun noun constructions, she also refers to noun noun constructions with compositional meanings as constructions with phrase-like semantics, referencing an old tradition within the compound noun community starting with Sweet's (1891: 288) observation on nouns with "even stress" that "the logical relation between the elements of the compound resembles that between the elements of a free group, especially when the first element is felt to be equivalent to an adjective". Semantic compositionality is then operationalized as shown in (10), her (3.10):

(10)   A NN is semantically compositional when its meaning entails one of a small number of relations between N1 and N2, which can usually also be expressed phrasally, and can be described schematically.

The entailed relations that were considered were the following 4 (cf. Table 3.4, Bell 2012: 65): (1) N2 IS (MADE OF) N1, (2) N2 IS AT/ON/IN N1, (3) N1 HAS N2, and (4) NN IS NAME. The entailment criterion can best be illustrated by a concrete example from the N2 IS AT/ON/IN N1 group. A(n) NN was classified as belonging to this dataset if the statement in (11), applied to the NN of interest, resulted in a true statement.

(11)   X is (an) NN entails X is (an) N2 and X is at/in/on N1
         Bell (2012: 69)

Bell (2012: 69) gives *London school* and *Monday morning* as examples that fulfill this condition. While this so far does not look different from other relational classifications, Bell shows that the entailment criterion can be used for further, non-trivial distinctions. For the at/in/on group, it is used for the distinction between "NNs where N1 simply gives the location of NN, and those where N1 defines a type of NN, irrespective of its location" Bell (2012: 69). Thus, Bell (2012: 69) excludes an item like *door bell* from this group, since, according to her argumentation, a door bell remains a door bell independent of its actual location, whereas *office ceiling* was judged to entail that the ceiling is located in an office. Note that while this is an important difference, discussing this difference under the term of entailment is somewhat unfortunate, as what seems to have been judged here are typical relations between the referents of the compound and the referents of its constituents that need not always hold. On top of that, speakers might vary in their judgments on this typicality. Bauer, Lieber & Plag (2013: 447), discussing the issue of individual variation in relation to the terminological distinction between ascriptive and associative interpretations made in Giegerich (2009), remark: "linguists may disagree as to whether *door* in *doorknob* is associative (the knob is associated with a door) or ascriptive (the knob has the property of being on a door) in nature".

Bell (2012) tested her hypothesis by building models for NN prominence, and all 4 relations emerged as significant predictors of rightward stress in a logistic regression model that also included other predictors usually associated with rightward stress. Interestingly, Bell (2012) also compared her regression model with several rule-based models, and discovered that the best rule-based model was one that only made use of the 4 semantic relations discussed above; its results were only slightly worse than those of the regression model (cf. Bell 2012, Table 3.11).

3.1.3 Conclusion: semantic transparency and other phenomena

As the extent of the discussion above has shown, semantic transparency has rarely been used in concrete attempts to explain observed language patterns. While the relationship between semantic transparency and outbound anaphora sounds very plausible, the value and the extent to which the observations are generalizable is unclear, as none of the studies used empirical measures for semantic transparency. The approach by Bell (2012) used a clear operationalization of semantic transparency; however, it is not clear to what extent this categorization actually captures the same notion of semantic transparency that was used in the psycholinguistic operationalizations described in Chapter 2.

3.2 Other measures and notions relating to semantic transparency

3.2.1 Quantitative measures

There are a number of quantitative measures that, to varying degrees, target semantic aspects of complex nominals. I will introduce these in detail in Chapter 5, which contains sections on informativity related measures and on measures based on the word space model (such as Latent Semantic Analysis).

3.2.2 Semantic overlap

Odegard, Lampinen & Toglia (2005), studying effects on memory and recollection, consider the semantic overlap between compound triplets consisting of 2 parents, e.g. *handball* and *shotgun*, and a recombined child, e.g. *handgun*. For this particular example, they see a high semantic similarity between *shotgun* and *handgun*, and considerable semantic overlap between the meanings of *hand* in both compounds. As an example with little similarity and overlap they give the 2 parents *blackmail* and *jailbird* and the recombined child *blackbird*. For their experiments, they manually constructed a set of 40 compound word triplets which was then rated by 24 participants for "the level of similarity shared between the meaning of a parent word and its conjunction (e.g., blackmail to blackbird)" (Odegard, Lampinen & Toglia 2005: 419) on a 5-point Likert-type scale (ranging from 1, "not similar whatsoever", to 5, "highly similar").

Leding et al. (2007) used a large-scale questionnaire study (185 participants) to establish, besides familiarity and memorability, semantic overlap measures for 96 compound triplets.

3.2.3 Compositionality and literality

There are 2 notions that are also often discussed together with the notion of semantic transparency, namely the notion of compositionality and the notion of literality. I will discuss these 2 notions in turn.

3.2.3.1 Compositionality

In lieu of the term semantic transparency, some psycholinguistic and linguistic studies use the term 'semantic compositionality' to refer to similar phenomena. This usage of the term also occurs in some studies within distributional semantics, e.g. Reddy, McCarthy & Manandhar (2011), whose approach to establishing compositionality of compound nouns was already described in Chapter 2, Section 2.2.2. In formal semantics, compositionality is usually discussed in connection with the compositionality principle, cf. (12) for the formulation of this principle in Partee (1984: 281).

(12)   The meaning of an expression is a function of the meanings of its parts and of the way they are syntactically combined.

An expression is compositional if its meaning can be computed in accordance with this principle. The problem is that it is very unclear which formalisms do and which do not fit under this principle. This in turn is related to questions pertaining to the exact meaning of 'meaning' in (12). Thus, if we accept underspecified semantic representations, and if we distinguish between a proper semantic and a proper pragmatic level of interpretation, then almost all meanings are compositional. For example, taking *milkman* again, one can argue that its semantic meaning is composed by combining the 2 predicates MILK(x) and MAN(x) with the help of the underspecified template in (13), where R represents an underspecified relation (note that it is not relevant to the point illustrated here when and how this relation is eventually existentially bound).

(13) $\lambda B \, \lambda A \, \lambda y \, \lambda x \, [A(x) \ \& \ R(x,y) \ \& \ B(y)]$

This yields (14), which, up to this point, is technically semantically fully compositional.

(14) $\lambda y \, \lambda x \, [MILK(x) \ \& \ R(x,y) \ \& \ MAN(y)]$

In order to arrive at the final, correct interpretation of *milkman*, the relational parameter needs to be specified. For the appropriate specification, access to pragmatic information is needed, but this could be argued to lie outside of the realm of semantics proper. On this view, semantic transparency could easily be linked to compositionality. One approach would be to argue that semantic transparency correlates with the amount of additional pragmatic input that is involved in arriving at the pragmatic meaning of a complex expression whose semantic meaning has been calculated via the principle of compositionality.

   In contrast to such a view, some authors have argued for a clear distinction between transparency and compositionality. Sandra (1990: 550), for example, argues that transparency "refers to the relationship between compound and constituent meanings, the latter [compositionality] refers to the possibility of determining the whole-word meaning from the constituent meanings." This view is echoed in the final paragraph in Zwitserlood (1994):

> [S]emantic transparency is not the same as compositionality. Although the semantic relation between transparent compounds and their constituents might be easy to establish, the meaning of the compound as a whole is often more than the meaning of its component words.
> (Zwitserlood 1994: 366)

3.2.3.2 Literality

Within computational linguistics, literality is often linked to compositionality. In Chapter 2, Section 2.2.2, I included the study of Reddy, McCarthy & Manandhar (2011), who argued for viewing compositionality as literality. As pointed out there, their way of operationalizing literality corresponds to the methods others have used to establish semantic transparency. Others working in computational linguistics who also explicitly link literality and compositionality are for example Lin (1999), Katz & Giesbrecht (2006), and Biemann & Giesbrecht (2011) (Biemann & Giesbrecht 2011 are very similar to Reddy, McCarthy & Manandhar 2011 in that they annotated phrases for compositionality by asking 'How literal is this phrase'). Lin (1999) presents a method to detect non-compositional phrases which is based on the assumption "that non-compositional phrases have a significantly different mutual information value than the phrases that are similar to their literal meanings" (Lin 1999: 321). However, the exact understanding of 'literality' is often not made very clear. Thus, Lin (1999) gives *red tape* vs. the "compositional phrase" *economic impact* as a starting example. Indeed, when one considers the collocation *red tape* with its meaning 'obstructive official routine or procedure; time-consuming bureaucracy', one would intuitively judge it to be less literal than *economic impact*. Note, though, that the impact in *economic impact* can also be argued to be not a literal impact but only a metaphorical impact, as no physical contact takes place. Lin (1999) uses the operationalization of non-compositionality given in (15), cf. his (3).

(15)   A collocation α is non-compositional if there does not exist another collocation β such that (a) β is obtained by substituting the head or the modifier in α with a similar word and (b) there is an overlap between the 95% confidence interval of the mutual information values of α and β.

Thus, the actual criterion is exclusively based on frequencies, and no independent definition of literal or non-compositional meaning is given. Considering the contrast between *red tape* and *economic impact* in the light of the condition in (15), one might hypothesize that the decisive difference between the 2 combinations lies in the fact that *impact*, but not *tape*, already occurs often (if not mostly) in a non-concrete usage when it occurs on its own.

This is problematic, because standard dictionary definitions of *literal* as applied to meanings are clearly based not on frequencies, but on quite different concepts, cf. (16), a definition taken from the OED.

(16)   literal
        II.c
        Of, relating to, or designating the primary, original, or etymological sense
        of a word, or the exact sense expressed by the actual wording of a phrase
        or passage, as distinguished from any extended sense, metaphorical mean-
        ing, or underlying significance.
        OED

Importantly, a purely distribution-based approach like the one by Lin (1999) and the traditional understanding of literal meaning as illustrated in the quote from the OED might sometimes yield the same result, but this need not be the case. Take an example like *sacred cow* from the dataset of Reddy, McCarthy & Manand- har (2011). In the BNC, only one of 15 uses clearly refers to a real cow. In contrast, if looking at the word *cow* on its own, we find many uses referring to the real animal. Here, we would expect Lin's distributional approach to coincide with the notion of literality as described in the OED quote. However, it would be inter- esting to compare the intuitive literality of examples with rare animals like lion (rare at least from a broadly western point of view), e.g. in *stone lion*, with actual corpus occurrence of *lion* on its own, many of which do seem to refer to pic- tures, statues, or toy versions of lions. I will return to this issue when discussing the annotation of constituent meanings in the 2 empirical studies presented in Chapters 6 and 7.

Focusing on the state of the traditional idea of literality as illustrated by the OED quote, I cannot possibly do justice to all the literature written on this topic. However, I will illustrate the debates surrounding this notion by considering 2 viewpoints on the notion of literal meaning from psychology and formal seman- tics respectively.

In psychology, Gibbs (1989: 249), while agreeing that "[p]eople can sometimes judge some statements as literal and other as metaphorical", points out that this does not mean that literal meanings necessarily play a role in understanding non- literal meaning, and, perhaps more importantly, that there is no evidence to show that different cognitive processes are involved in processing these meanings.

For formal semantics, I will use Jaszczolt (2016) to illustrate a possible point of view. In general, Jaszczolt (2016) discusses the term *literal meaning* at several places, but, and that is most important for the discussion here, in her own model, called Default Semantics, this term does not occur anymore. In doing so, she does not abandon the idea of word meanings:

> ...: if we want a semantic theory that allows for the freedom of context-dependence and at the same time recognizes the fact that there *are* word meanings, that, to put it crudely, the word 'dog' is much more likely to refer to dogs than cats or food processors, we have to start with the assumption that words stand for concepts but that these concepts are situation-specific *not* because they shift according to some clear rules or that they are constrained by the possibilities of the grammar; neither are they situation-specific because they are built in the process of language use. Rather, they are dynamic simply because they are susceptible to new uses in virtue of past uses; the generalization over past uses does not produce an abstract concept but instead paves the way towards new uses.
> (Jaszczolt 2016: 133–134)

However, these word meanings are not literal meanings as traditionally understood. Rather, she argues "to retain the concept of word meanings as sufficiently to subsume such influences of context-driven inferences as well as automatic interpretations of different provenance" (Jaszczolt 2016: 136). Jaszczolt recognizes that some sentence meanings, and for that matter word meanings, are more easily arrived at when the sentences occur out of context. However, this is not because there is a literal meaning, but rather because she adapts a view she labels cognitive minimalism:

(17)   Cognitive minimalism
        Sentences issued out of context come with different degrees of plausibility and these degrees correlate with different intuitions concerning context-free evaluability with respect to truth and falsity. The plausibility and the intuitions all depend on the accessibility of a default, 'made-up' context that can be used as a tool for such a 'neutral', apparently context-free, evaluation. (Jaszczolt 2016: 58)

Importantly, she points out that the standard meaning one assigns to a sentence need not be the literal one. Consider (18), her (48) (Jaszczolt 2016: 59):

(18)   A star has died.

According to Jaszczolt, the default situation for (18) could be one that refers to the death of a movie star rather than to the death of a star in the astronomical sense (note that this point still seems to hold even if the predicate *die* is exchanged with something more neutral, e.g. *We saw a star*).

3.2.4 Semantic transparency as one dimension of idiomaticity

Nunberg, Sag & Wasow (1994), working on idioms, point out that existing attempts at defining idioms often fail to keep key semantic concepts apart. In particular, they argue that 3 semantic dimensions should be distinguished: an idiom's relative conventionality, an idiom's opacity/transparency, and an idiom's compositionality. The relative conventionality is "determined by the discrepancy between the idiomatic phrasal meaning and the meaning we would predict for the collocation if we were to consult only the rules that determine the meanings of the constituents in isolation, and the relevant operations of semantic composition" (Nunberg, Sag & Wasow 1994: 498). The opacity/transparency dimension stands for "the ease with which the motivation for the use (or some plausible motivation – it needn't be etymologically correct) can be recovered" (Nunberg, Sag & Wasow 1994: 498). And finally, compositionality stands for "the degree to which the phrasal meaning, once known, can be analyzed in terms of the contributions of the idiom parts" (Nunberg, Sag & Wasow 1994: 498). They introduce the term *idiomatically combining expressions* to refer to idioms "whose parts carry identifiable parts of their idiomatic meanings" (Nunberg, Sag & Wasow 1994: 496), in contrast to *idiomatic phrases*, where this is not the case. In this context, their discussion of the phrase *to pull strings* is particularly helpful. Clearly, the idiomatic meaning "exert a hidden influence" cannot be predicted on the basis of the meanings of its constituents and the relevant semantic construction rules for verb object combinations, there is therefore a large amount of conventionality involved. On the other hand, as Nunberg, Sag & Wasow (1994: 496) point out, on hearing a sentence like *John was able to pull strings to get the job, since he had a lot of contacts in the industry*, the hearer might be able to deduce the correct meaning of the phrase. Thus, the expression is not completely opaque, and more importantly, the hearer can now map parts of the idiom to parts of the meaning. Nunberg, Sag & Wasow, using the interpretation *exploit personal connections*, argue that *pull* can be mapped to *exploit*, and *strings* can be mapped to the exploited connections.

That conventionality should be kept apart from compositionality is illustrated by Nunberg, Sag & Wasow (1994) with the help of the contrast between American *thumb tack* and British *drawing pin*, which both denote the same types of objects:

Both are compositional and do not involve any figuration. Their double existence is solely due to different ways of conventionalization (cf. Nunberg, Sag & Wasow 1994: 495).

Titone & Connine (1999) provide a balanced overview of previous studies of idiomaticity which either argue for a non-compositional or a compositional approach. They explore the distinction between idiomatically combining expressions and idiomatic phrases from Nunberg, Sag & Wasow (1994) in an eye tracking study working with preceding and following contexts favoring either the literal or the non-literal interpretation. They interpret their results as supporting a hybrid model of idiom processing, according to which the idiomatic meanings are directly retrieved but a literal analysis of the respective phrase is also carried out.

Note that the research on idioms described above presupposes that a) there is a literal meaning and b) we know what that literal meaning is. As the discussion in the section on literality has shown, though, literal meaning by itself is not in any way well-understood. I suspect that one reason why the departure from literal meaning is taken as a given in the discussion of idioms lies in the fact that the expressions usually allow 2 interpretations, that is, we can use *kick the bucket* to refer to the action of striking the corresponding vessel, as well as using it to refer to the act of passing away. This is reminiscent of the contrast between *red tape* and *economic impact* discussed above: *Red tape* allows 2 interpretations, and the one that just refers to a narrow strip with the color red is used as a foil for the second interpretation. In contrast, *economic impact* only comes with one interpretation, which, since it is the only interpretation, is intuitively judged to be literal.

3.2.5 Semantic transparency and productivity

Just as one can hypothesize that there is a correlation between increased lexicalization and less semantic transparency, it seems intuitively plausible that productivity and semantic transparency might likewise be correlated, albeit with the effects going in the same direction: the more productive, the more transparent and vice versa. Baayen (1993: 199) points out that "semantic transparency, like phonological transparency, is a necessary but not a sufficient condition for productivity." He gives some examples from Dutch: the Dutch plural suffix *-eren* is fully semantically transparent, yet unproductive. Another example of phonologically and semantically fully transparent constructions are female personal nouns in *-ster*, which are less productive than constructions with an unmarked *-er* or a de-adjectival *-heid*. "Differences in the usefulness of items in *-ster*, *-er* and -*heid* to the language community, differences in markedness, the effects of paradigmatic rivalry, but also social convention as such – Dutch -*ster* is much less productive than its German counterpart -*in* – should not be neglected" (Baayen 1993: 199–200).

3.3 Transparency in other domains

In all of the examples for semantic transparency discussed so far, the 2 constituents making up the compound are still recognizable. If the individual constituents can no longer be recognized, considerations of semantic transparency become moot. Consider *lord*: Etymologically, it is a compound, according to the OED, derived from Old English *hláford*, in turn derived from the precursors of today's *loaf* and *ward* respectively. However, as pointed out by Dressler (2006: 40), it is not recognizable as a compound anymore, being the end product of fossilization. As witnessed by *lord*, fossilization can affect a construction's meaning as well as a word's phonology and orthography, with the latter usually trailing the latter. Both areas by themselves can also be described in terms of transparency.

3.3.1 Phonological transparency

In general, phonological transparency involves the relationship between the phonetic forms of a construction in isolation vs. the phonetic form of that construction when it is part of a larger, complex construction (this is in the spirit of Marslen-Wilson et al. 1994: 5, although they only discuss cases of affixation). Thus, the base *friend* in *friendly* is phonologically transparent, because the string [frend] occurs unchanged in [frendlɪ]. In contrast, the base *conclude* in *conclusive* is not phonologically transparent, because the [d] in [kənkluːd] is changed to [s] in [kənkluːsɪv]. In the case of compounds, changes with respect to the phonetic shape of the constituents in isolation can be as extensive as to make it doubtful whether, orthography aside, the compound status is still perceivable, consider e.g. *blackguard*, *boatswain*, and *shepherd*, pronounced /ˈblægərd/) and /ˈbəʊsn/, and /ˈʃepəd/ respectively. Phonological reduction is also a matter of degree. Thus, while *man* in *postman* [pəʊstmən] contrasts with the free form man [mæn] and is therefore not phonologically transparent, the pronunciation of the free form can be retrieved in situations calling for contrastive stress, e.g. *a post*[mæn] *not a postwoman*.

Phonologically opaque compounds bear some similarity to (and might in practice be indistinguishable from) pseudocompounds like *boycott*, an example used in Zwitserlood (1994).

3.3.2 Orthographic transparency

Orthographic transparency is, at least to a certain degree, unrelated to semantic and/or phonological transparency. Thus, 2 of the examples for phonologically opaque compounds of the previous section, *blackguard* and *boatswain*, are orthographically fully transparent. These 2 examples are also semantically opaque. In contrast, *shepherd* is not only phonologically opaque, but also orthographically opaque. However, the first element <shep> is not semantically opaque.

If, as in the case of *lord*, a construction is opaque with regard to its meaning, phonology and orthography, then it is typically impossible to synchronically recognize it as a compound.

3.4 Conclusion

The aim of this chapter was threefold. First, I gave an overview of 2 linguistic phenomena, anaphora resolution and stress placement, where semantic transparency is hypothesized to play a role. Second, I gave a short overview of other terms that are related to semantic transparency. Finally, I briefly discussed transparency in phonology and orthography.

As the first section has shown, while it seems plausible that semantic transparency plays a role with regard to whether internal constituents of complex words are accessible or not, the research so far has not used a clear criterion to identify transparency in the first place, or, in the case of my own research, the criterion was clear, but only insufficient empirical evidence could be found. With regard to the role of semantic transparency in stress assignment, Bell (2012) used very clear criteria, but these were very different in nature from the methods used in psycholinguistics to establish semantic transparency.

The second section started by pointing to work on semantic overlap, a notion that very likely at least partially taps into the same features that semantic transparency is after. However, given the very specific targets of that line of research (memory and recollection effects), and the overall very small number of compounds thus classified, it is hard to compare it to measures directly targeting semantic transparency. The section on compositionality and literality showed 2 points: (1) For many, transparency, compositionality and literality are one and the same thing. For those that distinguish between transparency and compositionality, compositionality refers to meaning predictability whereas transparency is already fulfilled when the constituent meanings can be recognized in the meaning of the complex expression. (2) Literality is a difficult concept.

The section on idiomaticity and semantic transparency showed that a distinction should be made between transparency, conventionality, and compositionality. While conventionality here is closely related to the difficult notion of literality, the combination of the transparency and the compositionality dimension is very close to the conception of semantic transparency as introduced in Chapter 1, namely a gradual notion with meaning predictability at one end and recoverability of constituent meanings at the other end. Finally, productivity can be argued to result in transparency. In contrast, semantic transparency does not automatically lead to or entail productivity.

The third section discussed the notion of phonological and orthographical transparency. These notions will not play a role in this work, but it is important to realize that a sufficient degree of transparency in a given construction in either of these 2 domains is a prerequisite for the question of semantic transparency to arise.

4 Compounds and the semantic analysis of complex nominals

Complex nominals, that is modifier-head combinations with a noun as their head, are traditionally distinguished into compounds and phrasal constructions. Compounds, because they are morphological units, are treated by morphologists, phrasal constructions are not.[1] At the same time, in works on noun noun compounds, one often finds reference to "phrase-like" noun noun combinations (cf. Giegerich 2009: 8), or "phrase-like semantics" of noun noun combinations (cf. Bell 2012: 48). While these formulations imply that there is a specific semantic analysis for phrasal modifier head constructions, a considerable body of work in formal semantics on the semantics of phrasal modifier head constructions, especially adjective noun constructions, has shown that this is not the case. In contrast, with notable exceptions like Fanselow (1981) and Meyer (1993), formal semantic treatments of compounds are rare.

Due to these differences in focus, the resulting analyses of complex nominals from the formal semantics and the morphological traditions also show major differences. In particular, early analyses in formal semantics are based on set-theoretic properties, while morphological analyses focus on relations. Newer approaches, in contrast, mix ideas from these 2 approaches. In this chapter, I will start by sketching the main ideas behind the set-theoretic and the relation-based approaches, and then introduce some mixed approaches.

While giving an overview of possible approaches to compound semantics, this chapter will also show why compound classifications based on the Levi system of classification are still so useful.

---

[1]Unless the phrasal constructions are themselves embedded in words, cf. Trips & Kornfilt (2017) for a recent edited volume on phrasal compounding.

4.1 Set-theoretic approaches: the semantics of adjective noun combinations

As mentioned in the introduction, formal semantics has focused on the analysis of phrasal constructions, and, when it comes to nominals, especially on set-theoretic analyses of adjective noun combinations. The set-theoretic approaches usually start from classifications for adjectives, which are differentiated into intersective and non-intersective adjectives, the latter set again being differentiated into subsective and non-subsective adjectives, cf. Partee (1995). Here, I follow this tradition by illustrating intersective, subsective, and non-subsective modification with the help of adjective noun constructions. In addition, I give pointers to similar behavior within the class of noun noun constructions.

4.1.1 Intersective modification

Intersective modification refers to combinations of modifier and modified that can semantically be analyzed as the intersection of the 2 sets denoted by modifier and modified respectively. The class of intersective adjectives is defined by its participation in the respective intersective modification patterns, illustrated below for the adjective *radioactive* in (1).

(1)   **Radioactive bumper cars** lie silent in the abandoned city of Priypat near the Chernobyl reactor. COCA

Assuming that *bumper car* denotes a set of individuals, that is, the set of bumper cars, and that *radioactive* likewise denotes a set of individuals, namely the set of radioactive things, the denotation of the combination of the 2 strings can be analyzed as the intersection of the 2 sets, cf. (2) (this representation format is directly adapted from Kamp & Partee 1995, cf. also Partee 1995).

(2)   *radioactive bumper car*
      $[\![$radioactive$]\!]$ $= \{x|x \text{ is radioactive}\}$
      $[\![$bumper car$]\!]$ $= \{x|x \text{ is a bumper car}\}$
      $[\![$radioactive bumper car$]\!] = [\![$radioactive$]\!] \cap [\![$bumper car$]\!]$
                        $= \{x|x \text{ is radioactive and } x \text{ is a bumper car}\}$

Intersective adjectives therefore allow the inference patterns given in (3) and (4).

(3)   This is a bumper car.
     This is radioactive.
     ―――――――――――
     → This is a radioactive bumper car.

(4)   This is a radioactive bumper car.

→ This is radioactive.
→ This is a bumper car.

Kamp (1975: 124) refers to these adjectives as *predicative*, and he mentions that technical and scientific adjectives like *endocrine, differentiable* and *superconductive* constitute typical examples. Keenan & Faltz (1985: 124) name *male, female* and *Albanian* as examples; Kamp & Partee (1995) and Partee (1995) use *carnivorous* as their example.

While the discussion revolves around adjectives, it is easy to come up with examples of noun noun combinations that behave similarly. In particular, material nouns like *plastic, nylon,* or *silk* give rise to similar inference patterns, cf. *silk shirt* in (5).

(5)   He wore his best suit, a clean **silk shirt** and shaved extra close.
       BNC/AC3 2081

Clearly, the same inference pattern arises here:

(6)   This is a silk shirt.

→ This is silk.
→ This is a shirt.

Note that the material nouns are typically mass nouns, and that, presumably due to this inference pattern, a standard dictionary practice is to simply assign them double class membership as nouns and adjectives (e.g., the noun sense of *silk* is the fiber, and the adjective sense is 'composed of or similar to silk', cf. the entry in the American Heritage College Dictionary 1993).

Another class of noun noun combinations that allows this inference are so-called copulative compounds, e.g. *singer-songwriter*, see also the remarks in Section 4.4.2.4.

4.1.2 Subsective modification

Subsective modification differs from intersective modification in that the combination of modifier and modified results in a subset of only the set denoted by the modified. Importantly, the denotation of the modifier by itself does not yield a single independent set denotation, because it is always relative to some scale or measure provided either by the linguistic or the extra-linguistic context. The class of subsective adjectives is defined by its participation in subsective modification patterns. Classic examples for this class are dimensional adjectives like *big* or *small*, cf. (7) for 2 combinations with *big*.

(7)   a.   A rat is not just a **big mouse**. COCA
       b.   There I was, face to face with a **big snake**, getting over my fears. COCA

The denotation of *big mouse* is not the intersection of the set of big things and the set of mice, and without further qualification, the inference patterns discussed for the intersective adjectives in the previous section are not available. In particular, a snake that is as big as a big mouse is not a big snake, and big mice are mice, but mice as a class are typically counted among the small things. The most obvious feature of these adjectives is thus that they display a certain context sensitivity or vagueness, cf. Kamp (1975), Partee (1995), Heim & Kratzer (1998) and Chierchia & McConnell-Ginet (2000). Note that this context sensitivity is not only influenced by the choice of the head noun. This is very convincingly demonstrated by Partee (1995) with (8), her (17).

(8)   a.   My 2-year-old son built a really **tall snowman** yesterday.
       b.   The D.U. fraternity brothers built a really **tall snowman** last weekend.

Although both sentences talk about tall snowmen, the size standards used to evaluate the adjective differ: One expects the snowman built by the 2-year old to be far smaller than the one built by the fraternity. In a similar way, information from previous utterances can influence which size standard is used in evaluation.

Note that once the context sensitivity is taken into account and the correct size standard has been chosen and is then fixed, subsective adjectives behave technically like intersective adjectives, cf. Partee (1995: 330–336).

There are various technical solutions on how vagueness can be accounted for. One popular implementation is Kennedy (2007), who analyzes gradable adjectives as functions from individuals to degrees. The degrees, in turn, constitute a scale, that is, a total ordering of the degree with respect to some dimension. The semantics of the positive form morpheme *pos* handles the vagueness, cf. (9), his (27).

(9) $[\![\, [_{Deg} pos] \,]\!] = \lambda g \lambda x . g(x) \geq s(g)$

Here, "[...] s is a context-sensitive function that chooses a standard of comparison in such a way as to ensure that the objects that the positive form is true of 'stand out' in the context of utterance, relative to the kind of measurement that the adjective encodes" (Kennedy 2007: 17).

Kennedy (2007: 6) points out that vagueness needs to be distinguished from indeterminacy, "the possibility of associating a single lexical item with several distinct but related measure functions". Thus, he argues that his example (4a), *Chicago is larger than Rome*, is ambiguous with regard to the exact measure function used; one could at least refer to either population or sprawl. Kennedy (2007: 6) views adjectives like *skillful* and *clever* as extreme examples for this kind of indeterminacy, because they are "highly underspecified for the precise feature being measured". However, whether vague or indeterminate, both types of adjectives lead to the same pattern of subsective modification (note that the examples for indeterminacy given here are also vague and require a standard of comparison once a measure function is selected).

Parallels to the behavior of subsective adjectives in the domain of noun noun constructions are not so obvious. However, *star* in the 2 examples in (10) parallels the behavior of indeterminate adjectives.

(10)   a.   Antonio was a **star dancer** and he could not take an objective view of the whole. BNC/A12 1732

        b.   As he was the NME 's **star writer** I guess Malcolm realised that once the band really started to get going, Nick would be able to help us out — whether he knew it or not. BNC/A6E 908

That is, after selecting a domain, here either the domain of dancing or writing, the modifier *star* is evaluated relative to the scale for this domain. And arguably, *star* also gives rise to the typical patterns for vague modification, since standards of starhood differ, consider the star writer of a high-school yearbook as opposed to the NME star writer in (10-b).

4.1.3 Non-subsective modification

Non-subsective modification refers to cases where the denotations of the modifier and the modified do not intersect. Classic examples of adjectives that are analyzed as non-subsective are e.g. *former* in (11) and *alleged* in (12).

(11)   These deaths occurred primarily among **former employees**. COCA

(12)   A fight ensued, and one of the **alleged vandals** was stabbed with a kitchen knife. COCA

What happens in the case of *former* is that any overlap with the current denotation of the head noun is excluded, that is, the set of people in the denotation of *former employee* does not overlap with the set of people in the current denotation of *employee*, cf. (13).

(13)   *former employee*
       [[former employee]] ≠ [[former]] ∩ [[employee]]

The case of *alleged* is a bit more complicated, because an overlap is not excluded. Both adjectives are also different from the adjectives discussed so far in that they require a more complicated semantic analysis in any case and cannot fruitfully be understood as one place predicates of alleged or former things respectively. This property is reflected in their inability to occur in predicative position.

   The *former*-type adjectives are also referred to as privative adjectives, cf. Partee (1995: 325). There, she gives *counterfeit* as an additional example.

   Within the group of constructions traditionally labeled as compounds, non-subsective usages can also be found. Thus, we have formations like *nonentity* in (14):

(14)   'Imagine them not even getting his name right, Weasley, it's almost as though he's a complete **nonentity**, isn't it?' he crowed.
       J. K. Rowling, Harry Potter and the Goblet of Fire, Chapter 13, Mad-eye Moody

Another example is *shadow cabinet* in (15), for additional examples from German cf. (43).

(15)   Mr Prescott is unquestionably closer to a large swathe of the rank and file than most other members of Labour's **Shadow Cabinet**. BNC/A1J 588

Shadow in *shadow cabinet* seems slightly similar to *former*, pointing to a virtual cabinet that might become the actual cabinet at a later point on the time axis.

4.1.4 Problems for a set-theoretic classification of adjectives

While the main differences between the 3 different types of modification are clear, it is not so clear whether adjectives can be classified with the help of these classes, or whether or not all adjectives are more or less subsective. For intersective adjectives, it has been the class of color adjectives which led to principled discussion of the question of intersectivity.

Another set of observations concerning the combinatorics of adjectives and nouns that is not accounted for by the set-theoretic approach is discussed in the section on pragmatic anomaly.

The non-intersectivity of specific adjectives is also sometimes questioned. Partee (1995: 325) discusses the adjective *fake* as a problematic candidate for the class of privative adjectives, pointing to questions like *Is that gun real or fake?* as rather suggesting otherwise.

4.1.4.1 Color adjectives

Color adjectives are typically taken to be good examples for the class of intersective adjectives, and combinations of color-adjective noun are often used to illustrate the expected inference pattern (cf. textbook discussions, e.g. Heim & Kratzer 1998: 62–70 on *gray cats* and Chierchia & McConnell-Ginet 2000: 459–461 on *pink tadpoles*, but also Fodor & Pylyshyn 1988: 43[2]). Many examples confirm this expectation, cf. *green chair* in (16), which gives rise to the 2 inferences in (16-a) and (16-b) and whose main clause, likewise, should be deducable from (16-a) and (16-b) treated as its 2 premises.

(16)   He sinks into a **green chair**, though James has not invited him to sit.
        COCA

      a.   He sinks into something green.
      b.   He sinks into a chair.

However, even here the situation is not always so straightforward. Consider the 2 occurrences of *blue wall* in (17) and (18).

(17)   So, if you wouldn't mind just standing over here against the **blue wall**.
        COCA

(18)   BRADLEY: I – i – is there a reluctance on the part of police officers to talk
        about other police officers and what some of them may have done?
        SCHWARZ: Are you referring to, like, a **blue wall**, what everybody else
        refers to? No, absolutely not.
        BRADLEY: There is no **blue wall**?
        SCHWARZ: No.   COCA

---

[2]Fodor & Pylyshyn (1988: 43) do not use the term 'intersective', but their example is clear enough: "Consider predicates like '...is a brown cow'. This expression bears a straightforward semantical relation to the predicates '...is a cow' and '...is brown'; viz. that the first predicate is true of a thing if and only if both of the other are."

In (17), meaning composition for *blue wall* follows the intersective pattern, i.e., the denotation of *blue wall* is the intersection of the set of walls with the set of blue things, and its meaning can likewise be seen as the addition of the 2 meanings of *blue* and *wall.* In contrast, *blue wall* in (18) clearly is used with another meaning, referring to the *blue wall of silence,* a euphemism for the police practice of stonewalling investigations into police misbehavior. While this usage of *blue* involves a clear meaning shift, the existence of true intersectivity has also been questioned for usages not involving obvious meaning shifts.

Some remarks by Quine (1960) throw first doubts on an intersective analysis for color adjectives. First, he points out that *red wine* can be treated as a compound mass term where "[r]ed wine is that part of the world's wine which is also part of the world's red stuff" (Quine 1960: 104). In contrast, "[r]ed houses and red apples overlap the red substance of the world in only the most superficial sort of way, being red only outside" (Quine 1960: 104). Secondly, Quine (1960: 132–133) mentions a suggestion by Jakobson to him, according to which, based on examples like *black bread, white wine* and *white man,* white and *black* should be construed as comparative adjectives (that is, along the lines of *white X* being interpreted as X is more white than the average X) due to the fact that "no wine is white stuff and no men are white things" (Quine 1960: 133). In a tradition dating back to Partee (1984), Quine (1960) is attributed with the contrasting pair *red apple* vs. *pink grapefruit,* with a red apple being red only outside (see above), and the pink grapefruit only being pink inside.

Lahav (1989) even uses the color adjective *red* to make a forceful attempt against the whole idea of compositionality. His exercise on what it means to be a red noun is worth citing in its entirety:

> Consider the adjective 'red'. What it is for a bird to count as red is not the same as what it is for other kinds of objects to count as red. For a bird to be red (in the normal case), it should have most of the surface of its body red, though not its beak, legs, eyes, and of course its inner organs. Furthermore, the red color should be the bird's natural color, since we normally regard a bird as being 'really' red even if it is painted white all over. A kitchen table, on the other hand, is red even if it is only painted red, and even if its 'natural' color underneath the paint is, say, white. Moreover, for a table to be red only its upper surface needs to be red, but not necessarily its legs and its bottom surface. Similarly, a red apple, as Quine pointed out, needs to be red only on the outside, but a red hat needs to be red only in its external upper surface, a red crystal is red both inside and outside, and a red watermelon is red only inside. For a book to be red is for its cover but

not necessarily for its inner pages to be mostly red, while for a newspaper to be red is for all of its pages to be red. For a house to be red is for its outside walls, but not necessarily its roof (and windows and door) to be mostly red, while a red car must be red in its external surface including its roof (but not its windows, wheels, bumper, etc.). A red star only needs to appear red from the earth, a red glaze needs to be red only after it is fired, and a red mist or a red powder are red not simply inside or outside. A red pen need not even have any red part (the ink may turn red only when in contact with the paper). In short, what counts for one type of thing to be red is not what counts for another. Of course, there is a feature that is common to all the things which count (non-metaphorically) as red, namely, that some part of them, or some item related to them, must appear wholly and literally redish. But that is only a very general necessary condition, and is far from being sufficient for a given object to count as red. (Lahav 1989: 264)

The same point is taken up again in Lahav (1993), cf. especially Lahav (1993: 76).

Blutner (1998), in discussing these data, also points to the phenomenon of lexical blocking. Lexical blocking in the case of color adjectives concerns for example the contrast between *pale green/blue/yellow* vs. *pale red*. Due to the availability of the word *pink*, the combination *pale red* is anomalous for some speakers, for others its domain is restricted to only the non-pink sub-part of the domain of pale red (Blutner 1998: 123 attributes this observation to Householder 1971).

Travis (2000) also discusses some examples containing color adjectives in connection with the notion of occasion-sensitivity. He writes:

The English sentence 'It's blue' represents (that is, is a means of representing) some contextually definite object as blue. That form, as produced in different surroundings, in different speakings of those words (of a given object at a given time) might engage with the world in any of indefinitely many ways. One might, in so producing it, say any of many different things to be so. For there are indefinitely many and various *possible* understandings of an object's being blue. (Travis 2000: 200, his emphasis)

As a consequence, the only rule for the predicate *blue* is "it is correctly used on an occasion only to describe what then *counts* as blue" (Travis 2000: 213, his emphasis). Again, his examples include the search for *blue ink* at a stationer, where on most occasions, *ink* will count as *blue ink* if it produces blue writing, and on these occasions, *ink* that looks blue but writes black will not count as *blue ink* (though on other occasions it perfectly well might count as blue ink).

4.1.4.2 Pragmatic anomaly of adjectives

Blutner (1998: 123) uses the data in (19), his (5), to illustrate what he calls the pragmatic anomaly of adjectives:

(19)   a.   The tractor is red.
        b.   The tractor is defective.
        c.   The tractor is loud.
        d.   The tractor is gassed up.
        e.   ?The tractor is pumped up.
        f.   ?The tractor is sweet.
        g.   *The tractor is pregnant.
        h.   *The tractor is bald-headed.

Blutner argues that pregnant and bald-headed tractors are simple cases of category violations, whereas the combinations in (19-e) and (19-f) are cases of pragmatic anomaly. Or, as Blutner writes, "[t]hat *sweet* is not an appropriate attribute of *tractors* can't be explained on grounds of an ontological category violation. A tractor *can* be sweet, by the way. Taste one: it might surprise you" (Blutner 1998: 123, his emphasis). Lahav (1989: 265–266) comes to the same conclusion, when he discusses the fact "that many adjectives do not apply to many objects at all" (Lahav 1989: 265), pointing to cases like *a straight house, a soft car,* or *a quiet stone,* or even *gradual rats* and *intense trees.* He continues:

> Notice, that the point is not that houses are never straight or that trees are never intense in the same way that trees never breath or talk. Rather, we have no agreed upon conception of what it would be for a house to count – or to fail to count – as straight, [...] (Lahav 1989: 265)

4.2 Relation-based approaches: the semantics of compounds

There is a considerable number of compound classifications that are in one way or another relation based. My aim in this section is not so much to compare all these approaches, instead, I want to focus on 2 important works from the same period, namely Levi (1978) and Fanselow (1981). I will start with a more detailed description of Levi's work, because her classification system or adaptions thereof are still used widely today. This holds both for psycholinguistic approaches (cf.

especially the discussion of the work relating to conceptual combination in Chapters 2 and 5), as well as for work in computational linguistics (cf. Ó Séaghdha 2008, who starts from Levi's proposal in order to arrive at a new annotation scheme). In addition, Levi already includes more than traditional compounds in her analysis, and, as pointed out in chapter 1, Levi's approach and usage of the term *complex nominal* is the starting point for my own, extended usage of the term.

For earlier work on semantic relations, a good starting point is the overview in Levi (1978: 77) which lists the traditional names of her relational predicates and points to relevant earlier literature. In particular, she refers to Koziol (1937), Jespersen (1942), Hatcher (1960), Brekle (1970), and Adams (1973) for English, and to Li (1971) for Chinese and Motsch (1981) for German.

4.3 Levi (1978)

4.3.1 Levi's complex nominals

Levi (1978: 1–2) introduces the term 'complex nominals' in order to cover 3 sets of expressions "which have generally been called 'nominal compounds', 'nominalizations', and 'noun phrases with nonpredicating adjectives'" Levi (1978: 1). Examples for each group, chosen from her original examples (1.1)–(1.3), are given in (20).

(20)	a.	nominal compounds:	*apple cake, windmill*
	b.	nominalizations:	*presidential refusal, dream analysis*
	c.	noun phrases with non-predicating adjectives:	*electrical conductor, musical talent*

Why does she treat these 3 distinct groups as one? The main reason, stated in Levi (1978: 4–5), is the observation that the third group, the noun phrases with nonpredicating adjectives, are very similar to noun noun constructions as far as their syntax and semantics are concerned, which leads Levi to the hypothesis that these adjectives are derived from underlying nouns. Following this hypothesis, she identifies complex nominals as a group encompassing the 3 subgroups mentioned above.

While Levi's understanding of complex nominals is thus wider than the traditional class of compounds, it nevertheless does not equate to a consideration of all sorts of traditional phrasal constructions. This can be seen very clearly when looking at the kind of data she considers as evidence for the introduction of her

new class. Of the 6 properties Levi (1978: 19) proposes, 3 are particularly interesting, namely nondegreeness, conjunction behavior, and case relations. The
first 2 of them are reminiscent of traditional compound tests, cf. the remarks in
Chapter 1, Section 1.2.

Levi (1978: 19) exemplifies the property of nondegreeness with the help of the
following examples, cf. her (2.4).

(21)   a.   *very urban riots
       b.   *very bodily injury
       c.   *a very electrical conductor
       d.   *very automotive emissions.

This property can also be found in items traditionally considered as compounds,
cf. *very blackbird* or *very blackboard.*

The conjunction behavior of interest is illustrated in (22) and (23), her (2.6)
and (2.7): As (22) illustrates, nonpredicating adjectives can be conjoined with
common nouns. In contrast, they cannot be conjoined with true adjectives, that
is, prototypical attributive adjectives, cf. (23).

(22)   nonpredicating adjectives conjoined with nouns:
       a.   electrical and mining engineers
       b.   a corporate and divorce lawyer
       c.   solar and gas heating
       d.   electrical and water services
       e.   domestic and farm animals

(23)   nonpredicating adjectives conjoin only with nonpredicating adjectives,
       not with true adjectives
       a.   a civil and mechanical/*rude engineer
       b.   anthropological and ethnographic/*respected journals
       c.   continental and oceanic/*expensive studies
       d.   literary and musical/*bitter criticism

While the co-ordination criterion also plays a role in the compound vs. phrase
debate (cf. Bauer 1998: 74–76, who discusses this issue extensively), the main
point here is that the nonpredicating adjectives follow the pattern of the nouns
and not the pattern of the other, more prototypical adjectives.

The data that Levi (1978: 27–28) discusses under the heading of case relations
concerns the observation that one can attribute the semantic relations of agent,
object, location, dative/possessive, and instrument to nonpredicating adjectives.

Her 'agentive' category is illustrated in (24), cf. her (2.12).

(24) a. presidential refusal
      b. editorial comment
      c. revisionist betrayals
      d. senatorial investigations
      e. national exports

Levi distinguishes between 2 distinct analyses (or, in her understanding, derivational pathways) for complex nominals. In Section 4.3.2, I give an overview of the first approach, the recoverably deletable predicates. Section 4.3.3 discusses her second approach, which involves predicate nominalizations.

4.3.2 Levi's recoverably deletable predicates

Levi (1978: 75–80) introduces 9 types of *recoverably deletable predicates*: CAUSE, HAVE, MAKE, USE, BE, IN, FOR, FROM, and ABOUT. The first 3, CAUSE, HAVE, and MAKE, come in 2 different versions.

The basic idea behind her analysis is that a construction like *tear gas* can be derived via an underlying relative clause in which the respective predicates serve as main verbs. Thus, *tear gas* is derived from *gas that causes tears*, and so on. Below, I give 2 of her examples for each predicate, one containing what is traditionally considered a compound noun, the other a phrase containing a nonpredicating adjective (cf. Table 4.1 in Levi 1978: 76–77).[3] The complex nominals are embedded in sentences retrieved via COCA. Behind the examples, I added paraphrases which make the intended interpretation clear. Note that since not all recoverably deletable predicates are verbs, the actual derivation pathways that Levi suggests are rather complex, cf. Levi (4.2, Derivations 1978: 118–153) for the details. Here, I will ignore this aspect of her work, focusing on the resulting semantic classification of complex nominals.

(25) CAUSE

      a. CAUSE1 [N2 causes N1]
          (i) You can no more deal with them in good faith than you can with a–a **disease germ**. COCA
               'germ that causes a disease'

---

[3]Due to zero occurrences in the COCA and the BNC, I replaced *nasal mist* with *nasal spray*. Likewise, *rural visitors* was replaced by *rural lawmakers*, *linguistic lecture* with *linguistic theory*, and *professorial friends* with *professorial staff*.

(ii)   The 9/11 attacks was a deeply **traumatic event** for our country. COCA
'event that causes a trauma'

b.   CAUSE2 [N1 causes N2]

(i)   As we have been reporting, **drug deaths** in Mexico skyrocketed. COCA
'deaths that drugs cause'

(ii)   Disease detectives are taking a serious look at the emerging link between **viral infection** during pregnancy and the later development of mental impairment in the fetus. COCA
'infection that viruses cause'

(26)   HAVE

a.   HAVE1 [N2 has N1]

(i)   The children narrated a wordless **picture book**. COCA
'book that has pictures'

(ii)   One teacher described the immediate area around the school as an **industrial area** with no houses and several major intersections. COCA
'area that has industry'

b.   HAVE2 [N1 has N2]

(i)   Instead, it has issued demolition notices throughout the slum, which sits illegally on **government land**. COCA
'land that the government has'

(ii)   Her **feminine intuition** told her that he was very definitely attracted to women, but she was pretty sure that he did not permit himself to cross the line that separated physical satisfaction from mind-spinning passion. COCA
'intuition that females have'

(27)   MAKE

a.   MAKE1 [N2 makes N1]

(i)   The town had a large-scale **silkworm** cultivation and many factories employed Korean workers. COCA
'worm that makes silk'

(ii)   A digital clock on the computer screen starts to tick down from sixty seconds, and a **musical clock** starts to sound too – something like the "Jeopardy" theme. COCA
'clock that makes music'

b.   MAKE2 [N1 makes N2]
  (i)   "I taught her how to make **daisy chains**," Essa said from the doorway. COCA
    'chains that daisies make'
  (ii)   The atmospheric reactions can create **molecular chains** heavy enough to rain out on Titan's surface. COCA
    'configurations that molecules make'

(28)   USE [N2 uses N1]

  a.   If you need to press the felt, use a **steam iron** or damp cloth. COCA
    'iron that uses steam'
  b.   It's hot, it's dirty, and it's undoubtedly **manual labor**. COCA
    'labor that uses hands'

(29)   BE [N2 is N1]

  a.   Grammar boxes – the **target structure** explained and exemplified for clarification and for reference. BNC/CLL 2985
    'structure that is a target'
  b.   Setzler had done graduate work at the University of Chicago, and he maintained strong ties with the **professorial staff** there. COCA
    'staff that are professors'

(30)   IN [N2 is in N1]

  a.   He hops out of the truck and goes inside to quickly say his **morning prayers**. COCA
    'prayers that are in the morning'
  b.   In addition, it should be noted that great **marital sex** is good for your health, in addition to the glow it puts on your face and the spirit it puts in your step. COCA
    'sex that is in a marriage'

(31)   FOR [N2 is for N1]

  a.   Kirghiz, the bay gelding, needs the **horse doctor**. COCA
    'doctor that is for horses'
  b.   Retrieving a **nasal spray** from an inner pocket of his waistcoat, he assumed a thoughtful expression: COCA
    'spray that is for the nose'

(32)   FROM [N2 is from N1]

  a.   Stir in the **olive oil**; it does not need to emulsify. COCA
    'oil that is from olives'

> b. Despite strong opposition from **rural lawmakers**, the bill passed the GOP-led House of Delegates with support from Democratic and Republican lawmakers throughout the urban crescent. COCA
> 'lawmaker that are from the countryside'

(33)   ABOUT [N2 is about N1]

> a. This has been **tax law** in, in America for almost 10 years now, existing **tax law**. COCA
> 'law that is about tax'
> b. He believed that an adequate **linguistic theory** should include not only just linguistic competence, but also the social-cultural aspects, which are "so salient" in any linguistics proper. COCA
> 'theory about linguistics'

Levi's study contains extensive commentary on these different classes. Here, I will only point to some of her remarks and findings that are particularly important as far as their interaction with or contribution to semantic transparency is concerned.

Levi (1978: 85–86) notes that her 9 recoverably deletable predicates are quite different in terms of their productivity (note, though, that from extensively studying Levi 1978 it has not become clear to me what exactly the data is that she uses to draw these conclusions). According to her, HAVE1, CAUSE, MAKE and FROM are least productive (cf. *picture book, disease germ/drug deaths, silkworm/daisy chains* and *olive oil* above). Moderately productive are USE, BE, and ABOUT. Finally, FOR, IN, and HAVE2 (cf. *government land* above) are most productive. In addition, for all 3 predicates with 2 configurations she finds a skew in her data towards those derived from passivized verbs (Levi 1978: 86). Interestingly, she mentions that she finds a 'surprisingly' similar distribution in an early study on Modern Hebrew, cf. Levi (1976).

Levi's system in many cases allows for multiple alternative analyses of one and the same complex nominal. Levi (1978) points out that a particular subgroup of those nominals that can be analyzed via the MAKE2 predicate have an alternative analysis via BE, again corresponding to a specific subset of complex nominals that fall under this predicate, cf. the examples in (34).

(34)   *landmass, chocolate bar, stone wall, sugar cube, bronze statue*
        [modifier denotes a unit, head denotes a configuration]

In general, MAKE2 nominals are derived from sources with what Levi (1978: 90) calls a 'compositional reading', corresponding to *make up of/made out of*, as opposed to MAKE1, where Levi (1978: 90) diagnoses "a sense of 'physically producing, causing to come into existence'". In (34), there are "head nouns that denote either a mass or an artifact of some sort, and modifiers that describe its constituent material". On the MAKE2 analysis, a complex nominal like *chocolate bar* is derived from *a bar that chocolate makes*, that is, *a bar made from/made of chocolate*. On the BE analysis, it is derived from an underlying *a bar that is chocolate*. Crucially, these 2 analyses are available for the same compound reading, that is, the compound itself is not ambiguous.

Other instances of 'analytic indeterminacy' (Levi 1978: 90) occur between MAKE1 and FOR (e.g. *musical clock, music box, sweat/sebaceous/salivary glands,* the analysis of *suspense film (film that causes suspense/has suspense)*, and *job tension (tension caused by the job, tension that the job has, tension on the job)*, cf. Levi (1978: 91) for all examples.

Levi (1978: 262–269) raises a number of issues connected with analytic indeterminacy. First, she notes that in many cases the analytic indeterminacy may in fact be regular and predictable, pointing to the MAKE2/BE pattern illustrated in (34). Secondly, in some cases analytic indeterminacy may in fact be non-existent on an ideolectal level. People may agree on the denotatum of a complex nominal, but nevertheless disagree if explicitly asked why a given complex nominal is called that way. Levi (1978: 265) mentions that an example like *tidal wave* is explained by some by *because it is caused by the tide*, others explain it by *because it sweeps in like the tide, only it's more powerful*. An important point that she makes in this context is that this kind of intersubject variation is not bound to high frequency complex nominals, but can also be expected for new nominals, exemplifying this by her first encounter with *athletic charges*, where even when being offered an explicit explanation she could either assign a FOR deletion or a nominalization based analysis (for the curious: "students on athletic scholarships had their book bills charged to the Athletic department" Levi 1978: 265).

Analytic indeterminacy, especially the case in which several non-conflicting analyses are held simultaneously, is also discussed by Jackendoff (2010: 427–428), who proposes to label the words in question as promiscuous, cf. the discussion in Chapter 6, Section 6.2.1.1.

4.3.3 Predicate nominalization

A predicate nominalization analysis is only relevant for nominals with deverbal nouns as heads. Again, the focus will be on the resulting classification rather than on the derivational system Levi introduces. Levi (1978: 167–174) works with 2 different axes of classification, one involving the type of nominalization, the other involving the syntactic status of the first, premodifying element, in the assumed underlying structure.

As far as nominalization types are concerned, she distinguishes between act, product, agent and patient nominalizations. Examples along with illustrating paraphrases, drawn from her (5.1) and (5.2), cf. Levi (1978: 168–169), and enriched with actual corpus occurrences and some additional explanatory paraphrases are given in (35).

(35)   a.   act nominalizations
- (i)   McPhee acknowledges that **dream analysis** isn't a highly respected element in psychology. COCA
  'act of analyzing dreams'
- (ii)   Until now the pan-German press had, however thinly, veiled its attacks in the rhetoric of **musical criticism**, but now they savaged Anna with unrestrained glee. COCA
  'act of criticizing music'

     b.   product nominalizations
- (i)   Cognitive science is a young, changing discipline subject to **human error** and ambition; only recently, a Harvard evolutionary biologist has been accused of fabricating data about animal cognition. COCA
  'that which is produced by (the act of) humans erring'
- (ii)   Ten most common misconceptions regarding **musical critique**. WEB
  'that which is produced by (the act of) criticizing music'

     c.   agent nominalizations
- (i)   My father worked in the post office, first as a **mail sorter** and then as station manager. COCA
  'x such that x sorts mail'
- (ii)   He was a successful Hollywood attorney; she was a **film cutter** for Hollywood movies. COCA
  'x such that x cuts film'

     d.   patient nominalizations
- (i)   **Student invention** could save kids in overheated cars WEB
  'y such that students invent y'
- (ii)   He has also served as a **presidential appointee** to the National Museum and Library Services Board since 2006. COCA
  'y such that presidents appoint y'

For the second axis of classification, Levi distinguishes between subjective, objective, and multi-modifier nominals. In the case of subjective nominalizations, the premodifier is analyzed as the subject in the corresponding derivational source, for the objective nominalizations, it is the object, and in the case of multi-modifier nominalizations, both subject and object of the underlying forms are realized as premodifiers. These 3 types are illustrated in (36), drawn from her (5.6–5.8), cf. Levi (1978: 173–174).

(36) a. subjective:
      (i)   **parental refusal** to allow initiative and creativity; COCA
             'act of parents refusing'
      (ii)   Anna Chau's 2010 Fulton County and Johns Creek tax bills
             were sent to the wrong address because of a **clerical error**.
             COCA
             'that which clerics making errors produce'
      (iii) Then Surapati and his men left Kartasura, reportedly with
             some of the Susuhunan's horses and fine firearms as **royal**
             gifts. COCA
             'that which royals give as gifts'

   b. objective:
      (i)   What kind of access should women have to **birth control**?
             COCA
             'the act of controlling birth'
      (ii)   Her income, from welfare, food stamps, rent and **tuition sub-**
             sidies and a $3,000 gift from her mother, puts Ms. Owens, a
             single mother, and her three children just above the official
             poverty line. COCA
             'that which subsidizes the tuitions'
      (iii) Privacy, hah! I slipped the **acoustic amplifier** out of my desk
             drawer and stuck it on the wall that my office shared with
             Sam's. COCA
             'that which amplifies the acoustics'

   c. multi-modifier:
      (i)   In the mid-1980s, the Indian government began an ambitious
             effort to clean up municipal and **industrial water pollution**
             in the Ganges River, where most of the 1.4 billion liters of
             sewage generated every day by cities and towns along the river
             is dumped without treatment. COCA
             'the industry's act of polluting water'

> (ii) Why should there be **government price supports** for sugar?
> COCA
> 'the products of governments supporting the price'

As can be seen from the examples, subjective constructions can be found with act, product, and patient nominalizations, objective constructions with act, product, and agent nominalizations, and multi-modifier constructions only with act and product nominalizations.

4.3.3.1 Scope restrictions of Levi's analysis

Levi (1978) aims "to demonstrate the pervasive regularities that may be discerned in the area of CN [complex nominal] formation" (Levi 1978: 269). To this end, she excludes certain sets of data from her analysis.

First of all, she is only interested in endocentric formations, that is, "those CN [complex nominals] whose referents constitute a subset of the set of objects denoted by the head noun" (Levi 1978: 6). With this, she in particular excludes the 3 groups illustrated in (37), cf. Levi (1978: 6).

(37) a. metaphorical names, e.g.:
          the usage of *ladyfinger* for a type of pastry, of *tobaccobox* for a sunfish, of *silverfish* for an insect, of *foxglove* for a flower.
      b. synecdochical reference (using a part to present the whole), e.g.:
          peg leg, blockhead, birdbrain, eagle-eyes in reference to people, or *razorback, glasseye, hammerhead, cottontail* in reference to animals.
      c. coordinate structures "such that neither noun may be taken as head", e.g.:
          speaker-listener, participant-observer, player-coach, secretary-treasurer, screwdriver-hammer, sofa-bed, library-guestroom

Secondly, she excludes proper nouns that resemble complex nominals in form but contain a first element used primarily to name a single and definite referent, e.g. *Kennedy Library* or *Sheridan Road*. Levi (1978: 7) notes that these usually denote places or businesses. Thirdly, she excludes constructions which contain non-predicating adjectives that, in her opinion, are derived from underlying adverbs, cf. the examples in (38), from her (1.9).

(38) a. potential enemy
      b. occasional visitor
      c. former roommate
      d. alleged attacks

Paraphrase possibilities like those in (39), cf. (1.10) in Levi (1978: 8), are taken by her as suggestive evidence for an underlying derivation from adverbs.

(39)   a.   They are all potential enemies/potentially enemies.
       b.   She is a former roommate/was formerly a roommate.

Finally, she wants her theory to be a theory about productive processes and therefore excludes metaphorical, lexicalized, or idiomatic meanings. She distinguishes between lexicalized meaning and idiomatic meanings as follows: lexicalized meanings are meanings of complex nominals that have idiosyncratic meaning added on to a predicted literal reading, cf. her example *ball park*, which is predicted to have the meaning 'park for ball' but has developed the lexicalized meaning 'park or stadium designed for people to play baseball in [rather than football, basketball, or handball]', cf. (1.16) in Levi (1978: 10). In contrast, idiomatic meanings are those meanings where the choice of the specific constituents is 'more or less' irrelevant. Thus, she considers *fiddlesticks, horsefeather*, and *bullshit* with their meaning 'nonsense' as fully idiomatic, cf. (1.20) in Levi (1978: 12) for more examples. Complex nominals are also excluded if only one of the constituents is idiomatic. Levi (1978: 12) illustrates these constructions with complex nominals containing an idiomatic prenominal modifier, e.g. *polka dot* as the name for a dot-based pattern, or *cottage cheese* as the name for a type of cheese.

4.3.4 Evaluating Levi's approach

Levi's approach has been much discussed, starting with Downing (1977) (she discusses Levi 1975, Levi's dissertation which forms the basis of the 1978 book).

Downing (1977: 827) points out that when reducing the semantics of a compound to the formulas proposed by Levi, "it is unclear how much of essential semantic content of the item is lost". In addition, she points out that her experimental results and some of the attested novel compounds "would be very difficult to reduce to any of these categories", illustrating this claim with the examples in (40), cf. her (14).

(40)   a.   interpretations of novel compounds from a context free interpretation task:
            (i)   *cow-tree*: a tree that cows like to rub up against
            (ii)   *egg-bird*: a bird that steals other birds' egg
            (iii) *pea-princess*: a genuine princess, who passes the test of a pea under 20 mattresses

b. rankings of novel compounds (rating of given interpretations as 'likely', 'possible', 'impossible')
   (i) *pumpkin-bus*: 'a bus that turns into a pumpkin at night' one likely, 6 possible, one impossible
   (ii) *oil-bowl*: 'a bowl designed to hold oil or syrup' 3 likely, 5 possible, zero impossible
c. attested compounds (from a scene-description task, a newspaper, and 2 novels, cf. Downing 1977: 817 for details): *thalidomide parent*; *cranberry morpheme*; *pancake-stomach* 'a stomach full of pancakes' *plate-length* 'what your hair is when it drags in your food'

However, Downing (1977: 828) acknowledges that the fact that many of the compound taxonomies proposed in the earlier literature are reducible to Levi's, and that, in addition, her own novel compounds are also reducable to a limited set of basic semantic categories akin to Levi's suggests that "these lists are something less than arbitrary". Downing (1977: 828–829) also points out that at least in her data there is a link between the semantic class of the head of the compound and the resulting preferred interpretation of the compound.

More principled criticism comes from Fanselow (1981: 151–154) who sees Levi's work in the tradition of Motsch (1981). He sees the resulting ambiguities in the classifications of individual compounds as problematic. Further, he doubts that the number of predicates can be kept as low as the respective authors assume, questioning the appropriateness of an analysis of, e.g., *Polizeihund* 'police dog' as 'dog that the police uses', and pointing to the exploitation of polysemies in the analyses of the different authors as indicative of this problem, citing Levi's analysis of both *cell block* as well as *silk worm* as formed with MAKE as an example (note that this criticism holds although the 2 are distinguished as MAKE2 and MAKE1 respectively). In general, he questions the usefulness of the resulting classification, which can only be a classification of those *Verrichtungen* 'doings' which dominate in our society, not a classification of possible ways of forming compounds. Finally, the system does not allow one to test whether a given classification is correct, since the final step from the predicates to the relation needed for the specific compounds is missing. If one acknowledges that the specific compound's constituents are responsible for the concrete specification of the relation in question, that is, when the constituents themselves allow to deduce the relation, then the underlying predicates are superfluous.

Devereux & Costello (2005) experimentally investigate the issue of analytic indeterminacy in a Levi-derived classification system, investigating the system used in establishing the CARIN model in Gagné & Shoben (1997) (for this system and the relations used, cf. Chapter 2, Section 2.1.3.1).[4] In their experiments, subjects could choose from 18 relations in classifying 60 compounds, and they were allowed to choose as many relations as fit. Although the compounds were presented along with an interpretation, subjects on average suggested 3.23 relations for every compound. One of the compounds where participants consistently chose several relations was *job anxiety*, where 'MODIFIER causes HEAD' and 'HEAD about MODIFIER' occur most often, with 13 (!) of the 18 relations chosen at least once.

4.3.5 Conclusion: the enduring appeal of Levi's system

As shown in the previous section, Levi's system has a number of weaknesses. However, if one is interested in compound formation from a cognitive point of view, one would like to be able to assess the productivity of different kinds of compounds. To assess the productivity, in turn, one needs to have access to some kind of frequency data. Here, the approaches to compound semantics that rely on a categorization in terms of different relations are in widespread use, and within these, the relations proposed by Levi (1978) have proven hugely influential. The reason for the success of her system is succinctly summed up in the following quote: "[...] Levi's proposals are informed by linguistic theory and by empirical observations, and they intuitively seem to comprise the right kind of relations for capturing compound semantics" (Ó Séaghdha 2008: 27). Often, the Levi-relations provide the starting point for classifications and are enriched with additional relations as needed (cf. especially the discussion of the works using the CARIN or RICE models of conceptual combination in Chapter 2 and Chapter 5). While these classifications are still very similar to Levi's original classification, other reworkings include a number of greater changes. The proposal by Ó Séaghdha (2008), who dubs Levi's and similar systems as inventory-style approaches (Ó Séaghdha 2008: 17), is a good example for a very extensive and careful reworking of Levi's system. Starting with her original 9 relations, he points out 4 main problems with her classification (cf. Ó Séaghdha 2008: 30–31):

1. The CAUSE relation is very infrequent.
2. The MAKE1 relation is also infrequent; in addition, alternative relations are possible for 'most, if not all' examples that Levi gives for this relation.
3. Nominalizations and recoverably deletable predicates are treated apart.

---

[4]For the purpose of their experiment, they add 2 additional relations, modifier IS head, and modifier MAKES head, cf. Devereux & Costello (2005: 495).

4. Levi does not provide explicit annotation guidelines and is unconcerned with regards to overlapping categorization or vague boundaries between categories.

Ó Séaghdha (2008: 31) singles out the overlapping categorization as the most critical of the problems, using the compound *car factory* to illustrate: whether categorized as FOR (factory for producing cars), CAUSE (factory that causes cars to be created), IN (factory in which cars are produced), or FROM (factory from which cars originate), all 4 categories still describe the very same meaning (cf. also Devereux & Costello (2005) discussed in section 4.3.4 above).

Ó Séaghdha works both aspects of Levi's analysis into one consistent annotation system, and adds detailed annotation guidelines for his system. Perhaps the most important changes are the removal of MAKE1, CAUSE, USE, and FOR, and the introduction of 2 new categories ACTOR and INSTRUMENT.

4.4 Fanselow (1981)

Working on German, Fanselow (1981) distinguishes between 2 major groups of compounds, *nominale Rektionskomposita* 'nominal relational compounds' and *Determinativkomposita* 'determinative compounds'. Following the structure of his work, I will start with the former in the next section and then discuss the *Determinativkomposita* in Section 4.4.2, cf. Part II and Part III in Fanselow (1981) respectively. Since Fanselow's approach is only published in German, I present his ideas here somewhat more extensively.

4.4.1 Compounds involving relational nouns

Fanselow not only discusses compounds with deverbal heads, but also other relational heads in some detail. Examples are words like *Sozialdemokratenfan* 'fan of the social democrats', *Professorenkomplize* 'professor accomplice' and *Kanzlerbruder* 'chancellor brother', cf. Fanselow (1981: 81). What they have in common with deverbal heads is that the noun in the head position has an open position for a term. Within this group, Fanselow distinguishes a number of subgroups. Here, I am not going to discuss these subgroups in any detail but simply point to several interesting observations in his work. Thus, he notes that for the deverbal cases, especially those formed with agent nominalizations like *LKW-Fahrer* 'truck driver', either a habitual or a non-habitual reading is possible. Corpus examples illustrating these 2 usages are given in (41), where *LKW-Fahrer* in (41-a) clearly requires a habitual interpretation, because it describes a specific function in a company. In contrast, in (41-b) the driver does not need to have been a habitual truck driver.

(41) a. Als die Familie Bauer Trans OG ihre Firma 2001 gründete, arbeitete Oswald Bauer noch bei der Firma Köck als **Lkw Fahrer**. DeReKo
'When family Bauer started their business, Trans OG, in 2001, Oswald Bauer was still working as a truck driver for Köck.'

  b. Ein dahinter fahrender 29-jähriger **LKW- Fahrer** konnte nicht mehr rechtzeitig bremsen und fuhr mit seinem LKW auf, teilt die Polizei mit. DeReKo
'The driver behind them, a 29-year old truck driver, didn't manage to stop in time and drove his truck into the preceding vehicle.'

In contrast to compounds with non-derived relational heads, compounds with deverbal heads also allow local interpretations of their first constituent. Thus, while both *Zeitungsverteiler* 'newspaper distributor (=newspaper boy)' and *Hochschullehrer* 'university teacher (=teacher at a university)' have deverbal heads, the modifier fills an argument position in the former case, but requires a location interpretation in the latter case, cf. Fanselow (1981: 93–94).

Besides their relational reading, compounds with a non-deverbal relational head like *Richterfreund* 'judge friend' might also have a simple coordinated reading, cf. (42).

(42) Der von Renaud Dély gekürte „Mann der Woche " ist Pierre Estoup, der heimliche **Richterfreund** von Bernard Tapie. WEB
'The man of the week chosen by Renaud Dély is Pierre Estoup, the secret judge friend of Bernard Tapie.'

Heimlicher Richterfreund 'secret judge friend ' in (42) needs to be interpreted as 'secret friend and judge'.

While in the examples so far the relational noun is always the head, Fanselow also presents numerous cases where a relational noun constitutes the first part of a compound. Among Fanselow's initial examples are *Mitgliedsbuch* member:book 'party book', *Freundeskreis* friend:circle 'circle of friends', and *Lieblingspolitiker* 'favourite politician'. Generally, these relational nouns yield compounds that are themselves relational. However, as Fanselow makes clear, there are very few general rules for these compounds, cf. e.g. *Lieblingspolitiker* vs. *Traumpolitiker* 'dream politician'. In passing, he notes a number of examples where the AB is not a B, cf. (43), Fanselow (1981: 104).

(43)   a.   *Scheingefecht*
                appearance:battle
                'mock battle'

       b.   *Kunsthonig*
                art:honey
                'fake honey'

       c.   *Schattenkanzler*
                shadow:chancellor
                'shadow chancellor'

       d.   *Ehrenpräsident*
                honor:president
                'honorary president'

       e.   *Falschgeld*
                wrong:money
                'counterfeit money'

       f.   *Pseudocleftkonstruktion*[5]
                pseudocleft:construction
                'pseudo-cleft construction'

For these cases, Fanselow (1981: 105) assumes an analysis where the first element operates on the intension of the second argument. In other cases with a relational first element, Fanselow (1981: 107) notes an asymmetry with regard to the examples in (44) as opposed to those in (45).

(44)   a.   **Fanprofessor*
                fan:professor
                'fan professor' (intended reading: professor of which somebody is the fan)

       b.   **Enkellinguist*
                grandchild:linguist
                'grandchild linguist' [intented reading: linguist who is the grandfather of someone]

(45)   a.   *Anfangskapitel*
                begin:chapter
                'first chapter'

---

[5] Note that the bracketing that Fanselow must have in mind here is [Pseudo[cleftkonstruktion]], contrasting with the bracketing suggested in the English translation equivalent. On the latter bracketing, the compound appears to be a regular determinative compound.

b.   *Schlußstein*
      end:stone
      'keystone'

Note that Fanselow is explicitly exluding readings where the first noun is not used as a relational noun. That is, Fanselow (1981: 107) acknowledges that *Vorstandspartei* 'steering committee party' could actually denote a party that only consists of the steering commitee or a party that supports the steering commitee. Given that, note that while he is correct that the first constituents in *Anfangskapitel* 'first chapter' and *Schlußstein* 'keystone' in (45) both still receive a relational interpretation, the relational argument place is not filled by the second noun, but is filled by something outside of the compound, as e.g. in *Anfangskapitel des Buches* 'first chapter of the book' or *Schlußstein des Gewölbes* 'keystone of the vault'. That is, the asymmetry is tied to whether the resulting compound is still relational, with the relationality deriving from the first noun. For compounds consisting of 2 relational nouns, he also distinguishes between those that yield relational nouns, e.g. *Zweigstellenleiter* 'branch manager', and those that do not, e.g. *Rektorentochter* 'headmaster daughter (=daughter of the headmaster)'. And again, there are sometimes ambiguities due to different readings of the compound constituents. Thus, *Kind* 'child' in *Kindsmörder* can either be taken as a common noun or as a relational noun, leading either to a reading 'set of persons who killed a child' or 'set of persons who killed their own child', cf. Fanselow (1981: 114).

Perhaps Fanselow's most important finding with regard to the compounds involving relational nouns is that deverbal heads are not so very special, since non-deverbal heads often function very similarly.

4.4.2 Common nouns with common nouns: *Determinativkomposita* 'determinative compounds'

4.4.2.1 Restrictions and the question of subsectivity

Fanselow (1981: 130) begins his treatment of determinative compounds by discussing the question whether there are any general restrictions on this type of compounds, starting with the categories that, according to Brekle (1970), play no role for compounds: quantification, tense, assertion, mode and negation. For negation, Fanselow (1981) agrees that this relation is in fact non-existent for compounds (contra Downing 1977, cf. also *nonentity* discussed in Section 4.1.3). As for quantification, he agrees with Brekle (1973) that it is usually indefinite (e.g., *car engine* ≈ engine of a car), and he likewise agrees with Brekle that the category of *assertion* is irrelevant for compounds, insofar as it has nothing to do with compound formation in particular. For mode, Fanselow (1981: 139) argues that it is needed, giving *Ziegellehm* 'brick clay' and *Kuchenmehl* 'cake flour' as examples: brick clay can be used to make bricks, and cake flour can be used to make cakes. On tense, Fanselow (1981: 133–139) argues that it is needed, but essentially restricted to perfect and co-temporality. A relevant pair of examples is *eine Nagelfabrik* 'a nail factory (= a factory that produces nails)' vs. *ein Fabriknagel* 'a factory nail (= a nail that has been produced in a factory)', illustrating co-temporality and perfect respectively. In this connection, he also points again to the different readings due to habitual vs. at least once interpretations, cf. *LKW-Fahrer* 'truck driver' in (41) above, and also notes their complementarity with what will be discussed in Section 4.4.2.2 as basic relations (cf. Fanselow 1981: 138–139).

In a next step, Fanselow considers the similarity between the first nominal element in these compounds and adjectives: "We can view the first constituent of a compound as a very special adjective with complicated semantics" [my translation] (Fanselow 1981: 142), and addresses to what extent they are subsective. He distinguishes 5 types of deviations from subsectivity. The first type subsumes combinations that do not fall into the common noun - common noun category, e.g. combinations of proper nouns like *Baden-Württemberg* 'Baden Württemberg', or combinations with a relational noun as the second element. The second type are compounds where either the first or the second element contain a 'regelmäßig bedeutungsverschiebende[n] Faktor', a regularly meaning-shifting element. An example is *Scheingefecht* 'mock battle', cf. (43-a) above, further examples are given in (46).

(46)   a.   *Saufbruder*
             drinking:brother
             'drinking companion'
       b.   *Ehrenjungfrau*
             honor:maiden
             'lady of honor'
       c.   *Boykottbrüder*
             boycott:brothers
             'guys involved in a boycott'

For these examples, compare also the comments following (43) above. Thirdly, he excludes so-called bahuvrihis, cf. the examples in (47), due to their low productivity and unsystematicity.

(47)   a.   *Dummkopf*
            stupid:head
            'idiot'
       b.   *Blaustrumpf*
            blue:sock
            'bluestocking'
       c.   *Einhorn*
            one:horn
            'unicorn'

Fourthly, some compounds (1) do not contain a regularly meaning-shifting element, (2) can be understood context-free, and (3) are not bahuvrihis. His examples are repeated in (48) and his further sub-classification is given in (49), cf. (4) in Fanselow (1981: 143).

(48)   a.   *Kindergeld*
            child:money
            'child benefit'
       b.   *Spielgeld*
            play:money
            'toy money'
       c.   *Stoffhund*
            cloth:dog
            'stuffed dog'
       d.   *Bronzegott*
            bronze:god
            'bronze god'
       e.   *Holzgewehr*
            wood:rifle
            'wooden rifle'
       f.   *Spielzeugauto*
            toy:car
            'toy car'
       g.   *Schokoladenzigarette*
            chocolate:cigarette
            'chocolate cigarette'

(49)   a.   A stands for a material from which the objects denoted by B cannot
            be made/consist of (for functional or other reasons):
            Schokoladenzigarette 'chocolate cigarette'

      b.   A stands for a function that normally is not the function of the B-objects:
          Spielzeugauto 'toy car'

      c.   A is normally not a participant in the activity associated with B:
          Kindergeld 'child benefit'

Finally, the fifth type of deviation subsumes compounds that would not receive the indicated interpretation without a specific context, Fanselow (1981: 143) gives the 3 examples in (50), corresponding to his (5).

(50)   Compounds that would not receive the indicated interpretation without a specific context:

      a.   *Fahrradbaby*
          bicycle:baby
          'somebody who just learned how to bicycle'

      b.   *Tribünensportler*
          tribune:sportsman
          'somebody who likes to watch sports from the grandstand'

      c.   *Juso-Oma*
          Juso-grandmother
          'somebody who supports Juso-aims but is, in the view of the speaker, already too old' [Juso: a youth organization of the social democratic party]

Fanselow (1981: 144) points out that the interpretation of a compound like *Bronzelöwe* 'bronze lion' does not present a compound-specific problem, as can be seen when looking at corresponding phrasal variants, cf. (51).

(51)   a.   *bronzener Löwe*
          bronze$_{ADJ}$ lion
          'bronze lion'

      b.   *Löwe aus Bronze*
          lion from bronze
          'bronze lion'

Further, Fanselow (1981: 144) points out that the required meaning shifts are not in any way different from shifts that are already needed for simplicia. This latter point can be easily demonstrated by passages like the one in (52):

(52) Der andere **Löwe** stammt von der einstigen Landesrechtspartei im Her-
      zogtum, die sich seit langem um die Wiedereinsetzung eines Welfen in
      Braunschweig bemüht hatte. Auch dieser **Löwe** erinnert an das welfische
      Wappentier. Nur hockt der **Löwe** auf einem Granitsockel, reißt das Maul
      auf und legt die Pranke auf das Wappenschild des Herzogtums. So wacht
      er symbolisch über das Land Ernst Augusts und Victoria Luises. DeReKo
      'The other lion comes from the former right-of-the-land party in the duke-
      dom [...] This lion, too, reminds one of the Welfian heraldic animal. But
      the lion crouches on a granite pedestal, yanks open his mouth and has
      his paw on the coat of arms of the dukedom. [...]'

In addition, Fanselow (1981: 145) notes that even for adjective noun combinations, one finds either reinterpretations of the noun (as in e.g. *bronzener Löwe*
'bronze lion') or reinterpretations of the adjectives (as in *scharfer Hund* 'sharp (=
aggressive) dog'). In general, "[w]hat exactly is re-interpreted is determined by
rules that crucially rely on questions of psychology and the state of things in the
world" [my translation] (Fanselow 1981: 147).

Fanselow comes to the following conclusion:

> We have thus reached a point where the compositional semantics must be
> silent and is allowed to assume that *Bronzelöwen* 'bronze lions' are indeed
> lions, and a *Juso-Oma* 'Juso grandmother' is indeed a grandmother, but
> *Löwe* 'lion' and *Oma* 'grandmother' understood with a re-interpreted de-
> notation. Thus the first constituents [*Vorderglieder*] are subsective. That is,
> every semantic rule should be of the kind: $\lambda x \ (R(A, B))(x) \ \& \ B(x))$. That
> the first constituents are subsective is also the only implication relation-
> ship [*Folgerungsbeziehung*] that we can defend for compounds consisting
> of 2 common nouns" [my translation] (Fanselow 1981: 147).

4.4.2.2 Two patterns for compounds: stereotypes or basic relations

Fanselow assumes that in many cases the relation that is not explicitly expressed
in a compound can be derived from the meaning of one of its 2 parts. The general
idea is best illustrated with his examples, cf. (53).

(53) a. *Zeitungsfrau*
          newspaper:woman
          'woman who delivers the newspaper'

    b.   *Buchgeschäft*
       book:store
       'book store'

According to Fanselow, the meaning of *Zeitung* 'newspaper' is the source of the inferred relation *zustellen* 'deliver' in (53-a), and the meaning of *Geschäft* 'store' is responsible for the inferred relation *verkaufen* 'sell' in (53-b). Some further examples from Fanselow (1981: 156) are reproduced in (54), with the compound part responsible for the inference set in boldface. The inferred relation itself is made explicit and set in boldface in the free paraphraes.

(54)   a.   *Taschenmesser*
         pocket:knife
         'knife **carried in** one's pocket'
    b.   *Fabrikgeige*
         factory:violin
         violin **made in** a factory
    c.   *Zugpassagier*
         train:passenger
         'paassenger **riding** a train'
    d.   *Gartenblume*
         garden:flower
         'flower **growing in** gardens'
    e.   *Düsenjäger*
         jet:hunter
         'jet fighter, i.e. fighter **powered by** jets'
    f.   *Roßarzt*
         horse:doctor
         'doctor **treating** horses'
    g.   *Tagfalter*
         day:butterfly
         'butterfly **flying** during the day'
    h.   *Zuhältermercedes*
         pimp:Mercedes
         'mercedes that pimps **drive in**'
    i.   *Sargnagel*
         coffin:nail
         'nail for **pounding into** coffins'

j.   *Sektflasche*
     champagne:bottle
     'bottle **containing** champagne'

Fanselow (1981: 156) argues that not all compounds fall under this generalization, compare *Politiker-Komponist* 'politician-composer', *Juso-Student* 'Juso student', or *Küstenstadt* 'coast town (= coastal town)', where Fanselow thinks that it
would be strange to argue that the *and* relation in *Politiker-Komponist* 'politician-
composer' or the *located by* relation in *Küstenstadt* 'coastal town' are linked to
the meanings of either *politician* or *town*. Therefore, he argues that 2 classes of
compounds need to be distinguished: A first, smaller class, whose members can
be generated with the help of the 5 basic relations *und* AND, *gemacht aus* MADE
OF, *ähnelt* SIMILAR TO, *ist teil von* PART OF, and *ist lokalisiert bezüglich* LOCATED
RELATIVE TO. And a second, larger class, where the meaning is derived from the
meaning of its constituents.

Fanselow (1981: 157) proposes the following operational distinction between
the set of basic relations and inferred relations:

> If the most explicit paraphrase of the compound AB contains nothing that
> has to do either with the meaning of A or B, then the relation is a basic
> relation. [6] [my translation] (Fanselow 1981: 157)

He motivates his operationalization by using the compound *Kinderzimmer* 'nurs-
ery', cf. (55).

(55)   *Kinderzimmer*
       children:room
       'nursery'

One could propose a reading à la *room meant for children*, and, based on this
reading, establish a basic relation MEANT FOR. However, there is a more explicit
paraphrase for this compound, namely *room in which usually the children live.*
And since *to live in* can be related to *room*, no basic relation is needed for a
successful interpretation. According to Fanselow, all basic relations (except BE
SIMILAR TO) can be linked to basic principles of the organization of the lexicon,
e.g. hyponymy, partonomy, and local inclusion (here Fanselow refers to Miller
1978: 79). In addition, Fanselow states:

---

[6]"Wenn die expliziteste Paraphrase des Kompositums AB nichts enthält, was mit der Bedeutung
von A oder B in Zusammnhang stünde, so liegt eine Grundrelation vor."

If one learns the meaning of, e.g., *hammer*, then one has to learn that it holds of things with a specific form and function, if one learns the meaning of *nail*, that these are things to be hammered into walls etc. But one does not need to learn that their denotations are located somewhere, that they can belong to other denotations, or that they are made out of something.

While therefore the inferred relations are something that needs to be learned when learning the meanings of the words, the basic relations are organizational principles of perception or of semantic classification that are constituted independent of the meanings of individual words. [my translation] (Fanselow 1981: 158)

4.4.2.3 More on compound interpretations based on stereotypes

For Fanselow, "[a] stereotype A_i of a word A is a typical property of things that fall under A. Its semantic type is therefore necessarily the same as the translation of A" [my translation] (Fanselow 1981: 169). In many cases, the stereotypes of 2 compound constituents will not generate the specific meaning of the compound. A case in point is his example *Taschenmesser* 'pocket knife'. *Tasche* 'bag, pocket' has the stereotype *carry in*, and one can therefore generate the meaning 'knife that can be carried in a bag'. In contrast, the more specific meaning, e.g. 'a small knife with one or more blades that fold into the handle', is due to the compound developing its own stereotype.

Fanselow (1981: 168) mentions the categories introduced in Shaw (1978), that is *vollmotiviert* 'completely motivated', *teilmotiviert* 'partially motivated', *unmotiviert* 'not motivated', and ponders the introduction of 2 categories building on these ideas: (1) *systemmotiviert* 'motivated by the system', where the production system almost, but not quite, yields the full meaning of the compound, and (2) *motiviert im engern Sinne* 'motivated in a strict sense', where the production system yields the full meaning of the compound. Shaw's categories are illustrated in (56), Fanselow's 2 categories in (57), cf. Fanselow (1981: 168).

(56) a. completely motivated
          Nagelfabrik
          nail:factory
          'nail factory'
      b. partially motivated
          (i) *Steinpilz*
               stone:mushroom
               'Boletus edulis (penny bun)'

(ii) *Butterblume*
butter:flower
'buttercup'

c. not motivated

Hahnenfuß
cock:foot
'buttercup/crowfoot'

(57) a. motivated by the system
(i) *Taschenmesser*
pocket:knife
'pocket knife'
(ii) *Blutbuche*
blood:beech
'blood beech'

b. motivated in a strict sense
(i) *Staudacherbruder*
Staudacher:brother
'Staudacher's brother'
(ii) *Nagelfabrik*
nail:factory
'nail factory'

Fanselow (1981: §18) discusses how best to formulate the stereotypes. Again, I report here only some of his observations. In general, if the inferred relation is stative, cf. e.g. *Rheinbrücke* 'Rhine bridge (= bridge over the Rhine)' or *Kandidatenplakat* 'candidate poster (= poster for a candidate)' (cf. Fanselow 1981: 157), there is no ambiguity between habitual and instantaneous ['instantiell'] readings. In all other cases, one finds an ambiguity, with the habitual reading being the preferred one. Fanselow (1981: 192) assumes that stereotypes are generally habitual, but allow the derivation of instantaneous readings. The relations inferred via the first constituent might be either efficient (as in *Fabriknagel* 'factory nail' → produce) or afficient (as in *Raketenbasis* 'missile base' → fire); among other things, this will influence the choice of tense. Words typically have several stereotypes that are relevant for compound composition, *Milch* 'milk' allows one to infer *drink in* in *Schulmilch* 'school milk' but *given by* in *Kuhmilch* 'cow milk'. As already shown in the examples in (54), some of the stereotypes contain a local relation, e.g. *Schulmilch* 'school milk' and *Teehaus* 'teahouse', which both use the relation *drink in*. Stereotypes come with constraints on their argument places, see *Professorenfabrik* 'factory for professors' in (58), his (9).

(58) Die Uni Konstanz ist eine richtige **Professorenfabrik**.
      The Uni Konstanz is a   right   professor.PL:factory
      'The University of Konstanz is a right factory for professors.'

Factories, according to Fanselow, produce inanimate things. Since professors are animate, the compound must be understood metaphorically.

According to Fanselow (1981: 201), the frequency adverbials that are most likely to modify a given inferred relation seem to be determined by the relevant stereotypes (or, as he puts it, the words determine this for their stereotypes). To illustrate this, Fanselow contrasts *Raketenbasis* 'base for firing missile in case of need for doing so' with *Gartenblume* 'flower that usually grows in a garden'. In addition, he notes that compounds like *Nagelfabrik* 'nail factory', 'a factory that usually produces nails', can be given a more precise paraphrase, e.g. 'usually, if this factory produces sth., it produces nails'. A similar step, according to Fanselow, is possible for *Gartenblume* 'garden flower' ('usually, if this flower grows somewhere, it grows in the garden') and *Sektflasche* 'champagne bottle' ('usually, if this bottle contains something, it contains champagne'). This is, however, not possible across the board, as he illustrates with *Silberbergwerk* 'silver mine', which not only excavates silver (technically, it excavates ore which contains silver, for one thing), and *Zuhältermercedes* 'pimp mercedes', which is not only driven by pimps. Finally, in a few cases, stereotypes of both compound parts are involved, see his example *Teehaus* 'teahouse', where, according to Fanselow (1981: 202), the inferred relation *drink in* is due to the contribution of both parts, *tea* being responsible for the *to drink* relation, and *house* being responsible for the *in* (as opposed to the local relation to be inferred for *Thekenbier* 'counter beer', 'a beer that is drunken at the counter').

4.4.2.4 More on Fanselow's basic relations

Fanselow (1981: §17) discusses the basic relations in more detail and gives further examples. For the combination of 2 common nouns, the first basic relation, *und* 'and', is analyzed as intersection, that is, for a compound AB, we have λ x (a'(x) & b'(x)), where a' is the semantic translation of A and b' that of B. Relevant examples are *Eichbaum* 'oak tree', *Juso-Student* 'Juso-student', *Hausboot* 'house boat', *Radio-Uhr* 'radio clock', *Negerfrau* 'negro woman'[7], and *Juso-Oma* 'Juso-grandmother'. Other examples, like *Mördergeneral* 'murderer general', are already more complex; he speculates:

---

[7]And yes, this is considered to be politically incorrect in German nowadays, too.

One might wonder whether words like *Mördergeneral* 'murderer general (= general who is a murderer)', *Mörderpolizist* 'murderer police man', *Mörderkanzler* 'murderer chancelor', and *Mörderpräsident* 'murderer president' are all *Analogiebildungen* 'analogical formations'. Because it further seems to hold that the interpretation of compounds via stereotypes constitutes an explication of that which is usually seen as *Analogiebildung* 'analogical formation', we can view *Mördergeneral* 'murderer general' and *Einbrecherpolizist* 'thief policeman' simply as a very specific case of a general word formation possibility. [my translation] (Fanselow 1981: 176)

Note that the difference between the 2 groups observed by Fanselow seems to correspond to compounds that, in Levi's system, would be analyzed with the BE relation, and, on the other hand, those combinations she refers to as coordinate structures and excludes from her analysis. In Bauer, Lieber & Plag (2013: 479–480), these 2 types are both subtypes of coordinative compounds, referred to as appositive and additive respectively.

The MADE OF relation is essentially treated by Fanselow as an extension of the AND-relation, so that e.g. an x is a *Roggenbrot* 'rye bread' iff x is bread and has been rye, and there is a process that caused the rye to be bread afterwards, cf. Fanselow (1981: 180).

For the basic relation PART OF Fanselow (1981: 184–185) gives the examples *Autokotflügel* 'car mudguard' and *Kammzinke* 'comb tooth'. Interestingly, he points out that "[w]e cannot simply translate *Autokotflügel* 'car mudguard' into: an x, that is a mudguard and part of a car. The mudguard can be dismantled, the corresponding car does not need to continue to exist, nor does there need to be a car at all in order for a thing to be a car mudguard."[my translation] Fanselow (1981: 184). Cf. Bell's entailment criterion discussed in Section 3.1.2, Chapter 3 for a similar point.

Fanselow (1981: 185–186) believes that the location-relation has fewer usages than commonly assumed; he takes *Küstenstraße* 'coast road (=coastal road)', *Hafenstadt* 'harbor town', and *Bergdenkmal* 'mountain monument (= monument in the mountains)' to be clear examples. In contrast, compounds like *Nachtarbeiter* 'night worker', *Automotor* 'car engine' and *Rheinbrücke* 'Rhine bridge' need stereotypes for their correct interpretation. In trying to find a good formal spell-out for location relation, he mentions an observation by Warren (1978) for English as support for what is essentially an underspecified localization relation: the conjunction with *und* 'and' is only possible, if the underlying relation is the same, cf. combinations like *Sekt- und Weingläser*. Since one can form combinations like *die Gruben- und Landarbeiter Boliviens* 'mine and farm laborers of Bolivia', with the mine laborers being in the mine and the farm laborers being on the farm land, this can be taken as support for an underspecified locative relation. However, he also notes that this idea does not generalize to all cases, as examples like *das Münchener Schnell- und Untergrundbahnsystem* 'the Munich express and subway railsystem' and *Schnell- und Güterzüge* 'express and freight trains' contain coordination with *and* even though the relationship between the head and the first elements cannot be the same, cf. Fanselow (1981: Footnote 10). A second rule to introduce location relations is needed for compounds like *Denkmalsberg* 'monument mountain' and *Stadtküste* 'town coast', which, according to Fanselow, are converses of the location relation as seen in the examples above. However, I think that instead of introducing a converse location relation one could also argue for other relations here, e.g. PART OF or AND.

The last basic relation to be discussed is BE SIMILAR TO, which comes in many forms. (59) gives a few examples from his overview.[8]

(59) a. B has the form of A:
  (i) *Flammenschwert*
    flame:sword
    'flame-bladed sword'
  (ii) *Einhornplastik*
    'unicorn sculpture'
  b. B has the color of A:
  (i) *Blutbuche*
    'blood beech'
  (ii) *Silberpappel*
    silver:poplar
    'white poplar'
  (iii) *Laubfrosch*
    foliage:frog
    'European tree frog'
  (iv) *Milchglas*
    'milk glass'

Fanselow's basic observations is that the exact type of the *being-similar-to* relation is determined via stereotypes, and he exploits this via a semantic rule that makes use of stereotypes. As a result, in his system compounds like *Blutbuche* 'blood beech' are explained with the help of a semantic rule, but a compound like *Bronzelöwe* with the help of a pragmatic rule, which Fanselow (1981: 191) justifies

---

[8]Fanselow (1981: Footnote 13, p. 188) points to a similar overview for English in Warren (1978).

by arguing that these semantic rules follow a clear pattern, whereas the shifts of the head seen in *Bronzelöwe* seem to behave more unruly. In addition, in his view explicit rules are always better than pragmatic explanations.

4.4.2.5 Context dependency and ambiguity in Fanselow's system

Fanselow argues that his system can derive most readings that compounds have. However, his system also generates ambiguity. In addition, nothing in his system as it stands is able to deal with context sensitivity. Thus, Fanselow mentions that combinations like *Taschenmesser* 'pocket knife' and *Fabrikgeige* 'factory violin' could also be used to mean 'knife to cut pockets with', or 'violin for usage in a factory' respectively.

He thinks that a hierarchy like (60), cf. Fanselow (1981: 215), is likely to be in place, and proposes the general hypothesis for compound interpretation in (61).

(60)   Hierarchy for compound rules:

    a.   stereotypes

    b.   and-rules

    c.   location-rules

    d.   similarity-rule

(61)   Hypothesis for the interpretation of nominal compounds
    In the interpretation of an AB compound, that relation R holds between A and B which is the most prominent relation in a given context among the relations whose linguistic realization occurs most often in sentences between A and B so that the compound interpreted with that relation R makes sense in the given context. [my translation] Fanselow (1981: 215)[9]

Based on this, Fanselow (1981: 215–216) thinks that it is not the case that every interpretation of a compound is possible in the respective contexts, and that the number of possible readings is smaller than the number of possible relations that are technically available.

He concludes his work by pointing out that it is still an open question which factors determine the most prominent relations/stereotypes in a given context, and illustrates the problem with the 2 examples in (62) and (63), examples (1)

---

[9]"Hypothese zur Interpretation der Nominalkomposita
    Bei der Interpretation eines Kompositum AB tritt genau die semantische Beziehung R zwischen A und B, die unter den Beziehungen, deren sprachliche Realisation mit großer Häufigkeit in Sätzen zwischen A und B tritt, im jeweiligen Kontext die prominenteste ist, so daß das Kompositum interpretiert mit R im Kontext sinnvoll ist" (Fanselow 1981: 215).

and (2) in Fanselow (1981: 221), where, according to Fanselow, in neither case the interpretation suggested in the sentence preceding the sentence containing the compound is able to win over a compound interpretation based on stereotypes.

(62)   Ich schlug einen Nagel in einer Fabrik ein. In dieser **Nagelfabrik** war es kalt.
'I pounded a nail into the factory. It was cold in this nail factory.'

(63)   Hedwig ist eine Lehrerin, die sich sehr für Geschichte interessiert. Diese **Geschichtslehrerin** treffe ich leider zu selten in der 'Schwedenkugel'.
'Hedwig is a teacher who is really into history. Unfortunately, I meet this history teacher all too seldomly in the 'Schwedenkugel'. '

That is, *Nagelfabrik* in (62) is not interpreted as 'factory into which I pounded a nail' but is still a factory that produces nails, and likewise the *Geschichtslehrerin* 'history teacher' in (63) is still somebody who teaches history, not a person who is interested in history and at the same time a teacher.

In general, he assumes that "the further one moves away from whatever one can call the pragmatically normal relation, the stronger the contextual marking needs to be" [my translation] Fanselow (1981: 221).[10] In addition, he assumes that the problem of selecting the pragmatically normal interpretation crops up in a similar way when it comes to the interpretation of genitives or attribute phrases.

4.4.3 Evaluating Fanselow's approach

Fanselow's work continues to impress through his analytic clarity and wide scope. The idea that stereotypes associated with the individual compound constituents play a major role in arriving at the most specific interpretation of a given compound is particular attractive. While this view of compound semantics might at first sight seem very different from Levi's 9 predicate system, aspects of both systems can be fruitfully combined in an approach in which the semantic relations are seen as tied to specific concepts. If the relations are not seen as independently existing objects but only relative to specific concepts, like in the conceptual combination approach pursued by Gagné and collaborators (cf. Chapter 2, Section 2.1.3), then categorizing compounds into these relations quite naturally leads to a localization of the set of Levi-relations to specific concepts. I

---

[10]"Je weiter man sich von dem fortbewegt, was man als die pragmatisch normale Relation beze-ichnen kann, desto stärker muß die kontextuelle Markierung sein" (Fanselow 1981: 221).

will come back to this issue in the description of the coding done for the analysis presented in Chapter 7, cf. especially Section 7.4.

4.5 Mixed approaches

Levi's and Fanselow's approaches have been discussed in detail because they show the range of possibilities in approaching compound semantics. The aim of this final section is not to give an overview of everything that followed but rather to introduce 2 further well-known strands of approaches. They are mixed in the sense that they introduce means that allow them to integrate knowledge that is not traditionally seen as belonging to the lexical meaning of words in the building of their semantic representations. The next section introduces Pustejovsky's generative lexicon and is followed by 2 sections discussing proposals that extend these ideas to compounds. The final section introduces approaches based on underspecification. On deciding to focus on these works, much other work is necessarily left aside, notably Meyer (1993). Focusing on German novel compounds, Meyer (1993) provides a theory of compound comprehension based on the 2-level semantics of Bierwisch (1989) and adapting Discourse Representation Theory (Kamp 1981) to represent lexical meaning and to model the process of arriving at an utterance meaning of new compounds. In addition, Meyer (1993: 12–38) provides a very useful overview of theories on compound semantics bridging the gap between Fanselow (1981) and the early 1990s.

4.5.1 Pustejovsky (1995)

Pustejovsky (1995) introduces a general approach to lexical semantics with no specific focus on compounds or complex nominals. However, as adjective noun constructions constitute one major class of his examples, and his approach is used elsewhere for the analysis of traditional compounds (cf. especially Jackendoff 2009 and Asher 2011, see also the discussion below), I will discuss his approach here, focusing especially on his discussion of adjective noun combinations.

Pustejovsky (1995: 32), pointing to earlier works by Katz (1964) and Vendler (1963), notes that the adjective *good* occurs with multiple different senses, depending on which noun it modifies, cf. the examples in (64), his (23) .

(64) a. a good car
      b. a good meal
      c. a good knife

Typical interpretations for *good* in (64-a) and (64-c) might be 'of high quality', while (64-b) is typically interpreted as 'delicious'. Illustrating this point further, he gives the following examples and paraphrases for *fast*, cf. his examples (7–14) (Pustejovsky 1995: 44–45).[11]

(65)   The island authorities sent out a fast little government boat, the Culpeper, to welcome us.
a boat driven quickly or *a boat that is inherently fast*

(66)   a **fast typist**
a person who performs the act of typing quickly

(67)   Rackets is a **fast game**.
the motions involved in the game are rapid and swift

(68)   a **fast book**
one that can be read in a short time

(69)   My friend is a **fast driver** and a constant worry to her cautious husband.
one who drives quickly

(70)   You may decide that a man will be able to make the **fast, difficult, decisions**.
a process which takes a short amount of time

(71)   The Autobahn is the **fastest motorway** in Germany.
a motorway that allows vehicles to sustain high speed

(72)   I need a **fast garage** for my car, since we leave on Saturday.
a garage that takes little time to repair cars

(73)   The **fastest road** to school this time of day would be Lexington Street.
a road that can be quickly traversed

As Pustejovsky (1995: 44–45) points out, these readings allow to distinguish between at least 4 distinct senses of *fast*, cf. (74).

(74)   a.   fast(1): to move quickly
       b.   fast(2): to perform some act quickly
       c.   fast(3): to do something that takes little time
       d.   fast(4): to enable fast movement

In addition, Pustejovsky (1995: 46) assumes blended senses for *fast garage* (blends senses 2 and 3) and *fast route* (blends senses 3 and 4). One important point is that

---

[11]For the corpus sources of Pustejovky's examples, cf. Pustejovsky (1995: 244, Endnote 2).

there is no principled limit to new senses or new blends of previous senses. There-fore, any system based on what Pustejovsky calls a sense enumeration lexicon is bound to fail. Instead, he proposes the system of the generative lexicon, which I will introduce in the next section.

4.5.1.1 The generative lexicon

Pustejovsky assumes that one can distinguish between different levels of seman-tic representation, and that one needs a set of generative devices that can be used to create new senses.

The 4 levels of representation he assumes are: (1) argument structure, (2) event structure, (3) qualia structure, and (4) lexical inheritance structure.

The set of generative devices includes the following semantic transformations: (1) Type coercion, that is, the semantic types can be shifted so that they match the type required by the functor they are to combine with. (2) Selective binding, that is, specific senses can be tied to specific aspects of meaning. (3) Co-composition, that is, information from both functor and argument is responsible for the cre-ation of new senses.

This allows rich meta entries, and in consequence a reduced size of the lexicon. The meta entries are called *lexical conceptual paradigms* (lcps).

I will not go into details of the presentation of argument and event structure, but instead focus here on the qualia structure, in my view the element of Puste-jovsky's approach that is usually considered to be its main innovation. Since I am interested in nominals, I will concentrate on them in the discussion of qualia structure, too.

4.5.1.2 Qualia structure

The *qualia structure* of a lexical item is intended to be "the structured representa-tion which gives the relational force of a lexical item" (Pustejovsky 1995: 76). The 4 essential aspects of a word's qualia structure are listed by Pustejovsky (1995: 76) as follows: (1) the constitutive aspect: "the relation between an object and its constituent parts"; (2) the formal aspect: "that which distinguishes it within a larger domain"; (3) the telic aspect: "its purpose and function"; and (4) the agen-tive aspect: "factors involved in its origin or 'bringing it about'". Importantly, "every [grammatical] category expresses a qualia structure", but "[n]ot all lexical items carry a value for each qualia role" (Pustejovsky 1995: 76). Qualia values themselves come with their own types and relational structures, cf. his example for *novel* in (75), reproducing (35) in Pustejovsky (1995: 78).

(75)
$$
\begin{bmatrix}
\textbf{novel} \\
... \\
\text{QUALIA} = \begin{bmatrix} \text{FORMAL} = \text{book(x)} \\ \text{TELIC} = \text{read(y,x)} \\ ... \end{bmatrix}
\end{bmatrix}
$$

Specifically for nominals, he introduces the concepts of dotted types in order to deal with cases like *door, book, newspaper,* and *window,* that is, cases of what he calls 'logical polysemy'. The intuition behind this terminology is that for a noun like *door* (at least) 2 word senses (the physical object and the corresponding aperture) can be distinguished, with both senses being related since both are arguments of the meaning of the the noun. The byword 'logical' seems to be used to indicate that this 'inherently relational' (Pustejovsky 1995: 91) characteristic of the nominal is located at the level of lexical semantics, as opposed to the level of concepts (cf. also Pustejovsky & Anick 1988). According to Pustejovsky (1995: 92), logical polysemy occurs in a number of nominal alternations. (76), his (11), reproduces his list of alternations along with examples.

(76) a. count/mass alternations   *lamb*
      b. container/containee alternations   *bottle*
      c. figure/ground reversals   *door, window*
      d. product/producer diathesis   *newspaper, Honda*
      e. plant/food alternation   *fig, apple*
      f. process/result diathesis   *examination, merger*
      g. place/people diathesis   *city, New York*

Each argument is of a specific type. The dotted types are the results of combining the 2 types to form a complex type. That it is possible to distinguish between the 2 senses in (76) and reference to a sense corresponding to the resulting complex type, or dot object, is illustrated by Pustejovsky (1995: 94) with the help of the 3 occurrences of *construction* in (77), his (17):

(77) a. The house's **construction** was finished in two months.
      b. The **construction** was interrupted during the rains.
      c. The **construction** is standing on the next street.

According to Pustejovsky, *construction* in (77-b) refers to the process, while it refers to the result in (77-c) and to the entire dotted type in (77-a).

4.5.1.3 Adjective noun combinations and qualia structure

Returning to adjective modification in a system with qualia structure, Pustejovsky comments on (78) and (79):

(78)   a.   a bright bulb
       b.   an opaque bulb

(79)   a.   a fast typist
       b.   a male typist

According to Pustejovsky (1995: 89), the 2 adjectives *bright/fast* in (78) and (79) are event predicates. The event they predicate over must in some way be associated with the qualia structure of the noun (*bulb* with the telic role of illumination, *typist* with the telic role making reference to the process of typing). In contrast, *opaque/male* access the formal role of their respective heads.

4.5.2 Extending the analysis to compounds 1: Jackendoff (2010)

Jackendoff (2010: 442–445)[12], in a section explicitly entitled 'Using material from the meanings of N1 and N2', gives a number of examples for which he assumes an analysis that is based on Pustejovskian co-composition. His first example is *water fountain*, "a fountain that water flows out of" (Jackendoff 2010: 443). Because it is the proper function of a fountain that liquid flows out of it, and because water is a liquid, water can fill this spot in the telic role of fountain. Jackendoff assumes a similar process for *coal mine, gas pipe, Charles River bridge,* and *toe-web,* and mentions several larger families (below always illustrated with one of his examples): N2 is a container (cf. *fishtank*), N2 is a vehicle (cf. *oil truck*), N2 is an article of clothing (cf. *ankle bracelet*), N2 is a location (cf. *liquor store*), and N2 is the incipient stage of something else (cf. *dinosaur egg*). In addition, there are also cases where N1 gives the topic of N2 (cf., *research paper*), or N2 is an agent or causer (cf., *pork butcher*), or an artifact (cf. *steak knife*). Likewise, he discusses cases where the proper function that drives the interpretation comes from the N1, like *cannonball.*

Jackendoff (2010: 443, Footnote 22) points to Brekle (1986), who discusses these types of compound under the heading of 'stereotype compounds' (cf. Brekle 1986: 42, Section 2.2). Brekle, in turn, refers to the analysis based on stereotype relations from Fanselow (1981), cf. the discussion in Section 4.4.2.3. I will come

---

[12]Cf. also Jackendoff (2009), an earlier, shorter version of the same article.

back to the connection between the Pustejovskian approach and stereotypes be-low. For an analysis of these types of compound in terms of Pustejovsky's (1995) qualia structure, Jackendoff points to Bassac (2006).

4.5.3 Extending the analysis to compounds 2: Asher (2011)

Asher (2011) is not an extension of Pustejovsky's analysis to compound nouns, but rather provides an alternative framework to Pustejovsky's approach, which Asher calls Type Compositional Logic or TCL. Nevertheless, for the data that concerns compounding in particular, the discussion and analysis can be seen as one way of spelling out the Pustejovskian approach. Asher (2011: 301–305) focuses on material modifiers, that is, adjectives like *wooden*, or nouns like *glass*, *stone*, etc. These, as the examples in (80), his (11.1) illustrate, "supply the material constitution of objects that satisfy the nouns these expressions combine with" (Asher 2011: 301).

(80)

$$\left.\begin{array}{c} glass \\ wooden \\ stone \\ metal \\ tin \\ steel \\ copper \end{array}\right\} bowl$$

Asher (2011: 302) notes that material modifiers are particular in being able to affect the typing of the head noun, cf. the examples in (81), his (11.2).

(81) a. stone lion (vs. actual lion)
b. paper tiger (vs. actual tiger)
c. paper airplane
d. sand castle
e. wooden nutmeg

Asher (2011: 301) notes that these constructions support different inferences, cf. (82), his (11.3).

(82) a. A **stone lion** is not a lion (a real lion), but it looks like one.
b. A **stone jar** is a jar.
c. ?A **paper airplane** is an airplane.

Crucially, *stone* in (82-a) does not allow the typical inference pattern known from intersective and subjective adjectives, while the very same noun in (82-b) allows the standard interference pattern expected for intersective and subsective modification. The question mark for (82-c) is explained by Asher as follows:

> I am not sure whether a paper airplane is an airplane. If one thinks of airplanes as having certain necessary parts like an engine or on board means of locomotion, then most paper airplanes aren't airplanes. On the other hand, many people tell me that their intuitions go the other way. (Asher 2011: 302).

Continuing his exploration of *paper plane*, he furthermore notes that it apparently gives rise to a similar bridging inference as *airplane*, cf. (83), his (11.4).

(83)   a.   John closed the door to the **airplane**. The engine started smoothly.
          b.   John made a **paper airplane** in class. The engine started smoothly.

Here, according to Asher, *paper* behaves more like an intersective modifier. This raises the question whether in the respective combinations the modifier itself is also having an effect. Asher then presents a formal analysis in which it is in fact the modifier that changes the typing of the head noun by specifying the "matter of the satisfier of the noun" (Asher 2011: 304). In addition, Asher assumes that the matter which may constitute an object is also specified in his type compositional logic. In this way, *stone jar* will, without type conflict, be interpreted as a jar made out of stone, allowing the inference in (82-b). In contrast, the combination of *paper* and *plane* will lead to a type conflict, and the corresponding inference is not available, explaining the question mark on (82-c). That *paper airplane* is nevertheless interpretable is due to reinterpretation processes that are available for "predications that don't literally work" Asher (2011: 305). How these kind of predications are to be handled in his framework is discussed by him in his section on *Loose Talk*, cf. Asher (2011: 305–309). The general idea is that "[l]oose talk relies on a set of distinctive and contingent characteristics associated with the typical satisfier of a predicate" (Asher 2011: 308). Whether a predicate P applies loosely or not then depends on whether the relevant object is closer to the elements that fall under the predicate P than it is to other relevant alternatives to P, cf. Asher (2011: 308) for a formal spell-out of the relevant conditions (however, also note that the idea of loose talk is again based on there being a clear notion of literal meaning, something that itself is very questionable, cf. the previous discussions of literal meaning in Chapter 3, Section 3.2.3.2).

What Asher shows us, then, is one way to spell out in detail how semantic characteristics inherent to compound constituents can be made to work in yielding an appropriate compositional meaning of a compound. Note that these semantic characteristics are very similar to Fanselow's stereotype relations.

4.5.4 Approaches using underspecification

What all the approaches discussed so far have in common is the general aim of providing a semantic analysis of complex nominals which in all cases also involved considerable parts that are independent of world knowledge and therefore truly semantic in nature. However, one can also find accounts where, apart from the acknowledgement that some interpretation exists between 2 compound constituents, the burden of interpretation is placed squarely on the pragmatic apparatus. Bauer (1979: 45–46), for example, argues that there is just one abstract 'pro-verb' that needs to be deleted in the generation of compounds, with the meaning of this proverb being something like 'there is a connection between' (Bauer 1979: 46). Thus, in order to arrive at at the actual interpretation of a compound, pragmatic knowledge is always needed. Similar points are made by Selkirk (1982: 23) and Lieber (2004: 49), both explicitly addressing non-deverbal compounds.

However, nothing is said about how the pragmatic apparatus would come to an interpretation. Levinson (2000) makes the following proposal: "Nominal compounds in English, and in many languages, have an unmarked N-N form. Assuming that the semantic relation between the nouns is no more than an existentially quantified variable over relations, the exact relation must be inferred" (Levinson 2000: 147). To infer the exact relation, conversational implicatures are used. The general idea becomes clear when looking at (84), cf. (47) Levinson (2000: 117), where the symbol "+>" is used to mark conversational implicatures.

(84)   noun-noun compounds (NN-relations)[13]
        The oil compressor gauge.
        +> 'The gauge that measures the state of the compressor that compresses the oil.'

In Levinson's system, the inference here is done via an I-implicature, that is, via an implicature to the most specific interpretation possible. An "I-induced interpretation, [...], is usually to a rich relationship between the nouns, as fits most plausibly with stereotypical assumptions" (Levinson 2000: 147).

---

[13]Levinson 2000: 117 here refers to Hobbs et al. 1993, cf. comments on that paper below.

Hobbs et al. 1993, who are credited by Levinson (2000: 117) with bringing the resolution of NN relations into pragmatics, start with the same observation, stating that "[t]o resolve the reference of the noun phrase 'lube-oil alarm', we need to find to entities *o* and *a* with the appropriate properties. The entity *o* must be lube oil, *a* must be an alarm, and there must be an implicit relation between them" (Hobbs et al. 1993). This implicit relation is treated as a predicate variable by them, following Downing (1977) in assuming that any relation is possible here. Interestingly, in their actual implementation they treat the relation as a predicate constant, encoding the most common possible relations, i.e., the Levi-relations, in axioms. This, in turn, is just one small aspect of the general system of weighted abduction they introduce in that paper (see also Blutner 1998 for another abduction-based approach to lexical semantics).

4.6 Conclusion

This chapter gave an overview of semantic analyses for compounds, including a discussion of approaches that either are originally focused on phrasal structures, like the set-theoretic approaches from formal semantics, or include both traditional compounds as well as a subset of phrasal constructions, like Levi's approach. The following points can be singled out as the most important ones:

1. There is no clear-cut difference between compounds and phrasal constructions in terms of the semantic analyses they can be subjected to. Some compounds can fruitfully be analyzed by using the set-theoretic classification originally developed for adjective noun combinations in formal semantics.
2. Compounds can in many cases be successfully classified using a relatively small number of categories, comprised of semantic relations and different nominalization patterns.
3. These classifications, originally meant to constitute semantic analyses, are not able to predict the final meanings of compounds, but seem to represent useful generalizations.
4. Stereotypes and analogies associated with specific concepts play a huge role in eventually arriving at a compound's correct interpretation.
5. Constituent specific information might be internally represented in different ways; proposals range from conceptual to semantic information to full underspecification.

5 Modeling semantic transparency: previous approaches

This chapter reviews in detail 3 studies which introduced different statistical models for semantic transparency. The first study by Reddy, McCarthy & Manandhar (2011) explores the usage of distributional semantics in order to model human judgments of transparency. The second study, by Pham & Baayen (2013), models human transparency judgments with the help of regression models employing measures related to the CARIN theory. Finally, the study by Marelli et al. (2015) explores the behavior of 2 different distributional semantics measures in predicting lexical decision times to reflect more or less compositional aspects of compound words. Because all 3 studies employ distributional semantics techniques in their modeling, this section starts with a short introduction to distributional semantics.

These different approaches will lead to a reflection of how semantic transparency is best conceptualized and the predictors considered in the models will partially reappear in the statistical models presented in Chapters 6 and 7.

5.1 Distributional semantics and word space models

The core idea behind distributional semantics is the distributional hypothesis, stated in (1), in this formulation taken from Sahlgren (2006: 21).

(1)   The distributional hypothesis:
       Words with similar distributional properties have similar meanings.

Early formulations of this idea can be found in the work of Zellig S. Harris, cf. (2), taken from Harris (1954), or the often-quoted "You shall know a word by the company it keeps!" from Firth (1957: 11) (for a more detailed look at the origins of the hypothesis, cf. Sahlgren 2006; 2008).

(2)   "[...] if we consider words or morphemes A and B to be more different in meaning than A and C, then we will often find that the distributions of A

and B are more different than the distributions of A and C. In other words, difference of meaning correlates with difference of distribution."

A word-space model of meaning (for this term, cf. Sahlgren 2006: 17, who builds on Schütze 1993) is a computational model of meaning that is based on this core idea. In particular, it assumes that word meaning can be spatially represented and, as Sahlgren (2006: 18) writes, "semantic similarity can be represented in n-dimensional space, where n can be any integer ranging from 1 to some very large number ...". What is missing at this point is a method to establish the actual vectors based on the distribution of the words one is interested in. This is done by collecting the co-occurrences of other words with the word of interest and storing this information in a vector, called context vector in Sahlgren (2006: 27). The distributional information is typically stored in a matrix of co-occurrence counts, the co-occurrence matrix, and the context vectors correspond to the rows or columns of the co-occurrence matrix (Sahlgren 2006: 31). Instead of word-by-word co-occurrence counts, one can also use word-by-document co-occurrences counts, as is often done in Latent Semantic Analysis (Dumais 2004).

5.1.1 The basics of distributional semantics: a toy example

I will use a toy example to explain the distributional semantics approach. Let us consider the 3 nouns *soldier, baker, butcher* and their co-occurrences with the 3 verbs *kill, knead* and *cut*. Let us assume that the nouns and the verbs co-occur as reported in the fictional distribution given in Table 5.1, the word-by-word co-occurrence matrix for this example.

Table 5.1: Fictional co-occurrences of the 3 nouns *soldier, butcher,* and *baker* with the 3 verbs *cut, kill,* and *knead*.

	cut	kill	knead
butcher	4	3	1
baker	2	0	4
soldier	3	4	1

This information can be used to construct a 3-dimensional space, with the 3 verbs providing the 3 axes. The co-occurrence counts of the nouns can now be used to place the 3 nouns in this geometrical space, cf. Figure 5.1.

Again, on the idea that meaning similarity corresponds to geometrical proximity in the word space, ocular inspection of Figure 5.1 suggests that *soldier* and

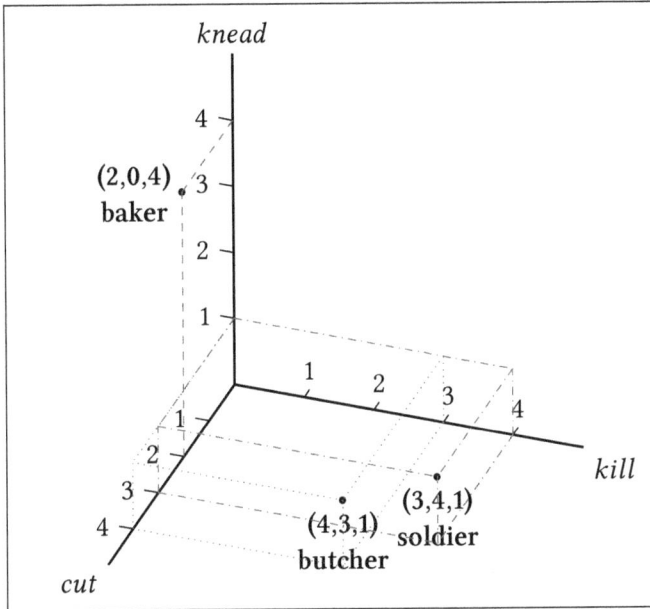

Figure 5.1: *Soldier, butcher,* and *baker* in 3-dimensional space. The 3 axes indicate the co-occurrences of the 3 nouns with the 3 verbs *cut, kill,* and *knead* respectively.

butcher are more similar to each other than either is to *baker.* Taking the co-occurrences as context vectors, that is, if the co-occurrence counts are the endpoints or the scalar components of the corresponding vectors, methods from vector algebra can be used to calculate their proximity, that is, their similarity. A common similarity measure for context vectors is the cosine similarity, that is, the cosine of the angles between the 2 items to be compared. Thus, to measure the similarity between *soldier* and *butcher,* one measures the cosine of the angle ϕ between their vectors, cf. Figure 5.2.

The equation in (3) shows how the cosine similarity is calculated.

$$(3) \quad sim_{\cos}(\vec{x}, \vec{y}) = \frac{x \cdot y}{||x||\,||y||} = \frac{\sum_{i=1}^{n} x_i y_i}{\sqrt{\sum_{i=1}^{n} x_i^2}\sqrt{\sum_{i=1}^{n} y_i^2}}$$

In (3), the cosine of the angle between 2 vectors, $\vec{x}$ and $\vec{y}$, is calculated by dividing their dot product, $x \cdot y$, by their norms, $||x||\,||y||$, where the dot product is the sum of the products of the corresponding scalar components, and the norm, or length, of the vectors is calculated by summing over the squares of their scalar components and taking the root.

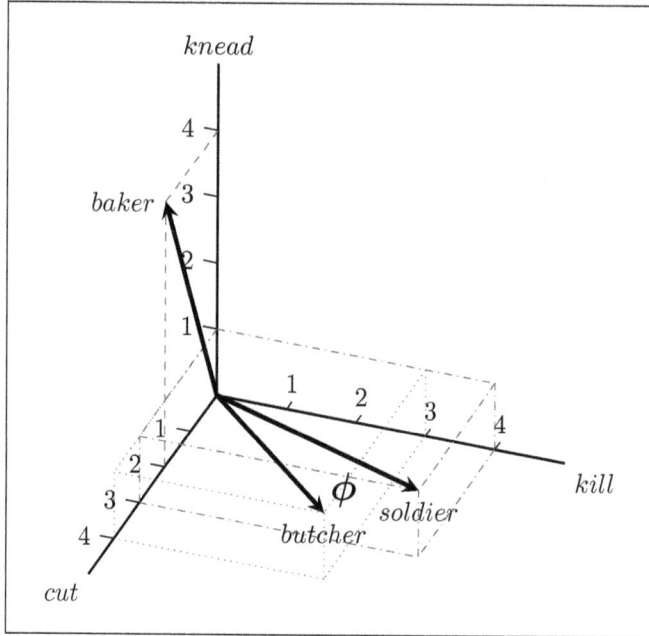

Figure 5.2: *Soldier, butcher,* and *baker* in 3-dimensional space. The 3 axes indicate the co-occurrences of the 3 nouns with the 3 verbs *cut, kill,* and *knead* respectively. The context vectors for the 3 nouns span from the origin to the respective coordinates. The angle ϕ between the vectors of *butcher* and *soldier* can be used to assess the similarity of the 2 words.

The cosine can only have values in the range between 1 and -1. The closer the value gets to 1, the more similar 2 vectors are. A cosine of 0, corresponding to a 90 degree angle, indicates unrelated scores and a cosine of -1, corresponding to a 180 degree angle, indicates opposite scores.

In my toy example, the cosine similarity between *soldier* and *butcher* is 0.96, cf. the calculation in (4).

(4) $\quad sim_{cos}(\overrightarrow{soldier}, \overrightarrow{butcher}) = \dfrac{soldier \cdot butcher}{||soldier|| \, ||butcher||}$

$$= \dfrac{3 \times 4 + 4 \times 3 + 1 \times 1}{\sqrt{9 + 16 + 1} \times \sqrt{16 + 9 + 1}} = \dfrac{25}{26} = 0.96$$

That is, the angle ϕ is 16°. For the pair *soldier/baker* the cosine value is 0.44, corresponding to an angle of 64°. And finally, for the pair *butcher/baker*, the cosine value is 0.53, corresponding to an angle of 58°. In other words, based on the toy distribution used here, the meaning of *butcher* and *soldier* are very similar, while both meanings are quite distinct from the meaning of *baker*, with *butcher* being slightly less distant, or dissimilar, from *baker* than *soldier* from *baker*.

5.1.2 Design decisions

In actual implementations, several decisions can and need to be made. The first decision concerns the co-occurrence counts. Here, one has to decide whether to use word-by-word or word-by-document co-occurrences. Furthermore, in both cases, additional decisions regarding the further procedure need to be made. For a word-by-word matrix, one has to decide which words to use to build the co-occurrence matrix. For example, one can decide to only use content words, or only the 10,000 most common content words. The number of words used to establish co-occurrences determines how many dimensions the geometrical space is going to have. Furthermore, the size of the context used to look for co-occurrences needs to be set. Both of these decisions crucially influence the computational tractability of the proposed models. For further dimension reduction techniques, cf. also the idea behind Latent Semantic Analysis explained in Section 5.1.3.1. The second question concerns the similarity measure used to assess context vector similarity. While cosine similarity is widely used, it is not the only possibility. The dot product alone can be used as a similarity measure, other common measures are distance measures. Distance measures measure the distance between 2 points in an n-dimensional space. These measures include e.g. Euclidean distance, Manhattan distance, or Minkowski distance (see Sahlgren 2006: 34–35 for discussion).

There are many other places where distributional semantic implementations can differ from each other. Thus, besides the raw counts, other measures can be used in the context vectors. For word-by-document approaches, the frequencies of the individual words (=terms) are often weighted against the inverse document frequencies, that is, in how many of the documents in the set of documents the terms occur, leading to the family of so-called TF-IDF-weight approaches (cf. Salton & Yang 1973. For word-by-word approaches, Mitchell & Lapata (2008) set the components "to the ratio of the probability of the context word given the target word to the probability of the context word overall" (Mitchell & Lapata 2008: 241). Reddy, McCarthy & Manandhar (2011) treat their context vector components in the same way, pointing out that this in effect corresponds to pointwise mutual information without logarithm (cf. Reddy, McCarthy & Manandhar 2011: 215, Footnote 4). Such steps are a departure from the simple geometric approach as outlined in the toy example, because now the context vectors are representing probabilities and not raw counts. While such steps have usually been taken because they delivered better results on the tasks at hand, they make the resulting models less intuitively accessible. Discussing the difference between geometric and probabilistic approaches, Sahlgren (2006: 28) points to work by Ruge (1992), who interprets her results to mean "that the model of semantic space in which the relative position of two terms determines the semantic similarity better fits the imagination of human intuition semantic similarity than the model of properties that are overlapping" (Ruge 1992: 328–329).

5.1.3 Two implementations: LSA and HAL

In order to get a feeling for the range of possibilities within distributional semantics, this section introduces 2 well-known implementations: Latent Semantic Analysis (LSA) and HAL, a Hyperspace Analogue to Language.

5.1.3.1 Latent Semantic Analysis (LSA)

Latent Semantic Analysis is a technique in Natural Language Processing that also uses distributional-semantics techniques. As Dumais (2004) points out, one of the main motivations behind LSA was to circumvent problems in information retrieval that stem from synonymy and polysemy. In order to address these problems, LSA uses a dimensionality reduction technique, so that fewer dimensions than unique terms are used. This dimensionality reduction induces similarities between terms that can then be used to solve the problems of synonymy and polysemy. The term 'latent' in the name alludes to the idea that this dimensionality reduction, metaphorically speaking, uncovers hidden relations between terms. Following Dumais (2004: 192–193), an LSA analysis can be divided into 4 steps:

1. A term-document-matrix is created: with each row standing for an individual word, the columns contain the occurrences of these words in the text units of interest (e.g. documents or sentences). Because LSA ignores order, this is also often referred to as a *bag of words* approach. This step corresponds to the establishment of a co-occurrence matrix as described above in Section 5.1.2.

2. The term-document-matrix might be transformed (e.g. using logs, or using probability/entropy based scores). This is not unique to LSA, cf. the remarks at the end of Section 5.1.2.

3. In a third step, dimension reduction is performed. This is done via singular value decomposition, a process by which a matrix is factorized, that is, in

the case of LSA, decomposed into a product of 3 matrices. These matrices contain so-called singular values, of which only the n-largest ones are retained, allowing calculation of a matrix which is an approximation to the original matrix, albeit with fewer dimensions (for more mathematical detail see Landauer, Foltz & Laham 1998).

4. Finally, similarities between terms can be computed in the dimensionally-reduced space. Here, again, cosine similarity is used.

5.1.3.2 A Hyperspace Analogue to Langague (HAL)

In contrast to LSA, HAL (Lund & Burgess 1996), a Hyperspace Analogue to Language, is based on word-by-word co-occurrences. The constructed matrix is direction sensitive and counts the co-occurrences before or after the word of interest in a given window. In addition, the co-occurrences are weighted, with words close to the word given greater weight. To measure similarity HAL uses distance measures, measuring proximity in geometrical space. In particular, HAL uses measures from the Minkowski family (this includes, e.g., Euclidean distances). In contrast to cosine similarity, these measures are sensitive to vector length. For this reason, the vectors are first normalized to unit length. The unit length of a vector is, in turn, related to the vector lengths/vector norms introduced in Section 5.1.1.

5.1.4 Conclusion

The aim of this section was to give an overview of the main ideas behind distributional semantics. The implementations used in the 3 papers to be discussed in the following 3 sections do not depart too much from the ideas presented here. Note, however, that the field is constantly developing. cf. Mikolov et al. (2013) who use a simple neural network architecture to compute high dimensional word vectors for large amounts of data (cf. also https://code.google.com/p/word2vec/).

5.2 Reddy, McCarthy & Manandhar (2011)

Reddy, McCarthy & Manandhar (2011) test several distributional semantic measures for semantic compositionality in compound nouns. Although the term 'semantic transparency' does not occur in their paper, their actual implementation of literality amounts to an assessment of semantic transparency. Reddy, McCarthy & Manandhar (2011: 211) adapt the following definition of compound compositionality proposed in Bannard, Baldwin & Lascarides (2003: 66): "[...] the overall semantics of the MWE [multiword expression] can be composed from the simplex semantics of its parts, as described (explicitly or implicitly) in a finite lexicon." This definition of compositionality is equivalent to semantic transparency if understood in terms of meaning predictability, cf. the quote below, taken from the discussion of derivational morphology in Plag (2003).

> [...], these forms are also semantically transparent, i.e. their meaning is predictable on the basis of the word-formation rule according to which they have been formed. (Plag 2003: 46)

If one can compose the meaning of a complex expression from the meanings of its parts, then its meaning is predictable. Likewise, if the meaning of a complex expression is predictable, then one can state the mechanism that allows one to compose this predictable meaning of the complex expression from the meanings of its parts. Whether this predictability comes about via a word-formation rule as suggested in Plag's definition or via some implicit mechanism is a separate issue. In a further step, Reddy, McCarthy & Manandhar (2011: 211) link compound compositionality to literality: "A compound is compositional if its meaning can be understood from the literal (simplex) meaning of its parts" (for more discussion of this issue see Chapter 3, Section 3.2).

Because the literality ratings from Reddy, McCarthy & Manandhar (2011) will also be used in the new studies presented in Chapters 6 and 7, their methodology is presented here in some detail.

5.2.1 Selection procedure

To arrive at a representative sample, Reddy, McCarthy & Manandhar (2011) first randomly selected 30 compounds for 4 classes, where the distribution across the 4 classes is based on the literal usage of the compound's constituents. Whether a given constituent was used literally was decided based on whether it occurred either in the hypernymy hierarchy or in the definition(s) of the compound in Word-Net (Fellbaum 1998; cf. the extended discussion in Chapter 7, Section 7.2). More specifically, the 4 classes in Table 5.2 were distinguished, each class illustrated by one example (the examples below are from their dataset, but the information from WordNet was added by me).

Because there were not enough candidates for group 2 (only the first constituent is used literally) and group 4 (no literal constituent), additional examples were added from Wiktionary (cf. https://www.wiktionary.org/). After these first steps, the compounds were merged and a set of 90 compounds was chosen, with

Table 5.2: The 4 classes distinguished in Reddy, McCarthy & Manandhar (2011) to create a representative sample. Each class is illustrated with one example from their dataset and the corresponding definitions and hypernyms from WordNet.

1.	**both constituents are used literally**:	*gold mine*
	WordNet definition (second entry):	*a mine where gold ore is found*
	Constituents in the WordNet hypernym hierarchy:	*mine*
2.	**only the first constituent is used literally**:	*speed limit*
	WordNet definition:	*regulation establishing the top speed permitted on a given road*
	Constituents in the WordNet hypernym hierarchy:	*none*
3.	**only the second constituent is used literally**:	*game plan*
	WordNet definition (second entry):	*(sports) a plan for achieving an objective in some sport*
	Constituents in the WordNet hypernym hierarchy:	*plan*
4.	**none of the 2 constituents are used literally**:	*agony aunt*
	WordNet definition:	*agony aunt (a newspaper columnist who answers questions and offers advice on personal problems to people who write in)*
	Constituents in the WordNet hypernym hierarchy:	*none*

every compound occurring at least 50 times in the ukWaC corpus, a large (> 2 billion tokens) web-based corpus of English (cf. Ferraresi et al. 2008).

5.2.2 Reddy et al.'s human judgment data

For every compound in their set, Reddy, McCarthy & Manandhar (2011) created 3 independent sub-tasks: (1) rating of the compound, (2) rating of its first constituent, and (3) rating of its second constituent.

The compound literality ratings were elicited by asking the subjects to give a score ranging from 0 to 5 for how literal the phrase AB is, with a score of 5 indicating 'to be understood very literally' and a score of 0 indicating 'not to be understood literally at all'. For the individual constituents, the subjects were asked for judgments on how literal the respective constituents are in the compounds, likewise on a 6-point scale. The concept of literality for phrases was explained in a qualification test, where it is stated that "A phrase is literal if you can understand the meaning of the phrase from its parts" (for the qualification test, cf. the downloadable material at http://sivareddy.in/papers/files/ijcnlp_compositionality_data.tgz). In contrast to all previous attempts to get transparency ratings, Reddy, McCarthy & Manandhar (2011) used a concrete task where (1) the target words were presented in context and (2) some precaution was taken that in cases of polysemous compounds it was clear which reading the annotators judged. One concrete example will make their procedure clearer.

For the target compound *brick wall*, annotators were presented with 2 definitions, cf. (5), and 5 different contextually embedded occurrences of the string, cf. (6), with normalized punctuation.

(5)   Definitions:

    a.   an obstacle

    b.   a wall built with bricks

(6)   Examples:

    a.   of the merits of the case. The 3 month limit though is not a brick wall, if circumstances demand an extention [sic] of time, then it is in the discretion

    b.   1975. A couple of years later another female who apparently vanished on reaching a brick wall, was observed near Traitor's Gate. Top WESTMINSTER ABBEY Victoria Street London SW

    c.   the landward side but sloping down steeply to a wooden door set in the high brick wall to seaward." 7 Tower 28 is recognisable not only from the above description

d.   for some time been aware of the outline of a structure in the form of brick walls at ground level. It was not until the end of April this year that

e.   'back, but we wont get them back by battling against a 'yellow brick wall'. Talking of 'exclusive clubs' thanks to Jes for getting me into

Based on the 5 examples, the annotators first have to choose that definition which occurs most often in the examples. Secondly, they have to give a score for how literal the phrase is (or, alternatively, for how literal either the first or the second constituent in the phrase is), basing their decision on the chosen definition.

They used the crowd-sourcing service Amazon Mechanical Turk (cf. https://www.mturk.com/mturk/welcome). Every task was randomly assigned to 30 annotators each. On average, every annotator worked on 53 tasks. In order to control for the quality of the contributions, the annotators first had to pass a qualification test. For the 151 annotators that passed the test, Reddy, McCarthy & Manandhar calculated the average Spearman correlation score (ρ) correlating all annotation values of all annotators. The annotations of 21 annotators with negative ρ were discarded, those of 81 annotators with a positive $\rho > 0.6$ were all accepted. The remaining annotations from 49 annotators were accepted or rejected for a given task depending on whether they fell within the range of $\pm$ 1.5 around the mean of the task. All in all, 383 annotations were rejected.

5.2.2.1 The relationship between the literality scores

Before developing their vector space model, Reddy, McCarthy & Manandhar investigated the relationship between the means of the different literality scores. In particular, they compared the fitting of 5 types of functions, cf. Table 5.3, where ST1 stands for the mean literality ratings for the first constituent, ST2 for the mean literality ratings for the second constituent, and ST-compound for the mean literality rating for the whole compound.[1] *a*, *b*, and *c* are coefficients.

The correlations between the scores are reported in Table 5.4, their Table 3.

As Reddy, McCarthy & Manandhar point out, the results clearly show that functions using literality scores of both constituents are superior to those involving only the first or only the second word. Interestingly, the correlation scores are obtained although the compounds are treated as types and not further distinguished according to the senses chosen by the raters.

---

[1] I used ST here instead of their usage of just *s* in order to make clear that at this point the variables refer to the mean literality scores, not to the scores based on cosine similarity introduced in Section 5.2.3.

Table 5.3: Types of functions used to investigate the relationship between the means of the different literality scores, cf. Reddy, McCarthy
& Manandhar (2011: 213).

function		formula
ADD	ST-compound =	$a \times ST1 + b \times ST2$
MULT	ST-compound =	$a \times ST1 \times ST2$
COMB	ST-compound =	$a \times ST1 + b \times ST2 + c \times ST1 \times ST2$
WORD1	ST-compound =	$a \times ST1$
WORD2	ST-compound =	$a \times ST2$

Table 5.4: Correlations between functions and phrase compositionality
scores reported in Reddy, McCarthy & Manandhar (2011). The R^2 value
shows how much of the variation in the original data is explained when
using these functions. It ranges from 0, no variation explained, to 1, all
variation explained.

function	ρ	R^2
ADD	0.966	0.937
MULT	0.965	0.904
COMB	0.971	0.955
WORD1	0.767	0.609
WORD2	0.720	0.508

5.2.3 Reddy et al.'s distributional semantics models

Reddy, McCarthy & Manandhar model the data with the help of distributional
semantics, using a vector space model of meaning or, in the terminology of
Sahlgren (2006), a word space model of meaning (cf. the introduction in Section
5.1). In the Reddy et al. study, the top 10,000 content words in the ukWaC corpus (Ferraresi et al. 2008) are used and the context window is set to 100. That is,
for every compound and every compound constituent, Reddy, McCarthy & Manandhar (2011) use the 100 word context around every occurrence in their corpus
and extract the co-occurrences with the top 10,000 content words. In addition,
"the context words in the vector are set to the ratio of probability of the context word given the target word to the overall probability of the context word"
(Reddy, McCarthy & Manandhar 2011: 215), cf. also Section 5.1.2. Reddy, Mc-

Carthy & Manandhar (2011) distinguish between 2 types of models, constituent based models and composition function based models.

5.2.3.1 Constituent based models

For the constituent based models, Reddy, McCarthy & Manandhar (2011) first model the literality score of the first and the second constituent separately, using the cosine similarity between the constituents and the corresponding compounds. Secondly, the model scores for the first or the second or both constituents are used as input to a function calculating the literality score for the whole compound. The functions explored are the same that were already considered for the constituent judgment based models, cf. Table 5.3 above.

The core hypothesis behind the idea that the literality scores of the constituents could be useful in determining the literality score of the whole compound is that constituents that are used literally in a compound are likely to share co-occurrence with the compound. Reddy, McCarthy & Manandhar (2011: 215) illustrate this with the example string *swimming pool*, which co-occurs with *water*, *fun*, and *indoor*, all of which also often co-occur with both *swimming* and *pool*. They model the literality of a given word in a compound in terms of the cosine similarity between the compound's and the constituent's co-occurrence vectors, cf. (7) and (8), where $s1$ and $s2$ stand for the calculated literality scores and $v1$ and $v2$ for the co-occurrence vectors of the first and second constituent respectively. The co-occurrence vector for the compound is represented by $v3$.

(7) $s1 = sim_{\cos}(v1, v3)$

(8) $s2 = sim_{\cos}(v2, v3)$

Having established the literality scores of the individual constituents, calculating the compositionality score for the whole compound is straightforward. Reddy, McCarthy & Manandhar (2011) use the same set of 5 functions they already used to investigate the relationship between the human judgments on the constituents and on the compound: ADD, MULT, COMB, WORD1, WORD2. This time, however, the input is not the human judgments but the modeled literality scores. Reddy, McCarthy & Manandhar (2011) point to the following works as partially motivating these models: Baldwin et al. (2003) used the similarity of verb and verb + particle combination in a Latent Semantic Analysis as a measure of decomposability. Sporleder & Li (2009) differentiate between literal and non-literal uses of words exploiting lexical chains, that is, one of the cohesion measures, lexical cohesion, proposed in Halliday & Hasan (1976). Bannard, Baldwin & Lascarides (2003), again investigating verb particle combinations, argued that compositionality could be measured by investigating the similarity between the co-occurrences of either verb or particle with the co-occurrences of the verb-particle combination. McCarthy, Keller & Carroll (2003), working on phrasal verbs and exploiting various measures for nearest neighbors, likewise argued for the usefulness of a comparison between individual constituents and a multiword expression.

5.2.3.2 Composition function based models

In contrast to the constituent based models, the composition function based models use the co-occurrence vectors for the constituents directly as input to a compositionality function $\oplus$.

Again, Reddy, McCarthy & Manandhar (2011) point to a number of papers that already employ this idea: Schone & Jurafsky (2001), in their equation (1), reproduced in (9), propose a general template for measuring non-compositionality of multi-word expressions.

(9) $g(\Psi(C), h(\Psi(X_1), ..., \Psi(X_n))) \geq 0$

In (9), C is a word n-gram, consisting of subcomponents X_1 to X_n. Ψ is a meaning function, e.g. a context vector or some probability based measure. The function h combines the meanings of the subcomponents of the n-gram represented by C and g measures the difference between the meaning of the multi-word expression and the combined meanings of its constituents. Working on German preposition-noun phrase-verb combinations, Katz & Giesbrecht (2006) used vector addition to estimate the compositional meaning of an expression. Giesbrecht (2009) compares additive and multiplicative models and finds that multiplicative models using tensor products fare best. Modeling human judgments on a sentence similarity task, Mitchell & Lapata (2008) compared the performance of additive vs. multiplicative models, showing the superiority of the latter. Guevara (2010) models the observed vectors of adjective noun combinations on the basis of the observed vectors of their 2 constituents and compares the performance of additive and multiplicative composition functions. In his models, vector addition performed better than vector multiplication.

Reddy, McCarthy & Manandhar (2011) compare the performance of 2 compositionality functions $\oplus$, simple addition and simple multiplication. Both functions operate on both constituent vectors *v1* and *v2*. (10) shows how the ith element of the composition *v1* $\oplus$ *v2* is defined in these 2 functions, cf. Reddy, McCarthy & Manandhar (2011: 216).

(10)   Compositionality functions:

    a.   simple addition:

        $(a \times v1 + b \times v2)_i = a \times v1_i + b \times v2_i$

    b.   simple multiplication:

        $(v1 \times v2)_i = v1_i \times v2_i$

Note that in the simple addition function 2 weights *a* and *b* are used; Reddy, McCarthy & Manandhar (2011) found best results by setting *a* to 0.60 and *b* to 0.40. In a final step, the compositionality score for the compound is calculated based on the cosine similarity between the composed vector and the corpus-based co-occurrence vector.

5.2.3.3 Evaluation

For the human judgments of the literality of the constituents and the calculated literality scores for the constituents (cf. (7) and (8) above), Reddy, McCarthy & Manandhar (2011) report a Spearman's ρ correlation of 0.616 for the first and 0.707 for the second constituent. They do not have an explanation for the greater correlation of the second constituent, hypothesizing that "[p]erhaps these constitute an easier set of nouns for modelling [...]" (Reddy, McCarthy & Manandhar 2011: 216).

    For the human judgments of compound literality, the different functions are compared using a linear regression analysis. The results are presented in Table 5.5, cf. their Table (5).

Table 5.5: Comparison of the performance of the different models for compound literality in Reddy, McCarthy & Manandhar (2011) (see their Table 5)

model	ρ	R^2
ADD	0.686	0.613
MULT	0.670	0.428
COMB	0.682	0.615
WORD1	0.669	0.548
WORD2	0.515	0.410
$a \times v1 + b \times v2$	0.714	0.620
$v1 \times v2$	0.650	0.501

Within the group of constituent based models, the ADD and COMB functions perform best, while the functions using only one constituent perform worst, with WORD1 leading to better results than WORD2.

Of the 2 compositionality functions, the additive function performs better. When comparing both the constituent and the compositionality function based approaches, the additive compositionality function performs best. Reddy, McCarthy & Manandhar, in contemplating a possible reason for the advantage of the approach based on the compositionality function, point out that "while constituent based models use contextual information of each constituent *independently*, composition function models make use of collective evidence from the contexts of both the constituents *simultaneously*" (Reddy, McCarthy & Manandhar 2011: 217). This statement seems a little misleading to me, as all models use exactly the same contextual information. What happens independently in the constituent based models is the comparison of this information against the contextual information coming from the compound. Another take on a possible explanation could thus be that compounding always involves some degree of actual composition over and above the semantic relation between the individual constituents and the whole compounds, and that the slight advantage of composition function based models reflects this.

5.3 Pham and Baayen (2013)

Pham & Baayen (2013) are mainly concerned with testing measures derived from assumptions of the CARIN theory (cf. the discussion of this approach in Chapter 2, Section 2.1.3, in particular in Section 2.1.3.1). However, in doing so, they use semantic transparency as a predictor and, in their Study 3, their dependent variable is a measure of human semantic transparency judgments. Their modeling of these judgments is the focus of this section. First, I will introduce their general selection procedure for the compounds used in their study and their semantic coding of these compounds as well as the measures they calculated for all of these compounds. Secondly, I will discuss the details of their Study 3. The goal of Pham & Baayen (2013) was to see to what extent CARIN based measures outperformed LSA measures; in their modeling of semantic transparency this seems to be the case, as the LSA measures are not mentioned. They also use several entropy-based measures; I will therefore start this section with a short overview of informativity based measures.

5.3.1 Informativity based measures

5.3.1.1 Informativity and entropy

All modern informativity measures can be traced back to Shannon (1948: 11), where he introduced the formula in (11) as an example for "measures of information, choice and uncertainty".

(11) $H = -K \sum_{i=1}^{n} p_i \log p_i$

H is usually referred to as entropy; if the logarithm is to the base of 2, H is measured in bits. K stands for some positive constant and is usually disregarded, typically only indicating the measure, and p_i gives the probability of i. Derived from this entropy measure are measures for the information content of particular words, e.g. the definition from Pan & McKeown (1999: 149) in (12).

(12)   information content of a word w = - log(P(w))

In (12), P(w) stands for the probability of a word w in a corpus, estimated via the frequency of the word w in the corpus divided by the accumulative occurrence of all the words in the corpus. The intuitive idea behind this measure is that the more likely a word is to occur, the less informative it is going to be. (13) gives some examples of single words and their information content, based on the BNC.[2]

(13)   a.   *agony*:
              922 hits in the BNC, a 98,313,429 corpus:
              information content:
              $-log_2(P(w)) = -log_2(922/98313429) = 5.029$
        b.   *aunt*: 2,744 occurrences
              information content: 4.554
        c.   *uncle*: 3,350 occurrences
              information content: 4.468
        d.   *column*: 2,775 occurrences
              information content: 4.549

Pham & Baayen (2013) introduce the new measure 'compound entropy', which they define over the probability distributions of modifier and head. The probability distributions, in turn, are based on the frequencies of the modifier and the

---

[2]For the sake of exposition, the numbers are based on non-lemmatized queries for only the word forms as they occur below.

head, cf. e.g. the procedure used in Baayen et al. (2008) to measure inflectional entropy via the frequencies of the singular and plural forms of a lexeme. Pham & Baayen (2013) do not give the exact formula, but I assume it is the same one that Baayen uses in a later paper, Baayen et al. (2011: 468), reproduced in (14), with *i* ranging over the probability of the modifier and the probability of the head.

(14) $H_{compound} = -\sum_{i=1}^{2} p_i log_2(p_i)$

Returning to our above examples, we can now calculate the compound entropy of *agony aunt, agony uncle* and *agony column*, re-using the BNC frequencies from (13).

(15)   a.   compound entropy of *agony aunt*:
$$-\left(\frac{922}{922 + 2744} \times log_2\frac{922}{922 + 2744} + \frac{2744}{922 + 2744} \times log_2\frac{2744}{922 + 2744}\right)$$
= 0.8136

b.   compound entropy of *agony uncle* = 0.7525

c.   compound entropy of *agony column* = 0.8103

Compound entropy, thus defined, picks up imbalances in the frequencies of the 2 constituents across their combined count.

   Pham & Baayen (2013) also use relative entropy, also known under the name of Kullback–Leibler divergence. Intuitively, this measure compares the difference between 2 different distributions.

   The equation (16), cf. (3) in Pham & Baayen (2013: 459), defines reC, a relative entropy measure comparing the distributions of conceptual relations across the modifier family and all compounds in the dataset.

(16) $reC = D(p||q) = \sum_i p_i \, log_2(p_i/q_i)$

In (16), p stands for the probability distribution of the conceptual relations within the modifier family $\mathcal{M}$, and q stands for the probability distribution of the conceptual relations in the lexicon $\mathcal{L}$. The way that Pham & Baayen (2013) classified the conceptual relations and the size of their lexicon will be discussed below. For purposes of illustration, let us take the *agony*-modifier family. In the BNC (again, considering only the singular word forms, cf. Footnote 2), this family only consists of the 3 compounds introduced above, all with the conceptual relation FOR between the 2 elements. Thus, the conceptual relation FOR has a probability of 1 and all other conceptual relations have a probability of 0 for this modifier family. In the whole corpus, however, all conceptual relations occur, so FOR necessarily cannot occur with a probability of 1, let us assume for the sake of the example that across all noun noun compound types FOR occurs with a probability of 0.5. The reC measure for *agony aunt* would thus be calculated as in (17) (note that the summation over all the other relations besides FOR can be disregarded, since the respective summands will always be zero).

(17) $reC = D(p||q) = \sum_i p_i \, log_2(p_i/q_i))$
        $= 1 \times log_2(1/0.5) + 0 + 0 \cdots = 2$

Finally, an entropy measure that is often used in combination with distributional semantics is mutual information or derivatives thereof. An example is positive pointwise mutual information, which is discussed in detail in Turney & Pantel (2010: 157–158). They walk through the steps needed to turn a word-context frequency matrix into a matrix on which positive pointwise mutual information has been applied. Here, I will closely follow their discussion, using the numeric examples from above, the baker-butcher-soldier matrix, adding in 2 further verbs for illustration, *have* and *be*. The frequency matrix F has 3 rows and 5 columns, and just as before the words of interest are *baker*, *butcher*, and *soldier*. The 5 verbs represent 5 different contexts.

Table 5.6: Fictional co-occurrences of the 3 nouns *soldier, butchers,* and *baker* with the 5 verbs *cut, kill, knead, have,* and *be,* with added margin totals

	cut	kill	knead	have	be	
butcher	4	3	1	10	12	30
baker	2	0	4	10	12	28
soldier	3	4	1	10	12	30
	9	7	6	30	36	

That is, a given element f_{ij} in the ith row and the jth column, f_{ij} gives the number of times that word w_i occurred in context c_j. Every row $f_{i:}$ corresponds to a word w and every column to a context $f_{j:}$, with the : standing for all of the columns/rows respectively. To calculate pointwise mutual information, Turney & Pantel (2010: 157) define 3 probabilities estimated via the frequencies, the estimated probability p_{ij} that word w_i occurs in context c_j, the estimated probability of the word w_i, p_{i*}, and the estimated probability of the context c_j, p_{*j}, cf. (18)-(20), based on their (1–3). Note that the denominator for all estimated probabilities is always the same, the sum of the summed frequencies of the word vectors.

$$(18) \quad p_{ij} = \frac{f_{ij}}{\sum_{i=1}^{n_r} \sum_{j=1}^{n_c} f_{ij}}$$

$$(19) \quad p_{i*} = \frac{\sum_{j=1}^{n_c} f_{ij}}{\sum_{i=1}^{n_r} \sum_{j=1}^{n_c} f_{ij}}$$

$$(20) \quad p_{*j} = \frac{\sum_{i=1}^{n_r} f_{ij}}{\sum_{i=1}^{n_r} \sum_{j=1}^{n_c} f_{ij}}$$

We can now calculate the estimated probability of the word *baker* to occur in the context of *knead*, cf. (21), or in the context of *have*, cf. (22).

$$(21) \quad p_{baker\text{-}knead} = \frac{4}{(30 + 28 + 30)} = \frac{4}{88} = \frac{2}{44} = 0.045$$

$$(22) \quad p_{baker\text{-}have} = \frac{10}{(30 + 28 + 30)} = \frac{10}{88} = \frac{5}{44} = 0.114$$

The estimated probability for the occurrence of the word *baker* is given in (23).

$$(23) \quad p_{baker} = \frac{28}{88} = \frac{14}{44} = 0.318$$

Finally, the estimated probabilities of the 2 contexts are given in (24) and (25).

$$(24) \quad p_{knead} = \frac{6}{88} = \frac{3}{44} = 0.068$$

$$(25) \quad p_{have} = \frac{30}{88} = \frac{15}{44} = 0.341$$

The definition for pointwise mutual information is given in (26), and the step from pointwise mutual information to positive pointwise mutual information is given in (27), cf. (4–5) in Turney & Pantel (2010: 157).

$$(26) \quad pmi_{ij} = log\left(\frac{p_{ij}}{p_{i*}p_{*j}}\right)$$

$$(27) \quad x_{ij} = \begin{cases} pmi_{ij} \text{ if } pmi_{ij} > 0 \\ 0 \text{ otherwise} \end{cases}$$

As the definition shows, pointwise mutual information is a measure of association between 2 variables. If the co-occurrence between 2 events is statistically
independent, then the pointwise mutual information will be zero. This follows
from the definition of statistical independence, according to which the joint probability of 2 events equals the product of their probabilities. In this case, the joint
probability divided by the product of the 2 probabilities equals 1, the log_2 of which
is 0. In contrast, PMI will be positive if word and context co-occur above chance
level, negative if they co-occur below chance level. Turney & Pantel (2010: 157)
point out that the distributional hypothesis is concerned with the co-occurrences
above chance level, which motivates the dismissal of all negative values in the
step from PMI to PPMI.

We can now turn the frequencies of *baker* in the context of *knead* and in the
context of *have* into positive pointwise mutual information, cf. (28) and (29).

(28) $pmi_{\text{baker-knead}} = log_2 \left(\dfrac{\frac{2}{44}}{\frac{14}{44} \times \frac{3}{44}} \right) = log_2 \dfrac{88}{42} = 1.067$

$ppmi_{\text{baker-knead}} = 1.067$

(29) $pmi_{\text{baker-have}} = log_2 \left(\dfrac{\frac{5}{44}}{\frac{14}{44} \times \frac{15}{44}} \right) = log_2 \dfrac{220}{210} = 0.067$

$ppmi_{\text{baker-have}} = 0.067$

The whole matrix transformed to positive pointwise mutual information is given
in table 5.7.

Table 5.7: PPMI transformation of the co-occurrence matrix of the 3
nouns *soldier, butchers*, and *baker* with the 5 verbs *cut, kill, knead, have,*
and *be.*

	cut	kill	knead	have	be
butcher	0.383	0.330	0	0	0
baker	0	0	1.067	0.067	0.067
soldier	0	0.745	0	0	0

What the PPMI transformed table shows is that now frequency counts that do
not help to distinguish between different words play a much smaller role than
before, even if their absolute counts are high.

5.3.1.2 Other informativeness measures

While the previous sections introduced the basics of entropy-based measures, I will use this section to introduce the informativity measures used in Bell & Plag (2012) in their study on noun noun compound stress assignment. They use 3 different informativeness measures, based on absolute and relative frequencies of the constituents and on what they refer to as semantic specificity. As an absolute measure, they used the frequency of the second constituent, the idea being that the more frequent the second constituent, the less informative it will be. The 2 other measures are more complex. The first relative measure that Bell & Plag (2012: 492) introduce is the conditional probability of N2 relative to N1, calculated by simply dividing the compound frequency by the N1 frequency. Again, the idea is clear: if the ratio of compound frequency to N1 frequency is high, then the probability of a specific N2 is also high and its information content therefore low. The 2 other relative measures are based on family size measures. Family size is a concept introduced in Schreuder & Baayen (1997: 121). The morphological family of a word denotes the set of all words that are either derivations from that word or that are compounds containing that word. The family size of a word is the number of different words in the morphological family, excluding the word itself. Bell & Plag (2012) used 2 type-based compound family size measures: (1) The N2 family size, i.e. the number of noun noun compound types in which N2 occurred as N2, in order to assess the probability of N2 occurring as the second member of a compound (see also Plag & Kunter 2010 who already use N1 and N2 family sizes as proxies for the informativeness of the respective compound constituents). (2) One divided by the type-based N1 family size, in order to assess the informativity of N2 (that is, the larger the N1 family is, the less probable is a particular N2 and thus the higher its informativity).

For their second measure gauging relative informativeness, Bell & Plag (2012: 493) are concerned with semantic specificity. Bell & Plag (2012) argue that highly-specific words can be considered to be more informative. They implement semantic specificity via the number of 'synsets' individual words have in the WordNet database (cf. Fellbaum 1998, see also Chapter 7, Section 7.2), where synsets are "A synonym set; a set of words that are interchangeable in some context without changing the truth value of the proposition in which they are embedded." For example, a word like the noun *dog* has a synset count of 7 (WordNet-Search 3.1), as compared to a word like *buttercup* with a synset count of 1. Bell & Plag (2012) argue that the number of synsets of N2 is linked inversely to N2 informativity and that N2 informativeness is affected by the synset count of N1 in that N2 is more informative if it is more specific than N1. Note that for words where no synset counts were available, Bell & Plag (2012) used the sense numbers in the OED online.

The study by Pan & McKeown (1999) mentioned above also introduces a second measure for informativity that could be categorized under the term of semantic specificity. In particular, they use TF-IDF weighting, cf. Section 5.1.2: the frequency of the word within a document is multiplied with the inverse document frequency. The inverse document frequency, in turn, is the logarithm of the ratio of the total number of documents to the number of documents containing the word (see their study for the concrete algorithm they used). Importantly, this measure of semantic specificity is always relative to a given document and thus not a global measure like all the other measures discussed so far.

5.3.2 Pham and Baayen: compound selection and variable coding

Since the CARIN measures require compounds annotated for their semantic relations, Pham & Baayen (2013) built a database of conceptual relations (cf. their Study 1). They started with a set of 783 randomly selected compounds. Although they do not state the source from which these compounds were randomly selected, it is clear that some other considerations must have been in play, given that the database contains only 50 different modifier families and 46 different head families. For these compounds, Pham & Baayen selected the constituent families, that is, all compounds sharing either the head or the modifier with these compounds, from the CELEX database. This resulted in a set of 3,455 compounds.

The first author, Hien Pham, coded the compounds with regard to semantic type, semantic relation, semantic modifier, and semantic head. Semantic type encodes semantic transparency, using a ternary distinction into transparent, partially opaque, or fully opaque compounds. Examples from their data are given in (30) (their data was at some point available at http://openscience.uni-leipzig.de/index.php/mr2/article/view/43[3]).

(30)   Examples for the different semantic types
    a.   transparent: *cartwheel, firebomb, railhead*
    b.   partially opaque: *cardboard, firearm, ragtime*
    c.   fully opaque: *candlewick, jackass, redcoat*
    Selected from the datasets used in Pham & Baayen (2013)

---

[3] As of December 2016, neither the .pdf of the paper nor their data is available from this location.

Note that, incidentally, these randomly picked examples already show typical problems in judging transparency. Take *cartwheel*, which has the meaning 'wheel of a cart' but also occurs in expressions such as 'to turn/do cartwheels', e.g. to perform sidewise somersaults. In the BNC, *cartwheel/s* yields 42 hits, with 17 of them clearly referring to the latter usage. If judged as transparent, probably its 'wheel of a cart' meaning is intended. And if we consider *railhead*, 'the farthest point reached by a railway under construction', the classification as transparent is somewhat surprising as it clearly contains a meaning shift for its head. Note further that in their actual datasets as far as accessible to me, only 35 compounds are judged as opaque, 243 compounds are judged as partially opaque, and the remaining 2,216 compounds are all judged as transparent. More disturbingly, of the 35 opaque compounds all but 5 start with the letter 'b', which makes one wonder whether this is even the correct dataset.[4]

To code the semantic relations, Hien Pham adapted the set of 15 relations from Gagné & Shoben (1997) (cf. Table 2.1 in Chapter 2) and added 4 relations, cf. the overview in Table 5.8, reproducing their Table 2. Note that of their 4 additions, the relation head-of-modifier is quite underspecified, in their data as available to me only used for *airspeed*, *bloodstream/s*, and *bombshell*. The relation LIKES is unclear. It does not occur in their database as available to me and its inclusion in the table is probably an error.

In coding, Hien Pham distinguishes between the meaning of a constituent in isolation and the meaning of the constituent in a compound. Thus, as illustrated in Pham & Baayen (2013: 461), in *airstrip* and *airport*, the modifier is *air*, but the semantic modifier is *airplane/aircraft*, and the conceptual relation for *airport* is coded as FOR. For *backlash*, the semantic modifier is *adverse*, the semantic head is *(violent) reaction*. The compound *backlash* is classified as head IS modifier, cf. Pham & Baayen (2013: 461). Their database also contained exocentric compounds, their treatment is exemplified by *camel-hair*, where Pham & Baayen (2013: 462) assume the semantic modifier *camel-hair* and a notional head *cloth*, so that the relation is coded as head MADE OF modifier. While the decision to encode the semantic relations after meaning shifts or reductions of individual constituents, that is, cases like *airport* and *backlash*, seem defendable to me, I think that classifying *camel-hair* as MADE OF is a strange choice, cf. the model to be discussed in Chapter 6, Section 6.3.2, where the semantic relation would be coded before the metonymic meaning shift (in that case, FROM being the obvious choice).

---

[4]This doubt is further backed by the fact that calculation of the CARIN measures based on their database does not lead to results matching with their calculations.

Table 5.8: Relational coding used in Pham & Baayen (2013), reproducing their Table 2 on page 457. The first 15 relations are adapted from Gagné & Shoben (1997), the final 5 relations are their own new additions.

	relation	example
1	head causes modifier	*flu virus*
2	modifier causes head	*job tension*
3	head has modifier	*college town*
4	modifier has head	*lemon peel*
5	head made of modifier	*chocolate bar*
6	head makes modifier	*honey bee*
7	head location is modifier	*office friendships*
8	head for modifier	*plant food*
9	head is modifier	*canine companion*
10	head uses modifier	*machine translation*
11	head is derived from modifier	*peanut butter*
12	head about modifier	*budget speech*
13	head during modifier	*summer clouds*
14	head used by modifier	*servant language*
15	modifier location is head	*murder town*
16	head by modifier	*student vote*
17	modifier likes head	*age-long*
18	head of modifier	*bombshell*
19	head made by modifier	*anthill*
20	head resemble modifier	*arrow-root*

Based on their database of conceptual relations, Pham & Baayen (2013) calculated 3 CARIN-related measures: (1) the strength measure C, (2) the generalized strength measure gC, and (3) the relative entropy measure reC.

The strength measure C is defined in (31), reproducing (1) in Pham & Baayen (2013). It gauges the relative frequency of a compound's conceptual relation relative to its modifier family.

$$(31) \quad C_i = \frac{n(s_i)}{\sum_{j \in r(M)} n(j)}$$

In (31), M stands for the modifier's family, s_i the for the conceptual relation of the i-th compound, and $n(s_i)$ for the type count of compounds with the same relation in M. $N(j)$ counts the compound types with relation j in M, where j ranges over the semantic relations. This measure is closely related to the strength measure proposed in Gagné & Shoben (1997) (cf. the definition (6) and the discussion in Chapter 2, Section 2.1.3.1). However, as Pham & Baayen (2013: 458) point out, the operationalization differs in 2 crucial places: (1) C is not restricted to the 3 highest ranked relations in the modifier family and (2) C is the probability of the relation of interest in the modifier family, whereas Gagné & Shoben (1997) use an exponential decay function.

The generalized strength measure gC is not based on the relations in a compounds modifier family but takes into account the full lexicon, cf. the definition in (32), reproducing (2) in Pham & Baayen (2013: 458).

(32) $\quad gC_i = \dfrac{m(s_i)}{\sum_{j \in r(\mathcal{L})} m(j)}$

In (32), $m(s_i)$ denotes the number of compounds in the lexicon that share the conceptual relation s_i, that is, the conceptual relation of the compound i. $r\mathcal{L}$ stands for the conceptual relations in the lexicon and $m(j)$ counts the types for each relation j.

Finally, Pham & Baayen (2013), use the reC measure introduced above.

(33) $\quad reC_i = D(p||q) = \sum_i p_i\, log_2(p_i/q_i))$

Here, p stands for the probability distribution of the conceptual relations within the modifier family M, and q for the probability distribution of the conceptual relations in the lexicon $\mathcal{L}$.

They also used 3 measures based on Latent Semantic Analysis, namely the LSA similarity (cf. Section 5.1.3.1) between modifier and head, modifier and compound, and head and compound.

5.3.3 Study 3: transparency rating experiment

In their Study 3, Pham & Baayen (2013) only used a subset of 1,313 randomly selected compounds from their set of 3,455 compounds. This subset was identical to the subset that was already used in their Study 2; in fact, Study 3 immediately followed Study 2 for the individual subjects. Between 125 and 147 compounds were presented to 33 subjects. The compounds were presented together with a sentence describing its meaning. The subjects were then asked to rate the transparency of a compound "specifically with respect to whether the constituents of a compound help to understand its meaning" (Pham & Baayen 2013: 467). They employed a 7-point scale ranging from 'not at all' to 'fully' transparent.

Pham & Baayen (2013) fitted a linear mixed effects model. Subjects and items were treated as crossed random effects. They report that "[t]he most parsimoneous yet adequate model incorporated 4 parameters for the random effects structure of the data, all of which were supported by likelihood ratio tests: standard deviations for the random intercepts for subjects and items, a standard deviation for by-subject random slopes for compound frequency, and a correlation parameter for the 2 by-subject random effect components" (Pham & Baayen 2013: 467). The coefficients of their model are given in Table 5.9.

Table 5.9: Fixed effects of the mixed effects model for transparency ratings, reference level for the predictor transparency is 'opaque' (from Pham & Baayen 2013)

	estimate	std. error	t value
intercept	4.1795	0.3705	11.2804
semantic type: partially opaque	1.2371	0.3442	3.5939
semantic type: transparent	1.9426	0.3244	5.9884
gC	1.3627	0.5583	2.4409
reC	-0.3475	0.0927	-3.7467
compound frequency	0.1262	0.0439	2.8774
modifier family size	0.0931	0.0382	2.4387
compound entropy	0.1075	0.0368	2.9259

The authors report that they also fitted generalized additive models, but no non-linearities were discovered. Further, they report that including the semantic relations as predictors also improved the model fit, but replacing them with the 2 CARIN measures led to better models. They do not report the exact numbers and as reported above, it is not possible for me to re-run their models.

Looking at the final model in more detail, the results with regard to the 3 levels of the semantic type come as no surprise; in effect, what is shown here is that the ratings for the semantic type and those for transparency addressed the same issue.

Of more interest is the next predictor, the generalized strength measure gC. The higher the gC, that is, the higher the probability of the compound's relation in the language, the more transparent it is judged. Note that gC is not a measure relative to a specific compound, as in the original formula for the strength measure. It could therefore be argued that this finding shows that the relations themselves, via their absolute type frequencies, do have some independent status. The authors do not report on the comparison of the generalized strength measure and the simple strength measure C, which only uses the relations in the compounds modifier family.

The negative value of the relative entropy measure reC indicates that the more different the distribution of the relations across the modifier family is in comparison to the distribution of the relations in the lexicon, the less transparent the compound is judged.

Compound frequency and modifier family size both make a compound seem more transparent. Both effects do not seem very surprising. If a compound is very frequent, it might be perceived as more transparent due to its relative familiarity. Likewise, if a modifier occurs in very many different compound types, it is likely to participate in recognizable patterns which give the appearance of transparency.

As for the role of compound entropy, Pham & Baayen (2013: 467) write that "[t]he enhancement in the ratings is consistent with the general effect of Compound Entropy in Study 2, where a greater Compound Entropy afforded reduced response latencies." Note, however, that in their Study 2, where they investigated familiarity responses, compound entropy participated in a 3-way interaction with the relative entropy measure and the strength measure C, which was dichotomized into C=1 and C<1. Recall that this measure is simply the proportion of the relation under investigation in the modifier family; its value is 1 only if the relation under consideration is the only relation in the modifier family. Pham & Baayen (2013: 464) point out that this has unwanted consequences for the relative entropy measure and "the statistical support for its predictivity is restricted." The effect of compound entropy with regard to reduced latencies is clearly observable only in the case of C<1. This merits closer investigation. Recall that the measure is the higher the more skewed the distributions of modifier and head are with respect to each other. It is not clear to me to what extent this should lead to increased transparency, or to what extent one would expect it to interact with the C value, as it did in their Experiment 2.

5.4 Marelli et al. (2015)

The starting point in Marelli et al. (2015) is the observation that semantic transparency can be conceptualized either via semantic relatedness or via semantic compositionality. While this is nothing new, the interesting point they make is that these 2 things do not necessarily go together, saying that semantic transparency in the latter conceptualization "measur[es] how well the combination of the constituents represents the compound meaning, independently of the degree to which the components, when treated as independent words, are related to the meaning of the whole" (Marelli et al. 2015: 1422). They illustrate this independence with the example *swordfish*:

> [T]he meaning of *swordfish* is not related to the meaning of *sword*; nevertheless, when *sword* and *fish* are considered together, it becomes apparent that *sword* underlines features which highly characterize the combined concept *swordfish*, hence *swordfish* is semantically compositional to a certain degree" (Marelli et al. 2015: 1422).[5]

Note that this illustration of the independence of the composition of compound meaning on the one hand and the relation between the compound meaning and the meanings of the individual constituents on the other hand is far from convincing: the name of the fish is clearly motivated by its bill having the shape of a sword and it is unclear why this fact should play no role when comparing the meaning of *sword* in isolation with the meaning of the compound.

Marelli et al. (2015) use distributional semantics based semantic transparency measures. They work with 2 different measures for every compound, reflecting occurrences as solid or open forms, where solid forms are occurrences of compounds written as unique orthographic strings and open forms are realizations with blank spaces separating the constituents. Hyphenated forms are not considered (Marelli et al. 2015: Footnote 1 point to Kuperman & Bertram 2013, who find that semantic factors do not play a role in explaining a preference for hyphenated vs. spaced realizations, in contrast to the preference for concatenated over spaced forms, cf. Kuperman & Bertram 2013: 960–962). The idea behind these 2 measures is that they "propose that semantic representations extracted from contexts in which a compound is written in open versus solid form will capture more or less compositional usages of the compound and that this orthographic cue can thus be used as a proxy for compositionality" (Marelli et al. 2015: 1424). They report 2 experiments, in Experiment 1, they investigate whether open and solid forms are actually associated with different meanings, in Experiment 2 they test whether their 2 semantic transparency measures serve as better or worse predictors for compounds in a lexical decision task dependent on the preferred spelling for these compounds. I will discuss both experiments in more detail below.

---

[5]Marelli et al. (2015: 2) point to Marelli & Luzzatti (2012) as already distinguishing between these 2 conceptualizations, cf. the discussion of their paper in Chapter 2, Section 2.3.3.2.

5.4.1 Experiment 1: the connotations of open and solid forms

Marelli et al. (2015) started with a random sample of 100 compounds drawn from the set of 2-constituent compounds listed in the English Lexicon Project database (cf. Balota et al. 2007 and http://elexicon.wustl.edu/). For these compounds, they collected sentence internal co-occurrences, using ukWaC, English Wikipedia, and the BNC. The co-occurrences were collected separately for the open and the solid forms. The compound meaning was then approximated by 2 vectors, one for the open and one for the solid form, both built by using the co-occurrence with the 10,000 most frequent content words in the corpus. Marelli et al. (2015) reweighted the resulting vectors using positive pointwise information as described in Turney & Pantel (2010), cf. the detailed description in Section 5.3.1.1.

For both the open and the solid forms, Marelli et al. (2015) evaluated the semantic connotations by extracting the 3 closest nearest neighbors, see the 2 examples *moonlight* and *football* in (34), taken from their table 1.

(34) a. *moonlight*
- (i) solid form: *dream, love, wonder*
- (ii) open form: *shine, light, dark*
  b. *football*:
- (i) solid form: *coach, soccer, team*
- (ii) open form: *kick, throw, round*

The resulting 6 words were paired with every compound constituent, yielding 12 word pairs. Via crowd-sourcing, each pair was rated by 10 different raters for meaning relatedness between the 2 words (using a 5-point scale ranging from 'unrelated' to 'almost the same meaning').

In a mixed effects model with the collected ratings as dependent variable, orthographic form emerged as a significant predictor, that is, constituent neighbors are judged as closer to the open form than to the solid form, corresponding to the authors' qualitative observation that the solid forms have neighbors "related to an extended (if not metaphorical) meaning of the compound word, often at an abstract level" (Marelli et al. 2015: 1426). They conclude: "open forms reflect productive, constituent-based combinatorial procedures, as opposed to solid forms reflecting a more lexicalized interpretation of the compound" (Marelli et al. 2015: 1426).

5.4.2 Experiment 2: semantic processing in the recognition of compound words

In Experiment 2, Marelli et al. (2015) use the 2 different semantic transparency measures in a regression analysis of lexical decision times, reasoning as follows:

> If S[emantic]T[ransparency] effects are purely dependent on the semantic relatedness between a compound and its constituents, and compositionality plays only a limited role, we should find very similar effects on response times for measures associated to open and solid compounds. However, the conceptual-composition hypothesis would predict that semantic similarity will be more reliable as a ST measure when calculated in contexts where the compound is used in an actively compositional way (i.e., *open compounds*), in comparison with contexts in which the compound is more lexicalized (i.e., *solid compounds*). (Marelli et al. 2015: 1427).

In contrast to Experiment 1, they extend the number of compounds from 100 to 1,176 2-constituent compounds. The lexical decision times, which constitute the dependent variable, were taken from the ELP. Since the ELP used only solid forms, the dependent variable was always the lexical decision time for the solid form of the compound. Further variables of interest were the frequencies for the constituents and the compounds from the CELEX database, and the compound length in letters. In addition, they also used the bias towards concatenated spelling (BiasC) measure introduced in Kuperman & Bertram (2013: 954). This measure is calculated by dividing the number of solid forms by the total number of compound realizations (Kuperman & Bertram 2013: 954 do not give the exact algorithm, but this checks with their description and the resulting range of the predictor). Marelli et al. (2015) calculated BiasC again on the basis of the concatenation of the ukWaC, English Wikipedia, and the BNC.

Vectors were obtained in the same way as in Experiment 1 (using again the concatenated corpus), but this time, 2 semantic transparency measures were obtained for each form: one relative to the modifier and one relative to the head. These were measured via the cosine similarity between the compound vector and the respective constituent vectors.

In model building, they used generalized additive models and started with a lexical baseline model, using the log-transformed frequencies and length variables, with BiasC as an additional covariate. The contribution of semantic transparency was then tested against this baseline model. However, because there was a correlation of 0.51 between modifier and head semantic transparency, "modifier ST was regressed on head ST, and the latter was replaced by the residuals of the resulting model" (Marelli et al. 2015: 1429).[6] In other words, modifier semantic transparency was left untouched, but head semantic transparency was replaced by the residuals.

As Marelli et al. (2015) report, inclusion of the semantic transparency measures increased the goodness of fit. Both transparency measures interacted nonlinearly with spelling form and BiasC. In contrast, the frequency measures were involved in linear interactions.

The semantic transparency measures from the open forms lead to more effects and they also show considerable interaction in that they are most helpful in boosting the reaction times when both are strongly related to the constituent meaning, whereas the measures from the solid forms show little interaction and only a small effect size. The finding that the measures from the open forms lead to more effects is interpreted by Marelli et al. (2015) as an indication that these measures are taken from contexts where active composition is taking place. Their interaction, in turn, is argued to point to combinatorial processing:

> The possibility to integrate both constituents is thus crucial for the semantic processing of compounds, an effect that is difficult to explain with a pure relatedness-based model (for which *fly* should be helpful in recognizing *butterfly*, irrespective of the unrelated constituent *butter*). A combinatorial procedure, on the other hand, would underline the importance of both constituent meanings, in line with the reported interaction between constituent-based ST measures. (Marelli et al. 2015: 1434)

Note that these effects hold even though, as mentioned above, the reaction times are based on solid forms, leading them to conclude:

> The properties associated to the everyday usage of a compound can thus dissociate from its actual form and arguably represent information stored in the mental lexicon. In other words, the properties observed for open forms are associated to the compound representation itself and play a role during processing irrespective of the way the compound is actually presented." (Marelli et al. 2015: 1434)

Marelli et al. (2015: 1434) argue that routine access to open and solid forms is also supported by the interaction observed for the BiasC measure: When the value is very large, that is, when the compound is almost always written as one word,

---

[6]Marelli et al. (2015: 1429) make reference to Kuperman et al. (2009), who use a similar procedure to orthogonalize the morphological family of the left compound constituent and their occurrences as free forms, cf. Kuperman et al. (2009: 879).

the reaction times are very fast and there is no interplay between constituent semantic transparency measures. In contrast, when BiasC is very low, the reaction times are very low, argued by them to be probably due to an interference effect of seeing a compound presented in its solid form which usually occurs in its open form. They interpret the results as support for a routinely combinatorial procedure.

5.5 Conclusion

This chapter discussed in detail 3 studies in which either semantic transparency was the dependent variable or a stand-in for semantic transparency was used that was not based on human judgments but on some distributional measure. In the process, I also introduced the basic ideas behind distributional semantics and entropy-based measures. Importantly, the 2 approaches are often combined and vectors based on co-occurrence counts are transformed into some probability-based measure.

As far as the 3 studies are concerned, the first study by Reddy, McCarthy & Manandhar showed that distributional semantics can be used to predict the transparency ratings of compounds. In addition, they showed that the individual constituent ratings of compounds are highly predictive of the compound transparency ratings. Of the different composition functions they tested, the additive compositionality function performed best. This function adds the weighted vectors of both constituents.

Pham & Baayen presented a regression model for semantic transparency. Here, the most interesting results are that CARIN-based measures turned out to be significant predictors of semantic transparency. At the same time, it is also interesting that of the CARIN based measures only the generalized strength measure and the relative entropy measure remained as significant predictors in the model. And finally, the model for semantic transparency presented in Pham & Baayen shows that purely distributional, that is, frequency of occurrence measures, and distributional measures derived from semantic annotations, here the distribution of relations in constituent families, can both occur as significant predictors in the same model. On the downside, since the semantic coding of the compound selection that served as the basis of the measures in Pham & Baayen (2013) is itself not very transparent, it is not clear to what extent the results of their modeling can be treated as reliable findings.

In the work of Marelli et al. (2015), semantic transparency functioned as an independent variable, however, and this is the reason why their work was discussed in this chapter, the semantic transparency measure they used was itself a distributional semantics measure. In addition, they used 2 transparency measures, distinguishing between open and closed forms, that is, occurrences of the 2 constituents of a compound written spaced or unspaced, and dismissing hyphenated occurrences. In a meaning relation experiment, the nearest neighbors of the open forms were judged as closer to the meanings of the compounds in their open form. In modeling lexical reaction times, the measures based on the open forms also turned out to be more important, leading Marelli et al. (2015) to the conclusion that these measures reflect semantic composition more than the measures based on closed forms.

Many aspects and points raised by these 3 studies will reappear in one form or another in the 2 empirical studies to be discussed in Chapters 6 and 7: clear examples are the finding by Reddy, McCarthy & Manandhar (2011) that there is a strong correlation between constituent transparency ratings and whole compound ratings and the usage of the distribution of semantic relations across compound families in Pham & Baayen (2013). The finding in Marelli et al. (2015) that measures based on open and solid forms make a huge difference is implicitly reflected in the spelling ratio which is used as a predictor there. However, many of the predictors used in their models are not further explored there and more work is needed to understand the interrelationship between the different measures and their effectiveness in capturing core aspects of human compound processing.

6 Modeling the semantic transparency of English compounds: piloting semantic factors

6.1 Introduction

This chapter introduces and critically discusses statistical models for the semantic transparency ratings of English compounds collected in Reddy, McCarthy & Manandhar (2011). The initial idea for the models presented here is quite simple: if the aim is to model semantic transparency, would the best predictors not be predictors that directly encode core aspects of the semantic structure of the compounds? In contrast to the distributional models used by Reddy, McCarthy & Manandhar (2011), the models presented here therefore include 2 semantic features of the target compounds as predictors: on the one hand, the semantic relation between the constituents of the compounds, and on the other hand, meaning shifts exhibited by the compounds and/or their constituents.

The semantic coding used in this chapter is joint work by Melanie Bell and me, and was already used for the analyses in Bell & Schäfer (2013). The models presented in Bell & Schäfer (2013) are reproduced in Section 6.3. What is new in this chapter is first a more thorough description of the data and the coding scheme. Secondly, in Section 6.4.1, the first model proposed in Bell & Schäfer (2013) is exemplarily subjected to a model criticism routine, and the effect of re-running the models on the same dataset after a more rigorous outlier-removal is presented. Thirdly, I show that by using statistically more appropriate models for the data, core results of Bell & Schäfer (2013) disappear (cf. Section 6.4.2). And finally, I argue that the semantic predictors that remain in the final models are doubtful because the annotation scheme we used itself was questionable (cf. Section 6.4.3.2).

This extensive reevaluation of Bell & Schäfer (2013) is the basis for the new way of modeling the data presented in the following chapter, Chapter 7.

6.2 The Reddy et al. data: a descriptive overview

The analysis presented in Reddy, McCarthy & Manandhar (2011) and the way in which they selected their data has already been described in detail in Chapter 5, Section 5.2. The aim of this section is to give a descriptive overview of the data, starting with the characteristics of the compounds themselves in Section 6.2.1, followed by the characteristics of the rating data in Section 6.2.2. Table 6.1 shows all the compounds rated in Reddy, McCarthy & Manandhar (2011) in alphabetical order.

Table 6.1: The compounds used in Reddy, McCarthy & Manandhar (2011)

[1]	acid test	agony aunt	application form	balance sheet
[5]	bank account	blame game	brass ring	brick wall
[9]	call centre	car park	case study	cash cow
[13]	chain reaction	cheat sheet	china clay	climate change
[17]	cloud nine	cocktail dress	couch potato	crash course
[21]	credit card	crocodile tears	cutting edge	diamond wedding
[25]	end user	engine room	eye candy	face value
[29]	fashion plate	fine line	firing line	flea market
[33]	front runner	game plan	gold mine	graduate student
[37]	grandfather clock	graveyard shift	gravy train	ground floor
[41]	guilt trip	head teacher	health insurance	human being
[45]	interest rate	ivory tower	kangaroo court	law firm
[49]	lip service	lotus position	mailing list	melting pot
[53]	memory lane	monkey business	nest egg	night owl
[57]	number crunching	panda car	parking lot	pecking order
[61]	polo shirt	public service	radio station	rat race
[65]	rat run	research project	rock bottom	rocket science
[69]	role model	rush hour	sacred cow	search engine
[73]	shrinking violet	silver bullet	silver screen	silver spoon
[77]	sitting duck	smoking gun	smoking jacket	snail mail
[81]	snake oil	speed limit	spelling bee	spinning jenny
[85]	swan song	swimming pool	think tank	video game
[89]	web site	zebra crossing		

6.2.1 Linguistic characterization of the selected compounds

In this section, I first describe purely form-based linguistic properties of the set of compounds, cf. Section 6.2.1.1. Secondly, in Section 6.2.1.2, I discuss whether those combinations in which the head is either formally identical to a verb or is deverbal allow an analysis of the corresponding compounds as argument-head combinations.

6.2.1.1 Word class and morphological properties of the constituents

All constituents belong either to the class of adjectives, verbs, or nouns. The majority of the compounds are standard noun noun combinations. Allowing for meaning shifts, all are endocentric. *Cloud nine* is the only compound that contains a numeral. Of this set of compounds, 3 are special with regard to their morphological structure: *cocktail dress*, *grandfather clock* and *graveyard shift* all have a first constituent that is itself a compound form. *Cocktail* and *graveyard* are noun noun combinations, whereas *grandfather* consists of the combining form *grand* and the noun *father*.

This section disregards the standard noun noun compounds and instead focuses on the minority cases, starting with combinations involving adjectives and ending with combinations involving verbs or deverbal nouns.

6.2.1.1.1 Compounds containing adjectives
Sacred cow presents the only example of an unambiguous adjective noun combination in the data. *Fine line*, although the adjective *fine* is homonymous with the noun *fine*, is also clearly an adjective noun combination, with the meaning contribution of *fine*, 'very thin', being that of the adjective. Since in both cases the main stress falls on the second element, both are traditionally considered not as compounds but as phrasal constructions.

Formally and semantically ambiguous between adjective noun and noun noun compounds are the 6 combinations in (1).

(1) a. *public service, graduate student, human being*
     b. *silver bullet, silver spoon, silver screen*

For the examples in (1-a), analyzing them as either adjective noun compounds or noun noun compounds leads to *promiscuity* (for this term, cf. Jackendoff 2010: 427–428; cf. also the discussion of analytic indeterminacy in Chapter 4, Section 4.3.2). Promiscuity is intended as a counterpart to ambiguity. Promiscuity captures those compounds which can be explained, that is, analyzed, in different ways, with the different analyses still leading to the same interpretation (in contrast to the different interpretations in the case of ambiguity).

To see the promiscuity exhibited by the compounds in (1-a), consider the combination *public service*: If we take the meaning *Service to the community, esp. under the direction of the government or other official agency; an instance of this* from the OED, then both *service for the public*, where *public* is used as a noun, as well as *service that is public*, where *public* is used as an adjective, are acceptable paraphrases, and, more importantly, they mean the same thing (note, too, that these 2 possibilities remain even when *service* is read as *religious service*).

In contrast, the compounds in (1-b) are ambiguous depending on whether *silver* is taken to refer to the material or to the color. This ambiguity is in principle independent of whether *silver* is analyzed as an adjective or a noun (cf. the remarks concerning material nouns in Chapter 4, Section 4.1.1). Take *silver bullet*. When paraphrasing the meaning as 'a bullet made from silver', one makes use of one of the noun senses of *silver*, refering to the metal. When the paraphrase is, instead, 'a bullet that is silver', one could argue that *silver* is used as an adjective, but as long as the adjective meaning still describes the material (e.g., *composed of silver*), it would only lead to promiscuity as discussed above. An ambiguity arises only when contrasting the material with the color reading. However, the color reading of *silver* by itself can also be analyzed as being linked to a noun or an adjectival use.

6.2.1.1.2 Compounds containing verbs

For verbs, it is helpful to distinguish between compounds containing *-ing* forms and those that do not contain *-ing* forms. Starting with the latter, and within this group with verb noun combinations, there are 2 clear cases of verb noun compounds, *think tank* and *cheat sheet*. In addition, there are 6 cases which are formally ambiguous between verb noun and noun noun compounds, cf. (2).

(2)   *research project, blame game, call centre, search engine, balance sheet, rush hour*

For all compounds in (2), whether we analyze the first element as a noun or as a verb seems to make no difference to the meaning we arrive at (see also the discussion of promiscuity above in the context of the examples in (1-a)).

While there are no true noun verb compounds in this group, 4 compounds contain second constituents that are homonyms of the verbs from which the nouns were converted: *climate change, case study, rat race*, and *rat run*.

Among the compounds containing V-*ing* constituents, *number crunching* is the sole example for an *-ing* form in second position. The 13 examples of compounds starting with V-*ing* forms are given in (3).

(3)   *parking lot, spelling bee, shrinking violet, smoking gun, smoking jacket, mail-
       ing list, melting pot, swimming pool, spinning jenny, firing line, cutting edge,
       sitting duck, pecking order*

The nouniness of the *-ing* forms differs. Some are lexicalized deverbal nouns
(e.g. *spelling* in *spelling bee*), others are gerund-participles used attributively (e.g.
smoking gun), or they are ambiguous between gerund-participles functioning as a
noun or gerundial nouns (e.g. *pecking* in *pecking order*) (the terminology follows
Huddleston, Pullum, et al. 2002: Chapter 3, §1.4).

6.2.1.2 Argument-structure based properties

For those cases where the head is or could formally be a verb, and for cases with
deverbal nouns as head, the question arises whether these constitute argument-
head structures. The dataset contains 3 deverbal noun heads formed by adding
the suffix *-er*: *teacher* in *head teacher*, *runner* in *front runner* and *user* in *end
user*. In all 3 cases, the first constituent does not correspond to an argument
of the underlying verbal base. For the 4 ambiguous cases, *climate change, case
study, rat race* and *rat run*, an argument-based analysis seems possible, with the
first constituent serving either as the theme or the agent. Similarly, for *number
crunching* the first constituent can be seen as expressing the theme argument
linked to the argument structure of the underlying verb.

6.2.1.3 Conclusion: linguistic characteristics

Most of the compounds in the dataset are standard noun noun compounds. Apart
from noun noun compounds, the dataset also contains adjective noun combinations and verb noun combinations, as well as a few combinations that have second constituents that are formally identical to nouns. Thus, the dataset is not
completely homogeneous.

As the semantic coding can be applied to all combinations regardless of their
characteristics, and as the number of items that are unambiguously not noun
noun compounds or exhibit a specific pattern within the group of noun noun
compounds is too small to include corresponding predictors in the statistical
analysis, these different characteristics will not play a further role in the analyses presented in this chapter. However, the non-homogeneity in the dataset is
one of the motivations to eventually use mixed effects regression models, cf. the
comments in Section 6.4.2. The distinction between standard noun noun compounds and other compound types in the dataset will also play a role in Chapter
7, cf. especially Section 7.5.4.

6.2.2 Descriptive overview of the rating data

The following descriptive statistics are all based on the means file provided with the Reddy et al. (2011) dataset. For all 3 transparency ratings, I give an overview of the distribution of the mean ratings across the data and comment on the distribution of the standard deviations.

6.2.2.1 Transparency of constituent 1

Figure 6.1 gives an overview of the means of the ratings for constituent 1 of the compound dataset. While the plot of the mean values in the left panel already shows that the mean values are clustered towards the lower and higher end of the Likert scale, this becomes much clearer when considering the histogram in the middle panel, where one can also observe an asymmetry in the distribution of the means towards the 2 ends of the scale, with more ratings at the higher end than at the lower end. The means are clearly not normally distributed, resulting in the Q-Q plot in the right-hand panel: instead of a straight line, the high number of low mean values lets the graph stay relatively low, only to rise very steeply and bend sharply to accommodate the even greater number of high and very high mean values.

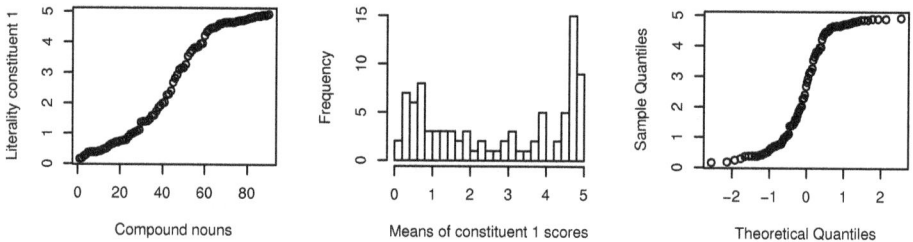

Figure 6.1: Mean transparency ratings of constituent 1: The panel on the left shows the mean compound ratings. The panel in the middle shows the distribution of the mean ratings. The Q-Q plot in the right panel compares the distribution of the mean ratings against the normal distribution.

Table 6.2 illustrates the data further by showing the 5 compounds with the lowest mean rating for their first constituent, the 5 compounds closest to the 2.5 value (the mean of the mean of the ratings is 2.68), and the 5 compounds with the highest rating for their first constituent.

Turning now to the standard deviations, the following observations can be made: The 5 items with the lowest standard deviations occur with words with

Table 6.2: Selected mean ratings for constituent 1. In the leftmost column the 5 items with the lowest mean ratings for the first constituent, in the middle column the 5 items whose mean constituent 1 ratings are closest to 2.5, and in the rightmost column the 5 items whose mean constituent 1 rating is closest to 5, the highest possible rating.

lowest ratings		medium ratings		highest ratings	
kangaroo court	0.167	shrinking violet	2.276	bank account	4.867
crocodile tear	0.185	cheat sheet	2.300	climate change	4.897
rat race	0.250	chain reaction	2.407	car park	4.897
gravy train	0.296	web site	2.679	research project	4.900
snake oil	0.370	game plan	2.821	speed limit	4.933

high transparency scores for the first constituent (ordered by increasing standard deviation: *speed limit, research project, climate change, bank account, human being*). The 5 items with the highest standard deviation, in contrast, have mean transparency scores between 2.00 and 3.73 (in increasing order of standard deviation: *web site, china clay, brass ring, game plan, brick wall*). Note that the final 3 all have been rated with 2 definitions, which in all 3 cases is one of the main reasons for the high standard deviation, in the case of *brick wall* it is the sole reason: 14 subjects chose the second meaning as the basis for their rating, and they consistently gave it the highest transparency rating, '5'. The first reading by itself, chosen by 11 subjects and a mean rating of 0.818, yields a standard deviation of 1.17, but its their combination which leads to a standard deviation of 2.29.

The transparency score and standard deviation of the first constituent are slightly negatively correlated (Spearman's ρ -0.29, p-value <0.01), that is, the lower the transparency score, the higher the standard deviation.

6.2.2.2 Transparency of constituent 2

Figure 6.2 gives an overview of the means of the ratings for constituent 2 of the compound dataset. Just as for constituent 1, it can be observed that the ratings are not normally distributed but concentrate towards the 2 ends of the scale, here with an even clearer tendency towards the high end of the scale.

Table 6.3 gives the 5 compounds with the lowest mean rankings for the second constituent, the 5 items closest to the 2.5 value (the mean of the mean values is 3.06), and the 5 highest rated items.

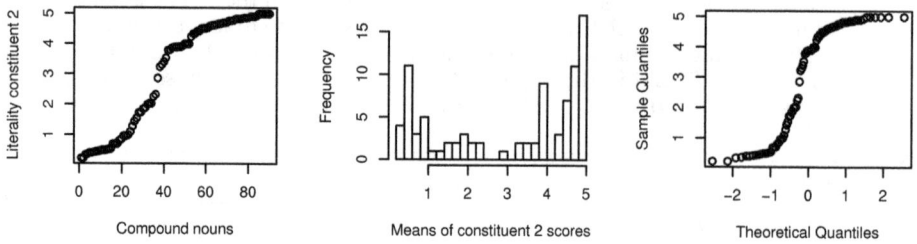

Figure 6.2: Mean transparency ratings of constituent 2: The panel on the left shows the mean compound ratings. The panel in the middle shows the distribution of the mean ratings. Q-Q plot in the right panel compares the distribution of the mean ratings against the normal distribution.

Table 6.3: Selected mean ratings for constituent 2. In the leftmost column the 5 items with the lowest mean ratings, in the middle column the 5 items whose ratings are closest to 2.5, and in the rightmost column the 5 items closest to 5, the highest possible rating.

lowest ratings		medium ratings		highest ratings	
shrinking violet	0.233	rat race	2.036	cocktail dress	5
cloud nine	0.233	search engine	2.250	video game	5
couch potato	0.345	rat run	2.333	polo shirt	5
cash cow	0.370	rush hour	2.862	graduate student	5
spinning jenny	0.414	silver screen	3.231	engine room	5

The highest ranked are also those with the lowest standard deviation, viz. zero. In contrast, the 5 items with the highest standard deviation for constituent 2 (in increasing order of standard deviations: *sacred cow, silver spoon, brick wall, brass ring, fashion plate*) have transparency scores ranging from 0.96 (*sacred cow*) to 3.87 (*brass ring*). Similar to the constituent 1 ratings, for the 3 items with the highest standard deviations subjects used both available definitions.

The transparency score and standard deviation of the second constituent are negatively correlated (Spearman's ρ -0.45, p-value <0.01), that is, the lower the transparency rating for the second constituent, the higher the standard deviation.

6.2.2.2.1 Transparency of the whole compound   Figure 6.3 gives an overview of the means of the whole compound ratings. Just as for the constituent 1 and the constituent 2 ratings, the graphs and plots show that the ratings are not normally distributed. However, in contrast to those 2 distributions, the concentration of the ratings towards the 2 ends of the scale is less extreme, and there are more mid-level rating means.

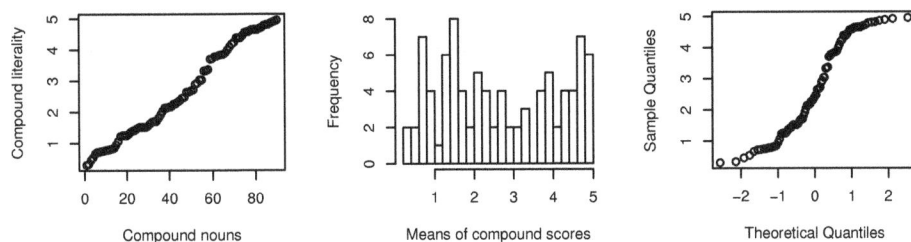

Figure 6.3: Mean transparency ratings for the whole compound. The panel on the left shows the mean compound ratings. The panel in the middle is a histogram showing the distribution of the mean ratings. The right panel is a Q-Q plot, comparing the distribution of the mean ratings against the normal distribution.

Table 6.4 gives the 5 lowest ranked, the 5 items closest to the 2.5 value (the mean of the mean values is 2.66), and the 5 highest rated items.

Table 6.4: Selected mean ratings for the whole compound. In the left-most column the 5 items with the lowest mean ratings, in the middle column the 5 items whose ratings are closest to 2.5, and in the right-most column the 5 items closest to 5, the highest possible rating.

lowest ratings		medium ratings		highest ratings	
gravy train	0.310	silver screen	2.379	speed limit	4.828
cloud nine	0.333	spelling bee	2.448	swimming pool	4.867
ivory tower	0.464	lotus position	2.483	graduate student	4.900
melting pot	0.538	grandfather clock	2.643	engine room	4.931
silver bullet	0.667	front runner	2.655	climate change	4.966

As far as standard deviations are concerned, the compounds with the lowest standard deviations (in order of increasing standard deviations: *climate change, engine room, graduate student, swimming pool, research project*) all have very high transparency scores (in fact, the top four exactly correspond to the transparency top four). For the compounds with the highest standard deviations (in order of increasing standard deviations: *sacred cow, silver screen, firing line, brick wall and brass ring*), the transparency ratings range from 1.52 (*sacred cow*) to 3.79 (*brass ring*). For all 5 items, subjects made use of 2 different definitions.

There is a slight negative correlation (Spearman's ρ -0.21, p-value <0.05), that is, the lower the transparency score, the higher the standard deviation.

6.3 Bell & Schäfer (2013)

This section presents Bell & Schäfer (2013). First, Section 6.3.1 describes the subset of the Reddy et al. dataset that we used. Second, Section 6.3.2 describes the semantic annotation scheme. This is followed by an overview of the annotation results in Section 6.3.3 and finally the 4 statistical models in Section 6.3.4. The main difference to the presentation in Bell & Schäfer (2013) lies in the more detailed discussion and more extensive illustration of the results of our study. This is particularly evident in the discussion of the annotation results.

6.3.1 Subsetting the Reddy et al. dataset

In Bell & Schäfer (2013), we did not use the whole dataset from Reddy et al. (2011), because we decided to use a within-subject design. The main reason for a within-subject design was that we wanted to include models that used the constituent ratings as predictors for whole compound transparency, and the usage of a within-subject design means that for a given rating on the whole compound, we always used the ratings by the same subjects on N1 and N2 transparency as the input to the regression formula. This has the main advantage that we can, at least to a certain degree, disregard the role of any individual differences between the subjects on the dependent variable, because these individual differences will also have influenced the other measures from the same subject. However, it also has the disadvantage that being exposed to the same item several times might affect one's rating on that item. In addition, the order of the presentation might play a role here. Since the Reddy et al. dataset does not contain any information with regard to the order of representation of the materials to individual subjects, we could not explore whether or not there was such a relationship. Extracting only those items for which the same rater had performed all 3 tasks from the total dataset produced a set of 1,337 tokens for which transparency judgments for each constituent as well as the compound as a whole had been given by a single person.[1] The ratings come from a total number of 40 raters, with individual contributions ranging from one token (6 raters) to more than 80 (9 raters). On average, every rater contributed ratings on 33 tokens. Within this set, 12 of the 90 compound types showed variation in the definition assigned, i.e. each of the possible definitions had been chosen by at least one rater. A list of these 12 compounds is given in (4).

---

[1]This number excludes the compound *number crunching*. Why we excluded it at this point is not clear to me (in contrast to its exclusion for the models presented in Chapter 7, cf. the explanation in Section 7.5.4).

(4)   List of compounds for which subjects differed in their choice of definition
        brass ring   brick wall   case study
        chain reaction   face value   fashion plate
        firing line   game plan   public service
        sacred cow   silver screen   snake oil

Because we were interested in the relationship between semantic structure and transparency ratings, we coded and analyzed these different readings separately from one another. A token-based analysis allowed us to do this since, for each token, the dataset indicates the definition assigned by the rater in question.

6.3.2 Semantic annotation of the compounds

In order to capture and classify the internal semantic relations involved in semantic transparency, we start from the underspecified predicate logic notation in (5), which repeats (13) from Section 3.2.3.1 in Chapter 3 (note that it is left open when and how this relation is eventually existentially bound). In (5), A stands for the first constituent of a complex nominal, and B for the second constituent.

(5) $\lambda B \, \lambda A \, \lambda y \, \lambda x \, [A(x) \, \& \, R(x,y) \, \& \, B(y)]$

We assume that an underspecified relation R links the denotations of A and B in a given construction. Based on this, we developed the scheme given in Figure 6.4, where, for reasons of perspicuity, we omitted the arguments of the predicates. Shifted predicates are followed by an apostrophe.

As the scheme indicates, we assume that context and world knowledge are responsible for any further specification of the meaning of an AB combination. Specifically, we assume that A as well as B can be shifted from their literal meaning to a secondary meaning, labeled A' and B'. Metaphors and metonyms present types of well-known shifts, other candidates would be e.g. the process of meaning differentiation, cf. Bierwisch (1982). However, even after a shift, they are still linked to the other part of the construction via the R relation. This kind of semantics for AB combinations therefore clearly falls into the category of radically underspecified approaches (cf. the characterization in Blutner 1998: 128, and the approaches discussed in Chapter 4, Section 4.5.4). At the same time, it is much in the spirit of the analyses of determinative compounds presented in Fanselow (1981), cf. Chapter 4, Section 4.4. With him we assume that the specification of the exact relationship between the denotations as well as the shifts of the A and B parts fall into the domain of pragmatics.

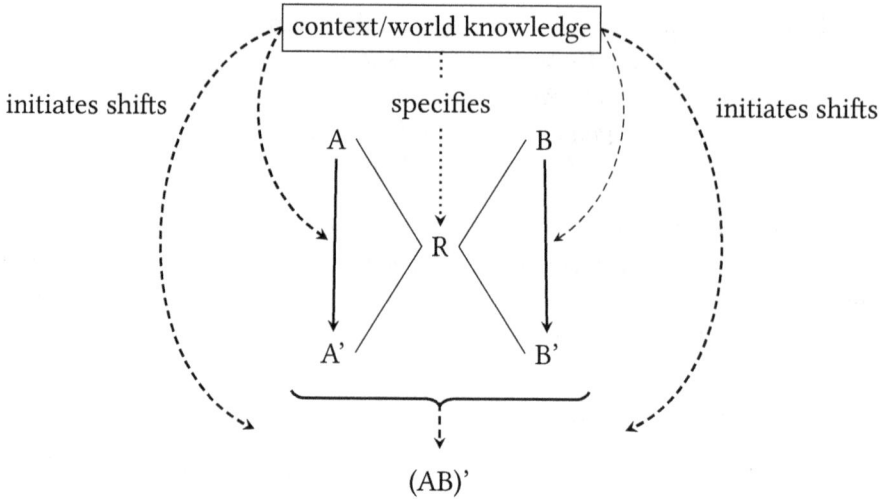

Figure 6.4: Scheme for A B combinatorics

The most basic configuration possible would be one where A and B retain their original meaning, and the relationship is set to identity. That is, the property expressed by A and by B hold of the very same entity, and the semantics is thus intersective. These combinations might be regarded as the most transparent AB combinations. Classic examples result from the combination of Kamp's (1975) predicative adjectives with a nominal head, e.g. *four-legged animal.* Feeding *four-legged* and *animal* into the underspecified template above, cf. (5) and setting the relation parameter to identity results in (6), and since x and y are identical, the formula can be simplified, cf. (7).

(6) $\lambda y \, \lambda \, x$ [FOUR-LEGGED(x) & =(x,y) & ANIMAL(y)]

(7) $\lambda \, x$ [FOUR-LEGGED(x) & ANIMAL(x)]

In our scheme, this configuration can be represented as in Figure 6.5.

However, even for standard examples of intersective modification further differentiation is needed, cf. the discussion in Chapter 4, Section 4.1.4. Examples for shifted As and Bs are presented in Section 6.3.3.

In order to use the abstract scheme for classification, we chose the classification scheme based on the recoverably deletable predicates introduced in Levi (1978). Levi's system has proven itself to be useful in computational linguistics as well as in psycholinguistic approaches (cf. the discussion in Chapter 4, where Section 4.3.2 introduces her recoverably deletable predicates in detail and Sec-

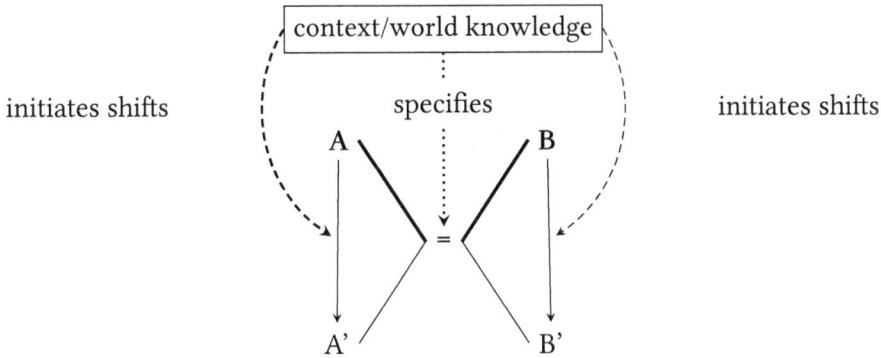

Figure 6.5: Schematic semantic representation of the combination *four-legged animal*. Both constituents remain unshifted, and the relation parameter is set to identity.

tion 4.3.5 discusses the continued popularity of her approach as a classification scheme).

For the 2 cases where we couldn't classify the compounds into one of her recoverably deletable predicates, we used the label NONE. In Levi's analysis, these 2 compounds, *rat race* and *number crunching*, fall into the category of predicate nominalizations.

In our scheme, we also allow for whole compound shifts. At this point, we just indicate this possibility by the (AB)' in the scheme, without distinguishing in detail between the further internal possibilities. A very clear example of a whole compound shift is the derogative *asshole*, examples from the Reddy et al. dataset used in the analysis include *ivory tower* and *cloud nine*. Concurrent shifts of constituents and the whole compound can be illustrated by a combination like *buttercup* which was already used as an example in the introductory chapter: both *butter* and *cup* are metaphorically shifted, standing for the color and the shape of the flower of the plant. The compound as a whole can be analyzed as metonymically shifted, referring to the plant and not just the flower of the plant.

6.3.3 Annotation results

We coded the set of compounds for the semantic variables that are contained in the scheme introduced in the last section, Section 6.3.2. For the shifts, we distinguished between metaphoric and metonymic shifts (for more on the encoding of shifts, including the distinction between the 2 types of shifts, compare the discussion in Section 6.4.3.2). The semantic codings used in that paper are available at www.martinschaefer.info/publications/TFDS-2013/TFDS-2013_Bell_Schaefer. zip. The semantic coding was reading-specific: each token was coded according to the reading chosen by the particular rater, so different tokens of the same compound did not necessarily receive identical coding. This coding was done by Melanie Bell and me; we first coded independently, and then discussed the results to reach a consensus about those items where we initially disagreed. For 2 compounds, *kangaroo court* and *flea market*, we were unable to reach consensus and these were therefore subsequently excluded. That no agreement could be reached on these 2 items is perhaps not surprising, since in both cases the etymology is quite unclear: For *kangaroo court*, a term originating from the US, one finds the following remark in the Merriam-Webster online dictionary (Merriam-Webster 2015): "A *kangaroo court* has never been a court by or for kangaroos, but beyond that, little is known for sure about the term's origins." *Flea market* is often explained with reference to the French *marché aux puces*, see Mike (2012) for this and alternative theories. Excluding the ratings for these 2 items left us with 1,310 ratings.

Figure 6.6 gives an overview of the distribution of the compound readings over the coded relations. What Figure 6.6 shows very clearly is that most of the relations occur in the dataset only very rarely. One relation, CAUSE1, does not occur at all. An overview of the semantic coding by relation can be found in Appendix A.

The following examples from the dataset illustrate our coding scheme: *application form*, in its reading as *a form to use when making an application*, was classified as having unshifted first and second constituents, and the parameter R was set to FOR ('a form for an application'). In contrast, *crash course*, defined as *a rapid and intense course of training or research*, contains a metaphorical shift of the first element ('something fast and intense'), and R is set to BE. A metaphorical shift of the second element is exemplified by *eye candy*, where *candy* is shifted to mean *something pleasing but intellectually undemanding*. Again, the relationship is FOR. *Ground floor* exemplifies the IN-relation, which includes temporal and spatial location, and *brick wall* exemplifies the MAKE2 relation.

We also coded whether the compound as a whole had been shifted, as in *ivory tower* for example. *Ivory tower* as a whole stands for 'A condition of seclusion or separation from the world' (OED online), and it is not possible to synchronically decompose it further in any sensible way. However, it is clear to the native speaker that there has been a shift; otherwise it is inexplicable why, although neither *ivory* nor *tower* have anything to do with its current meaning, the con-

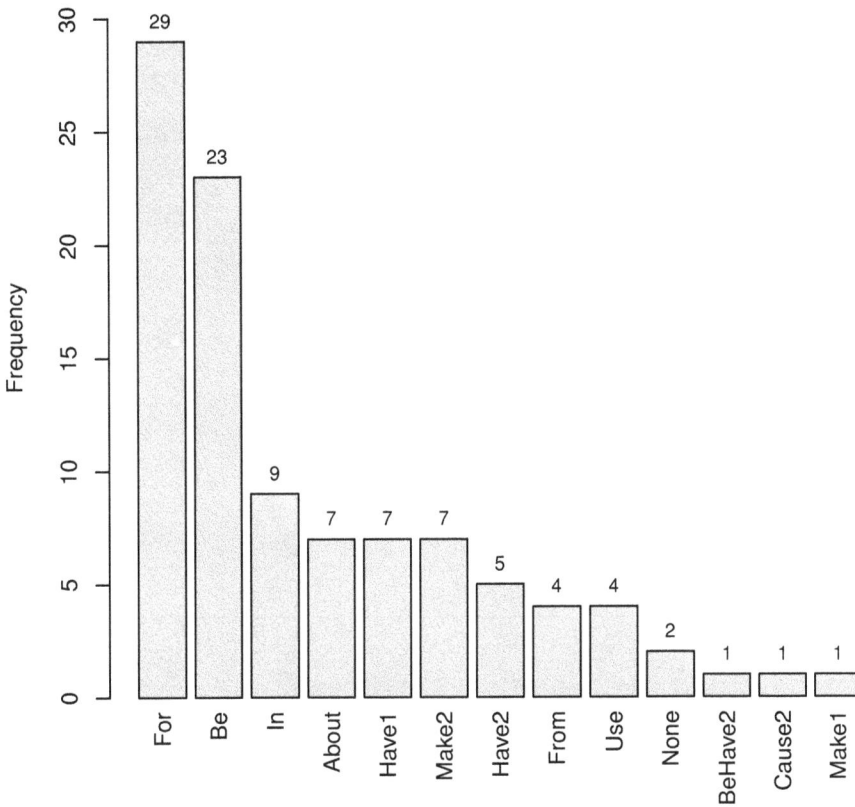

Figure 6.6: Distribution of compound readings over the semantic relations in the data used in Bell & Schäfer 2013.

cept of *tower* still shines through in expressions like *live in ivory towers/assault their ivory towers/geek atop an ivory tower.*

As the examples already show, in the case of constituent shifts the relation between the constituents was classified after the application of the shifts. In contrast, as noted in Section 4.3.3.1 in Chapter 4, Levi (1978) excluded shifted compounds, in fact, all lexicalized compounds.

Because we annotated the specific senses and not the compound types, we ended up with 100 annotated compound readings (2 of the 12 compounds where both definitions were used did not occur in our chosen subset of the data).

Figure 6.7 shows the distribution of compound readings over the different types of shifts.

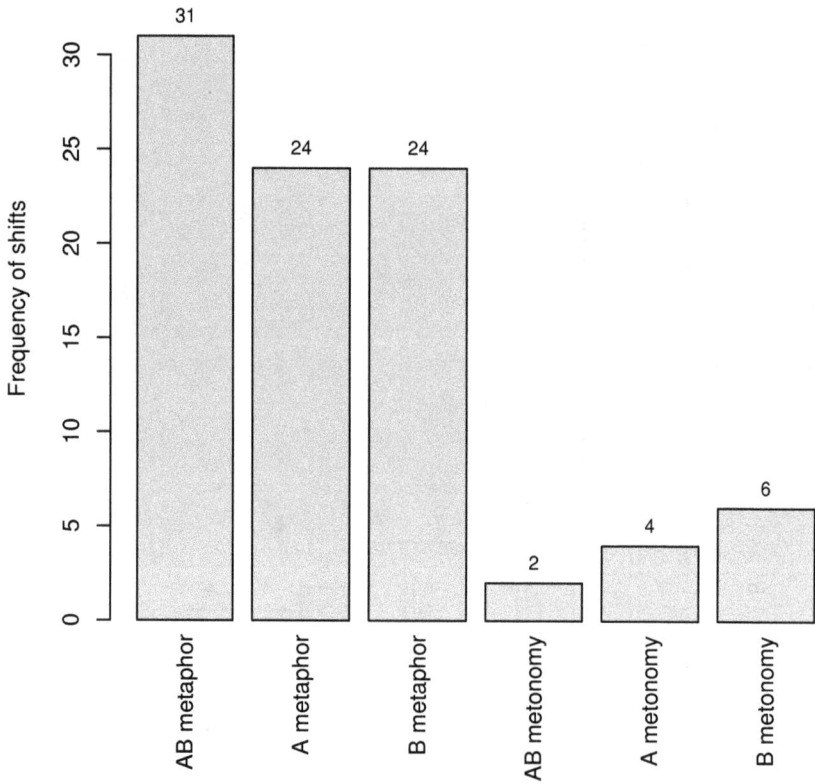

Figure 6.7: Frequency of compound readings per coded shifts in the data used in Bell & Schäfer 2013.

As the histogram shows, metaphoric shifts are relatively frequent in our data, whereas there are only very few compound readings that we coded as metonymic shifts. An overview of the semantic coding by shift can be found in Appendix A.

6.3.3.1 Additional frequency-based variables

In addition to the semantic variables, we extracted a number of frequency measures from the British National Corpus (cf. BNC 2007), namely the lemmatized frequencies of the individual constituents and of the whole compound. For the latter, we extracted the frequencies for all 3 possible forms, that is, spaced, hyphenated or concatenated (=written as a single word) occurrences. The concatenated and hyphenated occurrences were summed into the single category unspaced. All frequencies where logarithmized, using the natural logarithm. Because some frequency counts were 0, we always added 1 to all frequency counts. The effect of logarithmizing the data is that the effect of skewing is reduced and distributions become more symmetrical. Many statistical techniques do not work appropriately with skewed data (cf. Baayen 2008: 31). Kuperman & Bertram (2013: 954) use logarithmization on their dependent variable (lexical decision times) and all frequency-based measures "to attenuate the influence of outliers on the predictions of statistical models" (Kuperman & Bertram 2013: 954).

On the basis of the frequency measures, we calculated an additional derivative measure, the 'spelling ratio' for each compound: this is the proportion of tokens that are written unspaced. The formula we used for the calculation is given in (8) and illustrated with the help of 2 compounds from our data, *bank account* and *swan song*, in (9). This measure has previously been hypothesized to be a correlate of lexicalization, cf. Bell & Plag (2012: 496).

(8) spelling ratio: proportion of tokens that are written unspaced

$$\text{spelling ratio} = log(\frac{\text{unspaced freq}}{\text{spaced frequency}})$$

(9) a. bank account:
    (i) raw frequencies in the BNC:

                                \<bank account> 286
                                \<bank-account>   2
                                \<bankaccount>   0

    (ii) spelling ratio $= log(\frac{3}{287}) = -4.561$

  b. swan song:
    (i) raw frequencies in the BNC:

                                  \<swan song>   11
                                  \<swan-song>   11
                                  \<swansong>   29

    (ii) spelling ratio $= log(\frac{41}{12}) = 1.229$

Note that a measure very similar to the spelling ratio is introduced in Kuperman & Bertram (2013: 954) as BiasC, the bias towards concatenated spelling which is calculated by dividing the number of concatenated forms by the total number of compound realizations (cf. also the discussion of Experiment 2 of Marelli et al. 2015 in Chapter 5, Section 5.4.2).

6.3.4 Bell and Schäfer (2013): the models

A first decision to be taken when modeling data from a Likert scale rating exercise is to decide how to treat the data. On the face of it, Likert scales produce ordinal data, that is, the relationship between the values only establishes a ranking, nothing more. However, it is common practice to treat the results as interval-level measurements, and Bell & Schäfer (2013) follow this practice. For more detailed discussion, cf. the arguments against this practice in Jamieson (2004) and the arguments for this practice in Norman (2010).

The frequency and semantic variables were used as predictors in ordinary least squares regression analyses with transparency of the compound or its constituents as the dependent variables. Some of the semantic categories, including all metonymical shifts and several values of the free parameter R, applied to very few compounds in the dataset. This would greatly reduce the power of any statistical analysis involving these variables: failure to reach significance could be the result of low frequency in this particular set of compounds or significant effects could be due to other features of those particular types. We therefore included in the analyses only metaphorical shifts and the 3 most frequent values of R, namely FOR, IN and BE. Each of the classes coded was represented by at least 9 types (i.e. compound senses) and 140 tokens in our data.

All statistical analysis was done with R (R Core Team 2015). For the effect plots, I used the effects package, cf. Fox (2003).

We also investigated to what extent the different numerical predictors we intended to use are correlated with each other, that is, to what extent there exists collinearity in our data. For 2 explanatory variables to be collinear means that there exists an exact linear relationship between them, that is, when mapped against each other on a graph, the result is a straight line. To investigate and reduce the collinearity in our data, we follow the procedure in Baayen (2008: 181–183), using the condition number provided by the function collin.fnc() from Baayen (2013) to indicate the overall degree of collinearity (this way of calculating the condition number follows Belsley, Kuh & Welsch 1980). Further, we used the varclus() function from Harrell Jr (2015) to perform hierarchical cluster analysis allowing us to visually inspect the correlational structure. Based on this procedure, we decided to exclude all direct compound based frequency measures, and instead we just used the spelling ratio. This yields a condition number of 22.562, indicating a moderate but not harmful level of collinearity in the explanatory variables (cf. Baayen 2008: 182).

The explanatory variables used in the models are listed in (10).

(10)   a.   numerical explanatory variables
          (i)   logarithmized frequency N1
          (ii)   logarithmized frequency N2
          (iii)   spelling ratio
          (iv)   transparency rating N1
          (v)   transparency rating N2
      b.   categorical (binary) explanatory variables
          (i)   FOR
          (ii)   IN
          (iii)   BE
          (iv)   N1 metaphor
          (v)   N2 metaphor
          (vi)   whole compound metaphor

6.3.4.1 Model 1

We first modeled the overall transparency of the compound, as given by the human raters, using our semantic and frequency-based variables as predictors. Since BE is not significant, we removed it from the model, resulting in the final model shown in Table 6.5. Positive coefficients indicate a tendency towards higher transparency, while negative coefficients indicate a tendency towards lower transparency, i.e. opacity. The significant predictors are represented graphically in Figure 6.8. In all cases, the vertical axis represents the semantic transparency of the whole compound as given by the human raters. For the categorical variables, the dots indicate the mean transparency ratings in the presence or absence of the pertinent semantic feature. For the continuous variables, the graphs show regression lines. In addition, the rug plot on the horizontal axis gives the marginal distribution of the predictor, in other words, it shows the actual distribution of the values of that predictor in the data. Confidence bounds are indicated by error bars for the categorical variables and by confidence bands for the continuous variables, using 95% confidence limits. To show the effect of each predictor in turn, the other predictors are adjusted to their reference level (for categorical variables) or to their means (for continuous predictors). The reference level for the categorical variables is 'no': in other words, the model shows the effect of independently varying each predictor in a situation where none of the (other) semantic categories applies.

It can be seen that both types of predictor, semantic and frequency-based, were found to be statistically significant. Transparency rating is lower when either constituent, or the whole compound, is metaphorical. While the coefficients as-

Table 6.5: Final model for compound transparency using semantic and frequency-based predictors, adjusted $R^2 = 0.459$

	estimate	std. error	t	pr(> |z|)
(intercept)	-0.5861	0.3207	-1.83	0.0678
N1 metaphor	-0.6397	0.0939	-6.82	<0.0001
N2 metaphor	-0.4841	0.0920	-5.26	<0.0001
N1N2 metaphor	-1.8411	0.0910	-20.23	<0.0001
IN	0.6041	0.1273	4.75	<0.0001
FOR	0.2363	0.0882	2.68	0.0074
N1 frequency	0.2830	0.0243	11.63	<0.0001
N2 frequency	0.1535	0.0283	5.42	<0.0001
spelling ratio	-0.1240	0.0249	-4.98	<0.0001

number of observations: 1310, d.f. 1301

sociated with the metaphorical shifts of the constituents are relatively small, a metaphoric shift of the whole compound has a much bigger effect. In contrast, both semantic relations, FOR and IN, are associated with greater perceived transparency. This suggests that the relation between constituents, as well as the semantics of the constituents themselves, contributes to transparency. Transparency increases with increasing frequency of either constituent and falls as the proportion of unspaced tokens increases. Both of these findings are not unexpected. Higher frequency in general facilitates processing and might therefore also make items appear to be more transparent across the board. The negative correlation with spelling ratio is in line with the assumption that spelling ratio can be used as a stand-in for lexicalization, and, in turn, the additional assumption that lexicalization is associated with more opacity.

6.3.4.2 Model 2

Model 2 is a second model for whole compound transparency, this time including the ratings for constituent transparency as predictors. Why did we want to include those ratings? The main reason was that Reddy, McCarthy & Manandhar (2011: 213–214) show that there is a strong correlation between the average transparency scores for the compounds and those for their constituents (cf. also Chapter 5, Section 5.2.2.1), so it is to be expected that they would also be highly significant predictors in our model. More importantly, though, on the assump-

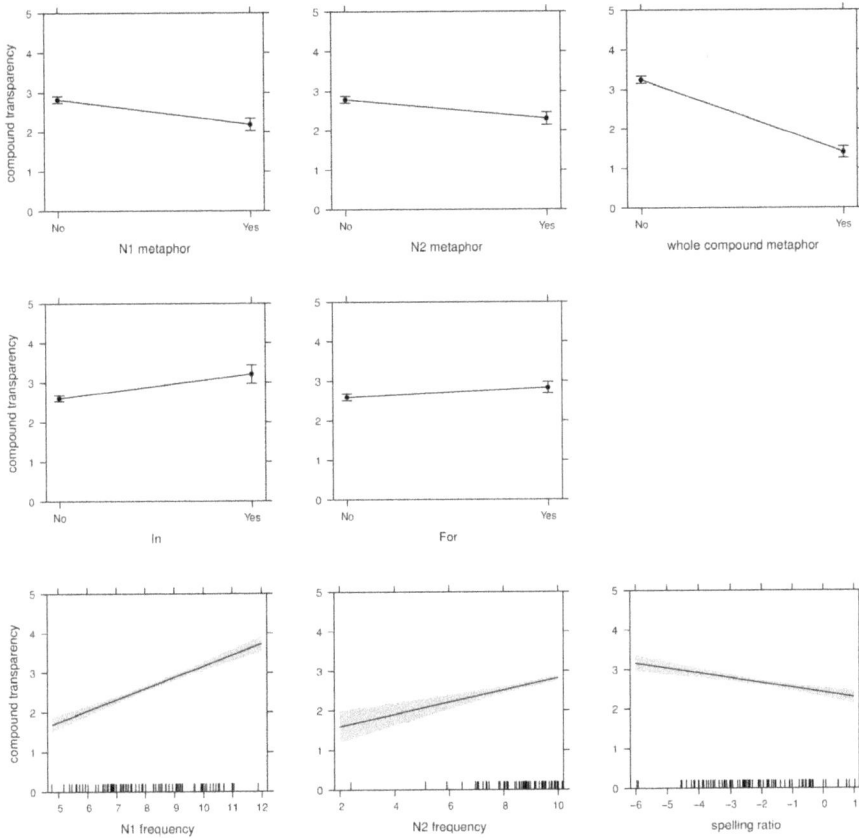

Figure 6.8: Effects in the final model for compound transparency using semantic and frequency-based predictors. The effects associated with meaning shifts are shown in the first row, the second row shows the effects associated with semantic relations and the frequency-based effects are shown in the third row.

tion that the properties of a constituent contribute to its degree of transparency, we hypothesized that the constituent transparency ratings would subsume the other constituent-based variables, namely constituent frequency and semantic shifts of the constituents. We therefore expected that these variables would become less significant or even insignificant in the presence of the 2 predictors for constituent transparency. On the other hand, we expected that the effects of semantic relations and whole-compound metaphorical shifts would remain significant, since they are properties of the whole compound, rather than either constituent.

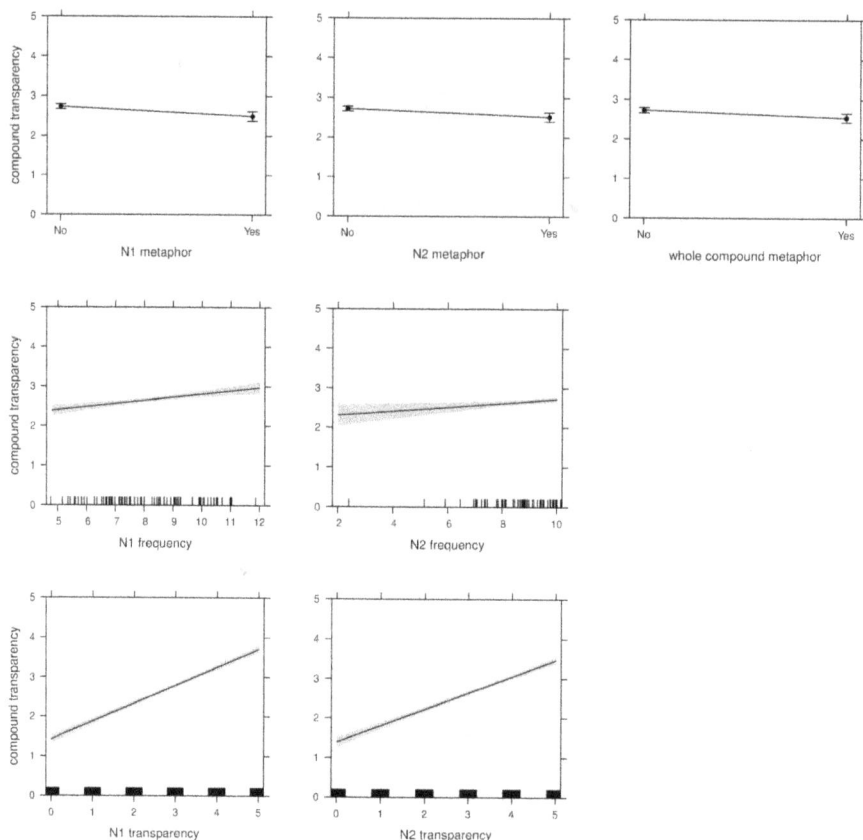

Figure 6.9: Effects in the final model for compound transparency including constituent transparencies as predictors. The effects associated with meaning shifts are shown in the first row, the second row shows the frequency-based effects and the effects of constituent transparency are shown in the third row.

The final model, from which all non-significant predictors have been eliminated, is shown in Table 6.6. The significant predictors are represented graphically in Figure 6.9. As expected, the transparency ratings of the constituents are highly significant predictors of overall transparency: in each case, the more transparent the constituent, the more transparent the compound. Surprisingly, however, the other constituent-based variables remain significant even in the presence of the constituent transparency ratings: though the effects are much weakened, an increase in frequency of either N1 or N2 still leads to greater over-

Table 6.6: Final model for compound transparency including constituent transparency ratings, $R^2 = 0.739$

	estimate	std. error	t	pr($> |z|$)
(intercept)	-0.8117	0.2211	-3.67	0.0003
N1 metaphor	-0.2361	0.0720	-3.28	0.0011
N2 metaphor	-0.2059	0.0726	-2.84	0.0046
N1N2 metaphor	-0.1849	0.0752	-2.46	0.0141
N1 frequency	0.0804	0.0179	4.50	<0.0001
N2 frequency	0.0506	0.0196	2.58	0.0100
N1 transparency	0.4558	0.0179	25.43	<0.0001
N2 transparency	0.4147	0.0180	23.03	<0.0001

number of observations: 1310, d.f. 1302

all transparency, while metaphorical shifts of either constituent lead to greater opacity. It might be argued that the strong effects in our models of metaphorical shifts are a result of the data collection method: asking subjects to rate literality may have led them actually to rate the presence or absence of metaphor. However, if this were true, we would not expect the effects of metaphorical shift of A or B to survive in Model 2 alongside the constituent transparency ratings, since both types of predictor would be accounting for the same portion of the variance. An even more unexpected finding is that, once constituent transparency ratings are included in the model, lexicalization and semantic relations become insignificant as predictors of overall transparency. This suggests that these relations are correlated with the transparency of the constituents, so that they account for the same portion of the overall variation.

6.3.4.3 Models 3 and 4

To test the hypothesis that the semantic relation between compound constituents influences the extent to which the constituents are perceived as transparent, we constructed 2 models with the transparency ratings of A and B respectively as the dependent variables, and our semantic and frequency-based variables as the predictors.

Table 6.7 shows the final model for transparency of the first constituent, with non-significant predictors removed. The significant predictors are represented graphically in Figure 6.10.

Table 6.7: Final model for transparency of N1 using semantic and frequency-based predictors. $R^2 = 0.499$

	estimate	std. error	t	pr(> |z|)
(intercept)	-0.3791	0.3418	-1.11	0.2676
N1 metaphor	-1.7234	0.1003	-17.19	<0.0001
N2 metaphor	0.8728	0.0987	8.85	<0.0001
N1N2 metaphor	-1.8728	0.0939	-19.95	<0.0001
IN	0.9275	0.1344	6.90	<0.0001
N1 frequency	0.3406	0.0262	12.99	<0.0001
N2 frequency	0.0953	0.0305	3.13	0.0018
spelling ratio	-0.0674	0.0268	-2.51	0.0122

number of observations: 1310, d.f. 1302

It can be seen that of the 3 semantic relations, only IN is a significant predictor, being associated with an increase in perceived transparency. Constituent 1 is also perceived as more transparent as the frequency of either constituent increases. On the other hand, when the compound has a higher spelling ratio, or when the whole compound has undergone a metaphorical shift, the first constituent is perceived as less transparent; similarly, when the first constituent itself has shifted metaphorically, it is perceived as less transparent.

However, in contrast to the effects associated with metaphorical shifts of the first constituent or the whole compound, a metaphorical shift of the second constituent leads to the first constituent being perceived as more transparent. One possible explanation for this is that the second constituent is used as a foil in assessing the transparency of the first constituent, e.g., the more opaque the second constituent, the higher the perceived transparency of the first constituent relative to the second constituent.

Table 6.8 shows the final model for transparency of the second constituent, again with non-significant predictors removed. The significant predictors are represented graphically in Figure 6.11.

This model is very similar to the model for constituent 1, both concerning the number of significant predictors as well as the direction of the effects. However, instead of the relation IN, which does not reach significance, it is the relation FOR that is associated with an increase in perceived transparency. Note that the magnitude of this effect is very small. The effect of the constituent frequencies is likewise smaller than the frequency effects in the model for constituent 1, and the magnitude of the effect associated with N2 frequency is only slightly bigger

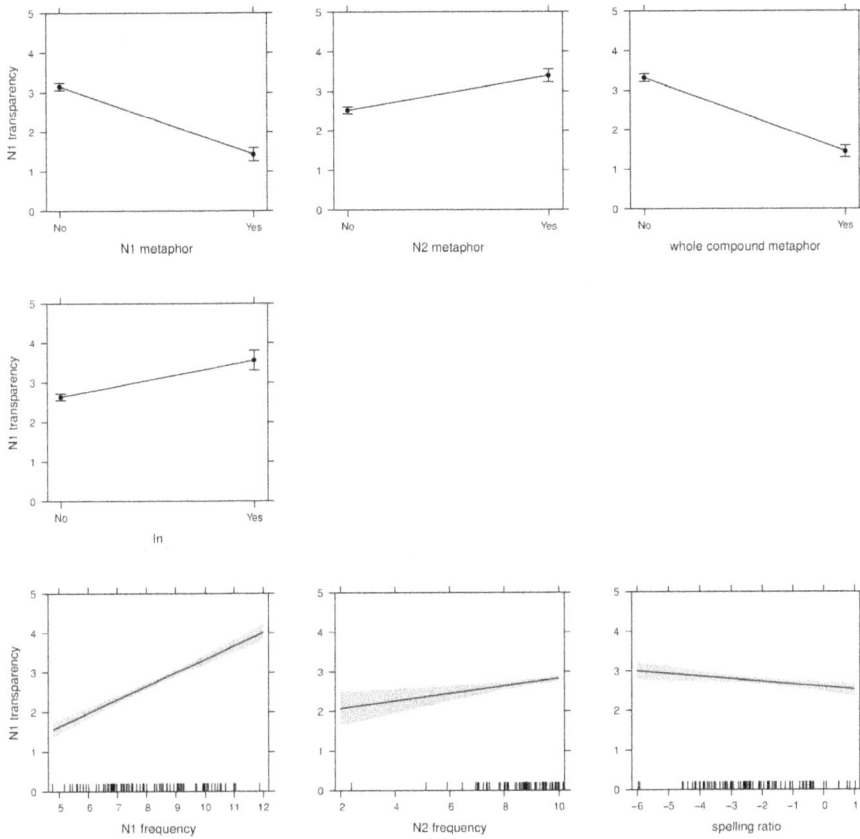

Figure 6.10: Effects in the final model for N1 transparency. The effects associated with meaning shifts are shown in the first row, the second row shows the effect of semantic relations, and frequency-based effects are shown in the third row.

than that associated with N1 frequency. Perhaps most interestingly, just as N2 metaphor was positively correlated with N1 transparency, N1 metaphor is positively correlated with N2 transparency. This supports the interpretation of the constituent ratings as always relative to the transparency of the respective other constituent.

That the effect of semantic relation on compound transparency is mediated through the transparency of the constituents, and that each constituent is associated with a different relation allows one to tie in the results with recent work

Table 6.8: Final model for transparency of N2, R^2 = 0.498

	estimate	std. error	t	pr(> |z|)
(intercept)	1.2383	0.3448	3.59	0.0003
N1 metaphor	0.8382	0.1009	8.31	<0.0001
N2 metaphor	-1.6511	0.0989	-16.70	<0.0001
N1N2 metaphor	-2.0563	0.0978	-21.02	<0.0001
FOR	0.2241	0.0929	2.41	0.0160
N1 frequency	0.1224	0.0259	4.73	<0.0001
N2 frequency	0.1443	0.0304	4.75	<0.0001
spelling ratio	-0.1563	0.0264	-5.93	<0.0001

number of observations: 1310, d.f. 1302

on prosodic prominence in English noun noun compounds. Plag et al. (2008), for example, demonstrate that the FOR relation is correlated with stress on N1, whereas IN is correlated with stress on N2. Furthermore Bell & Plag (2012) show that stress tends to fall on the most informative constituent. If FOR is associated with greater transparency of N2, that might explain why in such compounds stress tends to fall on N1, the assumption being that the less transparent constituent is also the more informative. The reverse pattern would hold in the case of compounds with R set to IN: N1 is more transparent, hence N2 is relatively more informative, hence prone to be stressed.

6.4 Bell & Schäfer (2013) revisited

This section has 3 aims. Firstly, in Section 6.4.1 I will subject the first model of Bell & Schäfer (2013) to a standard model criticism routine and report the results from running the models on slightly smaller datasets with more outliers removed. Secondly, Section 6.4.2 will argue that mixed effects regression should be used for the kind of data under investigation here, and all 4 models will be rerun using this regression technique. Finally, Section 6.4.3.2 will take a closer look at the role of the meaning shifts and discuss in detail why the approach taken to meaning shifts in Bell & Schäfer (2013) in retrospect does not seem to be a convincing idea.

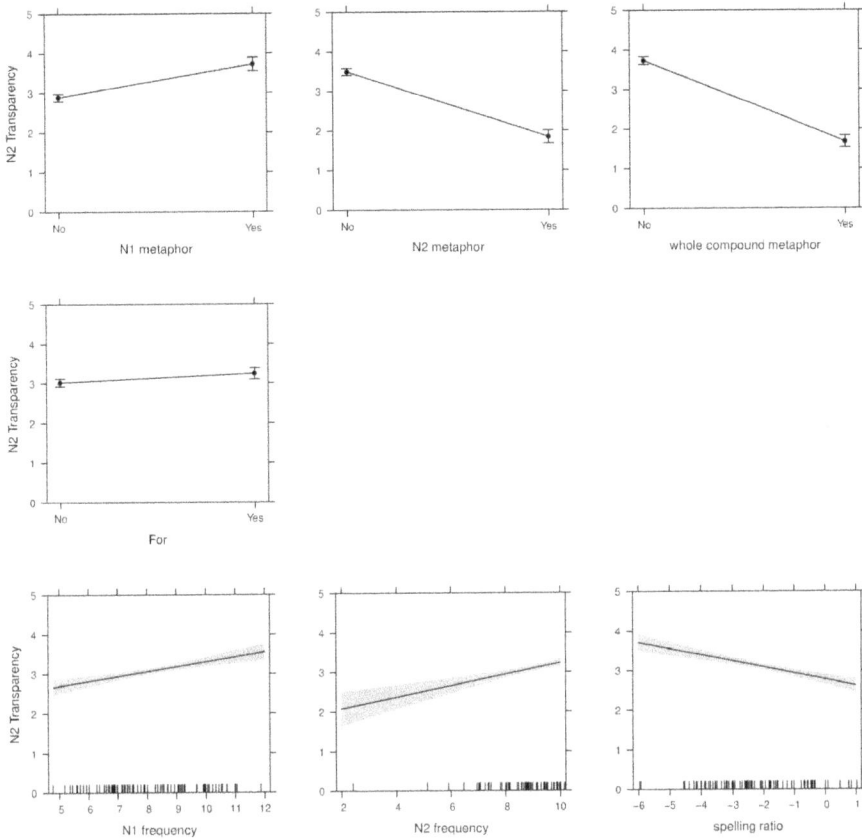

Figure 6.11: Effects in the final model for N2 transparency. The effects associated with meaning shifts are shown in the first row, the second row shows the effect of semantic relations, and frequency-based effects are shown in the third row.

6.4.1 Classic model criticism

In order to evaluate models using ordinary least square regression, one can use a variety of diagnostics. Here, I will go through the diagnostics for Model 1 from Bell & Schäfer (2013) in some detail, before giving short summaries of the results of using the same reduced dataset in re-running the 3 other models.

6.4.1.1 Model 1 revisited

Figure 6.12 shows the distribution of the residuals. By and large, their distribution follows the normal distribution, although, as the quantile-quantile plot shows, the distributions differ in their tails, with the residuals being larger in the lower tail, and smaller in the upper tail.

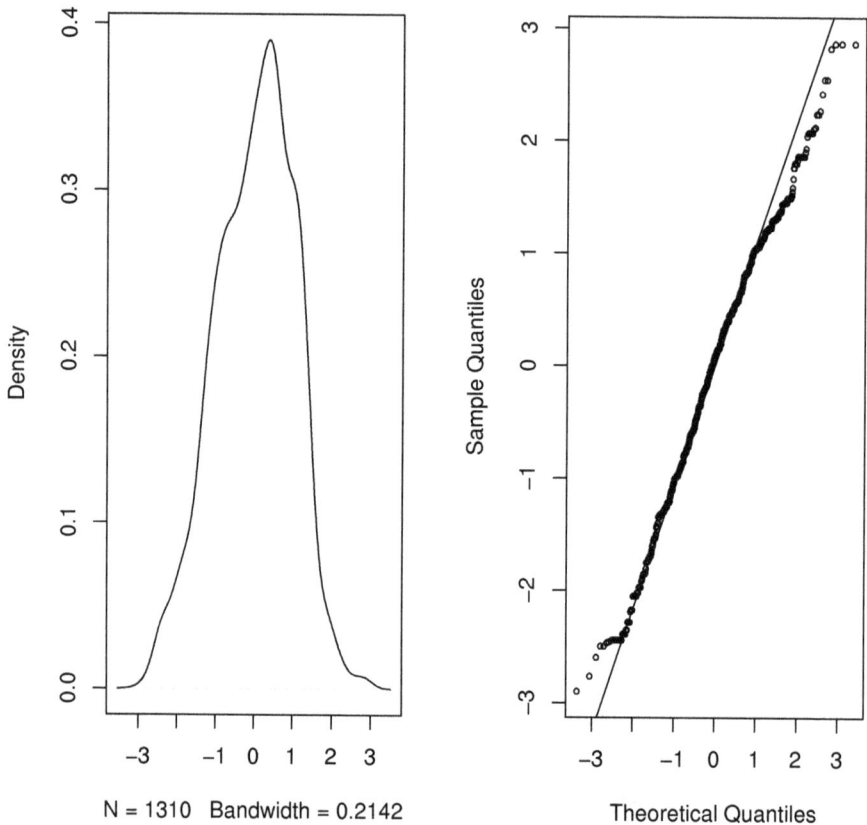

Figure 6.12: Density and quantile-quantile plot of the residuals of Model 1 presented in Bell & Schäfer (2013)

Plotting the standardized residuals against the fitted values, that is, the values predicted by the model formula allows us to check whether there is a correlation between the residuals and the fitted values. If there is no correlation, that is, the variance in the error term is constant across the x-values, then the assumption of homoscedasticity is fulfilled. Figure 6.13 shows the standardized residuals of Model 1 plotted against the corresponding fitted values. Ideally, the mean should

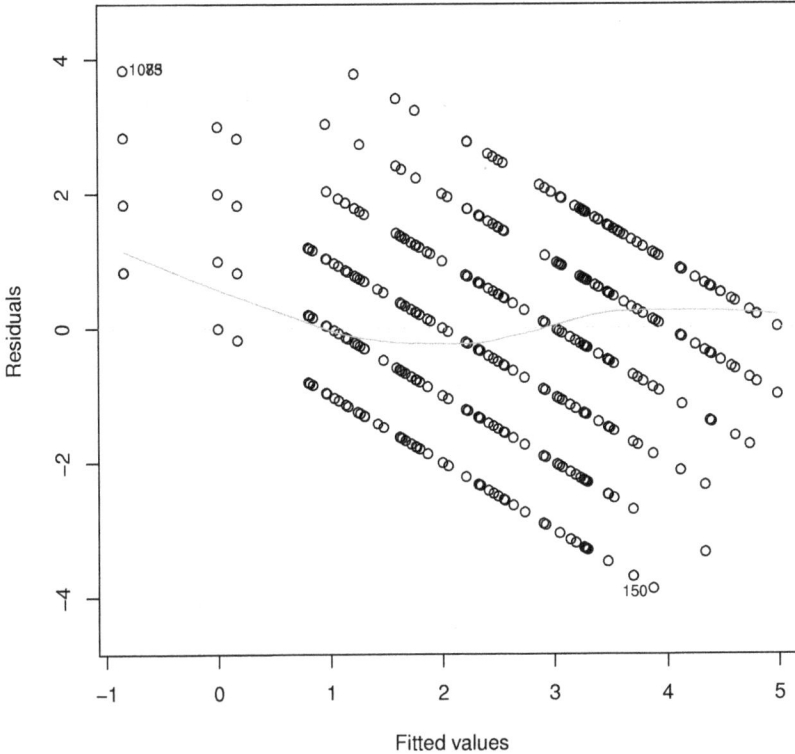

Figure 6.13: Standardized residuals vs. fitted values of the Model 1 presented in Bell & Schäfer (2013)

be on the horizontal line at 0, and there should be no change in variance across the fitted values. As the error terms should be randomly distributed, we also would not expect to see a pattern in the plot.

Inspecting the plot, we see that the mean does not form a straight line, note especially the upward swerve toward the left edge of the plot, where the prediction of values outside of the original scale used, '-1', led to large and unbalanced residuals. However, one can also see that this is caused by only a few data points which can be identified using dedicated outlier detection functions, see the discussion below. Furthermore, one notices a pattern as there are 6 horizontal evenly distanced stripes running from the upper left to the lower right. This pattern is due to the fact that the actual values to be modeled all come from a 6 point Likert scale. That is, fitted values with zero residuals are only possible at the 6 discrete values of the scale. This pattern is therefore a natural consequence of treating Likert scale ratings like continuous data.

Having seen that the model, as the standardized residuals vs. fitted values plot has shown, is still considerably influenced by a few single datapoints, I now turn to diagnostics for outlier detection. One method is to look at the differences in the fits, that is, the difference in the fitted value for an observed data point in a model that was built with that data point as opposed to a model where that data point has not been used in the model building. If the difference is large, this means that this single data point has high leverage on the resulting model, that is, its inclusion changes the model considerably. Figure 6.14 shows the values for Model 1.

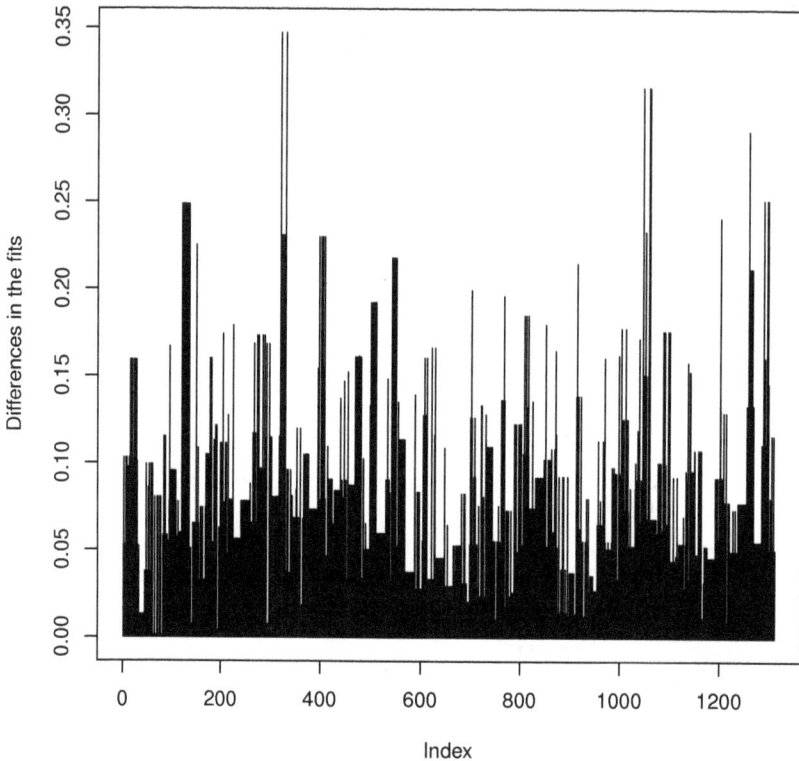

Figure 6.14: Differences in the fits for the Model 1 presented in Bell & Schäfer (2013)

The 5 spikes in the plot crossing the 0.25 value are caused by 2 datapoints for *crocodile tears*, and one each for *silver bullet*, *silver screen*, *silver spoon*, and *web site.* As all 5 compounds are only rated on one of their readings, the only difference between these datapoints and the other datapoints coming from the same compound types lies in the ratings themselves. Thus, the mean of the transparency ratings for *crocodile tears* is 1.727, and the 2 datapoints identified here are the only 2 points where the subjects chose a rating of 3, the highest rating selected for this compound type.

A further diagnostic, the dfbetas, allows us to detect datapoints not via their leverage for the whole model but via their influence on the model's individual predictors. Here, the only predictor unduly influenced is the logarithmized N2 frequency, and the responsible 7 datapoints come all from the ratings on *crocodile tears*. Not surprisingly, these 7 datapoints include the 2 points already identified by using the differences in fit. Notably, the ratings are those where the item was rated with 2 or 3, which is not in line with it having the lowest N2 frequency (the unsuspicious datapoints have been rated with 0 or 1). This finding is confirmed when looking at the flagged output of the generic outlier detection function for regression models build with the `lm()` function, `influence.measures()`. Just as we have seen for the datapoints identified before, the common pattern in the compounds containing the outliers is huge variation in the given transparency ratings.

What this suggests is that it would be helpful to exclude outliers in the ratings more thoroughly. Reddy et al. did not accept all judgments and applied a 1.5 deviation from the mean criterion to exclude outliers, but this was only applied when subjects fell under a certain correlation threshold, not across the board (cf. the remarks in Chapter 5, Section 5.2). If applying the ±1.5 deviation from the mean across the board, the 1,310 observations are reduced by 163 datapoints, leaving 1,147 transparency judgments. Note that other procedures, e.g., examining the contribution of every subject and of every item in terms of its conformity with the normal distribution, do not make sense here, because (1) many subjects made too few contributions and (2) the distribution of the ratings overall does not follow the normal distribution in the first place (see the discussion and especially Figure 6.3 in Section 6.2.2 above). Table 6.9 shows the final model for compound transparency using the reduced dataset.

As the adjusted R^2 value of 0.577 shows, the resulting model has a much better fit to the data (cf. the adjusted R^2 value of the original model, 0.459). The magnitude and direction of the predictors themselves do not change very much. The predictors for the meaning shifts and the relations and N1 frequency become slightly more pronounced, with the effect of N2 frequency and spelling ratio is slightly reduced. Note that both models do not differ much with regard to overfitting. When validating the models using bootstrap sampling with replacement on

Table 6.9: Final model for compound literality using semantic and frequency-based predictors, with outliers removed across all subjects and items, adjusted $R^2 = 0.5766$

	estimate	std. error	t	pr($> |z|$)
(intercept)	-0.81071	0.30576	-2.651	0.00813
N1 metaphor	-0.73237	0.08952	-8.181	7.45e-16
N2 metaphor	-0.51709	0.08803	-5.874	5.59e-09
N1N2 metaphor	-1.97219	0.08550	-23.067	< 2e-16
IN	0.59291	0.12281	4.828	1.57e-06
FOR	0.35582	0.08261	4.307	1.80e-05
N1 frequency	0.32807	0.02318	14.156	< 2e-16
N2 frequency	0.14550	0.02730	5.329	1.19e-07
spelling ratio	-0.11825	0.02321	-5.095	4.09e-07

number of observations: 1147, d.f. 1138

1000 bootstrap runs, using the validate function provided by Harrell Jr (2016), all factors are retained and we get minimal adjustments of the unadjusted R^2 value by 0.0066 and 0.0068 respectively. That is, the models do not overfit.

6.4.1.2 The other 3 models

Instead of going through the model criticism individually, I will here just present the results of running similar outlier cleaning algorithms on the corresponding data.

Model 2 shares the dependent variable, building a model using the same predictors on the reduced dataset considerably increases the fit, yielding an adjusted R^2 of 0.813. Using the cleaned transparency judgments for N1 and N2 leaves 979 observations and again increases the fit considerably (adjusted R^2 of 0.840).

For Model 3, the fit increases from an adjusted R^2 of 0.499 to an adjusted R^2 of 0.608. Note that the small effect associated with spelling ratio becomes less significant, and a model without it results in an R^2 of 0.607.

For Model 4, the fit increases from an adjusted R^2 value of 0.498 to an adjusted R^2 of 0.587. As with models 1 and 2, the predictors are retained and the size and direction of the effects is similar.

6.4.2 Linear mixed effects modeling

Model 1 was based on 1,310 observations for 99 compound readings given by 40 different raters. That is, the transparency ratings include multiple contributions by the same subjects as well as multiple ratings for each compound reading. Therefore the individual data points are not statistically independent of one another. In other words, the simple least square regression models are actually not appropriate for this kind of data. A statistically sound solution that allows one to retain all the data even though statistical independence is not given is the usage of mixed effects regression models. These models allow the inclusion of effects associated with particular subjects and items as random effects. Note that this is not just a step motivated by the requirements of statistics. Quite on the contrary, idiosyncratic effects associated with individual raters as well as individual items are to be expected.

The individual raters might use different strategies for their ratings on the Likert scale, resulting e.g. in the usage of different ranges of values from the scale, and in different usage of the steps given on the scale. In addition, raters might react differently to the aspects of the compounds encoded by the explanatory variables. Take, e.g., the distributional variables frequency and spelling ratio. Here, raters will react according to their individual experience with the language, for spelling ratio in particular in accordance with their exposure to written language. This individual experience will be the same regardless of which item any given rater rates, but it might differ considerably across the range of raters.

The individual items contribute to the model via the selected predictors, while all their other properties are left out of consideration. However, these other properties, and there are many more than just the linguistic characteristics discussed in Section 6.2.1, might affect transparency judgments. Consider for example effects due to differences in age of acquisition, preference for certain text types, or reference to either concrete or abstract objects etc. Even embeddings in collocations spanning more than 2 words might play a role, take e.g. *cloud nine*, which usually occurs in the phrase *on cloud nine*. Furthermore, these properties might also lead to differentiated patterns of interaction with the other predictors. Consider the predictor spelling ratio, which we used as a stand in for lexicalization, and an item like *agony aunt*. Since *agony* ends in a vowel and *aunt* starts with a vowel, or alternatively, because the letter sequence <yau> does not occur in the orthography of English, concatenation of the 2 words is not expected, regardless of how lexicalized the sequence is.

Note that the item and rater specific influences are of 2 different types. On the one hand, the baseline transparency might vary. On the other hand, the effect of the other predictors on transparency might vary. To take the example of individual raters and their employment of the Likert scale: Raters A and B might employ a different baseline transparency in that rater A always uses '3' to indicate medium transparency, but rater B always uses '2'. This kind of variance is handled in a mixed effects model by adjusting the intercept for the individual raters accordingly. The random effects can also capture a difference in sensitivity to the effects of the predictors. Thus, let us say that rater A and rater B both use '3' to indicate medium transparency, but that they are influenced more or less strongly by N1 frequency: High N1 frequency leads rater A to rate items with '5', but rater B only rates them with '4'. Similarly, low N1 frequency leads rater A to rate items with '1' but rater B with '2'. This variance is captured by allowing the slopes for the various predictors to vary with the individual subjects.

Catering for all these possible influences on rating choice via random effects ensures that the remaining effects in the model, the fixed effects, are in fact due to the semantic and distributional predictors and not to any other peculiarity of either specific items or specific annotators.

There are different types of mixed models. In the following, I will use linear mixed effects regression models including crossed random effects for annotators and items (for an introduction to these types of linear mixed effects models, see Baayen, Davidson & Bates 2008).

In building the mixed effects models, I started with the maximal model for compound transparency with all the explanatory variables used in coming to the original Model 1. The maximal model is a model that includes random intercepts for items and for subjects as well as possibly interacting random slopes for all explanatory variables. This model fails to converge. Models without interaction terms for the random slopes likewise fail to converge. In a next step, I considered only random slopes for the distributional predictors, that is, frequency N1, frequency N2, and spelling ratio. Again, these models did not converge, and I ended up comparing models with random slopes for both frequencies and with random slopes for spelling ratio. Using ANOVAs for model comparison, I arrived at a model with random intercepts for items and subjects and random slopes for the influence of N2 frequency on subjects and items. This random effect structure was then used for the other 3 models, too.

Marginal and conditional R^2 values were calculated with the `r.squaredGLMM()` function in the MuMIn package (Bartoń 2016), an implementation which is in turn based on R code from Nakagawa & Schielzeth (2013) and Johnson (2014). For mixed effects models, marginal R^2 values give the variance explained by the fixed factors, and conditional R^2 values represent the variance explained by the whole model, that is, by the random and fixed effects taken together.

6.4.2.1 Compound transparency with mixed effects models

Just as in Bell & Schäfer (2013), I will first consider a model without the N1 and N2 ratings as predictors, and then look at a model that includes these as predictors. The final model for semantic transparency excluding constituent transparency as predictors is shown in Table 6.10 and graphically represented in Figure 6.15.

The top section of Table 6.10 shows the random effects: the model includes random intercepts for items, as well as random intercepts for raters. In addition, for both items and raters it includes random slopes for the effects of N2 frequency. The bottom section of Table 6.10 shows the fixed effects.

Table 6.10: Final mixed effects model for compound transparency, marginal $R^2 = 0.46$, conditional $R^2 = 0.78$

random effects: groups	name	variance	std. dev.			
wordSenseID	(intercept)	7.291617	2.70030			
	logFreqN2	0.044884	0.21186			
workerID	(intercept)	1.681205	1.29661			
	logFreqN2	0.009137	0.09559			
Residual		0.790487	0.88909			

number of obs: 1310, groups: wordSenseID, 99; workerID, 40

fixed effects:	estimate	std. error	df	t value	pr(> |t|)
(intercept)	-0.34407	0.98678	70.00000	-0.349	0.728375
N1 metaphor	-1.00774	0.22692	71.08000	-4.441	3.22e-05
N2 metaphor	-0.54721	0.24503	88.30000	-2.233	0.028060
N1N2 metaphorYes	-2.14365	0.21611	74.21000	-9.919	3.11e-15
N1 frequency	0.23668	0.06189	73.20000	3.824	0.000274
N2 frequency	0.23596	0.09170	47.82000	2.573	0.013231

Although the proportion of variance explained by the explanatory variables in this model is equal to the proportion of variance explained by Model 1 in Bell & Schäfer (2013) (adjusted R^2 for Model 1 and marginal R^2 for this model are both 0.46), this variance is accounted for in this model by just 5 explanatory variables. Note also that the conditional R^2 value (the R^2 value showing the total variation accounted for by the model) is 0.78, far higher than the adjusted R^2 value for the model using the cleaned data (R^2 0.58). The crucial difference between this and the original model are the missing predictors. Whereas in the original model and

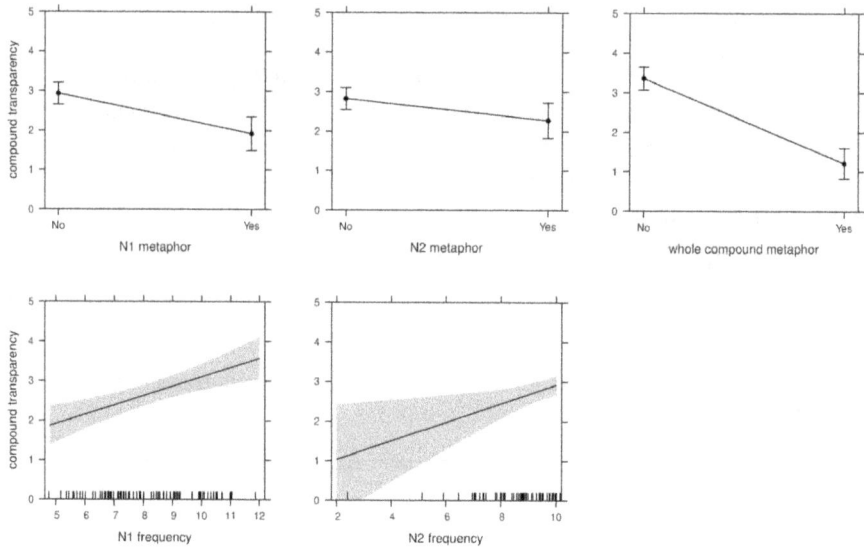

Figure 6.15: Partial effects in the final mixed effects model for compound transparency using distributional and semantic predictors.

in the model run on the cleaned data the predictors IN and FOR positively correlated with transparency, none of the variables encoding semantic relations survives in the mixed effect model. Spelling ratio also does not make a significant contribution. The explanatory variables that stay in the final model, however, come with coefficients that are, generally speaking, similar to the coefficients in the original model. Thus, all meaning shifts are associated with less semantic transparency, with the largest effect again coming from whole compound meaning shifts. The magnitude of the effect is slightly higher in this model than in Model 1. Similarly, the effect associated with N1 metaphor is more pronounced in this model than in Model 1. Just as in the previous model, the constituent frequencies are associated with more transparency, that is, the more frequent either constituent, the more transparent the compound. Differing from model 1, the magnitudes of the effects are the same for both N1 and N2 frequency.

The random effects in the model are illustrated in Figure 6.16 and Figure 6.17.

Figure 6.16 shows the random effects associated with the different raters. In the left hand plot, the dots represent the adjustment of the intercept for each of the 40 raters. Dots to the right of the vertical line at 0 indicate a positive adjustment, that is, the rater exhibits a tendency to give higher ratings. Dots to the left of the vertical line at 0 indicate a tendency towards lower transparency rat-

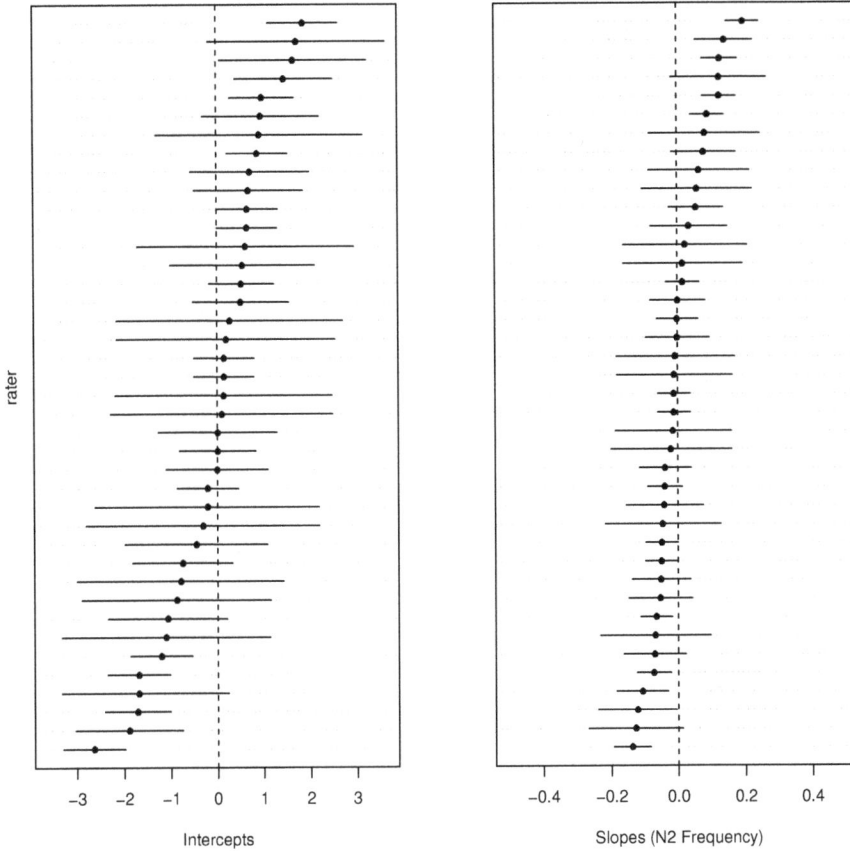

Figure 6.16: By-rater random intercepts and by-rater random slopes for the effect of N2 frequency in the final mixed effects model for compound transparency excluding constituent ratings.

ings. The horizontal lines show the 95% confidence intervals for these intercept adjustments. While for 28 raters 0 is included in this interval, 12 show a clear tendency towards either higher or lower ratings. The individual adjustments range from -3.6 to 3.6 and show considerable variation. The right hand plot shows the adjustments of the slope of the N2 frequency predictor for the individual raters, which range from -0.27 to 0.27. Again, for 12 out of the 40 raters the adjustments show clear positive or negative tendencies, while 28 include 0 in their confidence intervals.

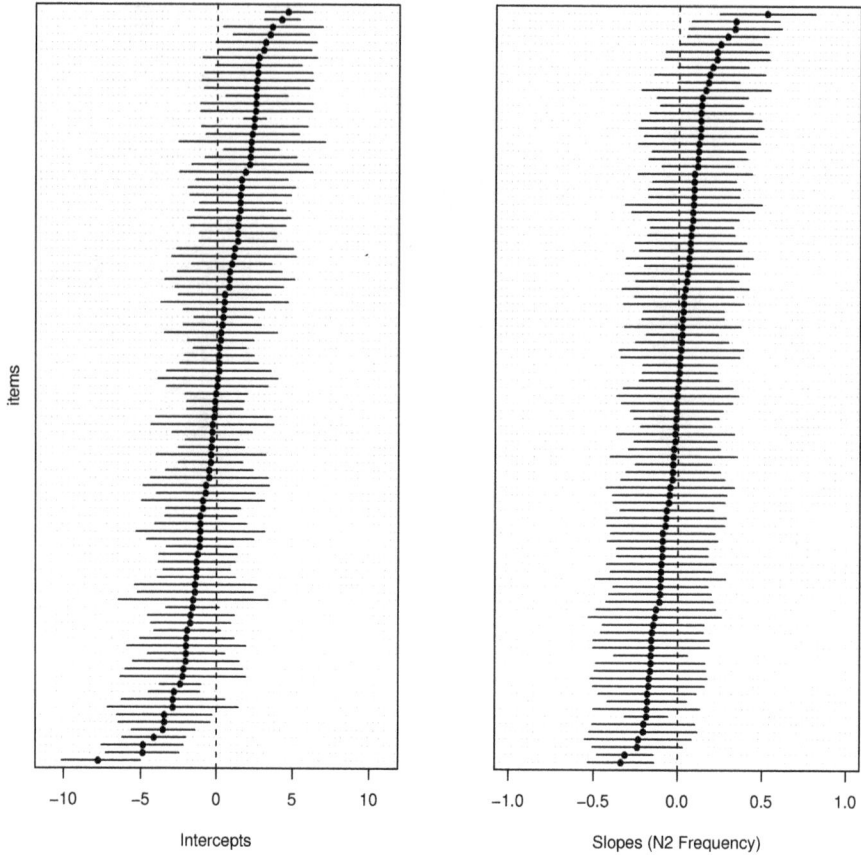

Figure 6.17: By-item random intercepts and by-rater random slopes for the effect of N2 frequency in the final mixed effects model for compound transparency excluding constituent ratings.

Figure 6.17 shows the random effects associated with the different items. As in Figure 6.16, the left hand plot represents the adjustment of the intercepts, while the right hand plot shows the adjustments of the slope associated with the predictor N2 frequency. For the intercepts, 16 of the 99 items lead to a clear preference for lower or higher ratings, while 83 include 0 in their confidence intervals. The adjustments themselves range from -10.5 to 7.0, the variance is very high. For the slopes, 8 items show a clear preference, and adjustments range from -0.55 to 0.81. For both the adjustments of the intercepts as well as the adjustments of the slopes, the random effects associated with the items are far more pronounced than those associated with the individual raters.

Including constituent transparency as predictors leads to the final model in Table 6.11, graphically represented in Figure 6.18.

Table 6.11: Final mixed effects model for compound transparency, including N1 and N2 constituent transparency as predictors, marginal $R^2 = 0.70$, conditional $R^2 = 0.78$

random effects:

groups	name	variance	std. dev.
wordSenseID	(intercept)	0.16305	0.4038
workerID	(intercept)	0.09023	0.3004
residual		0.65733	0.8108

number of obs: 1310, groups: wordSenseID, 99; workerID, 40

fixed effects:

	estimate	std. error	df	t value	pr(> |t|)
(intercept)	0.02528	.29028	9.50000	.087	0.930812
N1 metaphor	-0.31868	.12246	3.20000	.602	0.010963
N2 metaphor	-0.28440	.12231	4.00000	.325	0.022476
N1N2 metaphor	-0.51419	.12331	7.70000	.170	6.6e-05
N1 frequency	0.11151	.03114	5.90000	.581	0.000602
N1 transparency	0.37030	0.02169	735.20000	17.069	< 2e-16
N2 transparency	0.35393	0.02224	629.50000	15.916	< 2e-16

This time, all but one of the fixed effects in the original model also occur in the mixed effects model. The predictor variable N2 frequency does not play a significant role in this model. Since N2 frequency is no longer a fixed effect, it is not featured in the random part of the model. For the remaining predictors, the direction of the influence is always the same as in the original models. However, the strengths of the effects of the individual predictors differ slightly. The negative effects of the shifts are stronger, only slightly so in the case of the constituent shifts, but considerably stronger in the case of a metaphoric shift of the whole compound, where the negative coefficient increases from -0.18 to -0.52. The positive effect associated with N1 frequency is smaller. The effect of constituent transparency becomes slightly smaller. This can be explained by assuming that some of the variance originally accounted for by constituent ratings is now accounted for by the random effects. This explains also why the marginal R^2 value of the mixed effects model is lower than the R^2 value of the original model (0.70 vs. 0.74). The variance in the random effects for the items is much lower than in the previous model. This is a side effect of the rater and item specific constituent

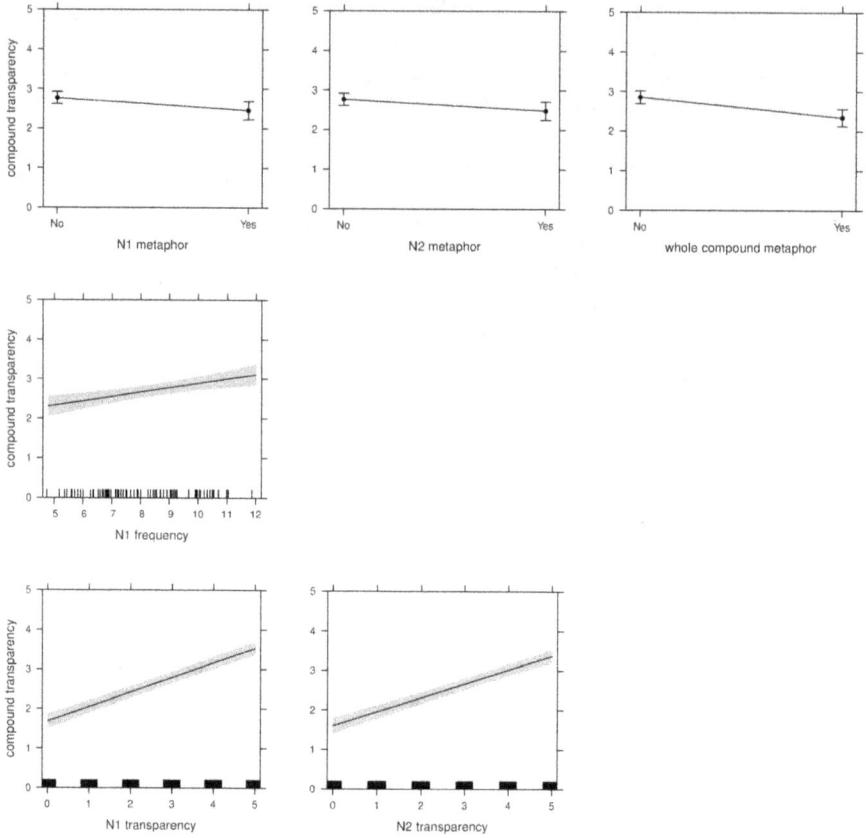

Figure 6.18: Partial effects in the final model for compound transparency, including N1 and N2 constituent transparency as predictors

ratings. That is, as explained in Section 6.3.1, we only included data where we had ratings on both constituents and the whole compound by the same rater, using a within subject design. Plausibly, much of the influence of the individual items not encoded in the predictor variables had a similar influence on the subject regardless which transparency rating (N1, N2, or the whole compound) they were making.

6.4.2.2 Constituent transparency with mixed effects models

The final mixed effects model for the transparency of the first constituent is given in Table 6.12, and graphically represented in Figure 6.19. Again, I started by using the same random effect structure as for the first model. However, since N2 frequency was not significant, the corresponding random slopes were also taken out of the model. The variance coming with the random intercept by item is higher than the variance in the second model, but still lower than the variance in the first model.

Table 6.12: Final mixed effects model for the semantic transparency of first constituent (N1) transparency, marginal $R^2 = 0.48$, conditional $R^2 = 0.80$

random effects:

groups	name	variance	std. dev.
wordSenseID	(intercept)	1.27456	1.1290
workerID	(intercept)	0.09922	0.3150
residual		0.86663	0.9309

number of obs: 1310, groups: wordSenseID, 99; workerID, 40

fixed effects:

	estimate	std. error	df	t value	pr($> |t|$)
(intercept)	0.8507	0.6902	93.4900	1.233	0.22084
N1 metaphor	-1.8480	0.2856	91.9600	-6.470	4.68e-09
N2 metaphor	0.7838	0.2818	90.5700	2.781	0.00659
N1N2 metaphor	-1.9549	0.2703	91.7400	-7.231	1.40e-10
IN	0.8567	0.4104	88.5700	2.087	0.03972
N1 frequency	0.3281	0.0754	91.9000	4.352	3.50e-05

Comparing this model to the original Model 3, we see that the variation explained by the fixed effects corresponds closely to the variation explained by the original model (cf. the marginal R^2 of 0.48 to the adjusted R^2 of 0.50 of Model 3). However, spelling ratio and N2 frequency are not significant in the mixed effects model, which therefore needs 2 predictors less to explain almost the same variation. Looking at the predictors that are shared by both models, we see that the 2 negative predictors, N1 metaphor and N1N2 metaphor become more pronounced, while the predictor N2 metaphor becomes slightly smaller (but remains positive). Likewise, the predictor IN becomes slightly less pronounced, as does the remaining frequency-based predictor, frequency N1.

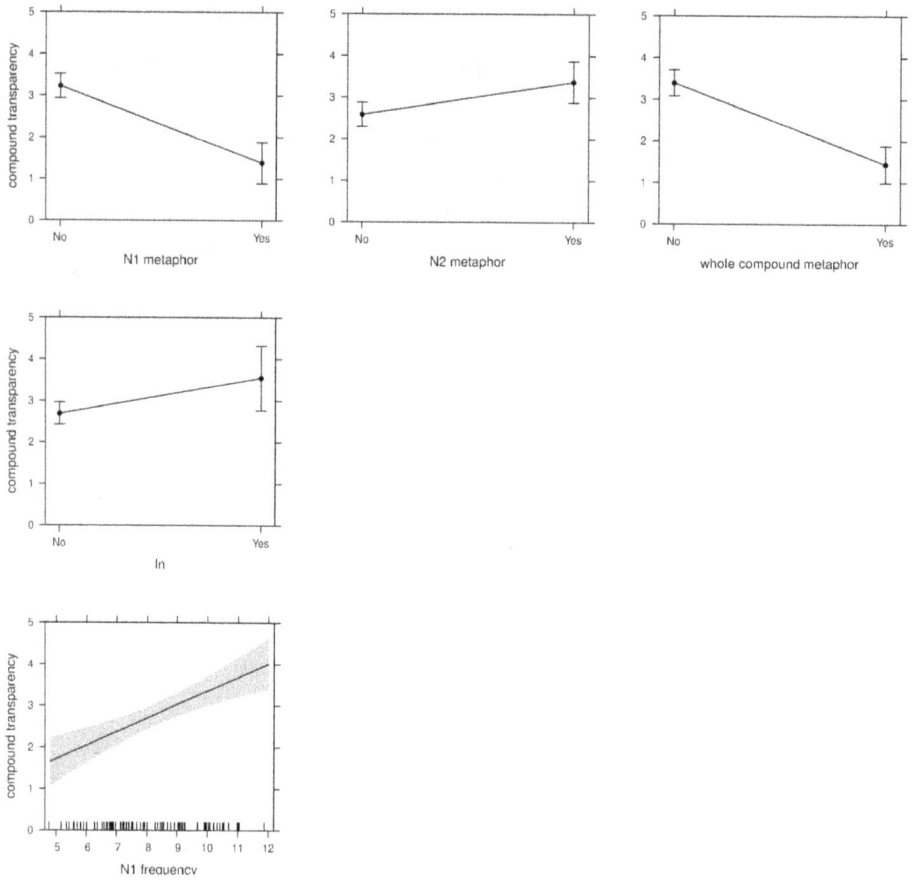

Figure 6.19: Partial effects in the final model for N1 transparency

The mixed effects model for N2 transparency is shown in Table 6.13 and graphically represented in Figure 6.20. What we see here is first of all a massive increase of variance in the adjustment to the intercept by item. Why is that? If we look at the 4 items with the highest adjustments in the positive and negative direction, we can throw some light on the issue. The 2 items with the highest negative adjustments are one word sense of *gold mine*, with a mean N2 rating of 0.54, and *gravy train*, with a mean N2 rating of 0.08 respectively. Although *gold mine* came with 2 senses to choose from, it was only rated with the word sense *a good source of something that is desired*. In the semantic annotation, it is marked as not shifted. *Gravy train* only has one possible word sense, *income obtained with a minimum of effort*. As far as the shifts are concerned, it is annotated as containing metaphorically shifted first and second constituents, N1 and N2, whereas the whole compound, N1N2, is annotated as unshifted. So here, both items are given extremely low transparency values, but neither of them falls under the strong negative predictor N1N2 metaphor (though *gravy train* falls under the less strongly negative predictor N2 metaphor). For the positive predictors, the logarithmized N1 frequency of *gold* and *gravy* are 8.92 and 5.59 respectively, placing them in middle and low regions of the frequency spectrum exhibited by the N1 constituents. In contrast, both logarithmized N2 frequencies, 8.99 for *mine* and 9.54 for *train*, place them in the highest region of the frequency spectrum exhibited by the N2 constituents.

The 2 items with the highest positive adjustments are one word sense of *face value*, with a mean N2 rating of 4.78, and one word sense of *acid test*, with a mean N2 rating of 3.92. For *face value*, raters chose actually both of the available senses, the one in question here is *the apparent worth as opposed to the real worth*. It is coded as N1 metaphor and N1N2 metaphor. For *acid test*, the only definition chosen by raters was *a rigorous or crucial appraisal*. It is coded as N1N2 metaphor. So in both cases, there are very high respectively high transparency ratings, but items falling under the strongest negative predictor for N2 transparency, N1N2 metaphor. Of the logarithmized constituent frequencies, the values for both *face* and *value* correspond to the top spectrum, with 10.71 for N1 and 10.18 for N2, while for *acid test* the values are slightly lower, with 8.69 for N1 and 10.02 for N2, placing *acid* in the middle of the spectrum, and *test* again in the top region.

As for the fixed effects, one can again observe that the variation explained by them is lower than the variation explained by the original Model 4, with a marginal R^2 of 0.40 against an adjusted R^2 value of 0.50. In contrast to the original model, the relational predictor FOR does not become significant. Likewise, and just as in the 3 previous mixed effects models, the predictor spelling ratio does not become significant. Of the meaning shifts, only the 2 predictors that were negatively correlated with N1 transparency, N1N2 metaphor and N2 metaphor, survive. Comparing the predictors occurring in both models, the effect associated with N2 metaphor is less pronounced in the new model, while the effect associated with N1N2 metaphor is slightly more pronounced in the new model. As far as the frequency-based predictors are concerned, we see a massive increase of the role of N2 frequency while the role of N1 frequency decreases. As the p-values show, the effect associated with N1 frequency is also not significant. However, models without this predictor did not converge.

The high variance in the random effects led me to reconsider the random effects structure for this model. Recall that the reason for using the random effect

Table 6.13: Final mixed effects model for the semantic transparency of N2, the second constituent, marginal $R^2 = 0.404$, conditional $R^2 = 0.823$

random effects:

groups	name	variance	std. dev.
wordSenseID	(intercept)	27.222122	5.21748
	logFreqN2	0.201389	0.44876
workerID	(intercept)	0.166860	0.40848
	logFreqN2	0.003522	0.05935
Residual		0.783607	0.88522

number of obs: 1310, groups: wordSenseID, 99; workerID, 40

fixed effects:

	estimate	std. error	df	t value	pr(> |t|)
(intercept)	-0.03739	1.05793	94.86000	-0.035	0.971879
N2 metaphor	-1.28548	0.24290	46.93000	-5.292	3.12e-06
N1N2 metaphor	-2.10421	0.19513	34.36000	-10.784	1.43e-12
N1 frequency	0.08553	0.05341	26.29000	1.601	0.121223
N2 frequency	0.37295	0.09838	91.97000	3.791	0.000268

structure was based on the testing done for the first model, and following the general logic that since the sources for the random effects remain the same across all 4 models, so should the random effect structure. Given the high variance in the random effects and the failure to converge when trying to build a model without N1 frequency as a predictor, it seems amply justified to test whether or not a simpler random effect structure would perhaps lead to better results. However, comparing the models in question via ANOVA shows that the random effect structure including the random slopes yields models with significantly lower AICs and BICs than those models without the random slopes.

6.4.2.3 Conclusion: the results of the mixed effects modeling

At the beginning of this section, I argued that the nature of the data that was used in Bell & Schäfer (2013) required mixed effect modeling. Thus, the models discussed in this section are preferable over the models discussed in Section 6.3.4 which only used ordinary least square regressions. Any predictors occurring in the models reported in Bell & Schäfer (2013) but not in the mixed effects models are best seen as artefacts of idiosyncrasies of either the individual raters or the individual items. The most important result from the mixed effects models is

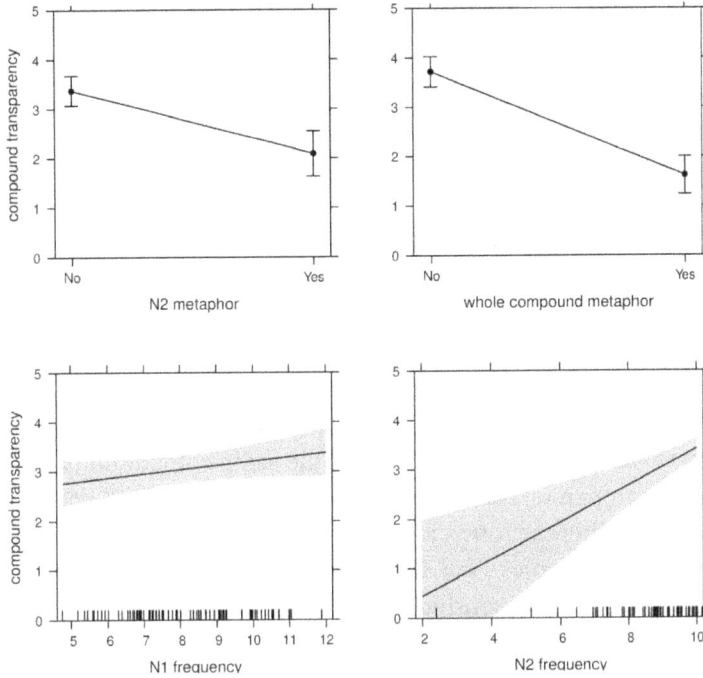

Figure 6.20: Partial effects in the final model for N2 transparency

that the semantic relations almost completely disappear from the models. Only IN survives in the model for N1 transparency. In contrast, except for the absence of an effect of N1 metaphor on N2 transparency, the 3 semantic shifts remained as significant predictors in all models. These results are very intriguing; as far as the relations are concerned, the fact that the relations as such are not associated with more or less perceived transparency is expected from the point of view of the conceptual combination models by Gagné and collaborators (cf. the discussion of the CARIN and RICE models in Chapter 2, Section 2.1.3): the relations only play a role relative to the constituents involved, that is, a given relation might be associated with increased transparency for some constituent while at the same time being associated with decreased transparency for some other constituent.

As far as the distributional predictors are concerned, it is interesting that both constituent frequencies together only become significant predictors in the model for whole compound transparency excluding constituent transparency judgments. Another interesting finding is the failure of spelling ratio to become significant in any of these models. There are a number of possible explanations for this. Assuming that spelling ratio is a good stand-in for lexicalization, this finding could be taken to show that there is no significant correlation between lexicalization and transparency. Alternatively, the role of lexicalization could also be already subsumed by the codings for the meaning shifts. Finally, spelling ratio might not be suitable to effectively represent lexicalization. Consider in this respect also the nature of the dataset: since part of the original criteria for selection was that the combinations have to occur at least 50 times in the ukWaC corpus, none of the compounds are new or ad-hoc formations. Therefore, it might well be that the proportion of items in this set that are not spelled as one word is disproportionately influenced by the phonological and/or orthographic properties of the items (cf. the remarks on *agony aunt* in Section 6.4.2), thus distorting the assessment of a possible role of concatenation as indicator of semantic opaqueness. Note in this context also the findings by Marelli et al. (2015) with regard to distributional models for one and the same compound based on its occurrence in either open or solid form discussed in Chapter 5, Section 5.4: if it is correct that these different forms are regurlarly associated with different meanings, then spelling ratio picks out the balance of these meanings (if both forms are possible) rather than presenting lexicalization as such.

6.4.3 The role of the meaning shifts

The innovative aspect of Bell & Schäfer (2013) was the usage of semantic annotations in the modeling. As evidenced by the mixed effects models, the semantic relations do not contribute significantly to transparency, except in the model for N1 transparency, where IN is a significant predictor, though barely so. In contrast, the meaning shifts reoccurred in all mixed effects models, moreover, except for the model of N2 transparency, all 3, that is N1 metaphor, N2 metaphor, and N1N2 metaphor were significant predictors.

Here, I want to argue that there are more fundamental problems with these predictors. In order to do so, I will proceed in 2 steps. First, I will take a closer look at the relationship between the codings for the shifts and the actual annotator judgments. Secondly, I will argue that these relationship but also principled considerations show that a binary category shift/no shift is not able to adequately capture the nature of the data (for these points, cf. also Bell & Schäfer 2016).

6.4.3.1 Relationship between the shift codings and the actual annotator judgments

One reason for the meaning shifts remaining in all models is likely to be the very nature of the original task: Recall that raters were asked for the literality of compounds and constituents. So if we model these ratings with meaning shifts, which arguably are based on the idea that there is a departure from a literal meaning to some other interpretation, we are actually coding the same thing that the raters have rated (note that it is not coded in quite the same way, though, as in the coding, 2 categories of shifts, metaphoric and metonymic, were used, and the decisions were only categorical, while the raters had a 6 point scale at their disposal). But if the predictors encode the same things as the dependent variable, it is not surprising that the predictors become significant. In fact, if anything, it is surprising that the predictors did not perform even better than they did. One straightforward way of delving into this issue is by simply plotting the actual ratings against the semantic annotation. Below, this is done for the 3 possible metaphoric shifts (N1, N2, N1N2) and the constituent as well as the whole compound ratings.

Figure 6.21 shows the distribution of the rater judgments for N1, N2, and N1N2 respectively against whether the compound was annotated as containing a metaphorically shifted first constituent.

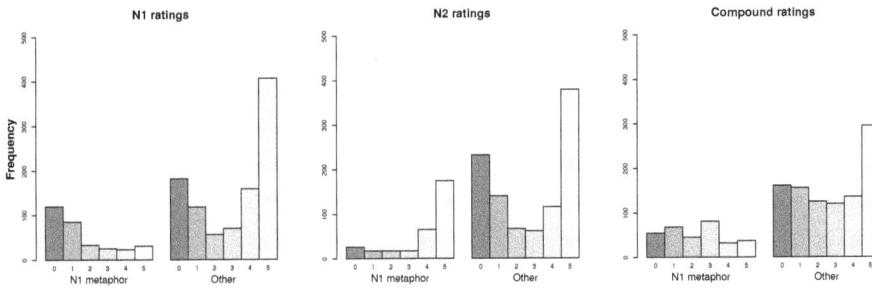

Figure 6.21: The N1 is metaphor coding vs. rater judgments on N1, N2, and whole compound transparency. The 3 panels are all divided into 2 parts. On the left, they show the distribution of the transparency ratings for those items that are annotated as containing a metaphorically shifted first constituent, on the right, they show the distribution over the other items. The histograms on the left show the distribution of the N1 transparency ratings. The histograms in the middle show the distribution of the N2 transparency ratings. The histograms on the right show the distribution of the compound transparency ratings.

The panel on the left hand side depicts the distribution of the N1 ratings, the panel in the middle depicts the distribution of the N2 ratings, and the panel on the right hand side depicts the distribution of the N1N2 ratings. The Likert scale ratings are ordered form 0, the lowest rating, to 5, the highest rating, with the lowest rating in black and the higher ratings in increasingly lighter shades of gray.

The patterns in Figure 6.21 are partially reassuring: in the left panel, one sees that for those items that have been coded as N1 metaphor, there is a clear trend in the ratings for lower transparency judgments, while the right-hand panel with the whole compound ratings shows no clear trend. Of interest is also the clear trend for high N2 ratings given an N1 coded as metaphorically shifted. Of central interest for the discussion here, though, is the fact that although there is a clear trend in the left-hand panel, it is also clear that many N1 constituents were rated as being quite or even fully transparent, although they are annotated as shifted. This misalignment of rater judgments and semantic annotation is even more apparent in the data for N2 transparency. Figure 6.22 shows similar plots for the distribution of the ratings against whether the items were annotated as containing a metaphorically shifted second constituent. Focusing on the middle panel, where N2 ratings are plotted against the N2 metaphoric shift, one can see that even though the lowest 2 ratings still account for the 2 most highly populated bins, many constituents received very high transparency ratings, so that it is difficult to speak of a general trend in the distribution. Again, there is a still clearer trend for the other constituent in the other direction, whereas there does not appear to be a trend in the distribution of the whole compound ratings.

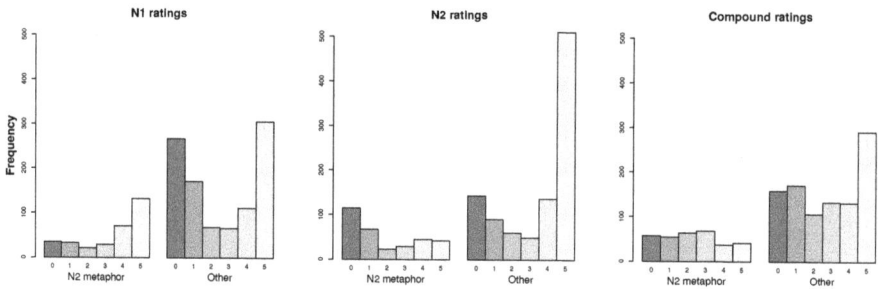

Figure 6.22: The N2 is metaphor coding vs. rater judgments on N1 (left), N2 (middle), and whole compound transparency (right). The 3 panels contrast the distribution of the ratings for items coded as containing a metaphorically shifted N2 (left) with those that do not (right).

Finally, Figure 6.23 shows the distribution of the ratings against whether the whole compound was annotated as metaphorically shifted. Here, we see the expected pattern: as the right hand panel shows, for those items coded as containing whole compound shifts, almost none of the raters gave a high transparency rating, and the trend towards low ratings is very clear. Interestingly, this trend also occurs in the other 2 panels, resulting in a much clearer pattern for the N2 ratings than what we found for the N2 ratings of items rated as containing a shifted second constituent, cf. the middle panel in Figure 6.22.

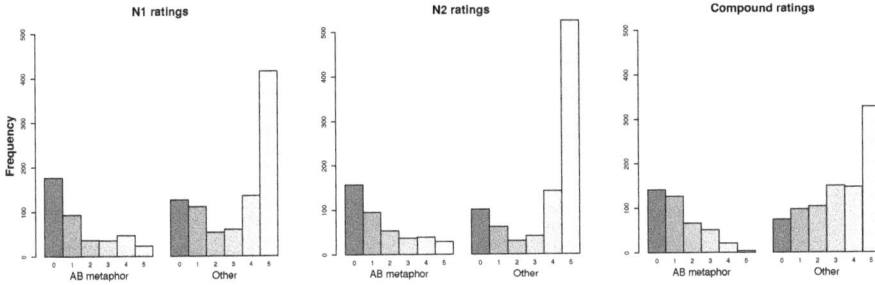

Figure 6.23: The whole compound is metaphor coding vs. rater judgments on N1, N2, and whole compound transparency

Another interesting observation is that the total number of items coded as containing shifts is actually higher than the number of items judged by the raters as departing from literality. As seen earlier, in Figure 6.7, the individual shift categories contain at most 31 compound readings, however, since the different shifts are distributed over all the items, there are actually only 28 compound readings that are annotated as containing no shift at all. In contrast, 40 compound readings where given unanimously '5' ratings on all 3 transparency categories, that is, N1, N2, and N1N2. Thus, although the semantic annotators had to make a categorical decision and the raters could choose from a scale, the semantic annotators were more prone to judge items as departing from literality than the raters.

In the following section, I want to argue that the actual coding of the meaning shifts and the conclusion one can draw from the annotation results go a long way towards explaining this discrepancy.

6.4.3.2 Coding the meaning shifts

In Bell & Schäfer (2013: 3), we just mention that the shifts that we coded, *metaphor* and *metonymy*, are well-known, and refrain from any further explanation. In fact, both types of meaning shifts are part of, if not everyday knowledge, then at least common knowledge that linguists acquire at the very early stages of their education. If we look at introductory semantics textbooks, we find definitions like cf. (11) and (12), taken from Löbner (2013: 52–53), his Definition 5 and 6 respectively.

(11)   Metonymy
        An expression is used metonymically if it is used to refer to things that
        belong to the kind of objects to which the expression refers in its literal
        meaning.

(12)   Metaphor
        An expression is used metaphorically if it is used to refer to things that are
        in crucial aspects similar to the kind of objects to which the expression
        refers in its literal meaning.

In annotating the compounds for meaning shifts, I think that we had definitions
of this kind in mind. Note that both definitions use the concept of 'literal meaning', a point we will come back to later (see also the discussion of the term in
Chapter 3, Section 3.2.3.2).

6.4.3.3 Coding metonymic shifts

As mentioned above, the metonymic shifts were not very frequent and were
therefore not considered in the statistical models. Even so, if I look at the coding
by us in Bell & Schäfer (2013), I find it very hard to reconstruct the coding of some
of the metonymical shifts. Coding *cocktail* in *cocktail dress* as metonomy seems
straightforward to me: the whole compound refers to a dress worn at cocktail parties, and cocktails belong to cocktail parties (note that this holds independently
of whether one knows the exact literal meaning of 'cocktail'). But why did we
classify *cash* in *cash cow* and *wedding* in *diamond wedding* as a metonymic shifts?
Likewise, why did we classify *silver spoon* as whole compound metonomy? Constructing metonymical analyses is not impossible, but the analyses do not seem
to be very compelling. Thus, the image associated with *cash cow*, at least for me,
is of a cow that gives coins instead of milk, and since cash consists of banknotes
and coins, the definition of metonymy is fulfilled. However, on reflection, this
seems to be a rather idiosyncratic interpretation, and other interpretations are
equally plausible.

6.4.3.4 Coding metaphoric shifts

At first sight, the coding of the metaphorical variables seems much more straightforward than the coding of metonymy, consider e.g. *head* in *head teacher, aunt*
in *agony aunt*, and the whole compound shift assumed for *swan song*, with representative usages given below:

(13) At the beginning of the school year, Mr Bailey, the **head teacher**, would remind the staff about various rules at the school and he would also give us his view about clothes. BNC/A6V 2190

(14) I am still friends with my ex-husband who takes it on himself to be my personal **agony aunt**. BNC/CH1 6758

(15) Gazing out into the blue, he asked himself if this assignment was his **swan song**. BNC/AC2 496

Head in *head teacher* is clearly used metaphorically, indicating that the referent is the person whose role with respect to whichever institution the person is head teacher of resembles the role of the head with respect to the body, i.e., that part that makes decisions for and guides the whole. Similarly clearly, *aunt* in *agony aunt* clearly does not refer to the speaker's real aunt, but to her ex-husband taking over a role that resembles the role and status of an agony aunt. In both cases, the metaphorically shifted elements are, to quote Löbner's definition from (12) above, "in crucial aspects similar" to the meaning of *aunt* as caring and trustworthy female relative and head as the body part. And finally, the whole compound shift of *swan song* is equally obvious, as here, although the expression refers to an assignment executed by a human, not a swan, the similarity lies in the metaphor being used to indicate one final, substantive effort.

Other decisions are not so clear, but for different reasons (cf. also the discussion in Bell & Schäfer (2016). However, in one way or the other all of the decisions are linked to the notion of literal meaning. Here, I will first focus on compounds where it is unclear whether shifts are involved and if so, which. Secondly, I will discuss the more fundamental aspect of the availability of a given literal meaning.

I already reported in Section 6.3.3 that 2 items, *kangaroo court* and *flea market*, had been excluded from the semantic annotation, because we could not agree on an annotation, and pointed to their murky etymology as a likely reason for this disagreement. However, similar points can be made with regard to some of the other compounds in the dataset. I will illustrate this here with the help of *grandfather clock* and *gravy train*.

Grandfather in *grandfather clock* is coded as being metaphorically shifted. We identified BE and HAVE2 as possible semantic relations, which is already a first indicator that we had trouble coding this item, since no other compound reading is coded with 2 different relations, and, according to the logic of the coding, the 2 relations cannot refer to the same construal of the compound meaning. Construing the compound with the BE relation, *grandfather* clearly requires a metaphoric shift. Note, though, that it is not at all clear which metaphorical shift this should be, it could be from grandfather to something as old or old-fashioned as a grandfather, or perhaps to something as big as a grandfather. This is quite different from other items coded as containing a metaphoric shift in the first constituent, cf. the above-mentioned *head teacher* or items like *panda car* or *snail mail*, where in both cases the crucial aspect involved in the shift, for *panda* the white-black pattern, for *snail* the speed of movement, is very straightforward. The construal with the HAVE2 relation, that is, a clock that grandfathers have, does not necessarily require a meaning shift of the constituent, although a widening from biological grandfather to all kinds of old people seems likely, that is, a clock that old people have. Thus, depending on the construal, *grandfather* is either shifted or unshifted, and if shifted, different crucial aspects can be selected, partly depending on the construal. All of the shifts involve considerable interpretational work and are not immediately obvious. Etymologically, all appear to be wrong: According to the OED, the name *grandfather clock* for a tall, floor-standing clock, originates from the song, *My Grandfather's Clock*, and not from a shift in the meaning of *grandfather*.

Gravy in *gravy train*, a compound which was already mentioned in Section 6.4.2.2 in the discussion of mixed effect models for constituent transparency, likewise is annotated as containing a metaphorically shifted first constituent. Again, though, it is quite unclear what the exact nature of the shift is supposed to be. The OED lists the whole compound under a word sense of *gravy* that comes from U.S. slang usage: 2. d. "Money easily acquired; an unearned or unexpected bonus; a tip. Hence **to ride (board) the gravy train (or boat)**, to obtain easy financial success." Is this a metaphor for any other sense of *gravy*? It is certainly not very straightforward, and it is not helping that the role of trains in all of this is unclear (*gravy train* is the topic of numerous blog entries, cf. Quinion (n.d.) for a good overview).

I now turn to the second issue, the necessity of having a literal meaning to start with: in order to classify something as metaphorically shifted, it has to be clear what the literal meaning is supposed to be. Thus, we rated *card* in *credit card* as metaphorical shifted. Our reasoning was that a *card* is made from cardboard and not from plastic like credit cards. Therefore, *card* needs to be shifted. Likewise, we coded *web* in *website* as metaphoric, reasoning that it does not refers to a real web, that is, a spider's web or anything tangible resembling one. These decisions were based on our intuitions about these words; the average ratings of *2.7* for *web* and *4.9* for *card* show that the raters saw medium and almost no deviation from the literal meaning for the 2 constituents. How can this be? First, as the discussion in Chapter 3, Section 3.2.3.2 has already shown, literal mean-ing is not a well-defined notion. Second, neither were the raters instructed to make decisions based on etymology, nor were our own annotations meant as exercises in etymology. What we annotated was whether we intuitively thought that something was metaphorically shifted or not. There are a number of factors that influence one's perception of words as shifted. Recall the reasoning by Jaszc-zolt (2016) from the earlier discussion that being able to easily come up with a meaning in isolation is linked to being able to envision contexts for the respec-tive meaning. In other words, if a word sense requires a very specific context, we might perceive it as somehow shifted from the original. Also, in the same section, I pointed to the role of contrasting pairs as driving such perceptions. In the case of *credit card*, once you start considering the card made from cardboard against the plastic version it seem plausible to consider the latter as somehow derivative. However, in many cases it is unclear when an additional contrast with another meaning is considered. Among other things, the frequencies of specific senses alone and in other compounds are likely to play a role. Further, specific proper-ties of the referents might play a role, so that for example animal names (*swan*, *crocodile* etc.), which refer to concrete and specific living entities, are more likely to give rise to senses that are seen as derived even if this does not necessarily correspond to frequency of usage of that specific word sense (in this context, re-call that of the 5 lowest rated first constituents in the Reddy et al. dataset, 4 are animal terms, cf. Table 6.2 in Section 6.2.2).

6.5 Conclusion and consequences

This chapter started with the idea to model the semantic transparency of com-pounds by including predictors that represent core aspects of their semantics: meaning shifts and the relations holding between a compound's constituents. Af-ter introducing the dataset from which the dependent variables, the transparency ratings for compounds and their constituents, were drawn, I introduced the an-notation scheme used in Bell & Schäfer (2013), as well as the results of their annotation. Section 6.3.4 presented the models from Bell & Schäfer (2013). The central part of this chapter, however, is Section 6.4. In Section 6.4.2, I first explain why the nature of the data requires one to use mixed effects models. Secondly, using mixed effects models shows that semantic relations, when considered as predictors independent of particular constituents, do not play a role in models of compound transparency. In contrast, meaning shifts as coded in Bell & Schäfer (2013), play a role. However, I argue in Section 6.4.3.2 that the way in which meaning shifts were coded throws doubt on the meaningfulness of the results. All in all, this chapter has thus shown that the goal behind the paper by Bell & Schäfer (2013), namely to show that the internal semantic structure of compounds plays a role for their perceived transparency, turns out not to have been achieved.

In the next chapter, I will therefore report on work that takes a different, expectancy-based approach on the role of semantic relations as well as on the role of meaning shifts.

7 Modeling the semantic transparency of English compounds: compound family based models

What other ways are there to exploit the underlying semantic structure of compounds in modeling their semantic transparency? And, more crucially, how can the problems and pitfalls encountered in the previous chapter be avoided? This chapter presents a new, alternative approach using semantic features of compounds in models of semantic transparency. In contrast to the method presented in the previous chapter, in which all semantic predictors were based on features of the target compounds alone, the approach presented here is based on semantic features of the constituents and the whole compound relative to the patterns found in the respective compound's constituent families. This chapter includes a detailed introduction to the approach and the models presented in Bell & Schäfer (2016). The choice of semantic explanatory variables for the models presented in this chapter is a result of the conclusions drawn from the models discussed in the previous chapter. In the mixed effects models presented there, the semantic relations used in the individual compounds did not emerge as significant predictors (except for IN in the model for N1 transparency). Furthermore, I have argued that the coding of meaning shifts is not empirically sound. The dependent variables in the statistical models are again the semantic transparency ratings collected in Reddy, McCarthy & Manandhar (2011) which have been introduced earlier.

In order to make use of constituent family information, I annotated a large set of compounds with information on semantic relations as well as constituent senses. Since this dataset constitutes a unique resource that can be used independently, its creation is described in detail.

This chapter is structured as follows: Section 7.1 discusses previous studies using semantic relations relative to compound families and motivates the procedure used to derive the corresponding explanatory variables for the models to be discussed in this chapter. Section 7.2 extends the expectancy-based approach used for the semantic relations to the coding of constituent senses. Section 7.3 describes the methods used by Melanie Bell and me to arrive at a representative set of compound families for the Reddy et al. items. My subsequent semantic coding of the compounds in these families is described in Section 7.4. Section 7.5 introduces the explanatory variables and the predictions from Bell & Schäfer (2016). The models from Bell & Schäfer (2016) are presented and discussed in Section 7.6. Section 7.7 starts from the inspection of the residuals of the models introduced in the previous section and shows the results of running models on the data after cleaning it using a more consistent outlier removal algorithm. Section 7.8 concludes.

7.1 Measuring semantic relations relative to constituent families

While in works like Plag, Kunter & Lappe (2007), Plag et al. (2008), and Bell & Schäfer (2013) the different semantic relations between compound constituents were treated as predictors across the whole set of data considered, works within the framework of conceptual combination offer a very different perspective on the nature of the relational information in compound processing. Central to this understanding is the following quote: "[...] the difficulty of any particular combination is a function neither of its frequency in the language nor of the complexity of the relation. Instead, we contend that the difficulty is a function of the likelihood of the thematic relation for the particular constituents" (Gagné & Shoben 1997: 73). If one wants to test whether this constituent-centric view of semantic roles can explain the role of semantic relations in rating semantic transparency, then 2 core issues need to be decided: (1) What should be used as the basis for the distribution of the semantic relations for a specific constituent? (2) How should the place of a particular compound in this distribution be represented, that is, what measure should be used to capture the distribution of relations as it pertains to a specific compound and its constituents.

   After introducing the methods used in Gagné & Shoben (1997) to assess the distribution of semantic relations, I will discuss some criticism brought against their approach, including the attempt by Maguire et al. (2007) to compare the results of Gagné and Shoben's method to an alternative way of establishing the relational distributions. Finally, the way semantic relations were treated in Pham & Baayen (2013) is summarized, and conclusions for the procedure to assess the distribution of semantic relations for the target data used in this chapter are drawn.

7.1.1 Gagné and Shoben

The CARIN model, the Competition Among Relations In Nominals models introduced in Gagné & Shoben (1997), was already discussed in Chapter 2, Section 2.1.3.1, and along with it also one specific measure they used to assess the distributions of semantic relations over a constituent family, the strength ratio. Here, I will describe in more detail which data they used to establish the distribution of the relations over a compound's constituent family, and which measures they used to operationalize these distributions.

7.1.1.1 Establishing the distributions of the relations

As mentioned in Chapter 2, Section 2.1.3.1, the distribution of relations within a constituent compound family were drawn from Gagné and Shoben's own artificial corpus, which was derived from combinations in the appendix of Levi (1978) and permissible permutations thereof. What exactly does this mean? Gagné & Shoben (1997: 74) report that they started with the 91 modifiers and 91 heads taken from the Shoben and Medin corpus which was created by sampling 100 combinations from the appendix of Levi (1978) and removing duplicates (they refer to Shoben 1991 but there the corpus is described only vaguely). The appendix of Levi (1978) is not very large and contains 3 pages listing examples of all of her proposed derivations, ranging from just 8 types of complex nominals for the MAKE1 category to larger groups, e.g. HAVE2 with 26 compound types. There is no information concerning the sources of these examples in her appendix. From these 2 sets of modifiers and heads, Gagné & Shoben (1997: 74) created all possible permutations (91 x 91 = 8,281). They selected only those permutations which were sensible, yielding a set of 3,239 sensible permutations. This procedure is the reason for my labeling of this corpus as artificial: while it is still very likely to contain the original sample of compounds from the Levi appendix whose constituents were used to generate the permutations, the permutations might or might not be attested in English. These 3,239 sensible combinations were then classified into 15 categories by both authors (the Levi categories plus some additions, cf. Chapter 2, Section 2.1.3.1 for the details). The resulting counts yielded the distribution of semantic relations across constituent families in their corpus.

7.1.1.2 Measuring a relation's place

As already discussed in Chapter 2, Section 2.1.3.1, Gagné & Shoben (1997) introduce the strength ratio, repeated in (1) for convenience, as a measure to capture the competition between the relation relevant for a specific compound and the other relations occurring in the compound's constituent families.

(1) $$\text{strength} = \frac{e^{-ap_{\text{selected}}}}{e^{-ap_{\text{selected}}} + e^{-ap_1} + e^{-ap_2} + e^{-ap_3}}$$

The way this formula works and the reason why the later renaming of strength ratio to *competition* is conceptually preferable were also already discussed in Section 2.1.3.1.

Gagné & Shoben (1997) introduced the above measure in a post-hoc analysis; throughout the paper, they use the distributional data in 2 other ways: (1) in the preparation of the experimental materials, they used an arbitrary 60% cut-off point to distinguish between constituents occurring with high relational frequency and those occurring with low relational frequency. In other words, any relation within a constituent family that accounted for 60% of the combinations was considered a high frequency relation for that constituent family. If no single relation accounted for 60%, all relations that occurred within the 60% bracket were taken as high frequency relations. This classification was used to construct 3 classes of experimental items: a combination High-High frequency, e.g. *mountain bird*, a combination Low-High frequency, e.g. *mountain magazine*, and a combination High-Low frequency, e.g. *mountain cloud*. (2) In the regression analyses for their experiments, they used the rank of the relation in the constituent family as well as the number of high-frequency relations in a constituent family as predictors.

7.1.2 Criticism and a corpus-based re-implementation

Storms & Wisniewski (2005: 854–855) point out 3 areas of concern with regard to the distributional frequencies established by Gagné & Shoben (1997): Firstly, the relational frequencies should ideally reflect how often these relations occur in combinations that people are familiar with (through reading or hearing). The way in which Gagné and Shoben constructed their corpus does not guarantee this, as they arbitrarily paired modifiers and heads and did not take familiarity of the combinations into account. Secondly, Storms & Wisniewski (2005) wonder whether the restriction to just 91 heads and modifiers actually resulted in a broad enough sample to accurately reflect the relation frequencies for the nouns. In particular, they point to their intuition that specific modifiers have a preference for certain types of heads and vice versa, which, if true, would require a much larger sample to accurately reflect distributional differences. Thirdly, they criticize that the sampling procedure did not take token frequencies into account, a point first made in Wisniewski & Murphy (2005), who in turn also take up the 2 other points.

Maguire et al. (2007) present a corpus study trying to test the representativity of the original Gagné and Shoben corpus. In particular, they tried to derive measures for 38 words, namely the 19 heads and 19 modifiers used in Experiment 1 in Gagné & Shoben (1997), from the BNC (in the process, they replaced the adjective modifier *musical* by *music* and using *flower* in addition to the original *floral*). For the compound heads, singulars and plurals where considered, leaving 4 heads with smaller samples. All in all, they extracted 1,832 compounds sharing the respective compound modifier constituent and 1,669 compounds sharing the respective head constituent. These were classified into the 15 relations used in Gagné & Shoben (1997), with one of the authors each classifying half of the compounds, using the actual BNC context sentence in order to determine the appropriate relation. Inter-rater agreement was checked on a sample of 10 combinations for each noun, with the authors reporting agreement at the 68% level. In coding, noun ambiguities were ignored (that is, usages of e.g. *plant* as standing either for the organism or for a factory were not differentiated). Maguire et al. (2007: 813) point out that in doing so they follow the procedure in the original paper (as evidenced by e.g. the experimental items). At the same time, Maguire et al. (2007: 813) note that according to the CARIN theory, the different distributions should be calculated individually for each unique concept associated with a given string, since, according to the theory, the frequencies of the different relations are stored with the concepts.

Furthermore, the authors observed that in many cases more than one relation could reasonably be chosen, citing *family activities* and *storm cloud* as examples, where the former could be classified with either HAS, LOCATED, FOR, CAUSES or BY, and the latter by either CAUSES, LOCATED, DURING, or HAS. Nevertheless, only a single relation was selected even in those cases. While the 2 examples might be extreme cases, note that this problem of multiple possible relations for one and the same compound is in fact the norm and not the exception (see also the discussion in Section 7.4), calling any absolute comparability of these labels across different modifiers and heads into question. For 7.5% of the modifier compounds and 4.3 % of the head compounds, thematic relations did not 'realistically' fit the combinations (their examples are *chocolate eater, water supply, family commitments* and *music journalist*). It is not clear how these combinations were treated.

When comparing their data to the data of Gagné & Shoben (1997), Maguire et al. (2007) noted the following differences: (1) The compound types identified for the respective heads and modifiers are very different. Only 5% of the compound types in Gagné & Shoben's modifier families and 7% of the head families also occur in the BNC sample. (2) Spearman's ρ for the correlation between the relational frequencies of the heads and modifiers in the 2 datasets was on average 0.64 and 0.63 for the modifiers and the heads respectively, with 10 of the modifier distributions and 9 of the head distributions significantly correlated at the 0.01 level. Maguire et al. (2007) contrast the correlation between the 2 datasets to the correlation that results when randomly splitting their BNC data in 2 halves. For their split dataset, the correlation is much better, with 0.83 and 0.88 as average values for modifiers and heads respectively, and a correlation at the 0.01 level for 17 of the modifier and 18 of the head distributions. Spalding & Gagné (2008) point out that the sampling procedure used by Maguire et al. (2007) resulted in non-unique modifier-head combinations, with items like *chocolate biscuit(s)* appearing 12 times, and *chocolate cake* and *chocolate bar* each appearing 8 times. Based on the numbers of unique modifier-head combinations, that is, compound types, the sample used by Maguire et al. (2007) is only roughly 20% larger than the original Gagné & Shoben (1997) sample (Spalding & Gagné 2008: 1576). Spalding & Gagné (2008) further point out that if only the compound types are considered, the artificial corpus used in Gagné & Shoben (1997) yields relational distributions very similar to those of the random sample from the BNC used by Maguire et al. (2007).

Should only compound types be considered? Spalding & Gagné (2008: 1577) argue that "research on compound-word processing sometimes finds that type frequencies are more appropriate and might reflect more central semantic levels of processing" and cite the comparison between family size vs. family frequencies of compounds in De Jong, Schreuder & Baayen (2000) as evidence to this effect.

Maguire et al. (2007) also critically discuss the mathematical features of the strength ratio, pointing especially to the results of using negative exponentials. Their first point concerns the fact mentioned earlier that a high strength ratio does stand for a high degree of competition (hence the renaming of strength ratio to competition in Spalding & Gagné 2008: 1574). Their second point is more interesting: given the way the strength ratio is calculated, the term standing for the relation with the lowest relation frequency will always have the largest influence on the strength ratio. To see why this must be so, cf. the plot in Figure 7.1.

As the plot shows, the result of using negative exponentials of the relation proportion in effect reverses the values associated with the different proportions. The lowest relation proportion possible is 0, the highest 1. The negative exponential, that is, Euler's number to the power of the negative relations proportion, reverses the situation, with the highest possible relation proportion resulting in the lowest possible value, and the lowest proportion in the highest value, cf. (2).

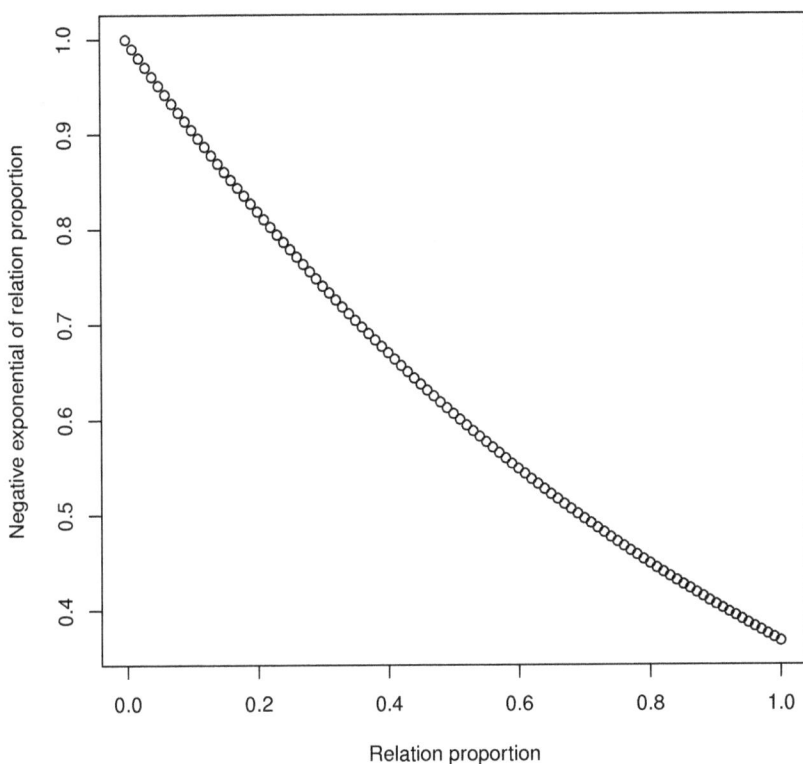

Figure 7.1: Relational proportion, ranging from 0 to 1, plotted against its negative exponentials

(2)   a. $e^{-0} = 1$
      b. $e^{-1} = 0.368$

Spalding & Gagné (2008: 1574) point out that "this pattern is actually a natural consequence of the RT [reaction time] data and of a particular kind of competition among the relations", and report similar patterns when modeling the influence of the 3 highest ranked competitors via individual weights.

7.1.3 Relational distributions in other studies

Pham & Baayen (2013) also use a database of semantic relations and 3 measures derived from this database. I discussed their approach in detail in Chapter 5, Section 5.3. In contrast to the previous 2 approaches, the main differences in establishing the relational distributions are: (1) they started with a much larger initial set of compounds (783 compounds). (2) they drew the compound families from the CELEX database, which contains only compounds drawn from dictionaries and is relatively small (see Section 7.3.2 below for additional discussion), resulting in 3,455 compounds. Using the CELEX database, Pham & Baayen (2013) calculated 3 measures based on the CARIN model of Gagné & Shoben (1997): the strength measure C, the generalized strength measure gC, and the relative entropy measure reC. Their strength measure C is based on Gagné & Shoben's strength ratio, but differs in (1) not being restricted to just 3 relations and (2) using proportions (instead of the exponential decay function). The generalized strength measure is based on the relational proportions across the full database (note that this measure is therefore a departure from the constituent-centred view of the CARIN model), and the relative entropy measure posits the probability of a relation in its modifier family against its probability across all modifier families (for the exact definitions of these measures, see the discussion in Chapter 5, Section 5.3).

7.1.4 Conclusion: semantic relations relative to constituent families

In exploring measures of semantic relations relative to constituent families, I discussed the original approach by Gagné & Shoben (1997), in which they constructed an artificial corpus and proposed the strength ratio to best capture the role the relational distributions relative to a given compound. Maguire et al. (2007) compare the result of sampling from the BNC with the distributions in the artificial corpus. Importantly, if one only considers compound types, the 2 corpora are very comparable. Pham & Baayen (2013) show yet another way of constructing a relational database, starting with a random compound sample and then using the CELEX database. In contrast to the BNC, the CELEX database is very small and all lemmata are derived from dictionaries, that is, lexicalized in the very sense of the word.

For the specific task set in this chapter, that is, establishing constituent families for a given set of compounds, the procedure chosen by Gagné & Shoben (1997) does not seem very promising for the simple reason that the starting point for an artificially constructed dataset, the Reddy et al. dataset, was not designed to reflect a variety of semantic relations. In contrast, this was the main concern of the appendix in Levi (1978). In addition, it seems plausible that the second selection step, judging all the combination for whether or not they make sense, is by itself heavily influenced by the frequencies of occurrence of the corresponding constituents and their preferred combinations. And finally, data from an actual corpus makes it possible to explore a fuller range of factors, for example the above-mentioned issue of type- vs. token-based measures for compounds.

When it comes to a decision between the BNC and CELEX, using the BNC has the advantage of not being restricted to lexicalized compounds. In addition, the CELEX database does not contain frequencies for compounds that are not written as one word. The construction of the database to be introduced below therefore will start from compound families drawn from the BNC (although CELEX data will also be used).

There are several proposals for measures assessing the role of the relational distribution for a particular compound. Once a database is available, these different measures can be compared and which measure works best in predicting compound transparency is an empirical question.

7.2 Assessing the role of constituent meanings

After concluding that the coding of the constituents and the whole compounds for meaning shifts as done in Bell & Schäfer (2013) is problematic for a number of reasons (cf. the discussion in Chapter 6, Section 6.4.3.2), an alternative to assess the role of meaning shifts for semantic transparency is needed. Here, an approach that closely mirrors the procedure for semantic relations is chosen. Recall that in order to be able to assess, for the individual constituents of a compound, how closely these constituents are associated with a specific relation, the distribution of relations in the individual constituent families is used. Transferring this idea to constituent senses, the distribution of different constituent senses across the constituent families can be used. This allows one to determine, for the specific constituent meaning used in a compound, how expected that meaning is in the given construction. This seems to me to be a very adequate way to encode uses of compound constituents that do not seem to be transparent. In this context, recall an important point from Jaszczolt (discussed in more detail in Chapter 3, Section 3.2.3.2): Nothing is ever interpreted in isolation; rather, "[t]he plausibility and the intuitions all depend on the accessibility of a default, 'made-up' context" Jaszczolt (2016: 58) (cf. the previous discussion for the quote in context). While she makes this point for sentences, it plausibly applies in a similar way to lower level construction such as, in this case, compounds. And arguably, for compound constituents, the constituent's compound families are the next place to look if one wants to emulate what language users will take to be a default context to be used as a guide in interpretation.

How, then, should one determine the distribution of constituent meanings in a compound family? One straightforward idea is to exploit the meaning differentiations made in existing lexical databases for this purpose. Here, the WordNet lexical database (Fellbaum 1998) is chosen, and I will introduce this resource in detail in Section 7.2.

An open question is what to use instead of manually coded meaning shifts of the whole compound. Recall that Bell & Schäfer (2013) also used spelling ratio, that is, the ratio of unspaced and hyphenated occurrences to spaced occurrences, which has been hypothesized to be a correlate of lexicalization (cf. Bell & Plag 2012: 496). This variable will also be used here, on the assumption that it is positively correlated with whole compound meaning shifts (but compare the discussion of spelling ratio in Chapter 6, Section 6.4.2.3).

WordNet and WordNet definitions

Data from WordNet already played a considerable role in the selection of the original items in the Reddy et al. study (cf. the discussion in Chapter 5, Section 5.2.1). Since it also forms the basis for coding the constituent meanings, this section introduces WordNet's general organization. Essentially, WordNet is a lexical database for English. Some of its distinguishing features can be seen when looking at an exemplary entry, cf. the entry for *rock* reproduced in (3).

(3)   WordNet entry for *rock*

    a. Noun

        (i)   S: (n) rock, stone (a lump or mass of hard consolidated mineral matter) "he threw a rock at me"

        (ii) S: (n) rock, stone (material consisting of the aggregate of minerals like those making up the Earth's crust) "that mountain is solid rock"; "stone is abundant in New England and there are many quarries"

        (iii) S: (n) Rock, John Rock (United States gynecologist and devout Catholic who conducted the first clinical trials of the oral contraceptive pill (1890-1984))

        (iv) S: (n) rock ((figurative) someone who is strong and stable and dependable) "he was her rock during the crisis"; "Thou art Peter,

and upon this rock I will build my church"–Gospel According
to Matthew

(v)   S: (n) rock candy, rock (hard bright-colored stick candy (typically flavored with peppermint))

(vi)   S: (n) rock 'n' roll, rock'n'roll, rock-and-roll, rock and roll, rock, rock music (a genre of popular music originating in the 1950s; a blend of black rhythm-and-blues with white country-and-western) "rock is a generic term for the range of styles that evolved out of rock'n'roll."

(vii)   S: (n) rock, careen, sway, tilt (pitching dangerously to one side)

b.   Verb

(i)   S: (v) rock, sway, shake (move back and forth or sideways) "the ship was rocking"; "the tall building swayed"; "She rocked back and forth on her feet"

(ii)   S: (v) rock, sway (cause to move back and forth) "rock the cradle"; "rock the baby"; "the wind swayed the trees gently"

Results of searching for *rock* on WordNet (WordNet Search 3.1, accessed 27.12.2014, http://wordnetweb.princeton.edu/perl/webwn)

The WordNet entry for *rock* is divided into 9 sub-entries, which are classified as either nouns or verbs. Each sub-entry constitutes a synset, a set of synonyms. These synonyms are interchangeable in some contexts (cf. Miller 1998b: 24). As Miller 1998b: 24 points out, "[i]t is convenient to think of a synset as representing a lexicalized concept of English." The resulting synsets might be connected by meaning shifts, and are thus etymologically related, cf. the synsets (3-a-i), (3-a-ii) and (3-a-iv), or they might be unrelated, as the stone-sense underlying the 3 synsets just mentioned and the music-sense of *rock* in (3-a-vi). Unsurprisingly, these cases are typically etymologically unrelated, in this case with the stone-sense being derived from a Romance noun and the music-sense being derived from a Germanic verb. WordNet incorporates a number of various sources, including large amounts of manual annotation, but also the results of automatic tagging based on a earlier versions of WordNet (cf. Miller 1998a: xviii-xxi). Note in particular that the explanatory glosses and the illustrative quotations were added manually, and that the unsystematic coverage of proper nouns in the set of synsets is due to the nature of the sources used in building WordNet. As Miller puts it: "No special attempt has been made to include proper nouns; on the other hand, since many common nouns once were names, no serious attempt has been made to exclude them." Miller (1998b: 23). While the basic unit for WordNet are words, Fellbaum (1998: 5–6) points out that WordNet also contains short phrases (her example is *bad person*) if these cannot be paraphrased by a single word. Technically, these short phrases seem to be non-distinct from compounds written as two words. All synsets are categorized as either nouns, adjectives, verbs or adverbs, and relations between synsets are always within their categorical boundaries (cf. Fellbaum 1998: 5).

7.3 A database of compound families

In this section, I describe the way in which Melanie Bell and I selected the items for the compound database used in Bell & Schäfer (2016). The selection of constituent families involved 4 steps: (1) Using the BNC to establish an initial set of families. (2) Adding items from CELEX. (3) Getting frequencies from USENET. (4) Further post-processing. I will describe and explain the rationale of the 4 steps in the following 4 sections.

7.3.1 Initial families from the BNC

We used the BNC XML edition to select all noun noun compounds from the BNC. The BNC, the British national corpus, is a 100 million word corpus, sampling written (90% of the total corpus) as well as spoken texts (10% of the total corpus). The spoken part comes from transcriptions of informal conversations and more contextualized spoken language (e.g. government meetings) dating from 1991 to 1994, that is, the time the corpus was built. The written part is mainly (92%) drawn from publications from 1985 to 1993, with the earliest publications dating from the 1960s. We accessed the BNC via the web interface provided by Lancaster University: the CQP-edition (Version 4.3) of BNCweb developed by Sebastian Hoffmann and Stefan Evert (cf. Hoffmann et al. 2008; BNCweb is accessible via http://bncweb.lancs.ac.uk/). We used the CQP query syntax to extract all strings of 2 nouns from the BNC, both the written and the spoken part. In order to minimalize manual corrections, the search was restricted to strings following the definite article, and excluded all strings that were themselves followed by a noun, an adjective, or a possessive marker. Since we also used the spoken part of the BNC, any strings containing pauses or interruptions or other additional material, be it linguistic or non-linguistic, were excluded. The exact query is reproduced in (4).

(4)   ([type="w"&word="the"][type="w"&pos="N.*"&
        flags_beforenotcontains"pause.*|vocal.*|event.*|shift.*|

trunk.*|unclear.*"][type="w"&pos="N.*"&
flags_beforenotcontains"pause.*|vocal.*|event.*|shift.*|
trunk.*|unclear.*"][:pos!="N.*|AJ.*|POS":])withins

We then used the constituents from the 90 compounds in the Reddy et al. dataset to extract those noun noun sequences from the BNC dataset that shared a constituent with any of those items. In doing so, we matched all items lemma-based, that is, regardless of whether they occurred in their singular or plural form. We decided to be as inclusive as possible with regard to regular spelling variants, searching for items regardless of whether they occurred with British or American spelling (for the 90 compounds from the Reddy et al. dataset, this concerns only the variation between *centre* and *center*). We created 2 sets of compound families: positional constituent families, that is, constituent families in which the constituent occurs in the same position as its position in the dataset, and reverse constituent families, that is, families where the constituent occurred in the opposite position. While the reverse families did not play a role in the creation of the semantically annotated database, they are needed for the calculation of the family size ratios, cf. the description and further explanation in section 7.5.2.

Note that at no point did we make any efforts to exclude proper nouns. Their inclusion is warranted for at least 3 reasons: (1) As far as we know, proper nouns are processed in the same way as other nouns (2) English does not have a clear formal distinction between nouns that are proper names and those that are not; in fact, conversions from and to proper names lead to the existence of doublettes (cf. Huddleston, Pullum, et al. 2002: 516) (3) The well-known variation in compound realizations between left and right-stress is among other things influenced by the proper name/proper noun status of the elements involved. Plag et al. (2008: 779) find both N1 and N2 forming a proper noun as well as N1 itself being a proper noun to be significant predictors of rightward stress in English noun noun compounds.

7.3.2 Adding items from CELEX

The search pattern described above is not able to find noun noun compounds that are written as one word, be it with or without hyphens. In general, it is not possible to search for these items in the BNC when using the tagging provided by the BNC, since it does not include compounds as a dedicated category. In order to also include those compounds that are always written as one word, we used CELEX, the database from the Dutch Centre for Lexical Information, cf. Baayen, Piepenbrock & Gulikers (1995). The English part of the CELEX database is compiled from two dictionaries, the 1974 edition of the Oxford Advanced Learner's Dictionary (41,000 lemmata) and the 1978 edition of the Longman Dictionary of Contemporary English (53,000 lemmata, with an overlap of approximately 30,000 lemmata with the other dictionary). Due to its origin, CELEX only contains lexicalized compounds (note that even though CELEX derives frequency information from the 17.9 million token COBUILD/Birmingham corpus, this corpus was not used to add new lemmata). The English morphological database distinguishes 52,447 word types. All in all, CELEX's morphological database contains 12,130 items marked as compounds. From these, all concatenated noun noun compounds sharing either the first or the second constituent with a compound from the Reddy et al. dataset were added to the respective constituent families (that is, to both the positional and the reverse families).

7.3.3 Usenet frequencies

Compounds have a comparatively low textual frequency (cf. Plag et al. 2008: 776). For English noun noun compounds, Baldwin & Tanaka (2004) report that between 2.6% (spoken part of the BNC) and 3.9% (Reuters corpus) of the respective corpus' tokens occur as part of a noun noun compound. Using a small corpus like the BNC to retrieve compound frequencies means that there is only limited insight into the distribution of low-frequency compounds. There are very many compounds that occur only once in the BNC (in the study by Lapata & Lascarides 2003, 70% of the candidate set of noun noun compounds drawn from the BNC are hapaxes, 60% of which are valid compounds), but within this group no further frequency distinction is possible. In order to get better insight into these lower frequency realms, we decided to use a much larger corpus as an additional filter, settling on the reduced redundancy USENET corpus (Shaoul & Westbury 2013). This corpus contains over 7 billion tokens. The corpus is a collection of public USENET postings collected between October 2005 and January 2011. The reduced redundancy version of the USENET corpus is the result of applying algorithms for the removal of text redundancy to the original collection of postings, shrinking the corpus to just over 7 billion tokens from originally 30 billion tokens. However, the shrunk corpus is still 700 times bigger than the BNC. Using this corpus has 2 side effects: (1) any highly context-bound ad-hoc formations are likely to be removed (2) the level of noise in the data might get slightly reduced, since noun noun combinations found in the BNC that are not compounds but are adjacent nonetheless might not occur adjacent in the USENET corpus.

The USENET corpus is not lemmatized. In order to get lemma frequencies, we searched for all inflectional variants of the compounds in question, as well as all spelling variants (spaced, hyphenated, and unspaced in British and American English). This was done via an R-script written by me. For the pluralization and singularization of words, I relied heavily on Conway (1998). We obtained frequencies for all the word forms from USENET. The actual extraction of these frequencies was kindly done for us by Cyrus Shaoul and Gero Kunter. We summed over these word form frequencies to get the lemma frequencies.

7.3.4 Further post-processing

Recall that we added items from CELEX because we could not search in the BNC for compounds written as one word. This, in turn, means that we also could not exclude the possibility that the items that were selected from the BNC included constituents that were themselves compounds written as one word. Because it is unclear in how far these 3 or 4 constituent compounds behave similarly to 2 constituent compounds, and because the current dataset can only contain those complex compounds as constituents that were written as one word, we decided to eliminate the 3 and more constituent compounds altogether. To achieve this, we proceeded as follows: (1) We filtered our search results against all English compounds and simplex words in the English part of the CELEX. (2) All compounds that consisted only of simplex words were left in the dataset, but all compounds with one or more constituents that were itself compounds were excluded. (3) Compounds with constituents not occurring in CELEX were checked manually, at which point we also excluded compounds in which either constituent consisted of an abbreviation.

We then restricted our constituent families to only those items that occurred with a lemma frequency of at least 5. We selected this cut-off point for 2 reasons: (1) to reduce the amount of noise, mishits, and ad-hoc formations and (2) to keep the data to be coded within manageable limits. This left a total of 2,893 compound lemmas in the N1 positional constituent families and 6,425 compound lemmas in the N2 positional constituent families.

7.4 Semantic coding

The semantic coding for the constituent families involved 2 steps: assigning a WordNet synset to the usage of the constituent in the respective families, and assigning a relation to the compound under consideration. In contrast to the coding in Bell & Schäfer (2013), only a single rater, me, annotated the data. The main reason why we opted for a single-rater based procedure is that inter-annotator agreement for coding compound relations is usually quite poor. Recall that Maguire et al. (2007) reported an inter-rater agreement of 68% for the test items in their study. Similarly, Ó Séaghdha (2008: 44–45), who worked out a very carefully worded annotation guideline based on an extension of the Levi-system, reports 66.2% agreement on a 500 item test set between himself and a second annotator experienced in lexicography who had been trained on two 100-compound batches previously. In case of disagreement, the corresponding items can either be discarded, or the disagreement can be resolved. Neither of these 2 options seemed desirable to us. The first option might lead to loss of predictive power due to loss of data as well as to a bias towards the more clear examples. The second option brings with it the danger of leading to an overall inconsistency in the annotations, depending on which annotation wins in the respective cases.

This section describes the coding of the semantic relations and the synsets. Appendix B contains a detailed overview of the coding results, especially focusing on the synset coding, but also containing notes on the relation coding.

7.4.1 Coding the semantic relations

In coding the semantic relations within a constituent family, I used the Levi classification system. In addition to Levi's (1978) categories, I used the relation VERB for deverbal heads with an argument in N1 position, and the category IDIOM for cases that did not fit any of the other relations. Coding examples from our positional families are shown in table (5).

The main idea behind the current approach is to investigate whether preferences of an individual constituent for a specific semantic relation play a role for the perception of semantic transparency. Therefore, all the semantic annotation was strictly compound family based. That is, all the compounds in the compound database were annotated twice, once in the N1 compound family, and once in the N2 compound family. In some cases, this resulted in different relational labels being assigned to the same compound in the N1 and N2 families. An example is *face value*, which in the N1 family was coded with the relation HAVE2 (value that the face has), along with e.g. *face price* and *face validity*, and in contrast to IN, which was used for e.g. *face ache*. On the other hand, in the N2 family *face value* was coded as IN (value on the face), as was e.g. *market value, cash value*, or *street value*, while examples for HAVE2 are e.g. *credit value, pixel value* and *probability value*. Note that when one is interested in the distribution of relations within a constituent family, the specific labels are irrelevant, as long as the coding scheme within the families is consistent and the overall level of granularity remains constant. On the other hand, this family specific way of coding the relations makes it impossible to compare their distribution across families.

Table 7.1: Examples of the coding of the semantic relations in the annotated dataset

	relation	examples
1	CAUSE1	*cost centre, result centre, collision course*
2	CAUSE2	*guilt feeling, night blindness, snake bite*
3	HAVE1	*ruby ring, coal mine, metal site*
4	HAVE2	*factory wall, death rate, staff reaction*
5	MAKE1	*cash cow, engine plant, law maker*
6	MAKE2	*copper plate, plastic clock, concrete floor*
7	USE	*video game, number lock, radio conference*
8	BE	*head man, gold grain, acid solution*
9	IN	*rock fissure, night class, bank teller*
10	FOR	*swimming club, rock station, fashion model*
11	FROM	*ground missile, interest charge, health advantage*
12	ABOUT	*fashion magazine, bank dispute, case study*
13	VERB	*credit granter, speed increase, video edit*
14	IDIOM	*monkey wrench, eye tooth, swann inn*

The compounds were annotated in isolation, that is, by inspecting them outside of their sentential context. However, when I could not decide on an annotation in isolation, I checked the sentential context in the BNC. Often, this led to the discovery of combinations that were in fact not compounds, either because they were part of 2 syntactic constituents or because they were hits that resulted from tagging errors. There were also cases where the compounds did not fit our original search query, usually because they were part of bigger complex expressions. All these cases were excluded.

7.4.2 Coding the constituent senses

The constituents were annotated with their respective WordNet synsets. This was done together with the coding of the semantic relations.

Table 7.2 shows some example codings from the constituent family of *bank* in N1 position, along with the number of compound types sharing the respective WordNet sense. For similar overviews of the synset coding decisions for all constituents, cf. Appendix B.

Table 7.2: Synset coding for bank in N1 position

wnSense	WordNet description	types	class	example
1	sloping land (especially the slope beside a body of water)	5	n	bank barn
2	a financial institution that accepts deposits and channels the money into lending activities	52	n	bank job
4	an arrangement of similar objects in a row or in tiers	2	n	bank switch
5	a supply or stock held in reserve for future use (especially in emergencies)	1	n	bank nurse
10	a flight maneuver; aircraft tips laterally about its longitudinal axis (especially in turning)	1	n	bank angle

As described in Section 7.2, WordNet does not differentiate between related or unrelated synsets, and the synset coding therefore simply shows the distribution of different senses across homonyms. In some cases, this distribution corresponds to the distribution of different senses related via meaning shifts, but this is not necessarily the case.

The specific word sense applicable to a given compound is usually clear, e.g. *rock music* vs. *rock arch*. In cases were the ambiguity persisted, e.g. *rock mix*, which could in principle mean a mix of different kinds of stones or a musical mix in the rock style, the meaning occurring in the BNC was used. If both meanings occurred in the BNC, the meaning that occurred most frequently was chosen.

A second difficulty I encountered were WordNet senses I could not distinguish, either conceptually or in application to the data. In these cases, the senses were collapsed into one sense. Finally, some compounds involved constituent senses that did not occur in WordNet, in which case I added the missing senses manually. Often, these missing senses involved proper names, e.g. *Ring* referring to the set of 4 operas by Richard Wagner.

The constituents were coded based on the compounds in isolation, similar to the way the semantic relations were coded. Whenever necessary for clarification, the sentential context in the BNC was checked. Any combination that turned out to be not a compound or part of a more complex compound was discarded.

The numbers of unique compound types accepted for further processing were 2,629 in the N1 families and 6,172 in the N2 families.

7.5 Bell & Schäfer (2016): explanatory variables and predictions

This section describes the explanatory variables used in the models described in this chapter. In Section 7.5.1, I describe the variables derived from the semantic annotations in our compound database. Section 7.5.2 explains the other variables used.

7.5.1 Variables derived from the semantic coding

To assess the place of a given compound in its constituent families relative to the distribution of relations and sysnsets in those families, we decided to use proportions and ranks as explanatory variables. Using these 2 types of variables allows one to bring the greatest amount of distributional information into the models. While we did not explore all other measures, initial exploration had shown that expressing the relations in terms of proportions explained more of the variation than using the strength ratio from Gagné & Shoben (1997).

The explanatory variables derived from the relation coding in the dataset are shown in (5).

(5)   a.   relation proportion:
                the proportion of positional family members that share a constituent's semantic relation
    b.   relation rank:
                the frequency-based ranking of a constituent's semantic relation in its positional family

The corresponding 2 explanatory variables encoding the synsets are given in (6).

(6)   a.   synset proportion:
                the proportion of positional family members that share a constituent's WordNet sense
    b.   synset rank:
                the frequency-based ranking of a constituent's WordNet sense in its positional family

I will use the compound *application form* to illustrate how these variables are derived. The calculations for the 4 variables pertaining to the N1 constituent family are shown in (7), while (8) shows the calculation of the 4 variables for the N2 family.

(7)   *application form*, N1 family
       relation: FOR
       synset: WordNet sense 2 (a verbal or written request for assistance or employment or admission to a school)

    a.   N1 relation proportion:

$$\frac{\text{number of compound types coded with FOR in N1 family}}{\text{total number of compound types in N1 family}}$$

$$= \frac{28}{42} = 0.67$$

    b.   N1 relation rank: 1

    c.   N1 synset proportion:

$$\frac{\text{number of compound types with WordNet sense 2 in N1 family}}{\text{total number of compound types in N1 family}}$$

$$= \frac{20}{42} = 0.48$$

    d.   N1 synset rank: 1 (no other synset occurs in more compound types)

(8)   *application form*, N2 family
       relation: FOR
       synset: WordNet sense 8 (a printed document with spaces in which to write)

    a.   N2 relation proportion:

$$\frac{\text{number of compound types coded with FOR in N2 family}}{\text{total number of compound types in N2 family}}$$

$$= \frac{77}{163} = 0.47$$

    b.   N2 relation rank: 1

    c.   N2 synset proportion:

$$\frac{\text{number of compound types with WordNet sense 2 in N2 family}}{\text{total number of compound types in N2 family}}$$

$$= \frac{76}{163} = 0.46$$

    d.   N2 synset rank: 1 (no other synset occurs in more compound types)

7.5.2 Further explanatory variables

7.5.2.1 Constituent frequencies and spelling ratio

Just as in the models discussed in Chapter 6, we use the constituent frequencies as predictors. Constituent frequencies are clearly not semantic predictors. However, they fit the general idea of modeling transparency in terms of expectedness: The more frequent the occurrence of a constituent in the language as a whole, the more expected it is.

As explained above in Section 7.2, we used the spelling ratio of a compound as a replacement of the coding of whole compound shifts used in the models described in Chapter 6. Spelling ratio was calculated as shown in (9):

$$(9) \quad \text{spelling ratio} = \frac{\text{unspaced frequency} + \text{hyphenated frequency})}{\text{spaced frequency}}$$

For an example of calculating the spelling ratio, cf. Chapter 6, Section 6.3.3.1.

7.5.2.2 Family size ratios

Besides the expectedness of the individual constituents themselves as measured via their overall frequency in the language, we added 2 variables assessing the expectedness of a constituent as either head or modifier of a compound, the family size ratios of N1 and N2 respectively. Bell & Plag (2012) introduced this measure to indicate the tendency of a given constituent to appear as a head or as a modifier in a compound. It is operationalized as the log of the positional family size divided by the reverse family size, cf. (10).

$$(10) \quad \text{family size ratio} = \frac{\text{positional family size}}{\text{reverse family size}}$$

As described in Section 7.3.1 above, the positional family of a constituent is the set of compounds in which a given constituent appears in the same position. In contrast, the reverse family is the set of compounds in which that constituent occurs in the alternative position. Take the compound *bank account*. The first constituent is *bank*, and its positional constituent family includes e.g. *bank emergency, bank fraud,* and *bank index*. The positional family of the second constituent, *account*, includes e.g. *summary account, insider account,* and *police account*. The N1 reverse family collects the compounds in which *bank* occurs as the second constituent, e.g. *asset bank, Beirut bank,* and *blood bank*. The N2 reverse family, correspondingly, collects the compounds in which *account* occurs as the first constituent, e.g. *account balance, account handler,* and *account number*. Again, the family size ratio is constituent specific. The calculation for the 2 constituents of *bank account* is shown in (11).

(11)   *bank account*

a.   N1 family size ratio = $\dfrac{\text{positional family size N1}}{\text{reverse family size N1}} = \dfrac{75}{101} = 0.74$

b.   N2 family size ratio = $\dfrac{\text{positional family size N2}}{\text{reverse family size N2}} = \dfrac{92}{33} = 2.79$

7.5.3 Tabular overview of the explanatory variables

The explanatory variables used in the modeling are listed in table 7.3

7.5.4 Restricting the target dataset

The compound dataset provided by Reddy, McCarthy & Manandhar (2011) consists of 90 compounds. In the discussion of the linguistic properties of these compounds in Chapter 6, Section 6.2.1, it already emerged that these compounds are not fully homogeneous. Some aspects turned out to be problematic for the approach taken in this chapter and the corresponding items were excluded.

As mentioned in Section 7.3.4, we used CELEX to prune the compound database, removing all compounds with 3 or more constituents. Following on the decision to exclude these items from the database, we also excluded the 3 Reddy et al. items that are internally complex, namely *grandfather clock, cocktail dress,* and *gaveyard shift,* from our analysis.

Because the construction of the compound database is based on noun noun patterns, we also excluded the adjective noun combinations *fine line* and *sacred cow* from our analysis. For the same reason, we excluded the 3 combinations that contained attributively used gerund-participles as modifiers: *shrinking violet, sitting duck,* and *smoking gun.* Finally, we excluded *number crunching* because *crunching* is exclusively classified as a verb in WordNet. This left 81 compound types in the analysis.

Note that since we did not intend to model compound transparency with the help of constituent transparency, we used the full set of ratings in the Reddy et al. dataset, accepting all ratings accepted in Reddy, McCarthy & Manandhar (2011). This left us with a total of 6,952 ratings for the 81 compounds: 2,307 ratings of whole compound transparency, 2,317 ratings of N1 transparency and 2,328 ratings of N2 transparency.

Table 7.3: Explanatory variables in the models from Bell & Schäfer (2016). All variables are logarithmized.

semantic explanatory variables		
1.	N1 relationship proportion	proportion of compound types sharing the target compound's semantic relation in the N1 constituent family
2.	N2 relationship proportion	proportion of compound types sharing the target compound's semantic relation in the N2 constituent family
3.	N1 synset proportion	proportion of compound types sharing the N1 synset of the target compound in the compound's N1 constituent family
4	N2 synset proportion	proportion of compound types sharing the N2 synset of the target compound in the compound's N2 constituent family
non-semantic explanatory variables		
4.	N1 frequency	summed occurrences of all forms of the N1 lemma
5.	N2 frequency	summed occurrences of all forms of the N2 lemma
6.	spelling ratio	sum of the unspaced and hyphenated frequency of the compound divided by the spaced frequency
7.	N1 family size ratio	number of compound types in the N1 positional family size divided by the number of items in the N1 reverse family
8.	N2 family size ratio	number of compound types in the N2 positional family size divided by the number of items in the N2 reverse family

7.5.5 Transparency in terms of expectancy: the predictions of Bell & Schäfer (2016)

The main hypothesis in Bell & Schäfer (2016) was that expectedness is the main explanation of perceived semantic transparency. We translated this into 14 explicit predictions, cf. Bell & Schäfer (2016: 172–174), distinguishing between effects of properties of the individual constituent on the 2 constituent transparencies and the whole compound transparency, and effects of properties of the whole compound on constituent as well as compound transparency. These predictions are reproduced in Tables 7.4 and 7.5.

Table 7.4: Predictions from Bell & Schäfer (2016), set A and B

set A	effects of a constituent's properties on that constituent's transparency
A1.	A constituent will be perceived as more transparent the more frequent it is, i.e. the more expected it is in the language in general.
A2.	A constituent will be perceived as more transparent, the more expected its particular sense within the positional family, i.e. the more likely it is to occur with that sense as the head (for N2) or modifier (for N1) of a compound.
A3.	A constituent will be perceived as more transparent, the more expected it is as the head (for N2) or modifier (for N1) of compounds in general, i.e. the more characteristic the relevant role for the constituent in question.
A4.	A constituent will be perceived as more transparent, the greater the proportion of compounds in its positional family that share the same semantic relation as the compound in question, i.e. the more expected the relevant semantic relation with that constituent.
set B	effects of a constituent's properties on the perceived transparency of the other constituent
B5.	A constituent will be perceived as more transparent the more frequent the other constituent, i.e. the more expected it is in the language in general. This is what we found in the study reported in Bell and Schäfer (2013); we expect to replicate this result.
B6.	A constituent will be perceived as more transparent, the less expected the relevant sense of the other constituent within its positional constituent family. In Bell and Schäfer (2013) we reported that a semantic shift in either constituent was associated with greater perceived transparency of the other constituent. If, as we hypothesize, sense frequencies can be used to estimate semantic shiftedness, then we would expect to find the same effect.
B7.	A constituent will be perceived as more transparent, the more expected the other constituent as the head (for N2) or modifier (for N1) of compounds in general, i.e. the more characteristic the relevant role for the other constituent. This is because we hypothesize that a more readily available semantic structure will lead to an increased perception of transparency all round.
B8.	A constituent will be perceived as more transparent, the greater the proportion of the other constituent's positional family that shares the same semantic relation as the compound in question, i.e. the more expected is the other constituent with the relevant semantic relation. This is because we hypothesis that the more easily accessible the semantic relation, the greater the perceived transparency all round.

Table 7.5: Predictions from Bell & Schäfer (2016), set C and D

set C	effects of constituent properties on the perceived transparency of the whole compound

C9.	A compound will be perceived as more transparent the more frequent either constituent, i.e. the more expected it is in the language in general. Greatest perceived transparency will occur when both constituents are frequent.
C10.	A compound will be perceived as more transparent, the more expected either constituent in the relevant role, i.e. as the head (for N2) or modifier (for N1) of compounds in general. Greatest perceived transparency will occur when both constituents occur in their characteristic roles.
C11.	A compound will be perceived as more transparent, the greater the proportion of either constituent's positional family that shares the same semantic relation as the compound in question, i.e. the more expected is either constituent with the relevant semantic relation. Greatest perceived transparency will occur when the relation occurs in a high proportion of both families.
C12.	The effect of constituent senses on whole compound transparency will be less pronounced than the effects on individual constituents, and less pronounced than the effects of the other predictors on whole compound transparency. This follows from our hypotheses that compound transparency is a function of constituent transparencies, and that a high sense proportion of a given constituent increases the perceived transparency of that constituent while decreasing the perceived transparency of the other.

set D	effects of properties of the whole compound

D13.	Both constituents will be perceived as less transparent, the greater the spelling ratio of the compound, i.e. the more frequently it occurs with non-spaced orthography relative to its frequency with spaced orthography. Bell and Schäfer (2013) found that semantic shifts of the compound as a whole were associated with lower perceived transparency of both constituents. We take spelling ratio to be a measure of the degree of semantic lexicalisation of a compound (after Bell and Plag 2012, 2013) and hypothesize that it can therefore be used to replicate the effect of whole-compound semantic shift.
D14.	The compound will be perceived as less transparent, the greater its spelling ratio, i.e. the more frequently it occurs with non-spaced orthography relative to its frequency with spaced orthography. As described above, we hypothesize that high spelling ratio is a correlate of whole-compound semantic shift.

I will use these predictions to discuss the models from Bell & Schäfer (2016) in the next section. However, note that some of the predictions are based on the findings in the models presented in Bell & Schäfer (2013), cf. the discussion in Chapter 6, Section 6.4.2. In the mixed effects regression models presented there, some of the predictors mentioned in Tables 7.4–7.5 are not significant. Thus, the finding underlying prediction B5, the positive correlation of the other constituent's frequency with perceived constituent transparency, occurs only in the mixed effects model for the second constituent. In contrast, the finding underlying prediction B6, a shifted other constituent as a foil for constituent transparency, occurs only in the mixed effects model for the first constituent.

7.6 The models from Bell & Schäfer 2016

We used mixed effects regression models with crossed random effects for the raters and the items. For the justification of why we used these kinds of models and the R-packages used, cf. the remarks in Chapter 6, Section 6.4.2.

All numerical variables were logarithmatized (cf. the remarks in Chapter 6, Section 6.3.3.1 for the reasons). In addition, the resulting variables were centred on their means. Baayen (2008: 254–255) explicitly recommends centering in his discussion of the random effect structure of mixed models, because centering allows to vary intercepts and slopes independently (see also the points on the advantages of centering in Chapter 2, Section 2.3.3.2).

We checked the set of explanatory variables for collinearity (as indicated by the condition number provided by the function collin.fnc() from Baayen 2013, cf. the remarks in Chapter 6, Section 6.3.4). Because including the proportions as well as the ranks for the synset and relation coding led to unacceptable levels of collinearity, we dropped the ranks from the analysis. We opted for the ranks because the proportions produce more fine-grained distinctions. The resulting set of predictors had very low condition numbers for the 3 different datasets used, ranging from 2.25 to 2.27. Note that these very low values are a side effect of centering the data. The possible influence of column scaling on the results of applying collinearity diagnostics is already mentioned in Belsley, Kuh & Welsch (1980: 183).

As well as the predictors individually, we also included an interaction between the relation proportions of N1 and N2: if the RICE theory of conceptual combination (Spalding et al. 2010) is correct, then we might expect some interaction between the strength of association of the relation with N1 and the strength of its association with N2.

The random effects structure was selected by comparing sequences of models with increasingly complex random effects structures using likelihood ratio tests.

Note that this procedure differs from the approach chosen in Chapter 6, where I started by using the maximal random effects structure. There is no agreement on the best way to approach this issue. For example, the procedures described in Baayen, Davidson & Bates (2008: cf. especially the remark on page 393) and Baayen (2008: Section 7.1) are hypothesis-driven: factors hypothesized to vary randomly are included in the random effect component. Regardless of the chosen procedure, the resulting models are compared using likelihood ratio tests, and only those random components are kept respectively added that yield significantly better fits.

The non-significant fixed effects were progressively removed from the models by stepwise elimination. The manual analysis was checked against the results of the step function in lmerTest, which performs automatic backward elimination on random and fixed effects in a linear mixed effects model.

7.6.1 N1 transparency

The final model for N1 transparency is presented in Table 7.6. Note that this model deviates slightly in its random effects structure from the N1 model presented in Bell & Schäfer (2016). However, this difference does not affect anything outside of the random effects structure to any noticeable degree. The fixed effects are presented graphically in Figure 7.2.

The random effects of the model are shown in the top section of Table 7.6, the fixed effects are shown in its bottom section. The random effects are grouped by item and rater. The model includes random intercepts for items. In addition, it contains random intercepts for the raters, and random slopes for the effects of spelling ratio and N1 frequency. These 3 random components are paired, and are allowed to correlate. This correlation makes sense conceptually, as the choice of one's personal rating range on the Likert scale influences both the intercept as well as the possible magnitude of the predictors at the same time. Note that the low variance indicates that the slope adjustments are in both cases rather small. For the adjustments of the intercepts we can observe that the items come with much more variance than the raters, that is, the adjustments to the intercepts for the individual items are greater than the adjustments due to peculiarities of the individual subjects.

Of the set of explanatory variables, 5 predictors are significant in the model. Of the semantic predictors, the proportion of a compound's relationship in the N1 family is positively correlated with the perceived transparency of N1. In contrast, the proportion of the synset of the compound's second constituent in the N2 constituent family is negatively correlated with semantic transparency. Of the

Table 7.6: Final mixed effects model for constituent 1 transparency, marginal $R^2 = 0.37$, conditional $R^2 = 0.77$

random effects:			
groups	name	variance	std. dev.
workerID	(intercept)	0.067673	0.26014
	spelling ratio	0.003092	0.05561
	N1 frequency	0.003479	0.05898
singBrUnderscore	(intercept)	1.627977	1.27592
residual		0.979093	0.98949

number of obs.: 2317, groups: workerID, 114; singBrUnderscore, 81

fixed effects:	estimate	std. error	df	t value	pr(> |t|)
(intercept)	2.84124	0.14840	81.94	19.146	< 2e-16
N1 relation proportion	0.37687	0.15973	75.02	2.359	0.020904
N2 synset proportion	-0.29064	0.14542	75.00	-1.999	0.049265
N1 frequency	0.69511	0.08637	76.17	8.048	8.79e-12
N2 frequency	-0.32050	0.13186	75.01	-2.431	0.017466
spelling ratio	-0.30710	0.08389	75.98	-3.661	0.000462

3 non-semantic predictors, only N1 frequency is positively correlated with the perceived transparency of N1, while both N2 frequency as well as spelling ratio are negatively correlated.

Figure 7.2 shows plots of the 5 significant predictors. In all cases, the vertical axis represents the semantic transparency of the first constituent as given by the human raters. Since all predictors are continuous variables, the graphs show regression lines. In addition, the rug plot on the horizontal axis gives the marginal distribution of the predictor, in other words, it shows the actual distribution of the values of that predictor in the data. Confidence bounds are indicated by confidence bands using 95% confidence limits. To show the effect of each predictor in turn, the other predictors are adjusted to their means. The predictors are presented in the same order as in the table with the semantic predictors first and the other predictors following.

How do the predictors fare with respect to our predictions? The top left-hand plot shows that the more frequent the relation of the target compound occurs within all the compounds in the N1 family, the more transparent is the first constituent rated. This corresponds to prediction A4. The top right-hand plot shows

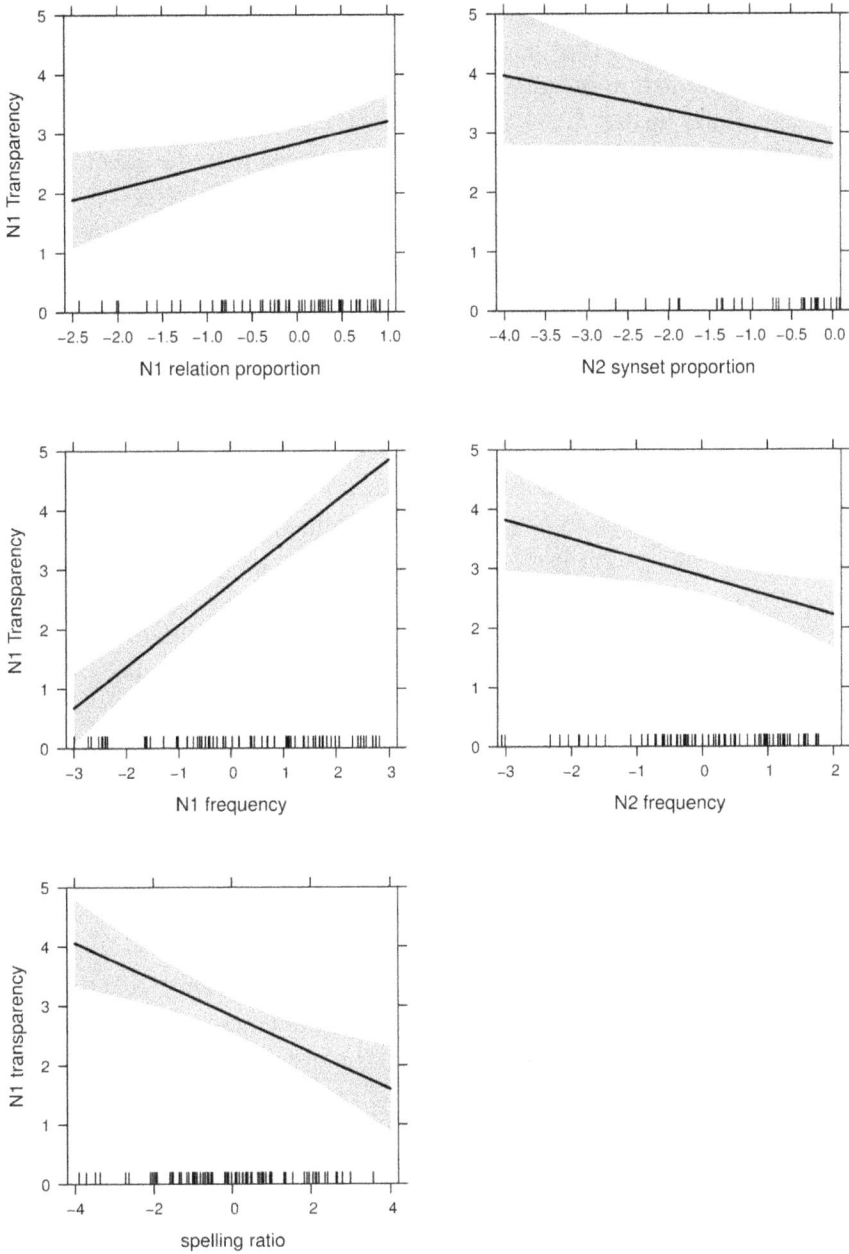

Figure 7.2: Partial effects in the final model for N1 transparency

that the more frequent the synset associated with the second constituent is used in the N2 family, the less transparent the first constituent is perceived. This corresponds to the prediction B6 and replicates the effect associated with metaphoric constituent shifts in Bell & Schäfer (2013) with the help of synset proportions. The next row shows the constituent frequency effects, with the effect associated with N1 frequency in the middle left-hand plot and the effect associated with N2 frequency in the middle right-hand plot. Again, the effect stemming from the same constituent is positively correlated with N1 transparency, while the effect stemming from the other constituent, in this case N2, is negatively correlated with N1 transparency. The positive correlation corresponds to our prediction A1. The negative correlation is exactly the opposite of our prediction B5. This prediction was again driven by a finding from Bell & Schäfer (2013). However, at least for N1, this finding disappeared when using random effects. One possible explanation for this finding is the same that we already used for the effects of metaphoric shifts and synset proportion of the other constituent: using the other constituent as a foil might lead to relative judgements. If the other constituent is very frequent, hence very expected, the constituent to be rated might appear to be less expected and hence less transparent relative to the other constituent. Finally, the bottom row shows the negative correlation of N1 transparency with spelling ratio. This corresponds to prediction D13.

7.6.2 N2 transparency

The final model for N2 transparency is presented in Table 7.7. Again, it departs slightly from the random effects structure used in Bell & Schäfer (2016), without in any way affecting the main findings. The fixed effects are presented graphically in Figure 7.3.

Table 7.7 is again divided into a top half showing the random effects structure and a bottom half showing the fixed effects. The random components are again grouped by items and raters. And just as in the previous model, this model has random intercepts for items. The random effects structure associated with the raters is different than the one used in the previous model: while the intercept is allowed to vary and the slopes are adjusted for the effects of spelling ratio, the random slopes for the effect of N1 frequency are replaced by random slopes for the effect of N2 frequency. While this is the justified result of our model selection procedure, it is not totally straightforward in its interpretation. After all, N2 effects played a role in the model for N1, too, and if the influence of the N2 frequency is adjusted by rater for this model, why should this not be the case for the first model? There are at least 2 possible reasons. On the one hand,

Table 7.7: Final mixed effects model for transparency of the second constituent, marginal $R^2 = 0.26$, conditional $R^2 = 0.77$

random effects:

groups	name	variance	std. dev.
workerID	(intercept)	0.059691	0.24432
	spelling ratio	0.002849	0.05337
	N2 frequency	0.012532	0.11195
singBrUnderscore	(intercept)	2.009065	1.41741
residual		0.953068	0.97625

number of obs.: 2328, groups: workerID, 108; singBrUnderscore, 81

fixed effects:

	estimate	std. error	df	t value	pr(> $|t|$)
(intercept)	3.09784	0.16357	82.40	18.939	< 2e-16
N1 relation proportion	0.45302	0.17608	77.01	2.573	0.0120
N2 frequency	0.68191	0.14249	78.74	4.786	7.83e-06
spelling ratio	-0.18673	0.08969	77.86	-2.082	0.0406

since rating transparency is a metalinguistic task, conscious focusing is involved, which might give more prominence to subtle aspects of the constituent that is being coded, resulting in adjusted slopes for N1 frequency when rating N1 transparency and similarly effects for N2. On the other hand, recall that, different from the models discussed in the previous chapter, the ratings on N1 and N2 transparency used here include all ratings, not just those from raters who rated N1, N2, and the whole compound for a given item. Thus, the set of raters differs, and, given the very small adjustments, this difference alone could be responsible for the differences in the random effects structure.

The top left-hand plot in Figure 7.3 shows that the relation proportion in the N1 constituent family, that is, the number of compound types in the N1 family that share the relation encoded in the target compound, is positively correlated with N2 transparency. This corresponds to our prediction B8, that is, the more accessible the relation in the target compound, the greater the overall transparency, including the transparency of the other constituent. The 2 non-semantic predictors presented in the second row, N2 frequency on the left-hand side and spelling ratio on the right-hand side, both point in the expected directions: N2 frequency is positively correlated with N2 transparency, and spelling ratio is negatively correlated with N2 transparency, again conforming to predictions A1 and D13 respectively.

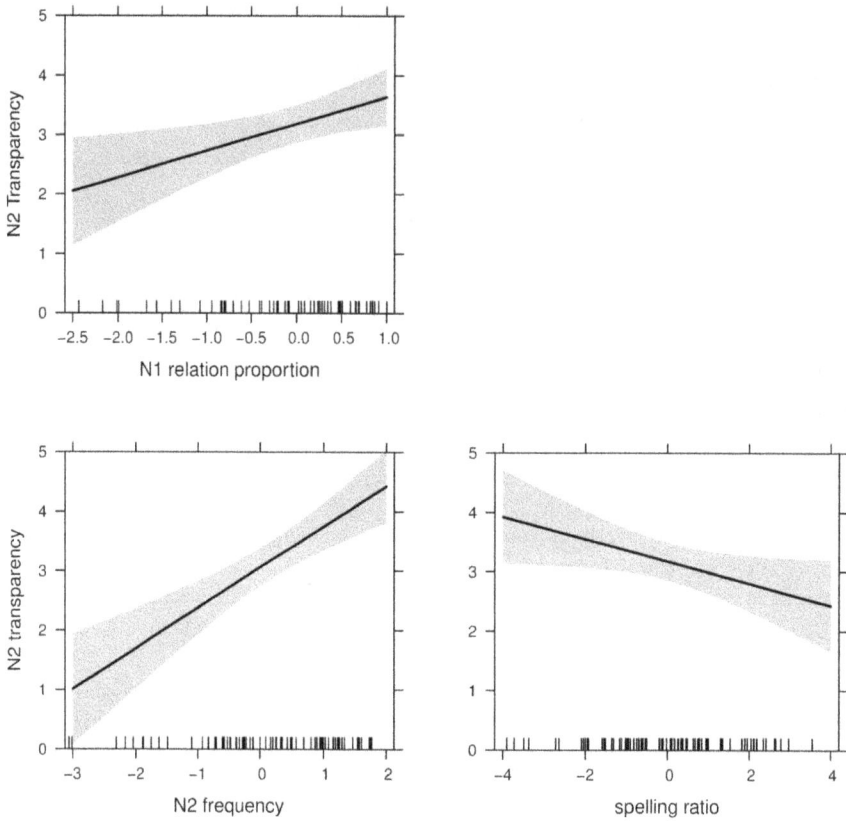

Figure 7.3: Partial effects in the final model for N2 transparency

7.6.3 Whole compound transparency

This section presents 2 models of whole compound transparency. The first model for N2 transparency, the final model including N2 synset proportion, is presented in Table 7.8. The fixed effects are presented graphically in Figure 7.4. The random effects include the random effects for items, as well as by-rater random intercepts and random slopes for the effect of spelling ratio.

The 4 significant fixed effects are shown in Figure 7.4. In accordance with our prediction D11, the greater the N1 relation proportion, the more transparent the whole compound is perceived to be. Note, however, that N2 relation proportion is not a significant predictor in this model. The second plot in the top row shows that the N2 synset proportion is negatively correlated with perceived compound

Table 7.8: Final mixed effects model for compound transparency, marginal $R^2 = 0.33$, conditional $R^2 = 0.72$

random effects:

groups	name	variance	std. dev.
workerID	(intercept)	0.150915	0.38848
	spelling ratio	0.004018	0.06339
singBrUnderscore	(intercept)	1.145611	1.07033
residual		0.930349	0.96455

number of obs.: 2307, groups: workerID, 119; singBrUnderscore, 81

fixed effects:

	estimate	std. error	df	t value	pr(> |t|)
(intercept)	2.83314	0.12886	95.57	21.986	< 2e-16
N1 relation proportion	0.41104	0.13442	76.04	3.058	0.003076
N2 synset proportion	-0.25046	0.12056	76.10	-2.077	0.041134
N1 frequency	0.52198	0.07116	75.97	7.336	2.04e-10
spelling ratio	-0.27239	0.06674	77.83	-4.081	0.000108

transparency. This is unexpected, and I will come back to this point below. The two plots in the bottom row show the non-semantic predictors. N1 frequency is positively correlated with perceived compound transparency, validating part of our prediction C9. Again, the predicted effect of N2 frequency is not significant in our model. Finally, in accordance with prediction D14, spelling ratio is negatively correlated with perceived compound transparency.

How can the unpredicted behavior of N2 synset proportion be explained? Recall that we predicted that both constituents' synset proportions individually are positively correlated with the respective constituent's perceived transparency (prediction A2) but negatively correlated with the perceived transparency of the respective other constituent (prediction A6). A likely explanation for the behavior with respect to the other constituent is that the other constituent is used as a foil in judging the transparency of the constituent under consideration, and we already explained the findings concerning the metaphoric shifts in the models described in the previous chapter this way. Based on this finding and the constituent transparency related predictions, we already predicted that the effect of synset proportion on whole compound transparency is more muted (prediction D12). In the constituent transparency models, we have only found an effect of N2 synset proportion on the perceived transparency of N1. While there is the

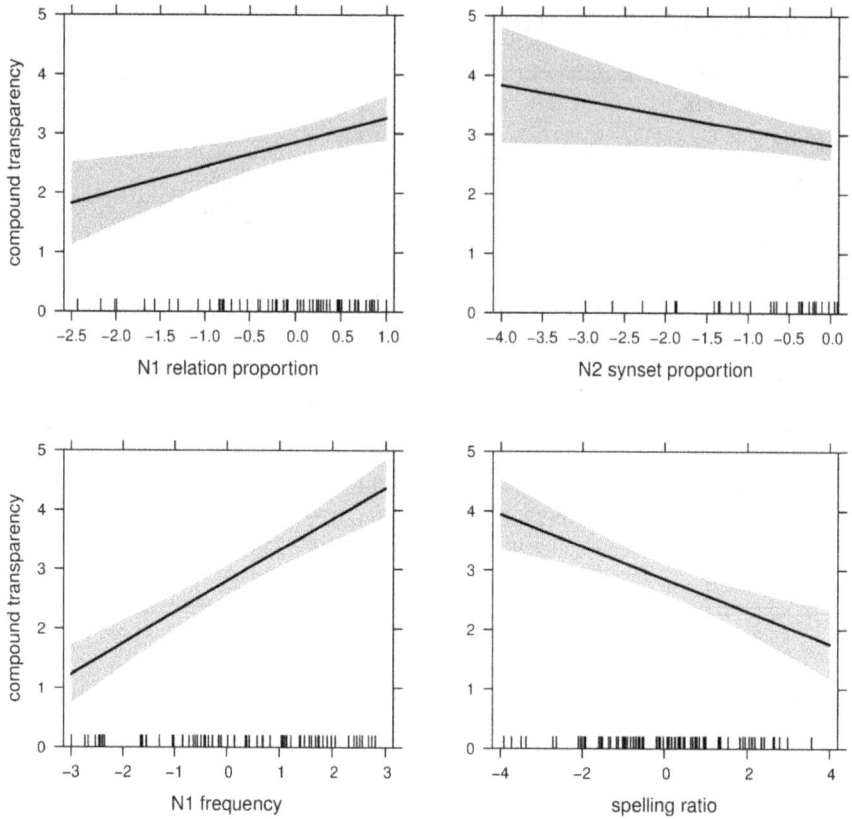

Figure 7.4: Partial effects in the final model for compound transparency

predicted negative correlation, I already pointed out that this effect is not found for N1 when re-running the models of Bell & Schäfer (2013) with mixed effects regression models. All in all it is surprising that sysnset proportion only occurs as a negative predictor. This led us to consider whether or not this effect might not be due to some other underlying factor not considered in our model, and warrants a closer look at the N2 synset proportion variable.

In our dataset, a high N2 synset proportion often arises in small N2 families. These families often only have a single synset to begin with, therefore the N2 synset proportion is maximally high, that is, one. In contrast, in large families the synset proportions are more varied, and the families are rarely restricted to just one synset. Note also that the family size puts a limit on how low the synset proportion can actually get. Since the synset proportion is calculated by dividing the number of compound types sharing the target synset by the number of compound types in the constituent family, the family size determines how small the proportion can possibly be. For example, if the family has 8 members, the lowest possible synset proportion is 0.125. Contrast this with the lowest synset proportion in our dataset, 0.006993007 for *model* from *role model,* with an N2 family with 143 members.

Because of the slight negative correlation between N2 family size and N2 synset proportion (the higher the family size, the lower the synset ratio), we decided to test the effect of adding positional family sizes as additional explanatory variables to the set of variables used in our models (this slightly increases collinearity, c-number = 3.777). The result is a model in which N2 family size in effect replaces N2 synset proportion.

This second model for compound transparency is shown in Table 7.9, and its significant predictors are graphically presented in Figure 7.5. Comparing the fit of the previous model with this model via R's anova function reveals that it is a significantly better model. However, the difference is small: the second model explains one percentage point more of the variance via its fixed effects.

Table 7.9: Final mixed effects model for compound transparency, including N2 positional family size as a predictor, marginal $R^2 = 0.34$, conditional $R^2 = 0.72$

random effects:

groups	name	variance	std. dev.
workerID	(intercept)	0.150796	0.38832
	spelling ratio	0.004011	0.06333
singBrUnderscore	(intercept)	1.107061	1.05217
residual		0.930388	0.96457

number of obs.: 2307, groups: workerID, 119; singBrUnderscore, 81

	estimate	std. error	df	t value	pr($> |t|$)
(intercept)	2.81222	0.12734	96.06	22.084	< 2e-16
N1 relation proportion	0.38949	0.13259	76.04	2.938	0.00438
N2 family size	0.25964	0.09793	76.01	2.651	0.00976
N1 frequency	0.47065	0.07170	75.97	6.564	5.75e-09
spelling ratio	-0.21449	0.06521	77.87	-3.289	0.00151

The 3 predictors that reoccur in this model, N1 relation proportion, N1 frequency, and spelling ratio, remain largely unchanged, differing only very slightly in their magnitudes from the magnitudes of the effects in the first compound

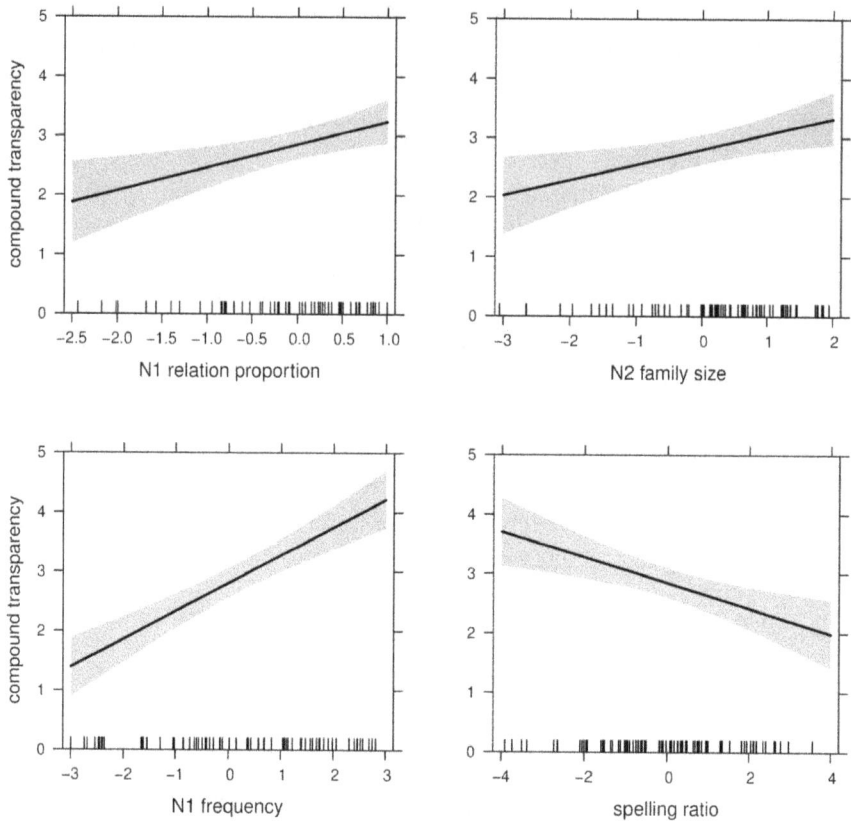

Figure 7.5: Partial effects in the final model for compound transparency, including N2 positional family size as a predictor

transparency model. The effect of N2 family size is depicted in the top right-hand plot of Figure 7.5. In contrast to N2 synset proportion, N2 family size is positively correlated with perceived compound transparency. While we did not predict any effects for family size per se, it is in line with the general logic of our predictions in that a large N2 family raises the expectedness of a given constituent to occur as the head of a compound. Note that the finding that the other predictors remain largely unchanged is a first sign that N2 family size and N2 synset proportion explain the same portion of the variance. This will be confirmed below in Section 7.6, when we look at the residuals of the models in detail.

Note that we consequently also re-ran the model for N1 transparency to check whether the N2 synset proportion effect would be replaced by the effect of N2 family size. However, this is not the case. One possible explanation for this is that the 2 variables in effect compete for significance in our models, and that, given that they explain a roughly similar part of the variation, small changes might lead to one predictor being chosen instead of the other predictor. Since the datasets are only partially produced by the same raters, this alone might make a decisive difference. Another explanation is that N2 synset proportion combines different underlying factors one of which might play a role for N1 transparency. Note incidentally that at least for small families synset proportion does not necessarily pick up anything related to semantic shifts per se. Thus, *agony aunt* is the only member of its N2 family. Therefore the synset proportion is 1, although *agony* would count as metaphorically shifted in the coding employed in Chapter 6.

7.6.4 The 2016 models: discussion and conclusion

This section presented the models from Bell & Schäfer (2016). Looking at all the 4 models, one can first of all observe that out of the set of explanatory variables considered (cf. Table 7.3), the 2 measures assessing the likelihood of a given constituent to occur as either the modifier or the head of the compound, family size ratio N1 and family size ratio N2, are not significant in any of the 4 models. For those explanatory variables that are significant, it is noticeable that the variables that are constituent specific usually only reach significance for either their N1 or their N2 version, with the exception of the role of N1 and N2 constituent frequency for N1 transparency.

As far as the general idea of compound transparency as a function of the 2 constituent transparencies is concerned, we can note that the first model for compound transparency looks like a combination of the effects observed for N1 and N2 transparency. The 2 predictors that correlate with both the N1 and the N2 constituent transparency ratings in the same direction, N1 relation proportion and spelling ratio, both re-appear in the first (and also in the second) model for whole compound transparency. In all models, N1 relation proportion is positively correlated with transparency, and spelling ratio is negatively correlated with semantic transparency. N2 frequency also emerges as a significant predictor in both constituent transparency models. However, in the model for N1 transparency it is negatively correlated with semantic transparency, while in the model for N2 transparency it is positively correlated with transparency. When it comes to whole compound transparency, these opposing tendencies seem to cancel each other out and N2 frequency does not emerge as a significant predictor. Finally, N2 synset proportion occurs only in the N1 but not in the N2 constituent transparency model, correlating negatively with N1 transparency. This negative correlation with transparency reoccurs in the model for whole compound transparency. Note, however, that at least for the whole compound, this predictor can be successfully replaced by N2 family size, again a positively correlating predictor in line with the general view of transparency as an expectancy driven phenomenon.

Going through the original list of predictions spelling out the hypotheses for all of the variables used, it can be observed that 8 of them are, albeit sometimes only partially, borne out by our models. In particular, the role of N1 relation proportion as a positive correlate of transparency in all 4 models shows that the attempt to reassess the role of semantic relations in terms of constituent family based expectancy payed off. In contrast, the synset proportions played a role in only 2 of the 4 models, namely the model for N1 transparency and the first model for compound transparency. However, N2 family size is a better predictor for compound transparency, apparently explaining the same portion (and a bit more) of the variation. There are at least 3 factors that might explain why synset proportion played such a small role in our models. Firstly, in contrast to the semantic relations in compounds which are bound to this specific construction type, the constituents also occur with different usages, that is, different synsets, outside of compounds. This distribution might play an important role for perceived transparency. Unfortunately, we had no way of assessing this distribution. Secondly, the number of synsets does not differentiate between the constituent families as much as the relation proportions do. Thus, for the 81 compound types from the Reddy et al. dataset, relation proportion yields 56 and 72 distinct proportions for the N1 and the N2 families respectively, compared to 41 and 56 for the N1 and N2 synset proportions. Thirdly, the synsets available for the constituents might have been too idiosyncratic in the way in which they distinguished between different meanings for the constituents (see the description of the WordNet senses in Section 7.2 and also my remarks on cases were it was difficult to understand or apply the WordNet distinctions in Section 7.4.2).

7.7 Re-modeling Bell & Schäfer (2016)

If we re-examine the models proposed in Bell & Schäfer (2016), one particular issue that signals room for improvement is the distribution of the residuals. Below, the standardized residuals for all 4 models discussed in the previous section are visualized in 2 ways: plotted against the fitted values and in Q-Q plots. Figure 7.6 shows the plots for the 2 models for constituent transparency.

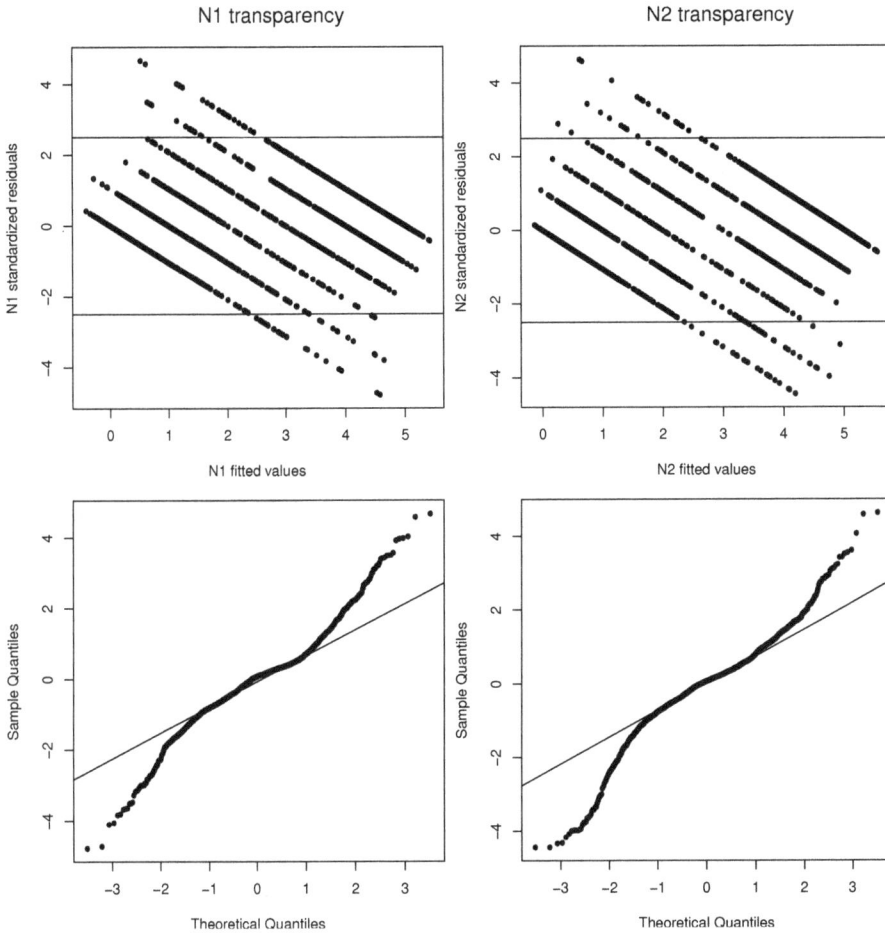

Figure 7.6: Standardized residuals of the models for constituent transparency. The plots for the N1 transparency model are shown on the left-hand side, the plots for the N2 transparency model on the right-hand side.

The top row shows plots of the standardized residuals against the fitted values. The 2 horizontal lines mark the ± 2.5 region. The bottom row shows Q-Q plots of the standardized residuals against the normal distribution. The plots for the N1 transparency model are shown on the left-hand side, while the plots for the N2 transparency model are shown on the right-hand side. The plots show very clear departures of the residuals from the normal distribution. Both models have problems predicting the high and the low ratings on the Likert scale.

Figure 7.7 shows plots for the residuals of the 2 models for compound transparency. Again, the top row shows the fitted values against the standardized residuals, and the bottom row shows the Q-Q plots. On the left-hand side are the plots for the first model for compound transparency which includes N2 synset proportion as a predictor. On the right-hand side are the plots for the second model of compound transparency, in which N2 synset proportion was replaced by N2 family size.

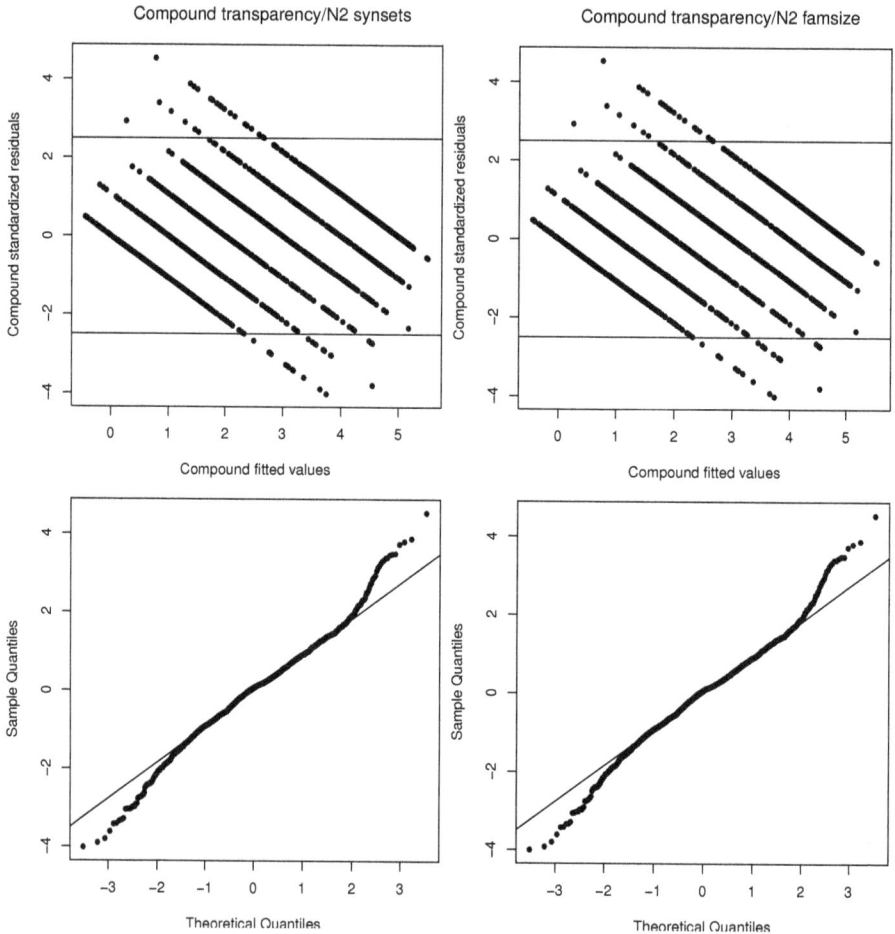

Figure 7.7: Standardized residuals in the models for compound transparency. The plots for the compound transparency model including N2 synset proportion are shown on the left-hand side. The plots for the compound transparency model including N2 family size instead are shown on the right-hand side.

Note that the distribution of the residuals is extremely similar in both models. Apart from that, the residuals depart less from normality than those for the constituent transparency models, but still noticeably so, again showing difficulties of the models in predicting the high and low ratings respectively.

In all 4 cases, the break in continuity outside of the ± 2.5 range points to outliers in the data. The existence of outliers in the data is not surprising, given that the outlier trimming procedure used by Reddy, McCarthy & Manandhar (2011) applied trimming only to the contributions of a subset of raters (see Chapter 5, Section 5.2). Using the same ±1.5 deviation from the mean cut-off point as previously for the models run on cleaned data in Chapter 6 (see Section 6.4.1.1), the distribution of the residuals changes as shown in Figure 7.8.

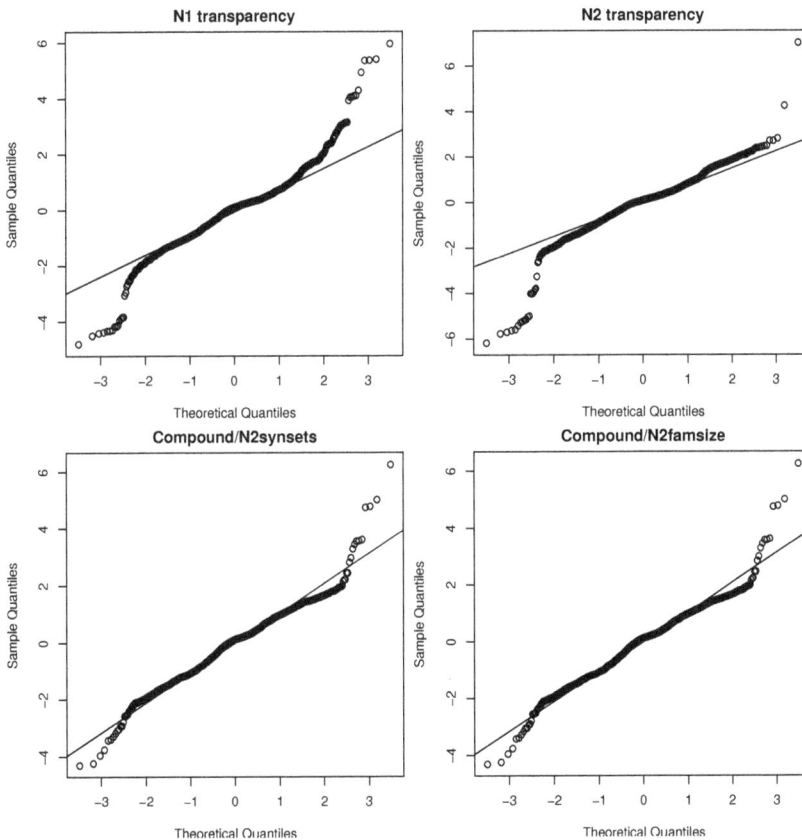

Figure 7.8: Standardized residuals for the 4 models in Bell & Schäfer (2016) run on trimmed data

Figure 7.8 shows the Q-Q plots of the standardized residuals against the normal distribution, with the plots for the constituent transparency models in the top row and the plots for the compound transparency models in the bottom row. Within the first row, the residuals for the model of N1 transparency are shown on the left-hand side, those for the N2 model on the right-hand side. At the bottom, the residuals for the model including the N2 synsets are shown on the left. The residuals for the model including the N2 family size are shown on the right-hand side. As the 4 plots show, trimming the data by using the word sense specific means results in residuals that are, in their majority, closer to the normal distribution than before. At the same time, there are in all plots, most noticeably in the plots of the residuals from the constituent transparency models, several strings of standardized residuals that are cut off from the main trend, exhibiting very large values. What caused this? Careful inspection of the residuals reveals that in almost all cases the existence of ratings on either of the 2 senses of a given compound is responsible for the outliers. Recall that whereas the models discussed in Chapter 6 are all word-sense specific, the models discussed here are item specific. That is, the semantic annotation did not take different interpretations of the same compound into account, but in all cases was based on what I believed to be the standard interpretation of the compound. Due to this procedure, the models cannot do justice to differences in the ratings that result from the raters actually rating different word senses of one and the same item. The effect of the trimming of the data was to bring out this difference more clearly, since the trimming was done on the individual compound senses, not on the items. For the final set of models to be discussed, I reduced the dataset again by taking out all ratings that yield standardized residuals exceeding the ± 2.5 range. This procedure eliminates many of those ratings which depart from the models' predictions because the raters apparently used different meanings of the compounds than the meanings used by me in annotating the data and by other raters in rating the data. Quite expectedly, this results in models with standardized residuals closer to the normal distribution, cf. Figure 7.9. However, not only the standardized residuals, also the models themselves change, particular those for constituent transparency.

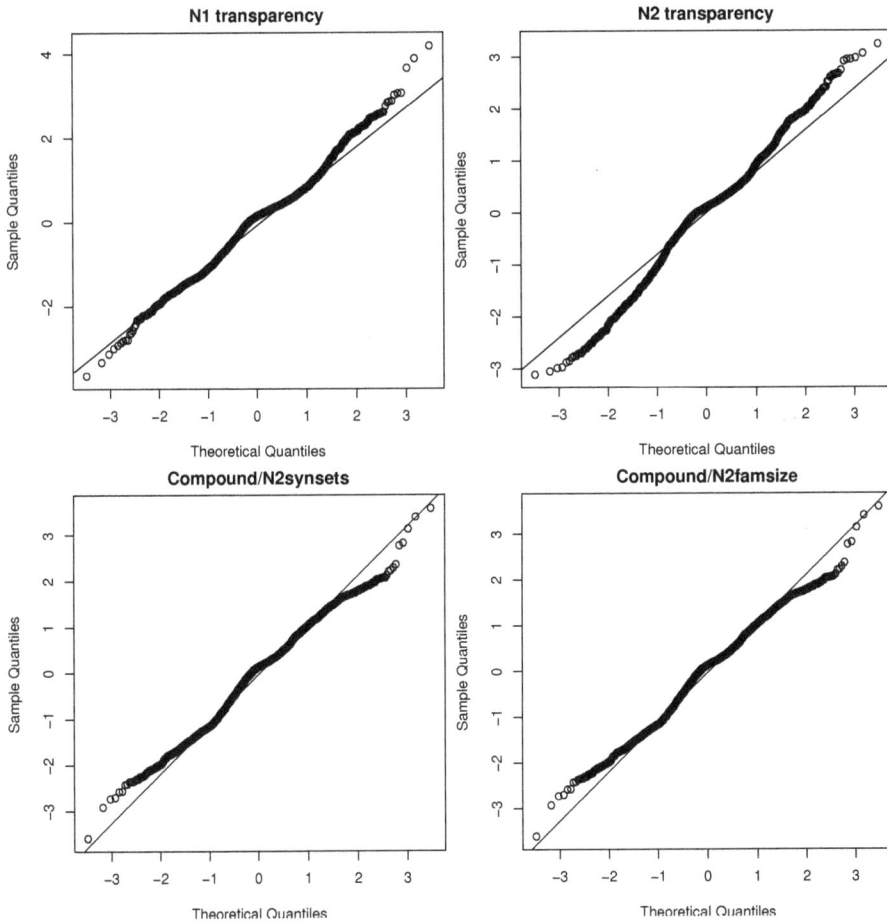

Figure 7.9: Standardized residuals in the models run on the datasets that were cleaned in a 2-step process. First, the datasets were trimmed using deviations from the mean ratings. Second, remaining outliers were removed by excluding those ratings that yielded standardized residuals exceeding the ±2.5 range in the models run on the trimmed dataset.

7.7.1 New models for constituent transparency

Using the same random effect structure and the same fixed effects in the model specification for the cleaned data leads to one of the originally 5 fixed effects to become insignificant. Eliminating this predictor, N2 synset proportion, leads to the model shown in Table 7.10. The fixed effects are presented graphically in Figure 7.10.

Table 7.10: Model for N1 transparency, using the cleaned dataset with outliers removed. Marginal R^2 = 0.40, conditional R^2 = 0.93

random effects:

groups	name	variance	std. dev.
workerID	(intercept)	0.0231369	0.15211
	spelling ratio	0.0003234	0.01798
	N1 frequency	0.0044793	0.06693
singBrUnderscore	(intercept)	2.2179216	1.48927
residual		0.3101274	0.55689

number of obs.: 2030, groups: workerID, 112; singBrUnderscore, 81

fixed effects:

	estimate	std. error	df	t value	pr(> $|t|$)
(intercept)	2.83970	0.16900	77.81	16.803	< 2e-16
N1 relation proportion	0.43872	0.18492	75.89	2.372	0.02020
N1 frequency	0.70623	0.09962	77.04	7.090	5.61e-10
N2 frequency	-0.31424	0.15035	75.94	-2.090	0.03997
spelling ratio	-0.27024	0.09380	76.01	-2.881	0.00515

Besides the missing predictor N2 synset proportion, the fixed effects are very similar to those in the original model, cf. Table 7.6. The magnitude of the positive correlation of N1 relation proportion is slightly higher, whereas the magnitude of the negative correlation due to the spelling ratio is slightly lower. The other 2 effects remain almost unchanged. Note that the higher R^2 values are to be expected given that I removed the outliers from the data.

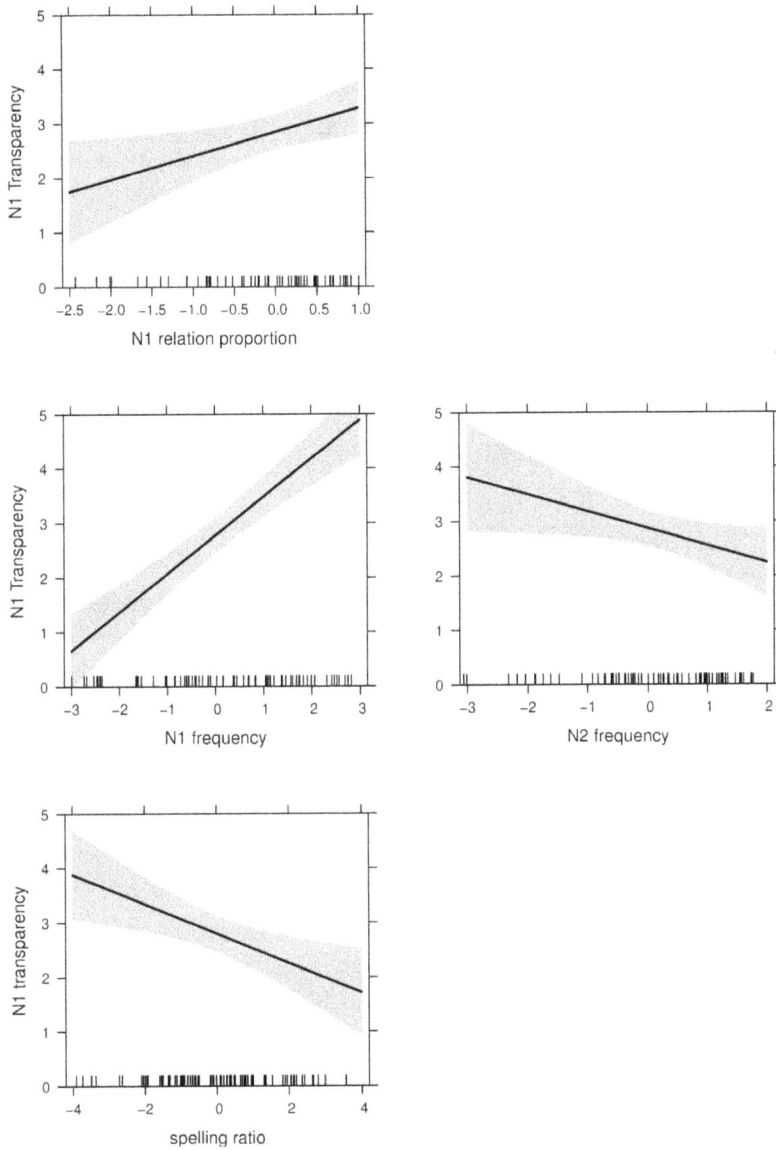

Figure 7.10: Fixed effects in the final model for N1 transparency, using the trimmed dataset with outliers removed

The result of using the same model specification but the cleaned data in modeling N2 transparency is shown in Table 7.11. The fixed effects are graphically presented in Figure 7.11.

Table 7.11: Model for N2 transparency, using the cleaned dataset with outliers removed. Marginal R^2 = 0.28, conditional R^2 = 0.92

random effects:			
groups	name	variance	std. dev.
workerID	(intercept)	0.012835	0.11329
	N2 frequency	0.008178	0.09043
singBrUnderscore	(intercept)	2.586534	1.60827
residual		0.308966	0.55585

number of obs.: 2075, groups: workerID, 108; singBrUnderscore, 81

fixed effects:

	estimate	std. error	df	t value	pr(> |t|)
(intercept)	3.1158	0.1813	79.03	17.188	< 2e-16
N1 relation proportion	0.5154	0.1984	77.95	2.598	0.0112
N2 frequency	0.8103	0.1530	78.92	5.295	1.04e-06

Just as in the new N1 transparency model, the new model for N2 transparency reduces the number of significant predictors: spelling ratio is not significant anymore, leaving the 2 predictors N1 relation proportion and N1 frequency. Note that since spelling ratio is not a significant fixed effect anymore, I also removed the corresponding random slope specification from the random part of the model specification.

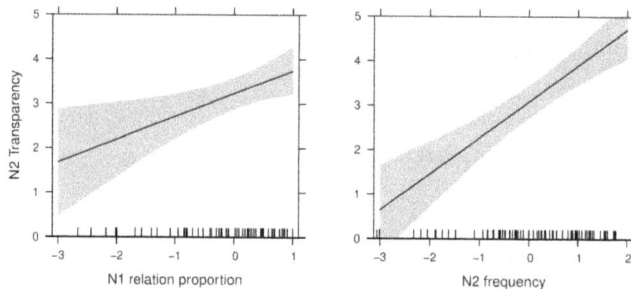

Figure 7.11: Fixed effects in the final model for N2 transparency, using the trimmed dataset with outliers removed

Just as in the previous model for N2 transparency, both remaining fixed effects are positively correlated with N2 transparency. In both cases, the magnitudes of the effects are slightly boosted.

7.7.2 New models for compound transparency

The 2 new models for compound transparency are shown in Table 7.12 and Table 7.13. Both models are very similar to the original models. In contrast to the models for constituent transparency, the fixed effects in both models remain the same as before.

Table 7.12: Final mixed effects model for compound transparency, including N2 synset proportion as a predictor, marginal $R^2 = 0.40$, conditional $R^2 = 0.87$

random effects:

groups	name	variance	std. dev.
workerID	(intercept)	0.043502	0.20857
	spelling ratio	0.001939	0.04404
singBrUnderscore	(intercept)	1.506764	1.22750
residual		0.420064	0.64812

number of obs.: 2005, groups: workerID, 116; singBrUnderscore, 81

fixed effects:

	estimate	std. error	df	t value	pr($> |t|$)
(intercept)	2.80437	0.13991	80.92	20.045	< 2e-16
N1 relation proportion	0.44567	0.15283	75.95	2.916	0.004656
N2 synset proportion	-0.27853	0.13709	76.04	-2.032	0.045671
N1 frequency	0.56859	0.08091	75.90	7.028	7.83e-10
spelling ratio	-0.27261	0.07560	76.69	-3.606	0.000551

In the compound transparency model including the N2 synset proportion, cf. Table 7.12, the 2 semantic predictors, N1 relation proportion and N2 synset proportion, are again correlated with compound transparency. And just as before, N1 relation proportion is positively correlated with compound transparency, and N2 synset proportion is negatively correlated with compound transparency. Both are slightly larger in magnitude than in the original model. In contrast, both non-semantic predictors, namely the positively correlated N1 frequency and the negatively correlated spelling ratio, are smaller in magnitude, although the former only slightly so.

Table 7.13: Final mixed effects model for compound transparency, including N2 positional family size as a predictor, marginal $R^2 = 0.41$, conditional $R^2 = 0.87$

random effects:

groups	name	variance	std. dev.
workerID	(intercept)	0.043520	0.20861
	spelling ratio	0.001941	0.04405
singBrUnderscore	(intercept)	1.457949	1.20746
residual		0.420060	0.64812

number of obs.: 2005, groups: workerID, 116; singBrUnderscore, 81

	estimate	std. error	df	t value	pr(> |t|)
(intercept)	2.78103	0.13814	81.08	20.131	< 2e-16
N1 relation proportion	0.42157	0.15080	75.96	2.796	0.00656
N2 family size	0.29016	0.11140	75.97	2.605	0.01106
N1 frequency	0.51130	0.08155	75.92	6.269	2.02e-08
spelling ratio	-0.20806	0.07388	76.72	-2.816	0.00618

In the compound transparency model including the N2 family size, cf. Table 7.13, the semantic predictor N1 relation proportion is also larger in magnitude, as is the replacement for N2 synset proportion, N2 family size. The positively correlated N1 frequency is larger in magnitude. The negatively correlated spelling ratio is slightly smaller in magnitude. The model including the N2 family size still fits the data better, but there is no significant difference between the 2 models anymore when comparing them via log likelihood testing.

7.7.3 Conclusion: re-modeling Bell & Schäfer (2016)

Starting from the observation of large residuals in the models from Bell & Schäfer (2016), this section showed that using a single consistent criterion to eliminate outliers across all ratings led to residuals containing even larger outliers, and also, and more conspicuously, bands of large outliers. Closer inspection revealed that these outliers were caused by ratings on compounds for which both meanings where selected by raters. Divergent ratings driven by different meanings of one and the same compound cannot be modeled by the predictor variables used in this chapter, because they were all bound to compound types, not compound senses. I therefore eliminated the entries causing the high residuals from the data, and presented the resulting 4 models.

The most notable changes occurred for the models of N1 and N2 transparency, resulting in more parsimonious models. In the model for N1 transparency, N2 synset proportion did not become significant; in the model for N2 transparency, spelling ratio did not become significant. Idiosyncratic properties of N2 synset proportion were already discussed at length earlier (cf. Section 7.6.4). Its diminished role in a model ran on cleaner data is thus reassuring. Why spelling ratio did not become significant in the model for N2 transparency is less clear. However, note that in the mixed effects models presented in Chapter 6, the model for N2 transparency was the only model that retained only 2 of the 3 predictors capturing meaning shifts. If spelling ratio, intended primarily as a replacement for whole compound shifts, also captures some part of the variation captured in the earlier models by constituent shifts, its smaller effect on N2 transparency is expected.

For compound transparency, the models remained unchanged as far as there significant predictors are concerned. Across all models, the remaining predictors exhibited the same direction and by and large similar magnitudes.

7.8 Conclusion

The aim of this chapter was to model semantic transparency based on information drawn from compound families. In particular, its aim was to explore whether the semantic predictors that emerged either as insignificant or as conceptually unsatisfactory in Chapter 6 could be turned into measures capturing the expectedness of a semantic configuration in view of a compound's constituent families.

Section 7.1 focused on previous attempts to assess semantic relations within compounds relative to their constituent families, extensively discussing the approach of using an artificial corpus by Gagné & Shoben (1997) and the BNC-based re-implementation by Maguire et al. (2007), and concluding that for the task at hand a BNC-based procedure is most promising. Section 7.2 extends the expectancy-based approach used for the semantic relations to the coding of constituent senses, proposing to use the distribution of WordNet synsets across constituent families instead of the coding of meaning shifts. In addition, it argues that spelling ratio, a variable already used in the models presented in Chapter 7, can be used as a stand-in for whole compound shifts. In addition, this section introduced WordNet, the lexical resource used to code the constituent senses.

Section 7.3 described the methods used by Melanie Bell and me to arrive at a representative set of compound families for the Reddy et al. items. Starting from the BNC, and adding items from CELEX, we used the USENET corpus in order to have more insight into the occurrences of low frequency items. In addition, we used CELEX to filter out compounds that themselves consisted of complex constituents. My subsequent semantic coding of the compounds in these families is described in Section 7.4.

Section 7.5 introduced the explanatory variables and the predictions from Bell & Schäfer (2016). The models from Bell & Schäfer (2016) were presented and discussed in Section 7.6. Core findings were an imbalance in the distribution of the contributions due to N1 and N2 predictors and the observation that the models for compound transparency can be seen as combinations of the predictors playing a role for the constituent transparency models. The majority of our predictions was at least partially borne out, and with the N1 relation proportion there was one predictor based on the semantic annotation that reoccurred in all models, always positively correlating with semantic transparency. Spelling ratio, in contrast, occurred in all but one model and was always negatively correlated with semantic transparency. However, while we motivated its inclusion with the assumption that it is positively correlated with whole compound meaning shifts, it is actually not so clear what exactly this variable represents in all individual cases, cf. again the pertinent remarks in Chapter 6, Section 6.4.2.3.

Section 7.7 showed that the dataset used so far still contained many outliers. After removing the outliers in a 2-step process, I presented the final models for semantic transparency. This resulted in more parsimonious models for N1 and N2 transparency, while the models for whole compound transparency remained essentially unchanged.

While thus only one predictor derived from the semantic annotation reoccurred in all models with a correlation in the expected direction, this is actually a very promising result, showing that viewing semantic relations as constituent-specific was a step in the right direction. Note also that in the 2 theoretical frameworks that argue for this view, the CARIN and RICE theories of conceptual combination, an imbalance in the contribution of the modifier and the head is expected.

8 Summary and outlook

The topic of this work has been the notion of semantic transparency and its relation to the semantics of compound nouns. The first part gave an overview of the place of semantic transparency in the analysis of compound nouns, discussing its role in models of morphological processing and differentiating it from related notions. After a chapter on the semantic analysis of complex nominals, this first part closed with a chapter on previous attempts to model semantic transparency. The second part introduced new models of semantic transparency. In the following, I first summarize the most important points of this work, and secondly, point to some remaining questions and discuss some avenues for further research.

8.1 Summary

The first 4 chapters established the backdrop for the 2 empirical chapters to follow. Chapter 2 focused on the role of semantic transparency in psycholinguistics. First, it explained the role of semantic transparency in different models of morphological processing. Secondly, it provided an overview of the measures used in psycholinguistics to assess the semantic transparency of compound nouns. Thirdly, the results and findings of studies involving semantic transparency as an independent variable were presented. Chapter 3 summarized the discussion of semantic transparency in works on anaphor resolution and compound stress, introduced a number of related terms and discussed transparency in other domains. Chapter 4 gave an overview of approaches to compound semantics, including discussion of work on the semantics of phrasal constructions in formal semantics. Chapter 5 provided an introduction to distributional semantics and discussed 3 studies which include distributional semantics measures in their statistical models of semantic transparency.

In the 2 chapters of the empirical part, I presented new empirical work on semantic transparency. Chapter 6, building on Bell & Schäfer (2013), first introduces models for semantic transparency that include the meaning shifts of the compounds and their constituents as well as the semantic relation between constituents as predictors. I show that after switching from ordinary least square regression models to mixed effects models, initially observed effects for semantic relations disappear. Furthermore, I argue that the coding of the meaning shifts was missing a principled basis. Chapter 7, building on Bell & Schäfer (2016), can be seen as a direct response to the conclusions drawn from the earlier set of statistical models. This time, all semantic-based predictors reflected expectancies drawn from the distribution of the respective features across the compounds' positional constituent families. In order to assess these distributions, Melanie Bell and I created a large compound database which I annotated for semantic relations and WordNet meanings of the compound constituents. The resulting models show that the semantic predictors representing the N1 and N2 families do not behave similarly. Furthermore, the distribution of semantic relations across the N1 families emerges as a stable, positive correlate of N1, N2, and whole compound transparency. In contrast, the only effects associated with the synset distribution were negative correlations which, in the case of compound transparency, led to extensive discussion of the nature of this variable.

8.2 Outlook

Semantic transparency is a rich and fascinating topic, and the research presented in this work opens up many new avenues of investigation. Here, I want to highlight 4 pathways which look particularly promising to follow.

1. Using the annotated compound database
   For the models presented in Chapter 7, I have annotated a large compound database. This database contains compound families of very different sizes, ranging from 1 member to 363 members. Compound families of comparable size sometimes differ considerably in the number and types of semantic relations and synsets used. A further variable that shows massive variation but was not considered in the studies presented here is the distribution of token frequencies across the members of a constituent family. In future studies, this database can be used to investigate the behavior of different compounds drawn from the same compound family against each other but also against the behavior of compound types drawn from groups that differ along the dimensions just mentioned. This will ideally lead to a much better understanding of the role of the distribution of the semantic features across the groups, but will also allow one to compare whether there are certain cut-off points, e.g. driven by family size or compound token frequency, that make certain compound types more important for the compositional

processes involved in language use. In addition, drawing balanced samples from this database allows one to compare between frequent and less frequent compound types. Recall that the current investigation focused on transparency measures for high frequency compounds only, since one of the original selection criteria was high frequency.

2. Comparing the different measures of semantic transparency experimentally

In the discussion of different ways to establish semantic transparency in Chapter 2, I pointed out that the differences in establishing semantic transparency for experimental items make a comparison of the experimental results difficult. One simply cannot know whether the same properties were measured in every case. An experimental comparison of responses to different ways of asking for semantic transparency would allow one to establish which measurements yield similar results, and can therefore be assumed to establish similar variables for experimental purposes.

3. Synchronizing the measures across tasks and approaches

While one can find some measures on compounds from the Reddy et al. dataset in other works on compounds, e.g. Juhasz, Lai & Woodcock (2015), or in databases of psycholinguistic measures like the English Lexicon Project (Balota et al. 2007), these items are too few in number to allow systematic comparison. In order to gain better insight into the nature of the semantic transparency judgments, getting psycholinguistic measures with better understood features (e.g. lexical decision ratings) on the items in the Reddy et al. dataset would be very helpful. Besides further psycholinguistic measures, models including distributional semantics and information theoretic measures together with the semantic predictors introduced in this work can lead to a deeper understanding of the ways in which semantic transparency and semantic aspects of meaning are reflected in the former measures.

4. Obtaining online measures

When less frequent compound types are used, it is likely that an off-line method like Likert scale ratings will not suffice to draw out nuances between compounds at the high end of transparency. To understand the influence of the distribution of semantic factors on the processing of less frequent, and therefore presumably not lexicalized compounds, data obtained by using an online task like eye-movement measurements allows one a more fine-grained look at the underlying processes. Such data would have maximal traction if obtained for a set of compounds that is already selected by using the annotated compound database as a guide in choosing the experimental items.

Appendix A: Semantic coding for Bell & Schäfer (2013)

This appendix contains the semantic coding used in Bell & Schäfer (2013). It is grouped into the coded semantic relations and the coded semantic shifts. The set of annotations is available at http://www.martinschaefer.info/publications/TFDS-2013/TFDS-2013_Bell_Schaefer.zip.

1 Relations

(1)   ABOUT: 5 compound types, 7 compound readings
      blame game   case study (2 readings)
      fashion plate (2 readings) rocket science
      spelling bee

(2)   BE: 21 compound types, 24 compound readings
      chain reaction (2 readings)   cloud nine
      crash course   diamond wedding
      fine line   graduate student
      grandfather clock   head teacher
      human being   interest rate
      lotus position   panda car
      research project   rock bottom
      sacred cow (2 readings)   shrinking violet
      silver screen (2 readings)   sitting duck
      smoking gun   speed limit
      zebra crossing
      For *grandfather clock*, cf. also HAVE2

(3)   CAUSE2: 1 type, 1 sense
      guilt trip

(4)   FOR: 25 tpyes, 28 readings

agony aunt	application form	call centre
car park	china clay	cocktail dress
credit card	cutting edge	eye candy
firing line (2 readings)	game plan (2 readings)	health insurance
law firm	mailing list	melting pot
parking lot	pecking order	polo shirt
public service (2 readings)	radio station	role model
search engine	smoking jacket	spinning jenny
swimming pool	think tank	

(5)   FROM: 3 types, 4 readings
crocodile tears   snake oil
swan song

(6)   HAVE1: 7 types

balance sheet	cheat sheet	engine room
gold mine	gravy train	memory lane
rush hour		

(7)   HAVE2: 5 types, 6 readings
climate change   face value (2 readings)
grandfather clock   monkey business
rat run
For *grandfather clock*, cf. also BE

(8)   IN: 9 types

bank account	couch potato	end user
front runner	graveyard shift	ground floor
nest egg	night owl	web site

(9)   MAKE1: 1 type
cash cow

(10)   MAKE2: 5 compound types, 7 readings
brass ring (2 readings)   brick wall (2 readings)   ivory tower
silver bullet   silver spoon

(11)   NONE: 2 types
number crunching   rat race

(12)   USE: 4 types
acid test   lip service
snail mail   video game

2 Shifts

(13) A metaphor: 23 readings

call centre	chain reaction (2 readings)
crash course	diamond wedding
end user	face value (2 readings)
game plan	grandfather clock
graveyard shift	gravy train
head teacher	lotus position
panda car	pecking order
rat race	rat run
role model	shrinking violet
smoking jacket	snail mail
web site	zebra crossing

(14) A metonymy: 4 compound types

cash cow	cheat sheet
cocktail dress	radio station

(15) B metaphor: 23 types, 24 readings

agony aunt	balance sheet	blame game
call centre	car park	cash cow
cheat sheet	couch potato	credit card
eye candy	firing line (two readings)	gravy train
guilt trip	lip service	memory lane
number crunching	rat race	search engine
shrinking violet	spelling bee	spinning jenny
think tank	web site	

(16) B metonymy: 5 types, 6 readings

chain reaction	diamond wedding
fashion plate (2 readings)	rat run
rush hour	

(17) AB metonymy: 2 types

silver screen	silver spoon

(18)   AB metaphor: 30 types, 31 readings

acid test	brass ring	brick wall
cloud nine	couch potato	crocodile tears
cutting edge	face value	fashion plate
fine line	firing line	front runner
ivory tower	lip service	melting pot
monkey business	nest egg	night owl
rat race	rat run	rock bottom
rocket science	rush hour	sacred cow
shrinking violet	silver bullet	sitting duck
smoking gun	snake oil (two readings)	swan song

Appendix B: Semantic coding for Bell & Schäfer (2016)

This appendix contains additional notes on the semantic coding of the dataset used in Bell & Schäfer (2016). The dataset is available at http://martinschaefer. info/publications/download/Bell_and_Schaefer_2016_semantic-coding.zip. The notes are also available as a standalone document at http://martinschaefer.info/ publications/download/Schaefer_2016_Notes-on-the-Semantic-Coding.pdf. Up-dated versions of this document will be made available there.

The presentation here follows the lemmas in the N1 and N2 families in alpha-betically order. The entry for every lemma starts with the compound containing this lemma in the respective position (N1 or N2) from the compound set rated in Reddy, McCarthy & Manandhar (2011). The following table gives an overview of the synset coding for the final dataset, using the following column headers:

column header	explanation
wnSense	value of the variable wnSense in the coded data, usually corresponding to the sense number in WordNet
example	example from the coded data
types	number of types in the data
class	word class according to WordNet
WordNet description	gloss (this is taken verbatim from WordNet unless otherwise indicated)

Following the table are any further comments on the WordNet senses as well as on the relational coding. In addition, known mistakes in the coding are listed here.

1 N1 families

1.1 acid (22 compound types)

Rated compound: *acid test*

wnSense	WordNet description	types	class	example
1	any of various water-soluble compounds having a sour taste and capable of turning litmus red and reacting with a base to form a salt)	17	n	acid alkali
2	street name for lysergic acid diethylamide	2	n	acid experience
3	harsh or corrosive in tone	2	adj	acid tongue
4	being sour to the taste	1	adj	acid tang

Notes:
Senses 3 and 4 are adjective synsets 1 and 2 in WordNet.

1.2 agony (3 compound types)

Rated compound: *agony aunt*

wnSense	WordNet description	types	class	example
1	intense feelings of suffering; acute mental or physical pain	3	n	agony column

Notes:
No distinction was made between sense 1 and the second WordNet sense (a state of acute pain).

1.3 application (42 compound types)

Rated compound: *application form*

wnSense	WordNet description	types	class	example
1	(the act of bringing something to bear; using it for a particular purpose)	1	n	application area
2	a verbal or written request for assistance or employment or admission to a school	20	n	application document
3	(the work of applying something)	1	n	application technique
4	(a program that gives a computer instructions that provide the user with tools to accomplish a task)	20	n	application server

Notes:

Application list occurs in the BNC with 2 meanings (chance discovery), bound to 2 different WordNet senses (in the coding, WordNet sense 2 and relation FOR is used):

(1) a. BNN 221 Much praised at the Evian conference for a bold offer to absorb up to 100,000 refugees, the Dominican Republic had closed its application list at 2000.

     b. JXG 19 Use the cursor keys to select "BASIC" from the application list.

1.4 balance (12 compound types)

Rated compound: *balance sheet*

wnSense	WordNet description	types	class	example
1	a state of equilibrium	6	n	balance beam
2	equality between the totals of the credit and debit sides of an account	3	n	balance sheet
9	(mathematics) an attribute of a shape or relation; exact reflection of form on opposite sides of a dividing line or plane)	1	n	balance value
10	a weight that balances another weight	1	n	balance engineer
11	(a wheel that regulates the rate of movement in a machine; especially a wheel oscillating against the hairspring of a timepiece to regulate its beat)	10	n	balance wheel

Notes:
WordNet sense 11 contains the type: balance wheel, balance (a wheel that regulates the rate of movement in a machine; especially a wheel oscillating against the hairspring of a timepiece to regulate its beat). Group is small but contains 3 single occurrence WordNet senses.
Mistakes:
Balance problem is coded as WordNet sense 2, while in the BNC it only occurs in the context of guitar design and music recording, corresponding to WordNet sense 1 or 10, or, for the latter, 9. *Balance change* does not occur as a compound in the BNC.

1.5 bank (61 compound types)

Rated compound: *bank account*

wnSense	WordNet description	types	class	example
1	sloping land (especially the slope beside a body of water)	5	n	bank barn
2	a financial institution that accepts deposits and channels the money into lending activities	52	n	bank job
4	an arrangement of similar objects in a row or in tiers	2	n	bank switch
5	a supply or stock held in reserve for future use (especially in emergencies)	1	n	bank nurse
10	a flight maneuver; aircraft tips laterally about its longitudinal axis (especially in turning)	1	n	bank angle

Notes:
Within WordNet sense 2, people working in a bank were either classified with the HAVE2 or the IN relation (cf. *bank boss* and *bank chief* vs. *bank clerk* and *bank cashier*).

1.6 blame (1 compound types)

Rated compound: *blame game*

wnSense	WordNet description	types	class	example
1	an accusation that you are responsible for some lapse or misdeed	1	n	blame game

Notes:
There is only one second WordNet sense *a reproach for some lapse or misdeed*; the compound meaning can also be construed from this meaning.

1.7 brass (49 compound types)

Rated compound: *brass ring*

wnSense	WordNet description	types	class	example
1	an alloy of copper and zinc)	43	n	brass foundry
2	a wind instrument that consists of a brass tube (usually of variable length) that is blown by means of a cup-shaped or funnel-shaped mouthpiece)	5	n	brass ensemble
3	the persons (or committees or departments etc.) who make up a body for the purpose of administering something)	1	n	brass hat

1.8 brick (26 compound types)

Rated compound: *brick wall*

wnSense	WordNet description	types	class	example
1	rectangular block of clay baked by the sun or in a kiln; used as a building or paving material	26	n	brick terrace

Notes:

Brick yard occurs in the BNC in both the FOR and the MAKE2 construal, cf. (2-a) and (2-b). Note that *brickyard* comes with its own WordNet entry, 'S: (n) brick-yard, brickfield (a place where bricks are made and sold)', and occurs in the OED as a sub-entry of *brick* n[1] with the meaning ' brickyard n. a place where bricks are made, a brickfield.'

(2)   a.   B0A 1380 Boulton and Watt beam engines pumped out water at both ends, and a brick yard was set up to make the bricks near the site — seven million were used.

b. CA0 47 Outside they admired a pink brick yard for twenty ponies, which looked like three sides of a Battenberg cake, and an indoor school, completely walled with bullet-proof mirrors.

1.9 call (17 compound types)

Rated compound: *call centre*

wnSense	WordNet description	types	class	example
1	a telephone connection	9	n	call log
7	a demand by a broker that a customer deposit enough to bring his margin up to the minimum requirement	1	n	call loan
9	a request	1	n	call button
10	an instruction that interrupts the program being executed	2	n	call instruction
13	the option to buy a given stock (or stock index or commodity future) at a given price before a given date	4	n	call option

1.10 car (109 compound types)

Rated compound: *car park*

wnSense	WordNet description	types	class	example
1	a motor vehicle with four wheels; usually propelled by an internal combustion engine	108	n	car commercial
2	a wheeled vehicle adapted to the rails of railroad	1	n	car flat

Notes:

Alternative construal for *car flat* compound is 'flat railroad car for cars'. This construal better fits the actual BNC context, while the coded construal corresponds to *flat car* or *flat wagon*.

1.11 case (37 compound types)

Rated compound: *case study*

wnSense	WordNet description	types	class	example
3	a comprehensive term for any proceeding in a court of law whereby an individual seeks a legal remedy	11	n	case file
5	a portable container for carrying several objects)	2	n	case lid
6	a person requiring professional services	18	n	case conference
11	nouns or pronouns or adjectives (often marked by inflection) related in some way to other words in a sentence	4	n	case ending
17	the enclosing frame around a door or window opening	2	n	case base

Notes:

Sometimes strings occurred as compounds and as non-compounds in the BNC, e.g. *case slots*. Due to the lexical ambiguity of *slots* (plural form of the noun or singular form of the verb), there are compound occurrences, cf. (3-a), as well as non-compound occurrences, cf. (3-b).

(3) a. EES 521 Typically, the program would look at the words from left to right, and test whether each word in the sentence was a likely candidate for the case slots of the main verb.

b. HAC 5089 Fitting a drive to the 2000 series can be tricky because of the way the case slots together and the need to use a 3.5" drive and mount.

While (3) contains an identical string, (4) illustrates a structural ambiguity that, at least in the BNC, is tied to the number of the first noun. When the first noun is in the singular, the string occurs as a compound, cf. (4-a). When the first noun is in the plural, the nouns in the string are part of 2 different phrases, cf. (4-b).

(4) a. EES 482 For a verb such as' collide ', all that is specified by the case restrictions is that the object case can be any inanimate entity.

b. K94 2424 In some cases restrictions placed against imports may take the form of complex (and unnecessarily prohibitive) safety or packaging regulations.

1.12 cash (78 compound types)

Rated compound: *cash cow*

wnSense	WordNet description	types	class	example
1	money in the form of bills or coins	77	n	cash point
3	United States country music singer and songwriter (1932-2003)	1	n	cash brother

Notes:

WordNet sense 3 used for any personal name usage of *cash* (it is not the singer's name in the BNC context).

1.13 chain (31 compound types)

Rated compound: *chain reaction*

wnSense	WordNet description	types	class	example
1	a series of things depending on each other as if linked together	7	n	chain letter
2	(chemistry) a series of linked atoms (generally in an organic molecule)	9	n	chain configuration
3	a series of (usually metal) rings or links fitted into one another to make a flexible ligament	13	n	chain brake
4	(business) a number of similar establishments (stores or restaurants or banks or hotels or theaters) under one ownership	1	n	chain store
9	a linked or connected series of objects	1	n	chain stitch

Notes:

Chain reaction is coded as VERB, modeled on *chain smoker*. The latter, though, did not make it into the final selection.

1.14 cheat (2 compound types)

Rated compound: *cheat sheet*

wnSense	WordNet description	types	class	example
5	a deception for profit to yourself	2	n	cheat mode

1.15 china (27 compound types)

Rated compound: *china clay*

wnSense	WordNet description	types	class	example
1	a communist nation that covers a vast territory in eastern Asia; the most populous country in the world	17	n	china lobby
2	high quality porcelain originally made only in China	10	n	china plate

Notes:
WordNet sense 4 *dishware made of high quality porcelain* can alternatively be used for some items, e.g. *china bowl* or *china plate*.

1.16 climate (11 compound types)

Rated compound: *climate change*

wnSense	WordNet description	types	class	example
1	the weather in some location averaged over some long period of time	11	n	climate model

1.17 cloud (20 compound types)

Rated compound: *cloud nine*

wnSense	WordNet description	types	class	example
2	a visible mass of water or ice particles suspended at a considerable altitude	20	n	cloud bank

1.18 cocktail (11 compound types)

Rated compound: *cocktail dress*

wnSense	WordNet description	types	class	example
1	a short mixed drink	11	n	cocktail lounge

1.19 couch (2 compound types)

Rated compound: *couch potato*

wnSense	WordNet description	types	class	example
1	an upholstered seat for more than one person	2	n	couch grass

1.20 crash (19 compound types)

Rated compound: *crash course*

wnSense	WordNet description	types	class	example
2	a serious accident (usually involving one or more vehicles)	15	n	crash barrier
3	a sudden large decline of business or the prices of stocks (especially one that causes additional failures)	1	n	crash period
18	sleep in a convenient place	1	n	crash pad
19	[very fast, rapid]	2	[adj]	crash dive

Notes:
WordNet sense 19 added to cover the almost adjectival usage ('very fast, rapid').

1.21 credit (63 compound types)

Rated compound: *credit card*

wnSense	WordNet description	types	class	example
1	approval	1	n	credit side
2	money available for a client to borrow	60	n	credit agreement
8	an entry on a list of persons who contributed to a film or written work	1	n	credit sequence
9	an estimate, based on previous dealings, of a person's or an organization's ability to fulfill their financial commitments	1	n	credit rating

Notes:

WordNet sense 9 contains coded compound in its entry: 'credit rating, credit (an estimate, based on previous dealings, of a person's or an organization's ability to fulfill their financial commitments)'. Since it was impossible to clearly distinguish WordNet sense 2 and 5 ('arrangement for deferred payment for goods and services'), only WordNet sense 2 was used.

1.22 crocodile (5 compound types)

Rated compound: *crocodile tears*

wnSense	WordNet description	types	class	example
1	large voracious aquatic reptile having a long snout with massive jaws and sharp teeth and a body covered with bony plates; of sluggish tropical waters	1	n	crocodile farm

1.23 cutting (34 compound types)

Rated compound: *cutting edge*

wnSense	WordNet description	types	class	example
1	the activity of selecting the scenes to be shown and putting them together to create a film	2	n	cutting room
3	the act of cutting something into parts	26	n	cutting knife
5	an excerpt cut from a newspaper or magazine	2	n	cutting book
9	[An open, trench-like excavation through a piece of ground that rises above the level of a canal, railway, or road which has to be taken across it.]	1	n	cutting side
A1	(of speech) harsh or hurtful in tone or character	1	adj	cutting disdain
A3	painful as if caused by a sharp instrument	1	adj	cutting wind

Notes:

WordNet sense 9 manually added. The description is a verbatim quote from the OED (cutting, n. 8.).

1.24 diamond (20 compound types)

Rated compound: *diamond wedding*

wnSense	WordNet description	types	class	example
1	a transparent piece of diamond that has been cut and polished and is valued as a precious gem	17	n	diamond industry
3	a parallelogram with four equal sides; an oblique-angled equilateral parallelogram	2	n	diamond logo
4	a playing card in the minor suit that has one or more red rhombuses on it	1	n	diamond lead

1.25 end (86 compound types)

Rated compound: *end user*

wnSense	WordNet description	types	class	example
1	either extremity of something that has length	49	n	end tent
2	the point in time at which something ends	16	n	end product
3	the final stage or concluding parts of an event or occurrence)	16	n	end game
4	the state of affairs that a plan is intended to achieve and that (when achieved) terminates behavior intended to achieve it	5	n	end objective

Notes:
Very many mishits due to *in the end* and similar constructions (e.g., *end families* resolves to *In the end families ...*). For the first 3 WordNet senses, the decision

between BE/IN proofed difficult. Decided to go with BE for wnSense 1, while for WordNet sense 2 IN was used (except 1 usage of BE for *end date*). For WordNet sense 3, both were used (cf. BE for *end section* vs. IN for *end game*). Due to both factors, coding this family took forever and almost every string was manually checked in the BNC.

1.26 engine (54 compound types)

Rated compound: *engine room*

wnSense	WordNet description	types	class	example
1	motor that converts thermal energy to mechanical work	52	n	engine mounting
3	a wheeled vehicle consisting of a self-propelled engine that is used to draw trains along railway tracks	2	n	engine driver

Notes:
Very clear differentiation between HAVE2/FOR, cf. e.g. *engine size* vs. *engine oil*.

1.27 eye (43 compound types)

Rated compound: *eye candy*

wnSense	WordNet description	types	class	example
1	the organ of sight	43	n	eye patch

Notes:
Eye witness coded as ABOUT, because all the other relations did not fit, and neither VERB nor IDIOM were really appropriate either.

1.28 face (20 compound types)

Rated compound: *face value*

wnSense	WordNet description	types	class	example
1	the front of the human head from the forehead to the chin and ear to ear	11	n	face cream
8	the side upon which the use of a thing depends (usually the most prominent surface of an object)	9	n	face sheet

1.29 fashion (45 compound types)

Rated compound: *fashion plate*

wnSense	WordNet description	types	class	example
3	the latest and most admired style in clothes and cosmetics and behavior	45	n	fashion trend

Notes:
Only WordNet senses 3 and 4 occur in our data. However, because 4 ('consumer goods (especially clothing) in the current mode') and 3 were mostly indistinguishable in the compounds, they were collapsed into 3.

1.30 fine (1 compound types)

Rated compound: *fine line*

wnSense	WordNet description	types	class	example
1	minutely precise especially in differences in meaning	1	adj	fine line

1.31 firing (compound types)

Rated compound: *firing line*

wnSense	WordNet description	types	class	example
1	the act of firing weapons or artillery at an enemy	14	n	firing pattern
3	the act of setting something on fire	4	n	firing process

1.32 flea (6 compound types)

Rated compound: *flea market*

wnSense	WordNet description	types	class	example
1	any wingless bloodsucking parasitic insect noted for ability to leap	6	n	flea bite

1.33 front (5 compound types)

Rated compound: *front runner*

wnSense	WordNet description	types	class	example
1	the side that is forward or prominent	5	n	front entrance

1.34 game (60 compound types)

Rated compound: *game plan*

wnSense	WordNet description	types	class	example
1	a contest with rules to determine a winner	17	n	game theory
2	a single play of a sport or other contest	5	n	game teacher
3	an amusement or pastime	13	n	game experience
4	animal hunted for food or sport	21	n	game bird
8	a secret scheme to do something (especially something underhand or illegal))	1	n	game plan
9	the game equipment needed in order to play a particular game	1	n	game fair
12	[proper name]	1	n	game stock

Notes:
WordNet sense 12 manually added (shares by a company named Game). Used WordNet Sense 1 as super-set in cases of doubt; WordNet senses 1-3 not always clearly distinguishable; WordNet Sense 2 used for physical education/games involving sports in school etc.
Mistakes:
The coding for *game stock* is wrong, as the BNC context makes it clear that Word-Net sense 4 is meant. This makes the added sense 12 superfluous.

1.35 gold (102 compound types)

Rated compound: *gold mine*

wnSense	WordNet description	types	class	example
1	coins made of gold	2	n	gold stater
2	a deep yellow color	38	n	gold embroidery
3	a soft yellow malleable ductile (trivalent and univalent) metallic element; occurs mainly as nuggets in rocks and alluvial deposits; does not react with most chemicals but is attacked by chlorine and aqua regia	54	n	gold mine
5	something likened to the metal in brightness or preciousness or superiority etc.	5	n	gold card
6	[gold medal/medallist]	3	n	gold winner

Notes:
Introduced WordNet Sense 6 for gold medal/medallist, in analogy to the WordNet entry for *silver*.

1.36 graduate (9 compound types)

Rated compound: *graduate student*

wnSense	WordNet description	types	class	example
1	a person who has received a degree from a school (high school or college or university)	9	n	graduate association

1.37 grandfather (1 compound types)

Rated compound: *grandfather clock*

wnSense	WordNet description	types	class	example
1	the father of your father or mother	1	n	grandfather clock

1.38 graveyard (1 compound types)

Rated compound: *graveyard shift*

wnSense	WordNet description	types	class	example
1	a tract of land used for burials	1	n	graveyard shift

1.39 gravy (4 compound types)

Rated compound: *gravy train.*

wnSense	WordNet description	types	class	example
1	a sauce made by adding stock, flour, or other ingredients to the juice and fat that drips from cooking meats	4	n	gravy bowl

Notes:
Used WordNet sense 1 for *gravy* in *gravy train*, with the relation IDIOM. Note, though, that WordNet gives WordNet sense 3, 'a sudden happening that brings good fortune (as a sudden opportunity to make money)', which might actually be related to its usage in the idiom. The OED establishes an explicit link between a somehow related sense and *gravy train*: 'd. Money easily acquired; an unearned or unexpected bonus; a tip. Hence to ride (board) the gravy train (or boat), to obtain easy financial success. slang (orig. U.S.).'

1.40 ground (84 compound types)

Rated compound: *ground floor.*

wnSense	WordNet description	types	class	example
1	the solid part of the earth's surface	71	n	ground game
4	a relation that provides the foundation for something	11	n	ground rule
5	a position to be won or defended in battle (or as if in battle)	1	n	ground threat
9	a connection between an electrical device and a large conducting body, such as the earth (which is taken to be at zero voltage)	1	n	ground plane

Notes:
Full alignment of WordNet sense 4 and BE.

1.41 guilt (5 compound types)

Rated compound: *guilt trip.*

wnSense	WordNet description	types	class	example
2	remorse caused by feeling responsible for some offense	5	n	guilt complex

1.42 head (compound types)

Rated compound: *head teacher.*

wnSense	WordNet description	types	class	example
1	the upper part of the human body or the front part of the body in animals; contains the face and brains	36	n	head gear
4	a person who is in charge	24	n	head servant
7	the top of something	19	n	head stone
9	(grammar) the word in a grammatical constituent that plays the same grammatical role as the whole constituent	2	n	head word
21	forward movement	1	n	head way
24	a line of text serving to indicate what the passage below it is about)	1	n	head line
27	(computer science) a tiny electromagnetic coil and metal pole used to write and read magnetic patterns on a disk	1	n	head arm
34		2	n	head start

Notes:
WordNet sense 21 contains coded compound as synonym. WordNet sense 34 added for *head start* and *head wind.* This group was cumbersome to do, WordNet sense 4 was also used for non-humans (e.g. *head quarter*). WordNet sense 7 for consistency always linked to IN (except for *head string*, coded as BE). As the numbers show, some very small groups with very specific WordNet senses are included.

1.43 health (112 compound types)

Rated compound: *health insurance*

wnSense	WordNet description	types	class	example
1	a healthy state of wellbeing free from disease	112	n	health sector

Notes:

No attempt was made to distinguish between the 2 available WordNet senses (*a healthy state of wellbeing free from disease* vs. *the general condition of body and mind*). This group contained many ABOUT/FOR relations (e.g. *health column* and *health authority*). While mainly unproblematic to code, some could be coded either way, e.g. *health education*.

1.44 human (1 compound types)

Rated compound: *human being*

wnSense	WordNet description	types	class	example
3	relating to a person	1	adj	human being

Notes:

WordNet sense 3 was chosen because the illustrating example fits (*"the experiment was conducted on 6 monkeys and 2 human subjects"*). The best fitting WordNet pointer is the one for the noun-sense. As the whole constituent family contains just one member, this decision does not matter here, anyways.

1.45 interest (25 compound types)

Rated compound: *interest rate*

wnSense	WordNet description	types	class	example
1	a sense of concern with and curiosity about someone or something	9	n	interest span
4	a fixed charge for borrowing money; usually a percentage of the amount borrowed	16	n	interest rate

1.46 ivory (11 compound types)

Rated compound: *ivory tower*

wnSense	WordNet description	types	class	example
1	a hard smooth ivory colored dentine that makes up most of the tusks of elephants and walruses	9	n	ivory carver
2	a shade of white the color of bleached bones	2	n	ivory wall

1.47 kangaroo (3 compound types)

Rated compound: *kangaroo court*

wnSense	WordNet description	types	class	example
1	any of several herbivorous leaping marsupials of Australia and New Guinea having large powerful hind legs and a long thick tail)	3	n	kangaroo skin

1.48 law (54 compound types)

Rated compound: *law firm*

wnSense	WordNet description	types	class	example
1	the collection of rules imposed by authority	53	n	law student
4	a generalization that describes recurring facts or events in nature	1	n	law table

Notes:

In the BNC, *law table* refers to the biblical tables of law. While the WordNet sense 4 does not match this exactly, it is better than any alternative lest covering it with WordNet sense 1, too. WordNet sense 1 has *jurisprudence* as a collocate, and the coded compounds all refer to worldly law. No attempt was made to distinguish between WordNet sense 1 and other, closely related senses, e.g. WordNet sense 6 ('the learned profession that is mastered by graduate study in a law school and that is responsible for the judicial system').

1.49 lip (6 compound types)

Rated compound: *lip service*

wnSense	WordNet description	types	class	example
1	either of two fleshy folds of tissue that surround the mouth and play a role in speaking	6	n	lip mike

1.50 lotus (8 compound types)

Rated compound: *lotus position*

wnSense	WordNet description	types	class	example
1	native to eastern Asia; widely cultivated for its large pink or white flowers	6	n	lotus pond
4	[brand name]	2	n	lotus product

Notes:
Introduced WordNet sense 4 to cover the brand name usage in the BNC (either for the racing team or for the software company). The car name *Lotus Elan* and the construction *Lotus name* where both classified as non-compounds. For *Lotus Elan*, this parallels the discussion of *the opera 'Carmen'* in Huddleston, Pullum, et al. (2002: 447, section 14.2).

1.51 mailing (3 compound types)

Rated compound: *mailing list*

wnSense	WordNet description	types	class	example
2	the transmission of a letter	3	n	mailing label

1.52 melting (10 compound types)

Rated compound: *melting pot*

wnSense	WordNet description	types	class	example
1	the process whereby heat changes something from a solid to a liquid	10	n	melting point

Notes:
Some members of this group could have been classified with the adjectival Word-Net sense (*melting frost/glacier/ice/wax*). This was not done, among other things because the relational coding already singles out this group.

1.53 memory (48 compound types)

Rated compound: *memory lane*

wnSense	WordNet description	types	class	example
1	something that is remembered	7	n	memory trace
2	the cognitive processes whereby past experience is remembered	19	n	memory span
3	the power of retaining and recalling past experience	2	n	memory drum
4	an electronic memory device	19	n	memory kernel
5	the area of cognitive psychology that studies memory processes	1	n	memory department

1.54 monkey (10 compound types)

Rated compound: *monkey business*

wnSense	WordNet description	types	class	example
1	any of various long-tailed primates (excluding the prosimians)	10	n	monkey wrench

1.55 nest (6 compound types)

Rated compound: *nest egg*

wnSense	WordNet description	types	class	example
1	a structure in which animals lay eggs or give birth to their young	6	n	nest area

1.56 night (116 compound types)

Rated compound: *night owl*

wnSense	WordNet description	types	class	example
1	the time after sunset and before sunrise while it is dark outside	116	n	night visitor

Notes:
Decided to only use WordNet sense 1, though WordNet provides a number of further senses. However, these are semantically very close to WordNet sense one and did not allow one any principled decisions between the senses. Noted a number of combinations that serve as or a contained in titles (e.g., all 3 *night kitchen* occurrences in the BNC are either from *In the night kitchen*, the title of a book by Maurice Sendak, or the name of a theater group he has).

1.57 number (24 compound types)

Rated compound: *number crunching*

wnSense	WordNet description	types	class	example
2	the property possessed by a sum or total or indefinite quantity of units or individuals	20	n	number theory
5	a symbol used to represent a number	3	n	number pad
13	[(Bible) Book of Numbers]	1	n	numbers story

Notes:
Added WordNet sense 13.

1.58 panda (2 compound types)

Rated compound: *panda car*

wnSense	WordNet description	types	class	example
1	large black-and-white herbivorous mammal of bamboo forests of China and Tibet; in some classifications considered a member of the bear family or of a separate family Ailuropodidae)	2	n	panda population

1.59 parking (23 compound types)

Rated compound: *parking lot*

wnSense	WordNet description	types	class	example
1	[The placing or leaving of a vehicle or vehicles in a car park or other designated area, at the side of a road, etc. Also: space reserved or used for the parking of motor vehicles (freq. with modifying word)]	23	n	parking bay

Notes:
The 2 noun WordNet sense are both not sufficient (*space in which vehicles can be parked* and *the act of maneuvering a vehicle into a location where it can be left temporarily*). The single sense for parking used instead is a verbatim copy of the OED entry parking 4.a.

1.60 pecking (1 compound types)

Rated compound: *pecking order*

wnSense	WordNet description	types	class	example
1	[The action of striking or picking up with the beak; an instance of this.]	1	n	pecking order

Notes:
There is no WordNet entry for the noun *pecking*. The description here corresponds to OED pecking, n.[1], 1.

1.61 polo (10 compound types)

Rated compound: *polo shirt*

wnSense	WordNet description	types	class	example
2	a game similar to field hockey but played on horseback using long-handled mallets and a wooden ball	10	n	polo match

Notes:
WordNet only contains one other sense for *polo*, designating Marco Polo. *Polo shirt* and *polo neck* were both classified as FOR and no new sense was added. Note that the OED has a separate entry 'polo n.[1] 3. b. A polo neck sweater or shirt; (also) a polo shirt.'

1.62 public (7 compound types)

Rated compound: *public service*

wnSense	WordNet description	types	class	example
1	people in general considered as a whole	7	n	public access

1.63 radio (106 compound types)

Rated compound: *radio station*

wnSense	WordNet description	types	class	example
1	medium for communication	27	n	radio telescope
2	an electronic receiver that detects and demodulates and amplifies transmitted signals	9	n	radio set
3	a communication system based on broadcasting electromagnetic waves	70	n	radio transmission

Notes:

This group contained many instances that could in principle be classified with a number of relations, e.g. *radio news*: news for the radio, news the radio has, news in the radio, news from the radio, or *radio preacher*, which allows all of these but also USE (preacher who uses the radio). Went by plausibility and group consistency.

1.64 rat (22 compound types)

Rated compound: *rat race, rat run*

wnSense	WordNet description	types	class	example
1	any of various long-tailed rodents similar to but larger than a mouse	21	n	rat poison
6	[name of a nucleotide/amino-acid sequence]	1	n	RAT part

Notes:

WordNet sense 6 added. Both *rat race* and *rat run* classed as HAVE2, while in Bell & Schäfer (2013) *rat race* was NONE.

1.65 research (160 compound types)

Rated compound: *research project*

wnSense	WordNet description	types	class	example
1	systematic investigation to establish facts	160	n	research training

Notes:

The 2 noun WordNet senses in WordNet were deemed identical (*systematic investigation to establish facts* and *a search for knowledge*).

1.66 rocket (14 compound types)

Rated compound: *rocket science*

wnSense	WordNet description	types	class	example
1	any vehicle self-propelled by a rocket engine	14	n	rocket launcher

Notes:

No attempt was made to distinguish the first 2 WordNet senses, e.g. the one given above and the second one, *a jet engine containing its own propellant and driven by reaction propulsion.*

1.67 rock (99 compound types)

Rated compound: *rock bottom*

wnSense	WordNet description	types	class	example
1	a lump or mass of hard consolidated mineral matter	11	n	rock field
2	material consisting of the aggregate of minerals like those making up the Earth's crust	45	n	rock arch
6	a genre of popular music originating in the 1950s; a blend of black rhythm-and-blues with white country-and-western	43	n	rock tour

Notes:
Rock bottom is coded as HAVE2, while in Bell & Schäfer (2013) it was coded as BE.

1.68 role (8 compound types)

Rated compound: *role model*

wnSense	WordNet description	types	class	example
1	the actions and activities assigned to or required or expected of a person or group	7	n	role reversal
2	an actor's portrayal of someone in a play	1	n	role play

Notes:
This group contained many false hits, e.g. reduced relative clauses like CRS 1842 *the role parents are allowed to play.*

1.69 rush (5 compound types)

Rated compound: *rush hour*

wnSense	WordNet description	types	class	example
1	the act of moving hurriedly and in a careless manner	2	n	rush job
3	grasslike plants growing in wet places and having cylindrical often hollow stems	2	n	rush seat
4	[proper name]	1	n	Rush concert

WordNet sense 4 used generically for the proper name *Rush* (instead of the Word-Net proper name use for Benjamin Rush, 1745-1813).

1.70 sacred (1 compound types)

Rated compound: *sacred cow*

wnSense	WordNet description	types	class	example
1	made or declared or believed to be holy; devoted to a deity or some religious ceremony or use	1	adj	sacred cow

1.71 search (56 compound types)

Rated compound: *search engine*

wnSense	WordNet description	types	class	example
1	the activity of looking thoroughly in order to find something or someone	26	n	search consultant
3	an operation that determines whether one or more of a set of items has a specified property	30	n	search window

1.72 shrinking (1 compound types)

Rated compound: *shrinking violet*

wnSense	WordNet description	types	class	example
1	process or result of becoming less or smaller	1	n	shrinking violet

1.73 silver (138 compound types)

Rated compound: *silver spoon, silver screen, silver bullet*

wnSense	WordNet description	types	class	example
1	a soft white precious univalent metallic element having the highest electrical and thermal conductivity of any metal; occurs in argentite and in free form; used in coins and jewelry and tableware and photography	43	n	silver bar
2	coins made of silver	5	n	silver dollar

3	a light shade of grey	77	n	silver mist
4	silverware eating utensils	12	n	silver plate
5	a trophy made of silver (or having the appearance of silver) that is usually awarded for winning second place in a competition	1	n	silver medal

Note:

WordNet sense 5 contains the compound type in its description: *silver medal, silver (a trophy made of silver (or having the appearance of silver) that is usually awarded for winning second place in a competition)*. Compounds with *silver* with WordNet senses 4 and 2 also allow WordNet sense 1. WordNet sense 3 used for everything that was not real silver.

1.74 sitting (3 compound types)

Rated compound: *sitting duck*

wnSense	WordNet description	types	class	example
3	the act of assuming or maintaining a seated position	3	n	sitting room

1.75 smoking (6 compound types)

Rated compounds: *smoking gun, smoking jacket*

wnSense	WordNet description	types	class	example
1	the act of smoking tobacco or other substances	5	n	smoking car
5	emitting smoke in great volume	1	adj	smoking gun

1.76 snail (3 compound types)

Rated compound: *snail mail*

wnSense	WordNet description	types	class	example
1	freshwater or marine or terrestrial gastropod mollusk usually having an external enclosing spiral shell	3	n	snail body

1.77 snake (13 compound types)

Rated compound: *snake oil*

wnSense	WordNet description	types	class	example
1	limbless scaly elongate reptile; some are venomous	8	n	snake charmer
5	something long, thin, and flexible that resembles a snake	5	n	snake cable

Notes:
Perfect example of different WordNet senses capturing a metaphoric shift.

1.78 speed (36 compound types)

Rated compound: *speed limit*

wnSense	WordNet description	types	class	example
1	distance travelled per unit time	36	n	speed indicator

Notes:
No attempt was made to differentiate the coded WordNet sense from the following 2 (*a rate (usually rapid) at which something happens* and *changing location rapidly*).

1.79 spelling (11 compound types)

Rated compound: *spelling bee*

wnSense	WordNet description	types	class	example
1	forming words with letters according to the principles underlying accepted usage	11	n	spelling mistake

1.80 spinning (1 compound types)

Rated compound: *spinning jenny*

wnSense	WordNet description	types	class	example
1	creating thread	1	n	spinning jenny

1.81 swan (10 compound types)

Rated compound: *swan song*

wnSense	WordNet description	types	class	example
1	stately heavy-bodied aquatic bird with very long neck and usually white plumage as adult	10	n	swan population

1.82 swimming (19 compound types)

Rated compound: *swimming pool*

wnSense	WordNet description	types	class	example
1	the act of swimming	19	n	swimming cap

1.83 think (2 compound types)

Rated compound: *think tank*

wnSense	WordNet description	types	class	example
1	an instance of deliberate thinking	2	n	think sign

Notes:

All other WordNet senses of *think* are verb-senses. Both compounds (*think tank* and *think sign*) can also plausibly be analyzed as VN compounds.

1.84 video (99 compound types)

Rated compound: *video game*

wnSense	WordNet description	types	class	example
1	the visible part of a television transmission	20	n	video cable
2	a recording of both the visual and audible components (especially one containing a recording of a movie or television program)	69	n	video department
3	(computer science) the appearance of text and graphics on a video display	10	n	video chip

Notes:

WordNet sense 4 was not used, unclear in how far it could be applied. Often, it was difficult to decide on the senses or multiple usages were possible. In the latter case, the most plausible one was chosen.

1.85 web (3 compound types)

Rated compound: *web site*

wnSense	WordNet description	types	class	example
5	computer network consisting of a collection of internet sites that offer text and graphics and sound and animation resources through the hypertext transfer protocol	1	n	web site
6	a fabric (especially a fabric in the process of being woven	2	n	web width

1.86 zebra (3 compound types)

Rated compound: *zebra crossing*

wnSense	WordNet description	types	class	example
1	any of several fleet black-and-white striped African equines	3	n	zebra tarantula

2 N2 families

2.1 account (92 compound types)

Rated compound: *bank account*

wnSense	WordNet description	types	class	example
1	a record or narrative description of past events	10	n	insider account
3	a formal contractual relationship established to provide for regular banking or brokerage or business services	61	n	bank account
4	a statement that makes something comprehensible by describing the relevant structure or operation or circumstances etc.	6	n	materialist account
7	a statement of recent transactions and the resulting balance	14	n	parish account
9	an itemized statement of money owed for goods shipped or services rendered	1	n	farm account

Notes:
No differentiation between the first 2 WordNet senses ('history, account, chronicle, story (a record or narrative description of past events)' vs. 'report, news report, story, account, write up (a short account of the news)'). Both were coded as WordNet sense 1. WordNet sense 3 extended to cover computer related usages such as *mail account* and *vms account* (vms = the proprietary Virtual Memory System operating system). WordNet sense 3 comes with clear cases of FOR vs. HAVE2, e.g. *savings account* and *Virgin account* (where virgin= the record company), but many cases could be either, e.g. *government account* or *client account*. Went with plausibility: HAVE2 if it is not per se or not likely per se a specific

kind of account. Highly specialized types of accounts/specialist banking terms classified with IDIOM (e.g. *trust account* or *nostro account*).

2.2 aunt (1 compound types)

Rated compound: *agony aunt*

wnSense	WordNet description	types	class	example
1	intense feelings of suffering; acute mental or physical pain	1	n	agony aunt

2.3 bee (7 compound types)

Rated compound: *spelling bee*

wnSense	WordNet description	types	class	example
1	any of numerous hairy-bodied insects including social and solitary species	6	n	bumble bee
2	a social gathering to carry out some communal task or to hold competitions	1	n	spelling bee

2.4 being (3 compound types)

Rated compound: *human being*

wnSense	WordNet description	types	class	example
1	the state or fact of existing	1	n	well being
2	a living thing that has (or can develop) the ability to act or function independently	2	n	half being

2.5 bottom (19 compound types)

Rated compound: *rock bottom*

wnSense	WordNet description	types	class	example
1	the lower side of anything	5	n	box bottom
2	the lowest part of anything	14	n	sea bottom

Notes:

Rock bottom coded as BE in Bell & Schäfer (2013), here coded as HAVE2.

2.6 bullet (5 compound types)

Rated compound: *silver bullet*

wnSense	WordNet description	types	class	example
1	a projectile that is fired from a gun	5	n	dumdum bullet

2.7 business (262 compound types)

Rated compound: *monkey business*

wnSense	WordNet description	types	class	example
1	a commercial or industrial enterprise and the people who constitute it	255	n	textile business
2	the activity of providing goods and services involving financial and commercial and industrial aspects	2	n	repeat business
5	an immediate objective	3	n	pound business
7	business concerns collectively	2	n	winter business

Notes:
WordNet sense 5 is illustrated with "gossip was the main business of the evening".
Assigning this sense relied in this case more on this quote, a more appropriate
paraphrase of *business* here would simply be 'activity/matter'.

2.8 candy (4 compound types)

Rated compound: *eye candy*

wnSense	WordNet description	types	class	example
1	a rich sweet made of flavored sugar and often combined with fruit or nuts	4	n	cotton candy

2.9 card (97 compound types)

Rated compound: *credit card*

wnSense	WordNet description	types	class	example
1	one of a set of small pieces of stiff paper marked in various ways and used for playing games or for telling fortunes	16	n	tarot card
2	a card certifying the identity of the bearer	24	n	security card
3	a rectangular piece of stiff paper used to send messages (may have printed greetings or pictures)	9	n	valentine card
4	thin cardboard, usually rectangular	31	n	vaccination card
7	a printed or written greeting that is left to indicate that you have visited)	4	n	business card

8	(golf) a record of scores (as in golf)	2	n	golf card
9	a list of dishes available at a restaurant	1	n	menu card
11	a printed circuit that can be inserted into expansion slots in a computer to increase the computer's capabilities	10	n	video card

2.10 car (100 compound types)

Rated compound: *panda car*

wnSense	WordNet description	types	class	example
1	a motor vehicle with four wheels; usually propelled by an internal combustion engine	80	n	dream car
2	a wheeled vehicle adapted to the rails of railroad	19	n	freight car
5	a conveyance for passengers or freight on a cable railway	1	n	cable car

WordNet sense 5 has *cable car* as collocate.

2.11 centre (268 compound types)

Rated compound: *call centre*

wnSense	WordNet description	types	class	example
2	an area that is approximately central within some larger region	11	n	village centre

3	a point equidistant from the ends of a line or the extremities of a figure	10	n	wheel centre
4	a place where some particular activity is concentrated	19	n	growth centre
8	a cluster of nerve cells governing a specific bodily process)	3	n	pleasure centre
9	a building dedicated to a particular activity	225	n	trade centre

Notes:

WordNet has 2 different entries for the UK/US spelling variants. Here, the *centre* version is used. Note the distinction between WordNet sense 4 and 9, where without context often both senses are OK. That is, *Africa centre* refers to a building (in the BNC, it is used for the Africa centre in London), whereas *banking centre* usually refers to larger places like towns (e.g. London). However, depending on context, a construal with the respective other WordNet sense should be possible, too.

2.12 change (126 compound types)

Rated compound: *climate change*

wnSense	WordNet description	types	class	example
1	an event that occurs when something passes from one state or phase to another	99	n	proportion change
3	the action of changing something	26	n	name change
11	[gear shift]		n	column change

Notes:

Added sense 11. Coding of WordNet senses 1 and 3 was linked to whether something changed or was exchanged. In the former case, the coded relation is IN (*script changes*: relation IN, WordNet sense 1), in the latter case, the relation is VERB (*tyre change*, WordNet sense 3 and relation VERB). Because of the many non-compounds, this group required manual look-up of almost every combination.

2.13 clay (4 compound types)

Rated compound: *china clay*

wnSense	WordNet description	types	class	example
1	a very fine-grained soil that is plastic when moist but hard when fired	4	n	pipe clay

2.14 clock (37 compound types)

Rated compound: *grandfather clock*

wnSense	WordNet description	types	class	example
1	a timepiece that shows the time of day	36	n	cuckoo clock
2	[A trivial name for the pappus of the dandelion or similar composite flower.]	1	n	dandelion clock

Notes:

Added sense 2. Description taken from the OED entry clock, n[1], 8.: "A trivial name for the pappus of the dandelion or similar composite flower. [So called from the child's play of blowing away the feathered seeds to find 'what o'clock it is'.]" Some clocks could be either HAVE2 or FOR; went with intuition (based on whether it results in a specific type or not, cf. *town clock* vs. *car clock*) and BNC contexts.

2.15 course (101 compound types)

Rated compound: *crash course*

wnSense	WordNet description	types	class	example
1	education imparted in a series of lessons or meetings	68	n	zoology
3	general line of orientation	1	n	compass course
5	a line or route along which something travels or moves	8	n	zigzag course
7	part of a meal served at one time	9	n	vegetable course
8	(construction) a layer of masonry	1	n	damp course
9	facility consisting of a circumscribed area of land or water laid out for a sport	14	n	mountain course

Notes:

Some combinations with WordNet sense 1 which were coded as ABOUT could also be classified as FOR (e.g. *fitness course*), but generally easily distinguishable. Did not attempt to distinguish sense 1 from sense 6, 'a body of students who are taught together', similarly for sense 5 and 4, 'a mode of action'.

2.16 court (83 compound types)

Rated compound: *kangaroo court*

wnSense	WordNet description	types	class	example
1	an assembly (including one or more judges) to conduct judicial business	15	n	Singapore court
4	a specially marked horizontal area within which a game is played	6	n	squash court
6	the family and retinue of a sovereign or prince	6	n	renaissance court
7	a tribunal that is presided over by a magistrate or by one or more judges who administer justice according to the laws	43	n	orphan court
8	the residence of a sovereign or nobleman	1	n	Fire court
9	an area wholly or partly surrounded by walls or buildings	12	n	prison court

2.17 cow (10 compound types)

Rated compound: *cash cow*

wnSense	WordNet description	types	class	example
2	mature female of mammals of which the male is called 'bull'	10	n	suckler cow

2.18 crossing (21 compound types)

Rated compound: *zebra crossing*

wnSense	WordNet description	types	class	example
1	traveling across	8	n	ferry crossing
3	a point where two lines (paths or arcs etc.) intersect	1	n	zero crossing
5	a path (often marked) where something (as a street or railroad) can be crossed to get from one side to the other	12	n	pedestrian crossing

2.19 crunching (1 compound types)

Rated compound: *number crunching*

wnSense	WordNet description	types	class	example
1	[the action of crunching]	1	n	number crunching

Notes:
Added sense 1. There is no WordNet entry for the noun *crunching*.

2.20 dress (25 compound types)

Rated compound: *cocktail dress*

wnSense	WordNet description	types	class	example
1	a one-piece garment for a woman; has skirt and bodice	21	n	cotton dress
2	clothing of a distinctive style or for a particular occasion	3	n	camouflage dress
3	clothing in general	1	n	head dress

2.21 duck (7 compound types)

Rated compound: *sitting duck*

wnSense	WordNet description	types	class	example
1	small wild or domesticated web-footed broad-billed swimming bird usually having a depressed body and short legs	6	n	plastic duck
3	flesh of a duck (domestic or wild)	1	n	peking duck

2.22 edge (57 compound types)

Rated compound: *cutting edge*

wnSense	WordNet description	types	class	example
1	the boundary of a surface	46	n	mirror edge
2	a line determining the limits of an area	2	n	city edge
3	a sharp side formed by the intersection of two surfaces of an object	9	n	sword edge

Notes:
WordNet sense 6 ('the outside limit of an object or area or surface; a place farthest away from the center of something') was not used, *leaf edge* classified with WordNet sense 1.

2.23 egg (14 compound types)

Rated compound: *nest egg*

wnSense	WordNet description	types	class	example
1	animal reproductive body consisting of an ovum or embryo together with nutritive and protective envelopes; especially the thin-shelled reproductive body laid by e.g. female birds	14	n	ostrich egg

2.24 engine (43 compound types)

Rated compound: *search engine*

wnSense	WordNet description	types	class	example
1	motor that converts thermal energy to mechanical work	35	n	combustion engine
2	something used to achieve a purpose	5	n	search engine
3	a wheeled vehicle consisting of a self-propelled engine that is used to draw trains along railway tracks	2	n	express engine
4	an instrument or machine that is used in warfare, such as a battering ram, catapult, artillery piece, etc.	1	n	siege engine

2.25 firm (69 compound types)

Rated compound: *law firm*

wnSense	WordNet description	types	class	example
1	the members of a business organization that owns or operates one or more establishments	69	n	mystery firm

Notes:

Security firm in the BNC is consistently used to refer to businesses providing private security, whereas *securities firm* is used to refer to banking businesses dealing in securities, that is, *securities* occurs here in its certificate of ownership sense.

2.26 floor (110 compound types)

Rated compound: *ground floor*

wnSense	WordNet description	types	class	example
1	the inside lower horizontal surface (as of a room, hallway, tent, or other structure)	79	n	wagon floor
2	a structure consisting of a room or set of rooms at a single position along a vertical scale	8	n	executive floor
4	the ground on which people and animals move about	4	n	jungle floor
5	the bottom surface of any lake or other body of water	4	n	ocean floor
6	the lower inside surface of any hollow structure	5	n	cavern floor

| 9 | the legislative hall where members debate and vote and conduct other business | 4 | n | senate floor |
| 10 | a large room in a exchange where the trading is done | 6 | n | trading floor |

Notes:
WordNet sense 10 has *trading floor* as collocate.

2.27 form (163 compound types)

Rated compound: *application form*

wnSense	WordNet description	types	class	example
1	the phonological or orthographic sound or appearance of a word that can be used to describe or identify something	11	n	root form
2	a category of things distinguished by some common characteristic or quality	6	n	life form
3	a perceptual structure	10	n	paper form
4	any spatial attributes (especially as defined by outline)	30	n	leaf form
5	alternative names for the body of a human being	7	n	dwarf form
6	the spatial arrangement of something as distinct from its substance	5	n	tensor form
8	a printed document with spaces in which to write	76	n	transfer form

10	an arrangement of the elements in a composition or discourse	14	n	verse form
12	(physical chemistry) a distinct state of matter in a system; matter that is identical in chemical composition and physical state and separated from other material by the phase boundary	3	n	compound form
14	an ability to perform well	1	n	fighting form

2.28 game (155 compound types)

Rated compound: *blame game, video game*

wnSense	WordNet description	types	class	example
2	a single play of a sport or other contest	67	n	relegation game
3	an amusement or pastime	60	n	war game
9	the game equipment needed in order to play a particular game	1	n	Simon game
10	your occupation or line of work	27	n	subsidy game

Notes:

Republic game, Newcastle game etc.: construal of these depends on the point of view: if Republic is your opponent, HAVE1 seems natural, if it refers to a game by your team, HAVE2 seems more appropriate. In the BNC, both usages occur. Decided to go with HAVE2 consistently. Note that the distribution of word senses used is interestingly different from the ones in the N1 family.

2.29 gun (40 compound types)

Rated compound: *smoking gun*

wnSense	WordNet description	types	class	example
1	a weapon that discharges a missile at high velocity (especially from a metal tube or barrel)	36	n	machine gun
3	a person who shoots a gun (as regards their ability)	1	n	advertising gun
7	the discharge of a firearm as signal or as a salute in military ceremonies	3	n	start gun

Notes:
WordNet senses 2, 'large but transportable armament', and 5, 'a hand-operated pump that resembles a pistol; forces grease into parts of a machine', where not distinguished, instead 1 was used.

2.30 hour (32 compound types)

Rated compound: *rush hour*

wnSense	WordNet description	types	class	example
1	a period of time equal to 1/24th of a day	31	n	peak hour
4	[for one hour]	1	n	kilowatt hour

Notes:
Added sense 4 for *kilowatt hour.*

2.31 insurance (9 compound types)

Rated compound: *health insurance*

wnSense	WordNet description	types	class	example
1	promise of reimbursement in the case of loss; paid to people or companies so concerned about hazards that they have made prepayments to an insurance company	9	n	fire insurance

2.32 jacket (25 compound types)

Rated compound: *smoking jacket*

wnSense	WordNet description	types	class	example
1	a short coat	22	n	cashmere jacket
2	an outer wrapping or casing	2	n	book jacket
5	the tough metal shell casing for certain kinds of ammunition	1	n	steam jacket

Notes:
A *steam jacket* is not a casing for certain kinds of ammunition, but it is usually a tough metal shell casing, so WordNet sense 5 was used.

2.33 jenny (1 compound types)

Rated compound: *spinning jenny*

wnSense	WordNet description	types	class	example
1	[personal name]	1	n	spinning jenny

Notes:

WordNet sense 1 refers to a specific person (Jenny, William Le Baron Jenny), here used for Jenny as a proper name.

2.34 lane (22 compound types)

Rated compound: *memory lane*

wnSense	WordNet description	types	class	example
1	a narrow way or road	11	n	country lane
2	a well-defined track or path; for e.g. swimmers or lines of traffic	11	n	emergency lane

2.35 limit (52 compound types)

Rated compound: *speed limit*

wnSense	WordNet description	types	class	example
1	the greatest possible degree of something	49	n	confidence limit
4	the boundary of a specific area	3	n	city limit

Notes:

Only the above 2 WordNet senses were used; all the other noun senses are very close to sense 1.

2.36 line (363 compound types)

Rated compounds: *fine line, firing line*

wnSense	WordNet description	types	class	example
1	a formation of people or things one beside another	3	n	picket line
2	a mark that is long relative to its width	14	n	chalk line
3	a formation of people or things one behind another	9	n	coffee line
4	a length (straight or curved) without breadth or thickness; the trace of a moving point	7	n	regression line
5	text consisting of a row of words written across a page or computer screen	22	n	solo line
7	a fortified position (especially one marking the most forward position of troops)	12	n	enemy line
8	a course of reasoning aimed at demonstrating a truth or falsehood; the methodical process of logical reasoning	19	n	appease-ment line
9	a conductor for transmitting electrical or optical signals or electric power	13	n	telegraph line
10	a connected series of events or actions or developments	3	n	plot line
11	a spatial location defined by a real or imaginary unidimensional extent	87	n	glacier line
12	a slight depression or fold in the smoothness of a surface	7	n	worry line

13	a pipe used to transport liquids or gases	8	n	fuel line
14	the road consisting of railroad track and roadbed	28	n	intercity line
15	a telephone connection	19	n	reception line
16	acting in conformity	1	n	policy line
17	the descendants of one individual	9	n	primate line
18	something (as a cord or rope) that is long and thin and flexible	24	n	trap line
20	in games or sports; a mark indicating positions or bounds of the playing area	10	n	goal line
21	(often plural) a means of communication or access	4	n	distribution line
22	a particular kind of product or merchandise	14	n	profit line
23	a commercial organization serving as a common carrier	13	n	tram line
25	the maximum credit that a customer is allowed	2	n	withdrawal line
26	a succession of notes forming a distinctive sequence	5	n	chorus line
29	a conceptual separation or distinction	23	n	wage line
30	mechanical system in a factory whereby an article is conveyed through sites at which successive operations are performed on it	7	n	canning line

Mistakes:

Birmingham line is misclassified with WordNet sense 10, it ought to be WordNet sense 14. In addition, in its occurrence in the BNC it is part of a complex construction (*London and Birmingham line*) and thus should be n1n2NotCompound:yes.

2.37 list (145 compound types)

Rated compound: *mailing list*

wnSense	WordNet description	types	class	example
1	a database containing an ordered array of items (names or topics)	145	n	waiting list

Notes:

Large numbers of FOR and HAVE1 compounds, e.g. *wedding list* vs. *witness list*. Often, both classifications are possible: *staff list* as list for the staff or as list that has the staff (e.g. list that lists the staff). Heuristic: went for HAVE1 if that interpretation is possible. In cases of doubt, checked against BNC usage.

2.38 lot (10 compound types)

Rated compound: *parking lot*

wnSense	WordNet description	types	class	example
1	(often followed by 'of') a large number or amount or extent	2	n	job lot
2	a parcel of land having fixed boundaries	8	n	studio lot

2.39 mail (13 compound types)

Rated compound: *snail mail*

wnSense	WordNet description	types	class	example
2	the bags of letters and packages that are transported by the postal service	3	n	air mail
4	any particular collection of letters or packages that is delivered	7	n	junk mail
5	(Middle Ages) flexible armor made of interlinked metal rings	2	n	chain mail
6	[newspaper]	1	n	Birmingham mail

Notes:
Added sense 6. Note that *snail mail* is coded here with WordNet sense 2 and the relation USE, in parallel to *air mail*. In the N1 family, it is coded as BE.

2.40 market (245 compound types)

Rated compound: *flea market*

wnSense	WordNet description	types	class	example
1	the world of commercial activity where goods and services are bought and sold	223	n	whisky market
3	a marketplace where groceries are sold	1	n	Com market
4	the securities markets in the aggregate	5	n	bull market
5	an area in a town where a public mercantile establishment is set up	16	n	Monday market

Notes:

No distinction made between WordNet sense 1 and 2 ('the customers for a particular product or service'), all classified as 1.

2.41 mine (22 compound types)

Rated compound: *gold mine*

wnSense	WordNet description	types	class	example
1	excavation in the earth from which ores and minerals are extracted	19	n	diamond mine
2	explosive device that explodes on contact; designed to destroy vehicles or ships or to kill or maim personnel	3	n	land mine

2.42 model (143 compound types)

Rated compound: *role model*

wnSense	WordNet description	types	class	example
1	a hypothetical description of a complex entity or process	16	n	regression model
2	a type of product	25	n	signature model
3	a person who poses for a photographer or painter or sculptor	1	n	life model
4	representation of something (sometimes on a smaller scale)	67	n	wax model
5	something to be imitated	1	n	artist model
6	someone worthy of imitation	1	n	role model

7	a representative form or pattern	25	n	ownership model
8	a woman who wears clothes to display fashions	7	n	agency model

Notes:
WordNet sense 6 has *role model* as collocate.

2.43 nine (1 compound types)

Rated compound: *cloud nine*

wnSense	WordNet description	types	class	example
2	the cardinal number that is the sum of eight and one	1	n	cloud nine

Notes:
First sense in WordNet.

2.44 oil (30 compound types)

Rated compound: *snake oil*

wnSense	WordNet description	types	class	example
1	a slippery or viscous liquid or liquefiable substance not miscible with water	11	n	massage oil
2	oil paint containing pigment that is used by an artist	1	n	landscape oil
3	a dark oil consisting mainly of hydrocarbons	8	n	mineral oil
4	any of a group of liquid edible fats that are obtained from plants	10	n	sesame oil

Notes:
Classified *whale oil* with the vegetable oils.

2.45 order (100 compound types)

Rated compound: *pecking order*

wnSense	WordNet description	types	class	example
1	(often plural) a command given by a superior (e.g., a military or law enforcement officer) that must be obeyed	8	n	draft order
3	established customary state (especially of society)	5	n	gender order
4	logical or comprehensible arrangement of separate elements	18	n	seating order
6	a legally binding command or decision entered on the court record (as if issued by a court or judge)	44	n	restriction order
11	a group of person living under a religious rule	3	n	dervish order
12	(biology) taxonomic group containing one or more families	2	n	primate order
13	a request for something to be made, supplied, or served	20	n	telephone order

Notes:
This group contains very many legal or half-legal terms. Many combinations can in principle be either FOR or HAVE2. For example, *question order* can refer to the ordering the questions have (in one's work for example), or the order for the questions (e.g. at a talk).

2.46 owl (4 compound types)

Rated compound: *night owl*

wnSense	WordNet description	types	class	example
1	nocturnal bird of prey with hawk-like beak and claws and large head with front-facing eyes	4	n	barn owl

2.47 park (49 compound types)

Rated compound: *car park*

wnSense	WordNet description	types	class	example
1	a large area of land preserved in its natural state as public property	4	n	nature park
2	a piece of open land for recreational use in an urban area	25	n	council park
3	a facility in which ball games are played (especially baseball games)	4	n	ball park
5	a lot where cars are parked	6	n	caravan park
7	[an area of land, often on the outskirts of a town, devoted to a particular activity or set of related pursuits]	4	n	science park
8	[used in district names formerly belonging to large estates]	6	n	grove park

Notes:

Added sense 7 and sense 8. Sense 7 corresponds to OED park n. 3.f ("With modifying word: an area of land, often on the outskirts of a town, devoted to a particular activity or set of related pursuits."), sense 8 to OED park 1.d ("Used in the names of suburban districts built on land formerly belonging to large estates, as Holland Park, Tufnell Park, and later in the names of other urban areas, housing estates, etc."). *Ball park* is collocate of WordNet sense 3.

2.48 plan (177 compound types)

Rated compound: *game plan*

wnSense	WordNet description	types	class	example
1	a series of steps to be carried out or goals to be accomplished	142	n	privatisation plan
2	an arrangement scheme	4	n	seating plan
3	scale drawing of a structure	31	n	factory plan

Notes:

Sometimes difficult to differentiate between HAVE2/MAKE2/FOR: an *army plan* is a plan the army has, the *Allon plan* was made by Allon, the *abolition plan* is for abolition; but especially for army etc., all 3 are possible. Person names usually linked with MAKE2, organizations with HAVE2. FOR was used for aims as well as target groups (cf. *recovery plan* vs. *staff plan*).

2.49 plate (82 compound types)

Rated compound: *fashion plate*

wnSense	WordNet description	types	class	example
1	(baseball) base consisting of a rubber slab where the batter stands; it must be touched by a base runner in order to score	1	n	home plate
2	a sheet of metal or wood or glass or plastic	48	n	aluminium plate
3	a full-page illustration (usually on slick paper)	2	n	colour plate
4	dish on which food is served or from which food is eaten	10	n	pie plate
6	a rigid layer of the Earth's crust that is believed to drift slowly	4	n	nazca plate
9	any flat platelike body structure or part	6	n	jaw plate
11	a flat sheet of metal or glass on which a photographic image can be recorded	3	n	printing plate
13	a shallow receptacle for collection in church	2	n	church plate
16	small label	1	n	book plate
17	[River Plate]	1	n	River Plate
18	[licence plate]	4	n	Texas plate

Notes:
Added senses 16, 17, and 18. Sense 18 used for licence plates (*licence plate* itself is contained in this group). Sense 16 and 17 both occur only for one single type. WordNet sense 1 has *home plate* as a collocate, WordNet sense 13 has *collection plate* as collocate.

2.50 pool (43 compound types)

Rated compound: *swimming pool*

wnSense	WordNet description	types	class	example
1	an excavation that is (usually) filled with water	14	n	hotel pool
2	a small lake	8	n	crocodile pool
3	an organization of people or resources that can be shared	20	n	player pool
8	something resembling a pool of liquid	1	n	moon pool

Notes:

WordSense 3 contains senses 4, 'an association of companies for some definite purpose', and 5, 'any communal combination of funds', and also 7, 'the combined stakes of the betters'. The latter 3 were therefore not used. *Moon pool* (OED: n. a shaft open to the sea in the centre of an (esp. oil-drilling) ship, through which equipment can be hoisted.) is coded with WordNet sense 8 and MAKE2 according to the etymology suggested in one of the OED quotations: "1981 'D. Rutherford' Porcupine Basin ii. 30 It was named moon-pool because on calm nights the water under a rig could reflect the moonlight and give the impression of a calm swimming pool."

2.51 position (161 compound types)

Rated compound: *lotus position*

wnSense	WordNet description	types	class	example
1	the particular portion of space occupied by something	55	n	word position
2	a point occupied by troops for tactical reasons	9	n	artillery position
4	the arrangement of the body and its limbs	20	n	lotus position

6	a job in an organization	8	n	manage-ment position
7	the spatial property of a place where or way in which something is situated	7	n	rotor position
9	(in team sports) the role assigned to an individual player	3	n	centre position
10	the act of putting something in a certain place	14	n	stock position
11	a condition or position in which you find yourself	19	n	monopoly position
12	a rationalized mental attitude	21	n	universalist position
14	an item on a list or in a sequence	5	n	pole position

Notes:
Used WordNet sense 10 for financial positions. Did not distinguish between sense 12 and 13 ('an opinion that is held in opposition to another in an argument or dispute').

2.52 potato (3 compound types)

Rated compound: *couch potato*

wnSense	WordNet description	types	class	example
1	an edible tuber native to South America; a staple food of Ireland	2	n	seed potato
3	[a person or character]	1	n	couch potato

Notes:
Added sense 3, cf. OED potato, n. 4. b. colloq. (chiefly humorous). A person or character, esp. of a specified sort (usually with negative or derogatory connotations).

2.53 pot (51 compound types)

Rated compound: *melting pot*

wnSense	WordNet description	types	class	example
1	metal or earthenware cooking vessel that is usually round and deep; often has a handle and lid	46	n	enamel pot
2	a plumbing fixture for defecation and urination	1	n	chamber pot
5	(often followed by 'of') a large number or amount or extent	2	n	place plot
8	a resistor with three terminals, the third being an adjustable center terminal; used to adjust voltages in radios and TV sets	2	n	volume pot

Notes:
Sense 1 contains 2 clearly distinguishable main relations: FOR and MAKE2.

2.54 project (118 compound types)

Rated compound: *research project*

wnSense	WordNet description	types	class	example
1	any piece of work that is undertaken or attempted	118	n	pilot project

Notes:
Used sense 1 without distinguishing it from sense 2, 'a planned undertaking'.

2.55 race (70 compound types)

Rated compound: *rat race*

wnSense	WordNet description	types	class	example
1	any competition	15	n	armament race
2	a contest of speed	41	n	marathon race
3	people who are believed to belong to the same genetic stock	10	n	elf race
6	a canal for a current of water	4	n	mill race

2.56 rate (249 compound types)

Rated compound: *interest rate*

wnSense	WordNet description	types	class	example
1	a magnitude or frequency relative to a time unit	82	n	acceleration rate
2	amount of a charge or payment relative to some basis	70	n	tax rate
4	a quantity or amount or measure considered as a proportion of another quantity or amount or measure	97	n	suicide rate

Notes:
Savings rate is the standard realization of the 2 lemmas, *saving rate* only occurs once in the BNC. WordNet sense 3, ('the relative speed of progress or change') deemed to close to sense 1, no attempt at a differentiation was made.

2.57 reaction (30 compound types)

Rated compound: *chain reaction*

wnSense	WordNet description	types	class	example
1	(chemistry) a process in which one or more substances are changed into others	10	n	fusion reaction
3	a bodily process occurring due to the effect of some antecedent stimulus or agent	8	n	anger reaction
4	(mechanics) the equal and opposite force that is produced when any force is applied to a body	1	n	torque reaction
5	a response that reveals a person's feelings or attitude	11	n	staff reaction

2.58 ring (56 compound types)

Rated compound: *brass ring*

wnSense	WordNet description	types	class	example
2	a toroidal shape	5	n	tree ring
3	a rigid circular band of metal or wood or other material used for holding or fastening or hanging or pulling	19	n	brass ring
4	(chemistry) a chain of atoms in a molecule that forms a closed loop	2	n	benzene ring
5	an association of criminals	2	n	spy ring

7	a platform usually marked off by ropes in which contestants box or wrestle	13	n	wrestling ring
8	jewelry consisting of a circlet of precious metal (often set with jewels) worn on the finger	14	n	engagement ring
10	[Wagner's Ring]	1	n	Decca ring

Notes:

Added sense 10 for Richard Wagner's *Der Ring des Nibelungen*. WordNet sense 7 also used for terms like *sale ring*, that is, a (circular) enclosure where sales take place etc.

2.59 room (292 compound types)

Rated compound: *engine room*

wnSense	WordNet description	types	class	example
1	an area within a building enclosed by walls and floor and ceiling	289	n	utility room
2	space for movement	3	n	leg room

Notes:

WordNet sense 2 has *elbow room* as collocate.

2.60 run (56 compound types)

Rated compound: *rat run*

wnSense	WordNet description	types	class	example
1	a score in baseball made by a runner touching all four bases safely	1	n	home run
2	the act of testing something	4	n	measure-ment run
3	a race run on foot	24	n	charity run
6	a regular trip	9	n	milk run
8	the continuous period of time during which something (a machine or a factory) operates or continues in operation	7	n	computer run
10	the production achieved during a continuous period of operation (of a machine or factory etc.)	2	n	print run
11	a small stream	3	n	gutter run
14	the pouring forth of a fluid	1	n	pot run
15	an unbroken chronological sequence	3	n	stage run
17	[An (often roofless) enclosure in which a (small) domestic animal may range freely.]	2	n	chicken run

Notes:
Added sense 17, pointer is a verbatim copy of OED run n.2, 15.b. *Pot run* as Word-Net Sense 14 is a misclassification, but its sense remains a solitaire (probably OED pot n.2 35. a. gen. An extent in length; a continuous stretch of something).

2.61 runner (10 compound types)

Rated compound: *front runner*

wnSense	WordNet description	types	class	example
1	someone who imports or exports without paying duties	4	n	drug runner
6	a trained athlete who competes in foot races	4	n	marathon runner
9	device consisting of the parts on which something can slide along	2	n	window runner

2.62 science (14 compound types)

Rated compound: *rocket science*

wnSense	WordNet description	types	class	example
1	a particular branch of scientific knowledge	14	n	defence science

2.63 screen (54 compound types)

Rated compound: *silver screen*

wnSense	WordNet description	types	class	example
1	a white or silvered surface where pictures can be projected for viewing	4	n	cinema screen
2	a protective covering that keeps things out or hinders sight	1	n	wind screen
3	the display that is electronically created on the surface of the large end of a cathode-ray tube	37	n	radar screen
4	a covering that serves to conceal or shelter something	2	n	Stevenson screen
5	a protective covering consisting of netting; can be mounted in a frame	2	n	insect screen
7	a strainer for separating lumps from powdered material or grading particles	2	n	security screen
8	partition consisting of a decorative frame or panel that serves to divide a space	6	n	silk screen

2.64 service (240 compound types)

Rated compound: *public service*

wnSense	WordNet description	types	class	example
1	work done by one person or group that benefits another	199	n	reservation service
3	the act of public worship following prescribed rules	29	n	funeral service
4	a company or agency that performs a public service; subject to government regulation	7	n	London service
6	a force that is a branch of the armed forces	2	n	field service
9	tableware consisting of a complete set of articles (silver or dishware) for use at table	1	n	tea service
12	(sports) a stroke that puts the ball in play	1	n	opening service
13	the performance of duties by a waiter or servant	1	n	court service

Notes:
This group often contained combinations that in principle could be used and hence classified in a number of ways, e.g. *student service* could be FOR/FROM/ HAVE2/USE. Went with plausibility, and hence mostly FOR.

2.65 sheet (79 compound types)

Rated compound: *cheat sheet*

wnSense	WordNet description	types	class	example
1	any broad thin expanse or surface	3	n	ice sheet
2	paper used for writing or printing	55	n	score sheet
3	bed linen consisting of a large rectangular piece of cotton or linen cloth; used in pairs	3	n	summer sheet
5	newspaper with half-size pages	2	n	scandal sheet
6	a flat artifact that is thin relative to its length and width	9	n	glass sheet
7	(nautical) a line (rope or chain) that regulates the angle at which a sail is set in relation to the wind	2	n	jib sheet
8	a large piece of fabric (usually canvas fabric) by means of which wind is used to propel a sailing vessel	5	n	fly sheet

Notes:

WordNet sense 3 has *bed sheet* as collocate. WordNet sense 1/HAVE2 used for *cell sheet*, which occurs in the context of a biological text (ASL). WordNet sense 8 not only used for sailing related sheets. WordNet sense 2: this sense is almost fully linked to FOR (e.g. *cheat/drawing sheet*). In some cases, HAVE1 is also possible or even more plausible then FOR, cf. e.g. *erratum sheet*. For consistency, the coding went always with FOR.

2.66 shift (17 compound types)

Rated compound: *graveyard shift*

wnSense	WordNet description	types	class	example
1	an event in which something is displaced without rotation	2	n	stick shift
2	a qualitative change	6	n	climate shift
3	the time period during which you are at work	7	n	evening shift
4	the act of changing one thing or position for another	2	n	paradigm shift

2.67 shirt (16 compound types)

Rated compound: *polo shirt*

wnSense	WordNet description	types	class	example
1	a garment worn on the upper half of the body	16	n	cotton shirt

Notes:
Small group with 3 clearly distinguishable relations (BE, FOR, MAKE2).

2.68 site (148 compound types)

Rated compound: *web site*

wnSense	WordNet description	types	class	example
1	the piece of land on which something is located (or is to be located)	138	n	stadium site
2	physical position in relation to the surroundings	5	n	attachment site
3	a computer connected to the internet that maintains a series of web pages on the World Wide Web	5	n	start site

Notes:

WordNet sense 3 has *web site* as collocate. When site is used a location, it occurs with either FOR (*golf site*), HAVE1 (*accident site*), or HAVE2 (*county site*). Tried to use FOR for less solid/stable things, but this is not fully consistent because a spill site is presumably the site of the spill, so HAVE1; other criterion was clear designation by somebody (again, quite soft, but see e.g. *colony site*); apart from the general difficulty, many things could be both (take e.g. *explosion site*), or FOR changed to HAVE1 over time. Sites the county has are also sites for the county.

2.69 song (46 compound types)

Rated compound: *swan song*

wnSense	WordNet description	types	class	example
1	a short musical composition with words	41	n	protest song
2	a distinctive or characteristic sound	2	n	siren song
4	the characteristic sound produced by a bird	3	n	bird song

WordNet sense 4 has *bird song* as collocate.

2.70 spoon (8 compound types)

Rated compound: *silver spoon*

wnSense	WordNet description	types	class	example
1	a piece of cutlery with a shallow bowl-shaped container and a handle; used to stir or serve or take up food	8	n	serving spoon

2.71 station (98 compound types)

Rated compound: *radio station*

wnSense	WordNet description	types	class	example
1	a facility equipped with special equipment and personnel for a particular purpose	93	n	petrol station
4	the position where someone (as a guard or sentry) stands or is assigned to stand	5	n	valley station

2.72 student (39 compound types)

Rated compound: *graduate student*

wnSense	WordNet description	types	class	example
1	a learner who is enrolled in an educational institution	39	n	divinity student

Notes:

If first part is a proper name, HAVE2 was used for places of learning (*Cornell student*), IN for general locations (*Beijing student*).

2.73 study (77 compound types)

Rated compound: *case study*

wnSense	WordNet description	types	class	example
1	a detailed critical inspection	42	n	usability study
2	applying the mind to learning and understanding a subject (especially by reading)	4	n	bible study
3	a written document describing the findings of some individual or group	17	n	research study
6	a branch of knowledge	12	n	computer studies
7	preliminary drawing for later elaboration	2	n	period study

Notes:

Many combinations allow several classifications; *computer studies* is a subject, but *computer study* is not. The distinction of WordNet senses 1 and 3 was done either via plausibility or with the help of the BNC context. In almost all cases, both readings should in principle be possible. The combination of proper name and study was always checked in its BNC context if it was recognized as a geographical location. As a result, either IN, FROM, or ABOUT was used.

2.74 tank (51 compound types)

Rated compound: *think tank*

wnSense	WordNet description	types	class	example
1	an enclosed armored military vehicle; has a cannon and moves on caterpillar treads	7	n	battle tank
2	a large (usually metallic) vessel for holding gases or liquids	44	n	water tank

Notes:

WordNet sense 1 has *army tank* as collocate.

2.75 teacher (50 compound types)

Rated compound: *head teacher*

wnSense	WordNet description	types	class	example
1	a person whose occupation is teaching	50	n	language teacher

2.76 tear (2 compound types)

Rated compound: *crocodile tears*

wnSense	WordNet description	types	class	example
1	a drop of the clear salty saline solution secreted by the lacrimal glands	2	n	salt tear

2.77 test (125 compound types)

Rated compound: *acid test*

wnSense	WordNet description	types	class	example
3	a set of questions or exercises evaluating skill or knowledge	15	n	language test
4	the act of undergoing testing	18	n	league test
5	the act of testing something	91	n	pregnancy test
7	[proper name]	1	n	River Test

Notes:

Added sense 7 for the River Test. WordNet sense 4 used for all rugby/cricket tests. WordNet sense 5: difficult decision between FOR or VERB 5: *merit test* as 'test for merit' or as 'test that tests the merit'? Decided by comparison to clear cases, with *drug test* and *cancer test* clearly FOR, *endurance test* and *connection test* clearly VERB; thus, *market test* is more 'a test for a market' and a *performance test* tests the performance. USE seemed sometimes more appropriate, e.g. for *dna test*, where the dna is determined and it is also clear that it does not concern the amount of dna or whether there is any at all.

2.78 tower (48 compound types)

Rated compound: *ivory tower*

wnSense	WordNet description	types	class	example
1	a structure taller than its diameter; can stand alone or be attached to a larger building	48	n	prison tower

2.79 train (54 compound types)

Rated compound: *gravy train*

wnSense	WordNet description	types	class	example
1	public transport provided by a line of railway cars coupled together and drawn by a locomotive	49	n	passenger train
2	a sequentially ordered set of things or events or ideas in which each successive member is related to the preceding	2	n	pulse train
3	a procession (of wagons or mules or camels) traveling together in single file	3	n	wagon train

2.80 trip (41 compound types)

Rated compound: *guilt trip*

wnSense	WordNet description	types	class	example
1	a journey for some purpose (usually including the return)	39	n	canoe trip
4	an exciting or stimulating experience	2	n	ego trip

2.81 user (39 compound types)

Rated compound: *end user*

wnSense	WordNet description	types	class	example
1	a person who makes use of a thing; someone who uses or employs something	36	n	computer user
3	a person who takes drugs	3	n	heroin user

Notes:
WordNet sense 3 has *drug user* as a collocate.

2.82 value (152 compound types)

Rated compound: *face value*

wnSense	WordNet description	types	class	example
1	a numerical quantity measured or assigned or computed	68	n	percentage value
2	the quality (positive or negative) that renders something desirable or valuable	20	n	entertain-ment value
3	the amount (of money or goods or services) that is considered to be a fair equivalent for something else	59	n	property value
5	(music) the relative duration of a musical note	1	n	sound value
6	an ideal accepted by some individual or group	4	n	school values

Mistakes:
lemma *sale value* occurs with 2 different relational codings, deriving from an earlier distinction between *sale value* as FOR and *sales value* as HAVE2.

2.83 violet (1 compound types)

Rated compound: *shrinking violet*

wnSense	WordNet description	types	class	example
1	any of numerous low-growing violas with small flowers	1	n	shrinking value

2.84 wall (179 compound types)

Rated compound: *brick wall*

wnSense	WordNet description	types	class	example
1	an architectural partition with a height and length greater than its thickness; used to divide or enclose an area or to support another structure	125	n	lavatory wall
2	anything that suggests a wall in structure or function or effect	1	n	wave wall
3	(anatomy) a layer (a lining or membrane) that encloses a structure	14	n	stomach wall
5	a vertical (or almost vertical) smooth rock face (as of a cave or mountain)	10	n	cliff wall
6	a layer of material that encloses space	7	n	tyre wall
7	a masonry fence (as around an estate or garden)	10	n	garden wall
8	an embankment built around a space for defensive purposes	12	n	compound wall

Notes:
Walls that plausibly form types coded as FOR (*balcony wall*), walls that don't as HAVE2 (*house wall*).

2.85 wedding (8 compound types)

Rated compound: *diamond wedding*

wnSense	WordNet description	types	class	example
1	the social event at which the ceremony of marriage is performed	8	n	church wedding

Notes:

Deemed it impossible to distinguish between WordNet sense 1 and 2 ('the act of marrying; the nuptial ceremony'); used only sense 1.

Appendix C: Reddy et al. items with multiple readings and the 2016 semantic coding

Below are all items from the Reddy et al. dataset for which raters used 2 different word senses, followed by the relation and word sense coding for Bell & Schäfer (2016) and comments indicating which reading is covered by the coding (recall that the 2016 annotations are not word-sense specific).

(1)   *acid test*

  a.   a rigorous or crucial appraisal
  b.   Any qualitative chemical or metallurgical test which uses acid
  Coded as:
       (i)   USE, 1 (N1 family)
       (ii)   USE, 5 (N2 family)
  Comments: coded is reading 2, but reading 1 is covered due to its being a
       whole-compound shift

(2)   *brass ring*

  a.   a rich opportunity or a prize
  b.   A ring made with brass
  Coded as:
       (i)   MAKE2, 1 (N1 family)
       (ii)   MAKE2, 3 (N2 family)
  Comments: reading 2 is coded, but reading one is covered, being a whole
       compound shift

(3)   *brick wall*

    a.   An obstacle.

    b.   a wall built with bricks

    Coded as:

        (i)   MAKE2, 1 (N1 family)

        (ii)   MAKE2, 1 (N2 family)

    Comments: reading 2 is coded

(4)   *case study*

    a.   a careful study of some social unit (as a corporation or division within a corporation) that attempts to determine what factors led to its success or failure

    b.   a detailed analysis of a person or group from a social or psychological or medical point of view

    Coded as:

        (i)   ABOUT, 6 (N1 family)

        (ii)   ABOUT, 1 (N2 family)

    Comments: both readings are coded, as both contain specific instances of cases

(5)   *chain reaction*

    a.   a series of chemical reactions in which the product of one is a reactant in the next

    b.   a self-sustaining nuclear reaction; a series of nuclear fissions in which neutrons released by splitting one atom leads to the splitting of others

    Coded as:

        (i)   VERB, 1 (N1 family)

        (ii)   BE, 1 (N2 family)

    Comments: both readings are covered, reading 2 being a specification of reading 1

(6)   *cheat sheet*

    a.   A sheet of paper containing notes used to assist (with or without permission) on a test.

    b.   Any summary or quick reference used as a shortcut or reminder, a crib sheet.

    Coded as:

        (i)   FOR, 5 (N1 family)

        (ii)   FOR, 2 (N2 family)

Comments: both readings are covered, as reading 1 is just more specific than reading 2

(7)   *cutting edge*

    a.   the position of greatest importance or advancement; the leading position in any movement or field

    b.   the sharp cutting side of the blade of a knife

Coded as:

    (i)   FOR, 3 (N1 family)

    (ii)   FOR, 3 (N2 family)

Comments: coded is reading 2, but reading 1 is covered (whole-compound shift)

(8)   *face value*

    a.   the value of a security that is set by the company issuing it; unrelated to market value

    b.   the apparent worth as opposed to the real worth

Coded as:

    (i)   HAVE2, 8 (N1 family)

    (ii)   IN, 3 (N2 family)

Comments: coded is reading 1, but reading 2 is a whole-compound shift

(9)   *fashion plate*

    a.   a man who is much concerned with his dress and appearance

    b.   a plate illustrating the latest fashion in dress

Coded as:

    (i)   ABOUT, 3 (N1 family)

    (ii)   ABOUT, 3 (N2 family)

Comments: reading 2 is coded, but reading 1 is covered, as it is a whole-compound shift

(10)   *firing line*

    a.   the line from which soldiers deliver fire

    b.   the most advanced and responsible group in an activity

Coded as:

    (i)   FOR, 1 (N1 family)

    (ii)   FOR, 11 (N2 family)

Comments: reading 1 is coded, but reading 2 is covered (whole-compound shift)

(11)   *game plan*

    a.   (figurative) a carefully thought out strategy for achieving an objective in war or politics or business or personal affairs

    b.   (sports) a plan for achieving an objective in some sport

    Coded as:

        (i)   FOR, 8 (N1 family)

        (ii)   FOR, 1 (N2 family)

    Comments: both readings are covered, as reading 1 is a whole-compound shift

(12)   *gold mine*

    a.   a good source of something that is desired

    b.   a mine where gold ore is found

    Coded as:

        (i)   HAVE1, 3 (N1 family)

        (ii)   HAVE1, 1 (N2 family)

    Comments: coded is reading 2, reading 1 is a whole-compound shift (and thus also covered)

(13)   *graveyard shift*

    a.   the work shift during the night (as midnight to 8 a.m.)

    b.   workers who work during the night (as midnight to 8 a.m.)

    Coded as:

        (i)   IN,1 (N1 family)

        (ii)   IN,3 (N2 family)

    Comments: reading 1 is coded, reading 2 is a whole-compound shift

(14)   *ground floor*

    a.   the floor of a building that is at or nearest to the level of the ground around the building

    b.   becoming part of a venture at the beginning (regarded as position of advantage)

    Coded as:

        (i)   IN, 1 (N1 family)

        (ii)   BE, 4 (N2 family)

    Comments: reading 1 is coded, reading 2 is a whole-compound shift

(15)   *nest egg*

    a.   a fund of money put by as a reserve

    b.   device consisting of an artificial egg left in a nest to induce hens to lay their eggs in it

    Coded as:

        (i)   IN, 1 (N1 family)

        (ii)   IN,1 (N2 family)

    Comments: covers both readings, as both are whole-compound shifts

(16)   *public service*

    a.   a service that is performed for the benefit of the public or its institutions

    b.   employment within a government system (especially in the civil service)

    Coded as:

        (i)   FOR, 1 (N1 family)

        (ii)   FOR, 1 (N2 family)

    Comments: covers both readings, because the second reading is a whole-compound shift

(17)   *rocket science*

    a.   the science or study of rockets and their design

    b.   anything overly complex, detailed or confusing

    Coded as:

        (i)   ABOUT, 1 (N1 family)

        (ii)   (N2 family)

    ABOUT, 1

    Comments: covers both readings, because reading 2 is a whole compound shift

(18)   *sacred cow*

    a.   a person unreasonably held to be immune to criticism

    b.   A cow which is worshipped

    Coded as:

        (i)   BE,1 (N1 family)

        (ii)   BE, 2 (N2 family)

    Comments: coding covers both readings, because reading 1 is a whole-compound shift

(19)   *silver bullet*

    a.   a simple guaranteed solution for a difficult problem

    b.   a bullet made with silver

    Coded as:

       (i)   MAKE2,1 (N1 family)

       (ii)   MAKE2,1 (N2 family)

    Comments: Coded is reading 2, but it covers reading 2, which is whole compound shift.

(20)   *silver screen*

    a.   the film industry

    b.   a white or silvered surface where pictures can be projected for viewing

    Coded as:

       (i)   BE, 3 (N1 family)

       (ii)   BE, 1 (N2 family)

    Comments: Both readings fall under the same coding, reading 2 literally, reading one is a whole compound shift

(21)   *snake oil*

    a.   (medicine) any of various liquids sold as medicine (as by a travelling medicine show) but medically worthless

    b.   communication (written or spoken) intended to deceive

    Coded as:

       (i)   FROM,1 (N1 family)

       (ii)   FROM,1 (N2 family)

    Comments: Both readings fall under the same coding, both corresponding being whole compound shifts

Appendix D: Corpus identifiers and material from online dictionaries

Below I list the sources for all of the examples drawn from the web, the DeReKo (Das Deutsche Referenzkorpus, IDS, n.d.) and the COCA (the Corpus of Contemporary American English, cf. Davies 2008–).

1 Corpus identifiers

1.1 Examples from the web

Example	Chapter	Source
(35-b-ii)	4	http://www.lastfm.pl/user/0k0k0k0/journal/2008/09/06/25g6hz_ten_most_common_misconceptions_regarding_musical_critique, accessed 2013-11-26.
(35-d-i)	4	http://hub.jhu.edu/gazette/2013/june/news-child-motion-detector-student-invention, accessed 2013-11-26.
(42)	4	http://www.arte.tv/de/homo-ehe-das-erste-jawort-managergehaelter/7534620,CmC=7534622.html, accessed on 2013-11-23

1.2 Examples from the DeReKo

Example	Chapter	Source
(41-a)	4	NON13/MAI.00132 Niederösterreichische Nachrichten, 02.05.2013, Ressort: Lokales; Lkw als Bonus
(41-b)	4	BRZ13/MAR.05371 Braunschweiger Zeitung, 14.03.2013, Ressort: 1SZ-Lok; 9000 Euro Schaden bei Verkehrsunfall

(52)	4	BRZ13/MAI.11357 Braunschweiger Zeitung, 31.05.2013, Ressort: 1BS-Lok; Braunschweigische Löwenals Hochzeitsgeschenke

1.3 Examples from the COCA

Example	Chapter	Source
(1-a)	1	Dyer, Serena (2015). Shopping, Spectacle & the Senses. *History Today*, 65(3), 30–36.
(1-b)	1	Lawler, Andrew (2008). Who Were the Hurrians? (cover story). *Archaeology*, 61(4), 46–52.
(1-c)	1	Ray Mark Rinaldi (2012). Off the football field, with a new goal in mind. *Denver Post*, 120318, FEATURES, 6E
(1-d)	1	Thomas Heath (2012). Tattooist's art helps breast cancer patients. *Washington Post*, 120227, A-SECTION; A11
(1-e)	1	Michaels, Fern (2006). *Pretty woman*. New York: Pocket Books pbk. ed.
(1-f)	1	Catherine Dennis (2003). Scary e-mail hoaxes. *Cosmopolitan*. 234(3), 172
(1-g)	1	Michele Bender (2001). The biggest communication mistakes women make. *Cosmopolitan*. 230(6), 198–
??	4	Zehner, Ozzie (2012). Nuclear Power's Unsettled Future. *Futurist*. 46(2), 17-21.
(7)	4	IRA FLATOW (2004). Interview: Richard Gibbs discusses nearing the completion of the mapping of the rat genome. *NPR_Science*, 20040409
(7-b)	4	Lybi Ma (2001). See Jane run. *Psychology Today*, 34(5), 36–
(11)	4	Radiographic Evidence of Nonoccupational Asbestos Exposure from Processing Libby Vermiculite in Minneapolis, Minnesota. *Environmental Health Perspectives*, 120(1), 44-49.
(12)	4	Anonymous (2012). Alexandria and Arlington crime report. *Chicago Sun-Times*. Metro; Pg. T21, (120614)
(16)	4	Brown, Suzanne Hunter (1990). High–Rise. *Southern Review*, 26(3), 604–

(17)   4   Anonymous (2011).   BURNING BED; ROLLER-
                     COASTER ROMANCE ENDS IN FLAMES. *20/20.*
                     (110325) 10:00 PM EST

(18)   4   Anonymous (1997). OFFICER CHARLES SCHWARZ
                     CLAIMS HE WAS MISTAKENLY IDENTIFIED AS BE-
                     ING INVOLVED IN THE ALLEGED POLICE BRUTAL-
                     ITY AND SODOMY AGAINST ABNER LOUIMA AT
                     THE 70TH PRECINCT IN NEW YORK CITY. *CBS_-*
                     Sixty. (19970824)

(25-a-i)   4   Poul Anderson (2001). Pele. *Analog Science Fiction &*
                     Fact, 121(10), 8–

(25-a-ii)   4   CNN_News (2010) (100815)

(25-b-i)   4   CNN_Situation. U.S. War Against Pirates; Obamas Re-
                     lease Tax Returns. 2009 (090415)

(25-b-ii)   4   Begley, Sharon (2011). A Viral Link to Mental Illness.
                     The Saturday Evening Post. Sep/Oct.

(26-a-i)   4   Allen, Melissa M., Ukrainetz, Teresa A., and Carswell,
                     Alisa L. (2012). The Narrative Language Performance of
                     Three Types of At-Risk First-Grade Readers. *Language,*
                     Speech & Hearing Services in Schools, 43(2), 205–221.

(26-a-ii)   4   BOSWORTH, KRIS, FORD, LYSBETH and HERNAN-
                     DAZ, DILEY (2011). School Climate Factors Contribut-
                     ing to Student and Faculty Perceptions of Safety in Se-
                     lect Arizona Schools. *Journal of School Health,* 81(4),
                     194–201.

(26-b-i)   4   RAVI NESSMAN (2010).   India: Land of many cell
                     phones, fewer toilets.   *Associated Press,* BUSINESS
                     NEWS (101030).

(26-b-ii)   4   Krentz, Jayne Ann (2004). *Dawn in Eclipse Bay.* Water-
                     ville, Me. : Wheeler Pub.

(27-a-i)   4   Anonymous (2003). The Great Kanto Earthquake and
                     the Massacre of Koreans in 1923: Notes on Japan's Mod-
                     ern National Sovereignty. *Anthropological Quarterly,*
                     76(4), 731–748.

(27-a-ii)   4   Anonymous (1993). Jurassic Park

(27-b-i)   4   Finch, Sheila (1996). Out of the Mouths. *Fantasy & Sci-*
                     ence Fiction, 91(6), 13–

(27-b-ii)	4	Yvonne J Pendleton (1997). Life: A cosmic imperative? *Sky and Telescope*, 94(1), 42–
(28-a)	4	Anonymous (1994). A homemade holiday: sew-easy costumes that are more treat than trick. *Todays Parent*, 11(7), 84.
(28-b)	4	Amanda Gold (2012). A do-it-yourself harvest; U-pick farms offer exceptional produce at reasonable prices. *San Francisco Chronicle*, Food, G1, (120617).
(29-b)	4	Anonymous (2004). Capturing the Public Imagination: The Social and Professional Place of Public History. *American Studies International*, 42(2/3),86–117.
(30-a)	4	Ilene R. Prusher (2006). The new walls of Jerusalem: Part 3 * From the West Bank, a circuitous road to market. *Christian Science Monitor*, (20061221)
(30-b)	4	Norment, Lynn (1993). 10 secrets to a happy marriage. *Ebony*, 48(10), 32–
(31-a)	4	William Boyd (2005). THE PIGEON. *The Kenyon Review*, 27(1), 1–
(31-b)	4	Brian Booker (2006). Train Delayed Due to Horrible, Horrible Accident. *Triquarterly*, 125, 44–
(32-a)	4	Lynne Char Bennett (2012). The power of sour; COOKING; Put leftover wine to good use by making your own vinegar. *San Francisco Chronicle*, Food; M1 (120226)
(32-b)	4	Fredrick Kunkle (2012). Fairfax frustrated by lack of urban coalition. *Washington Post*, METRO; B01, (120227)
(33-a)	4	Senate Minority Leader Source. 2010 (100822)
(33-b)	4	Zhongganggao, DR. Carl (2001). SECOND LANGUAGE LEARNING AND THE TEACHING OF GRAMMAR [1].*Education*, 122(2), 326–.
(35-a-i)	4	RODNEY HO (2002). What your dreams may mean. *Atlanta Journal Constitution*, (20021215).
(35-a-ii)	4	Ben Fountain III (2003). Fantasy for eleven fingers. *Southwest Review*, 88(1), 123.
(35-b-i)	4	HYMOWITZ, KAY (2011). Cogs in the Machine. *Commentary*, 131(3), 69–72.

(35-c-i)	4	Anonymous (2001). TRANSITION IN WASHINGTON; Excerpts From Judge's Testimony at Ashcroft Confirmation Hearing. *New York Times*, (0101).
(35-c-ii)	4	CBS_48Hours (2011). For May 28, 2011, CBS (110528).
(35-d-ii)	4	Anonymous (2011). A Celebration of Engineering ASME 2011 Honors. *Mechanical Engineering*, 133(11), 51–75.
(36-a-i)	4	Juni, Samuel (1998). The Defense Mechanisms Inventory: Theoretical and Psychometric Implications. *Current Psychology*, 17(4), 313–.
(36-a-ii)	4	M.B. Pell (2011). In tax lien limbo; Property owners caught in middle of policies. *Atlanta Journal Constitution*, NEWS, 1A, (110227).
(36-a-iii)	4	Ricklefs, Merle (1990). Balance and military innovation in 17th-century Java. *History Today*, 40(11), 40–.
(36-b-i)	4	CNN_Cooper (2012). Secret of Assad Regime Revealed; Contraception Controversy. (120315).
(36-b-ii)	4	LOUIS UCHITELLE (1999). DEVISING NEW MATH TO DEFINE POVERTY. *New York Times*, (19991018).
(36-b-iii)	4	Ben Bova (2003). Sam and the Flying Dutchman. *Analog Science Fiction & Fact*, 123(6), 114.
(36-c-i)	4	Livernash, Robert (1995). The future of populous economies China and India shape their destinies. *Environment*, 37(6), 6–.
(36-c-ii)	4	ABC_Special. FREELOADERS. 1997 (19970821).

2 Online dictionaries

The table below lists the words as discussed in the main text in the first column. The second column gives the specific entry in the online dictionary used.

Item	Source
cloud nine/cloud seven	"cloud, n.". OED Online. December 2016. Oxford University Press. http://www.oed.com/view/Entry/34689?rskey=hWbVMS&result=1&isAdvanced=false (accessed January 12, 2017). [II. Extant senses. 9.b.]
grandfather clock	"grandfather, n.". OED Online. December 2016. Oxford University Press. http://www.oed.com/view/Entry/80657?redirectedFrom=grandfather+clock (accessed January 18, 2017). [Compounds, C2]
gravy train	"gravy, n.". OED Online. December 2016. Oxford University Press. http://www.oed.com/view/Entry/81077?redirectedFrom=gravy (accessed January 18, 2017). [2. d]
hogwash/hogwash	"hogwash, n.". OED Online. June 2013. Oxford University Press. http://www.oed.com/view/Entry/87638?redirectedFrom=hogwash (accessed June 20, 2013).
kangaroo court	"Kangaroo Court." Merriam-Webster.com. Merriam-Webster, n.d. Web. 21 Oct. 2016. http://www.merriam-webster.com/dictionary/kangaroocourt
literal	"literal, adj. and n.". OED Online. September 2013. Oxford University Press. http://www.oed.com/view/Entry/109055?rskey=KNikjc&result=6&isAdvanced=false (accessed November 27, 2013)
lord	"lord, n. and int.". OED Online. December 2016. Oxford University Press. http://www.oed.com/view/Entry/110299?rskey=F85g77&result=1&isAdvanced=false (accessed January 13, 2017).
public service	"public service, n.". OED Online. December 2016. Oxford University Press. http://www.oed.com/view/Entry/239618?rskey=hM1uJ1&result=1 (accessed December 20, 2016)

References

Adams, Valerie. 1973. *An introduction to Modern English word formation.* London: Longman.

Arndt-Lappe, Sabine. 2011. Towards an exemplar-based model of stress in English noun-noun compounds. *Journal of Linguistics* 47(3). 549–585.

Arndt-Lappe, Sabine. 2014. Analogy in suffix rivalry: The case of English *-ity* and *-ness. English Language and Linguistics* 18. 497–548.

Asher, Nicholas. 2011. *Lexical meaning in context: A web of words.* Cambridge: Cambridge University Press.

Baayen, R. Harald. 1993. On frequency, transparency and productivity. In Geert Booij & Jaap van Marle (eds.), *Yearbook of morphology 1992*, 181–208. Dordrecht: Springer.

Baayen, R. Harald. 2008. *Analyzing linguistic data: A practical introduction to statistics using R.* Cambridge: Cambridge University Press.

Baayen, R. Harald. 2010. The directed compound graph of English: An exploration of lexical connectivity and its processing consequences. In Susan Olsen (ed.), *New impulses in word-formation* (Linguistische Berichte, Sonderheft 17), 383–402. Hamburg: Buske.

Baayen, R. Harald. 2011. Corpus linguistics and naive discriminative learning. *Brazilian Journal of Applied Linguistics* 11. 295–328.

Baayen, R. Harald. 2013. *languageR: Data sets and functions with "Analyzing Linguistic Data. A practical introduction to statistics".* R package version 1.4.1. http://CRAN.R-project.org/package=languageR.

Baayen, R. Harald. 2014. Experimental and psycholinguistic approaches to studying derivation. In Rochelle Lieber & Pavol Štekauer (eds.), *Handbook of derivational morphology*, 95–117. Oxford: Oxford University Press.

Baayen, R. Harald, Douglas J. Davidson & Douglas M. Bates. 2008. Mixed-effects modeling with crossed random effects for subjects and items. *Journal of Memory and Language* 59(4). Special Issue: Emerging Data Analysis, 390–412.

Baayen, R. Harald, Willem M. J. Levelt, Robert Schreuder & Mirjam Ernestus. 2008. Paradigmatic structure in speech production. In Malcolm Elliott, James

Kirby, Osamu Sawada, Eleni Staraki & Suwon Yoon (eds.), *Proceedings from the annual meeting of the Chicago Linguistics Society 43*, vol. 1, 1–29. Chicago.

Baayen, R. Harald, Petar Milin, Dusica Filipović Đurđević, Peter Hendrix & Marco Marelli. 2011. An amorphous model for morphological processing in visual comprehension based on naive discriminative learning. *Psychological Review* 118(3). 438–481.

Baayen, R. Harald, Richard Piepenbrock & L. Gulikers. 1995. *CELEX2*. Philadelphia: Linguistic Data Consortium.

Baldwin, Timothy, Colin Bannard, Takaaki Tanaka & Dominic Widdows. 2003. An empirical model of multiword expression decomposability. In *Proceedings of the ACL 2003 Workshop on Multiword Expressions: Analysis, Acquisition and Treatment* (MWE '03 18), 89–96. Sapporo, Japan: Association for Computational Linguistics.

Baldwin, Timothy & Takaaki Tanaka. 2004. Translation by machine of complex nominals: Getting it right. In *Proceedings of the Workshop on Multiword Expressions: Integrating Processing* (MWE '04), 24–31. Barcelona, Spain: Association for Computational Linguistics.

Balota, David A., Melvin J. Yap, Michael J. Cortese, Keith A. Hutchison, Brett Kessler, Bjorn Loftis, James H. Neely, Douglas L. Nelson, Greg B. Simpson & Rebecca Treiman. 2007. The English lexicon project. *Behavior Research Methods* 39(3). 445–459.

Bannard, Colin, Timothy Baldwin & Alex Lascarides. 2003. A statistical approach to the semantics of verb-particles. In *Proceedings of the ACL 2003 Workshop on Multiword Expressions: Analysis, Acquisition and Treatment* (MWE '03 18), 65–72. Sapporo, Japan: Association for Computational Linguistics.

Bartoń, Kamil. 2016. *MuMIn: Multi-Model Inference*. R package version 1.15.6. http://CRAN.R-project.org/package=MuMIn.

Bassac, Christian. 2006. A compositional treatment for English compounds. *Research in Language* 4. 133–153.

Bauer, Laurie. 1979. On the need for pragmatics in the study of nominal compounding. *Journal of Pragmatics* 3(1). 45–50.

Bauer, Laurie. 1998. When is a sequence of two nouns a compound in English? *English Language and Linguistics* 2(1). 65–86.

Bauer, Laurie, Rochelle Lieber & Ingo Plag. 2013. *The Oxford reference guide to English morphology*. Oxford: Oxford University Press.

Bell, Melanie J. 2011. At the boundary of morphology and syntax: Noun noun constructions in English. In Alexandra Galani, Glyn Hicky & George Tsoulas (eds.), *Morphology and its interfaces* (Linguistik Aktuell), 137–167. Amsterdam: John Benjamins.

Bell, Melanie J. 2012. *The English NN construct: Its prosody and structure.* University of Cambridge dissertation.

Bell, Melanie J. & Ingo Plag. 2012. Informativeness is a determinant of compound stress in English. *Journal of Linguistics* 48. 485–520.

Bell, Melanie J. & Martin Schäfer. 2013. Semantic transparency: Challenges for distributional semantics. In *Proceedings of IWCS 2013 workshop Towards a Formal Distributional Semantics*, 1–10. Potsdam, Germany: Association for Computational Linguistics.

Bell, Melanie J. & Martin Schäfer. 2016. Modelling semantic transparency. *Morphology* 26(2). 157–199.

Belsley, David A., Edwin Kuh & Roy E. Welsch. 1980. *Regression diagnostics: Identifying influential data and sources of collinearity.* New York: Wiley & Sons.

El-Bialy, Rowan, Christina L. Gagné & Thomas L. Spalding. 2013. Processing of English compounds is sensitive to the constituents' semantic transparency. *The Mental Lexicon* 8(1). 75–95.

Biemann, Chris & Eugenie Giesbrecht. 2011. Distributional semantics and compositionality 2011: Shared task description and results. In *Proceedings of the Workshop on Distributional Semantics and Compositionality* (DiSCo '11), 21–28. Portland, Oregon: Association for Computational Linguistics.

Bierwisch, Manfred. 1982. Formal and lexical semantics. *Linguistische Berichte* (80). 3–17.

Bierwisch, Manfred. 1989. Event nominalization: Proposals and problems. In Wolfang Motsch (ed.), *Wortstruktur und Satzstruktur. Linguistische Studien* 194, 1–73. Berlin: Akademie der Wissenschaften der DDR.

Blutner, Reinhard. 1998. Lexical pragmatics. *Journal of Semantics* 15(2). 115–162.

BNC. 2007. *The British National Corpus, version 3 (BNC XML Edition).* http://www.natcorp.ox.ac.uk/.

Brekle, Herbert Ernst. 1970. *Generative Satzsemantik und transformationelle Syntax im System der englischen Nominalkomposition.* München: Fink.

Brekle, Herbert Ernst. 1973. *Zur Stellung der Wortbildung in der Grammatik.* Trier: LAUT.

Brekle, Herbert Ernst. 1986. The production and interpretation of ad hoc nominal compounds in German: A realistic approach. *Acta Linguistica Academiae Scientiarum Hungaricae* 36(1-4). 39–52.

Browne, Wayles. 1974. On the topology of anaphoric peninsulas. *Linguistic Inquiry* 5(4). 619–620.

Bueno, Steve & Cheryl Frenck-Mestre. 2008. The activation of semantic memory: Effects of prime exposure, prime-target relationship, and task demands. *Memory and Cognition* 36(4). 882–898.

Bybee, Joan L. 1985. *Morphology: A study of the relation between meaning and form*. Amsterdam: John Benjamins.

Bybee, Joan L. 1988. Morphology as lexical organization. In Michael Hammond & Michael Noonan (eds.), *Theoretical morphology*, 119–141. Academic Press.

Bybee, Joan L. 1995. Regular morphology and the lexicon. *Language and Cognitive Processes* 10. 425–455.

Chierchia, Gennaro & Sally McConnell-Ginet. 2000. *Meaning and grammar: An introduction to semantics*. 2nd edn. Cambridge, Massachusetts: MIT Press.

Chomsky, Noam & Morris Halle. 1968. *The sound pattern of English*. Reprinted 1991 by MIT Press. New York: Harper & Row.

Conway, Damian. 1998. *An algorithmic approach to English pluralization*. Proceedings of the Second Annual Perl Conference.

Corum, Claudia. 1973. Anaphoric peninsulas. In Claudia Corum, T. Cedric Smith-Stark & Ann Weiser (eds.), *Papers from the ninth regional meeting*, 89–97. Chicago Linguistic Society.

Coulmas, Florian. 1988. Wörter, Komposita und anaphorische Inseln. *Folia Linguistica* 22(3-4). 315–336.

Danks, David. 2003. Equilibria of the Rescorla–Wagner model. *Journal of Mathematical Psychology* 47(2). 109–121.

Davies, Mark. N.d. *The Corpus of Contemporary American English: 450 million words, 1990–present*. Available online at http://corpus.byu.edu/coca/.

De Jong, Nivja H., Robert Schreuder & R. Harald Baayen. 2000. The morphological family size effect and morphology. *Language and Cognitive Processes* 15(4-5). 329–365.

Devereux, Barry & Fintan Costello. 2005. Investigating the relations used in conceptual combination. *Artificial Intelligence Review* 24(3). 489–515.

Downing, Pamela. 1977. On the creation and use of English compound nouns. *Language* 53(4). 810–842.

Dressler, Wolfgang U. 2006. Compound types. In Gary Libben & Gonia Jarema (eds.), *The representation and processing of compound words*, 23–44. Oxford: Oxford University Press.

Dumais, Susan T. 2004. Latent semantic analysis. *Annual Review of Information Science and Technology* 38(1). 188–230.

Fahim, Elsayed M. S. 1977. *Untersuchungen zum Modell substantivischer Komposita mit einem Primäradjektiv als erster unmittelbarer Konstituente*. Leipzig: Universität Leipzig dissertation.

Fanselow, Gisbert. 1981. *Zur Syntax und Semantik der Nominalkomposition* (Linguistische Arbeiten 107). Tübingen: Niemeyer.

Fellbaum, Christiane (ed.). 1998. *WordNet: An electronic lexical database*. Cambridge, Massachusetts: MIT Press.

Ferraresi, Adriano, Eros Zanchetta, Marco Baroni & Silvia Bernardini. 2008. Introducing and evaluating ukWaC, a very large web-derived corpus of English. In *Proceedings of the WAC4 workshop at LREC 2008*. Marrakech.

Firth, John Rupert. 1957. A synopsis of linguistic theory, 1930-1955. In *Studies in linguistic analysis. Special volume of the Philological Society*, 1–32. Oxford: Basil Blackwell.

Fodor, Jerry A. & Zenon W. Pylyshyn. 1988. Connectionism and cognitive architecture: A critical analysis. *Cognition* 28(1–2). 3–71.

Fox, John. 2003. Effect displays in R for generalised linear models. *Journal of Statistical Software* 8(15). 1–27.

Frauenfelder, Uli H. & Robert Schreuder. 1992. Constraining psycholinguistic models of morphological processing and representation: The role of productivity. In Geert Booij & Jaap van Marle (eds.), *Yearbook of morphology 1991*, 165–183. Dordrecht: Springer.

Frisson, Steven, Elizabeth Niswander-Klement & Alexander Pollatsek. 2008. The role of semantic transparency in the processing of English compound words. *British Journal of Psychology* 99(1). 87–107.

Gagné, Christina L. & Edward J. Shoben. 1997. Influence of thematic relations on the comprehension of modifier–noun combinations. *Journal of Experimental Psychology: Learning, Memory, and Cognition* 23(1). 71–87.

Gagné, Christina L. & Thomas L. Spalding. 2004. Effect of relation availability on the interpretation and access of familiar noun–noun compounds. *Brain and Language* 90(1–3). 478–486.

Gibbs, Raymond W. 1989. Understanding and literal meaning. *Cognitive Science* 13(2). 243–251.

Giegerich, Heinz J. 2009. The English compound stress myth. *Word Structure* 2(1). 1–17.

Giesbrecht, Eugenie. 2009. In search of semantic compositionality in vector spaces. In Sebastian Rudolph, Frithjof Dau & Sergei O. Kuznetsov (eds.), *Conceptual structures: Leveraging semantic technologies* (Lecture Notes in Computer Science 5662), 173–184. Springer Berlin Heidelberg.

Guevara, Emiliano. 2010. A regression model of adjective-noun compositionality in distributional semantics. In *Proceedings of the 2010 Workshop on Geometrical Models of Natural Language Semantics*, 33–37.

Halliday, M. A. K. & Ruqaiya Hasan. 1976. *Cohesion in English*. London: Longman.

Harm, Michael W. & Mark S. Seidenberg. 2004. Computing the meanings of words in reading: Cooperative division of labor between visual and phonological processes. *Psychological Review* 111(3). 662–720.

Harrell Jr, Frank E. 2015. *Hmisc: Harrell miscellaneous*. R package version 3.17-0. With contributions from Charles Dupont and many others. http://CRAN.R-project.org/package=Hmisc.

Harrell Jr, Frank E. 2016. *rms: Regression Modeling Strategies*. R package version 4.5-0. https://CRAN.R-project.org/package=rms.

Harris, Zellig S. 1954. Distributional structure. *Word* 10. 146–162.

Hatcher, Anna Granville. 1960. An introduction to the analysis of English noun compounds. *Word* 16. 356–373.

Heim, Irene & Angelika Kratzer. 1998. *Semantics in generative grammar* (Blackwell Textbooks in Linguistics 13). Oxford: Blackwell.

Hobbs, Jerry R., Mark E. Stickel, Douglas E. Appelt & Paul Martin. 1993. Interpretation as abduction. *Artificial Intelligence* 63(1-2). 69–142.

Hoffmann, Sebastian, Stefan Evert, Nicholas Smith, David Lee & Ylva Berglund Prytz. 2008. *Corpus linguistics with BNCweb – a practical guide*. Frankfurt am Main: Peter Lang.

Houghton Mifflin Company. 1993. *The American heritage college dictionary*. 3rd edn. Houghton Mifflin Company.

Householder, Fred W. 1971. *Linguistic speculations*. Cambridge: Cambridge University Press.

Huddleston, Rodney, Geoffrey Pullum, et al. 2002. *The Cambridge grammar of the English language*. Cambridge: Cambridge University Press.

IDS. N.d. *Das Deutsche Referenzkorpus DeReKo*. http://www.ids-mannheim.de/kl/projekte/korpora/. Institut für deutsche Sprache. Mannheim.

Jackendoff, Ray. 2009. Compounding in the parallel architecture and conceptual semantics. In Rochelle Lieber & Pavol Štekauer (eds.), *The Oxford handbook of compounding*, 105–128. Oxford: Oxford University Press.

Jackendoff, Ray. 2010. The ecology of English noun-noun compounds (2009). In *Meaning and the lexicon: The parallel architecture 1975–2010*. Expanded and revised version of Jackendoff (2009). Oxford: Oxford University Press.

Jamieson, Susan. 2004. Likert scales: How to (ab)use them. *Medical Education* 38(12). 1217–1218.

Jarema, Gonia, Céline Busson, Rossitza Nikolova, Kyrana Tsapkini & Gary Libben. 1999. Processing compounds: A cross-linguistic study. *Brain and Language* 68(1–2). 362–369.

Jaszczolt, Kasia M. 2016. *Meaning in linguistic interaction.* Oxford: Oxford University Press.

Jespersen, Otto. 1942. *A modern English grammar on historical principles.* Copenhagen: Ejnar Munksgaard.

Ji, Hongbo, Christina L. Gagné & Thomas L. Spalding. 2011. Benefits and costs of lexical decomposition and semantic integration during the processing of transparent and opaque English compounds. *Journal of Memory and Language* 65. 406–430.

Johnson, Paul C. D. 2014. Extension of Nakagawa & Schielzeth's R2GLMM to random slopes models. *Methods in Ecology and Evolution* 5(9). 944–946.

Juhasz, Barbara J. 2007. The influence of semantic transparency on eye movements during English compound word recognition. In Roger P. G. van Gompel (ed.), *Eye movements: A window on mind and brain*, 373–390. Elsevier Science.

Juhasz, Barbara J., Albrecht W. Inhoff & Keith Rayner. 2005. The role of interword spaces in the processing of English compound words. *Language and Cognitive Processes* 20(1-2). 291–316.

Juhasz, Barbara J., Yun-Hsuan Lai & Michelle L. Woodcock. 2015. A database of 629 English compound words: Ratings of familiarity, lexeme meaning dominance, semantic transparency, age of acquisition, imageability, and sensory experience. *Behavior Research Methods* 47(4). 1004–1019.

Kamp, Hans. 1975. Two theories about adjectives. In Edward Louis Keenan (ed.), *Formal semantics for natural languages*, 123–155. Cambridge: Cambridge University Press.

Kamp, Hans. 1981. A theory of truth and semantic representation. In Jeroen Groenendijk, Theo M. V. Janssen & Martin Stokhof (eds.), *Formal methods in the study of language Vol. I*, 1–41. Dordrecht: Foris.

Kamp, Hans & Barbara H. Partee. 1995. Prototype theory and compositionality. *Cognition* 57. 129–191.

Katz, Graham & Eugenie Giesbrecht. 2006. Automatic identification of non-compositional multi-word expressions using latent semantic analysis. In *Proceedings of the Workshop on Multiword Expressions: Identifying and Exploiting Underlying Properties* (MWE '06), 12–19. Sydney, Australia: Association for Computational Linguistics.

Katz, Jerrold J. 1964. Semantic theory and the meaning of 'good'. *The Journal of Philosophy* 61(23). 739–766.

Keenan, Edward Louis & Leonard M. Faltz. 1985. *Boolean semantics for natural language*. Dordrecht: D. Reidel.

Kennedy, Christopher. 2007. Vagueness and grammar: The semantics of relative and absolute gradable adjectives. *Linguistics and Philosophy* 30. 1–45.

Koziol, Herbert. 1937. *Handbuch der englischen Wortbildungslehre*. Heidelberg: Carl Winter's Universitätsbuchhandlung.

Kraemer, Helena C. & Christine M. Blasey. 2004. Centring in regression analyses: A strategy to prevent errors in statistical inference. *International Journal of Methods in Psychiatric Research* 13(3). 141–151.

Kučera, Henry & Winthrop Nelson Francis. 1967. *Computational analysis of present-day American English*. Providence, RI: Brown University Press.

Kuperman, Victor & Raymond Bertram. 2013. Moving spaces: Spelling alternation in English noun-noun compounds. *Language and Cognitive Processes* 28(7). 939–966.

Kuperman, Victor, Raymond Bertram & R. Harald Baayen. 2008. Morphological dynamics in compound processing. *Language and Cognitive Processes* 23(7-8). 1089–1132.

Kuperman, Victor, Robert Schreuder, Raymond Bertram & R. Harald Baayen. 2009. Reading polymorphemic Dutch compounds: Toward a multiple route model of lexical processing. *Journal of Experimental Psychology: Human Perception and Performance* 35(3). 876–895.

Lahav, Ran. 1989. Against compositionality: The case of adjectives. *Philosophical Studies: An International Journal for Philosophy in the Analytic Tradition* 57(3). 261–279.

Lahav, Ran. 1993. The combinatorial-connectionist debate and the pragmatics of adjectives. *Pragmatics and Cognition* 1(1). 71–88.

Lakoff, George & John Robert Ross. 1972. A note on anaphoric islands and causatives. *Linguistic Inquiry* 3(1). 121–125.

Landauer, Thomas K, Peter W. Foltz & Darrell Laham. 1998. An introduction to latent semantic analysis. *Discourse Processes* 25(2-3). 259–284.

Langacker, Ronald W. 1987. *Foundations of cognitive grammar: Vol. 1, theoretical prerequisites*. Stanford: Stanford University Press.

Langacker, Ronald W. 1988. A usage-based model. In Brygida Rudzka-Ostyn (ed.), *Topics in cognitive linguistics* (Current Issues in Linguistic Theory 50), 127–161. Amsterdam: John Benjamins.

Lapata, Mirella & Alex Lascarides. 2003. Detecting novel compounds: The role of distributional evidence. In *Proceedings of the tenth conference of the European chapter of the Association for Computational Linguistics– Vol. 1* (EACL '03), 235–242. Budapest, Hungary: Association for Computational Linguistics.

Leding, Juliana K., James Michael Lampinen, Norman W. Edwards & Timothy N. Odegard. 2007. The memory conjunction error paradigm: Normative data for conjunction triplets. *Behavior Research Methods* 39(4). 920–925.

Levi, Judith N. 1975. *The syntax and semantics of non-predicating adjectives in English.* University of Chicago dissertation.

Levi, Judith N. 1976. A semantic analysis of Hebrew compound nominals. In Peter Cole (ed.), *Studies in Modern Hebrew syntax and semantics: A transformational-generative approach*, 9–55. Amsterdam: North-Holland.

Levi, Judith N. 1977. The constituent structure of complex nominals or That's funny, you don't look like a noun! In Woodford A. Beach, Samuel E. Fox & Shulamith Philosoph (eds.), *Papers from the thirteenth regional meeting*, 325–338. Chicago Linguistic Society.

Levi, Judith N. 1978. *The syntax and semantics of complex nominals.* New York: Academic Press.

Levinson, Stephen C. 2000. *Presumptive meaning: The theory of generalized conversational implicature.* MIT press.

Li, Charles N. 1971. *Semantics and the structure of compounds in Chinese.* University of California at Berkeley dissertation.

Libben, Gary. 1994. How is morphological decomposition achieved? *Language and Cognitive Processes* 9(3). 369–391.

Libben, Gary. 1998. Semantic transparency in the processing of compounds: Consequences for representation, processing, and impairment. *Brain and Language* 61(1). 30–44.

Libben, Gary, Martha Gibson, Yeo Bom Yoon & Dominiek Sandra. 2003. Compound fracture: The role of semantic transparency and morphological headedness. *Brain and Language* 84. 50–64.

Lieber, Rochelle. 2004. *Morphology and lexical semantics.* Cambridge: Cambridge University Press.

Lin, Dekang. 1999. Automatic identification of non-compositional phrases. In *Proceedings of the 37th Annual Meeting of the Association for Computational Linguistics on Computational Linguistics* (ACL '99), 317–324. College Park, Maryland: Association for Computational Linguistics.

Löbner, Sebastian. 2013. *Understanding semantics.* 2nd edn. London & New York: Routledge.

Luce, Robert Duncan. 1959. *Individual choice behavior: A theoretical analysis.* New York: Wiley.

Lund, Kevin & Curt Burgess. 1996. Producing high-dimensional semantic spaces from lexical co-occurrence. *Behavior Research Methods, Instruments, & Computers* 28(2). 203–208.

Maguire, Phil, Barry Devereux, Fintan Costello & Arthur Cater. 2007. A reanalysis of the CARIN theory of conceptual combination. *Journal of Experimental Psychology. Learning, Memory & Cognition* 33(4). 811–821.

Manelis, Leon & David A. Tharp. 1977. The processing of affixed words. *Memory & Cognition* 5(6). 690–695.

Marelli, Marco, Georgiana Dinu, Roberto Zamparelli & Marco Baroni. 2015. Picking buttercups and eating butter cups: Spelling alternations, semantic relatedness, and their consequences for compound processing. *Applied Psycholinguistics* 36(6). 1421–1439.

Marelli, Marco & Claudio Luzzatti. 2012. Frequency effects in the processing of Italian nominal compounds: Modulation of headedness and semantic transparency. *Journal of Memory and Language* 66(4). 644–664.

Marslen-Wilson, William, Lorraine K. Tyler, Rachelle Waksler & Lianne Older. 1994. Morphology and meaning in the English mental lexicon. *Psychological Review* 101(1). 3–33.

McCarthy, Diana, Bill Keller & John Carroll. 2003. Detecting a continuum of compositionality in phrasal verbs. In *Proceedings of the ACL 2003 Workshop on Multiword Expressions: Analysis, Acquisition and Treatment* (MWE '03 18), 73–80. Sapporo, Japan: Association for Computational Linguistics.

McClelland, James L. & Karalyn Patterson. 2002a. 'Words or Rules' cannot exploit the regularity in exceptions. *Trends in Cognitive Sciences* 6(11). 464–465.

McClelland, James L. & Karalyn Patterson. 2002b. Rules or connections in past-tense inflections: What does the evidence rule out? *Trends in Cognitive Sciences* 6(11). 465–472.

Merriam-Webster. 2015. *Merriam-Webster Online Dictionary*. https : / / www . merriam-webster.com.

Meyer, Ralf. 1993. *Compound comprehension in isolation and in context: The contribution of conceptual and discourse knowledge to the comprehension of German novel noun-noun compounds* (Linguistische Arbeiten 299). Walter de Gruyter.

Mike. 2012. *History of flea markets*. Blog entry. https://web.archive.org/web/20120321163308/http://blog.aurorahistoryboutique.com/tag/fly-market/, accessed 2016-10-21.

Mikolov, Tomas, Kai Chen, Greg Corrado & Jeffrey Dean. 2013. Efficient estimation of word representations in vector space. *ArXiv e-prints*.

Miller, George A. 1978. Semantic relations among words. In Morris Halle, Joan Bresnan & Max Miller (eds.), *Linguistic theory and psychological reality*, 60–118. Cambridge, Massachusetts: MIT Press.

Miller, George A. 1998a. Foreword. In Christiane Fellbaum (ed.), *WordNet: An electronic lexical database*, xv–xxii. Cambridge, Massachusetts: MIT Press.

Miller, George A. 1998b. Nouns in WordNet. In Christiane Fellbaum (ed.), *WordNet: An electronic lexical database*, chap. 1, 23–46. Cambridge, Massachusetts: MIT Press.

Mitchell, Jeff & Mirella Lapata. 2008. Vector-based models of semantic composition. In *Proceedings of ACL-08: HLT*, 236–244. Columbus, Ohio: Association for Computational Linguistics.

Monsell, Stephen. 1985. Repetition and the lexicon. In Andrew W. Ellis (ed.), *Progress in the psychology of language*, vol. 2. Hove: Lawrence Erlbaum Associates Ltd.

Motsch, Wolfgang. 1981. Analyse von Komposita mit zwei nominalen Elementen. In Leonhard Lipka & Hartmut Günther (eds.), *Wortbildung*. Originally in Manfred Bierwisch & Karl Erich Heidolph (Eds.) (1970). Progress in linguistics. The Hague: Mouton. 208–223. Darmstadt: Wissenschaftliche Buchgesellschaft.

Nakagawa, Shinichi & Holger Schielzeth. 2013. A general and simple method for obtaining R2 from generalized linear mixed-effects models. *Methods in Ecology and Evolution* 4(2). 133–142.

Nelson, Douglas L., Cathy L. McEvoy & Thomas A. Schreiber. 1998. *The University of South Florida word association, rhyme, and word fragment norms.* http://w3.usf.edu/FreeAssociation/.

Norman, Geoff. 2010. Likert scales, levels of measurement and the "laws" of statistics. *Advances in Health Sciences Education* 15(5). 625–632.

Nunberg, Geoffrey, Ivan A. Sag & Thomas Wasow. 1994. Idioms. *Language* 70(3). 491–538.

Ó Séaghdha, Diarmuid. 2008. *Learning compound noun semantics.* Tech. rep. UCAM-CL-TR-735. University of Cambridge, Computer Laboratory.

Odegard, Timothy N., James M. Lampinen & Michael P. Toglia. 2005. Meaning's moderating effect on recollection rejection. *Journal of Memory and Language* 53(3). 416–429.

Olsen, Susan (ed.). 2010. *New impulses in word-formation* (Linguistische Berichte, Sonderheft 17). Hamburg: Buske.

Pan, Shimei & Kathleen R. McKeown. 1999. Word informativeness and automatic pitch accent modeling. In *Proceedings of EMNLP/VLC'99*, 148–157.

Partee, Barbara H. 1984. Compositionality. In Fred Landman & Frank Veltman (eds.), *Varieties of formal semantics*, 281–311. Reprinted in Partee, Barbara (2008). Compositionality in Formal Semantics. John Wiley & Sons, 153-181. Foris.

Partee, Barbara H. 1995. Lexical semantics and compositionality. In Lila Gleitman & Mark Liberman (eds.), *An invitation to cognitive science: Language*, 2nd edn., vol. 1, chap. 11, 311–360. Cambridge, Massachusetts: MIT Press.

Pham, Hien & R. Harald Baayen. 2013. Semantic relations and compound transparency: A regression study in CARIN theory. *Psihologija* 46(4). 455–478.

Pinker, Steven. 1984. *Language learnability and language development*. Cambridge, Massachusetts: Harvard University Press.

Pinker, Steven & Michael T. Ullman. 2002a. Combination and structure, not gradedness, is the issue. *Trends in Cognitive Sciences* 6(11). 472–474.

Pinker, Steven & Michael T. Ullman. 2002b. The past and future of the past tense. *Trends in Cognitive Sciences* 6(11). 456–463.

Plag, Ingo. 2003. *Word-formation in English*. Cambridge: Cambridge University Press.

Plag, Ingo & Gero Kunter. 2010. Constituent family size and compound stress assignment in English. In Susan Olsen (ed.), *New impulses in word-formation* (Linguistische Berichte, Sonderheft 17), 349–382. Hamburg: Buske.

Plag, Ingo, Gero Kunter & Sabine Lappe. 2007. Testing hypotheses about compound stress assignment in English: A corpus-based investigation. *Corpus Linguistics and Linguistic Theory* 3(2).

Plag, Ingo, Gero Kunter, Sabine Lappe & Maria Braun. 2008. The role of semantics, argument structure, and lexicalization in compound stress assignment in English. *Language* 84(4). 760–794.

Pollatsek, Alexander & Jukka Hyönä. 2005. The role of semantic transparency in the processing of Finnish compound words. *Language and Cognitive Processes* 20(1-2). 261–290.

Postal, Paul M. 1969. Anaphoric islands. In Robert I. Binnick, Alice Davison, Georgia M. Green & Jerry L. et al. Morgan (eds.), *Papers from the 5th regional meeting of the Chicago Linguistic Society*, 209–39. University of Chicago.

Pustejovsky, James. 1995. *The generative lexicon*. Cambridge, Massachusetts: MIT Press.

Pustejovsky, James & Peter G. Anick. 1988. On the semantic interpretation of nominals. In *Proceedings of the 12th Conference on Computational Linguistics - vol. 2* (COLING '88), 518–523. Budapest, Hungary: Association for Computational Linguistics.

Quine, Willard Van Orman. 1960. *Word and object*. Cambridge, Massachusetts: MIT Press.

Quinion, Michael. N.d. *World wide words. Entry for* Gravy train. http://www.worldwidewords.org/qa/qa-gra4.htm.

Quirk, Randolph, Sidney Greenbaum, Geoffrey Leech & Jan Swartvik. 1985. *A comprehensive grammar of the English language*. Harlow: Longman.

R Core Team. 2015. *R: A language and environment for statistical computing*. R Foundation for Statistical Computing. Vienna, Austria. https://www.R-project.org/.

Rastle, Kathleen, Matthew H. Davis & Boris New. 2004. The broth in my brother's brothel: Morpho-orthographic segmentation in visual word recognition. *Psychonomic Bulletin & Review* 11(6). 1090–1098.

Reddy, Siva, Diana McCarthy & Suresh Manandhar. 2011. An empirical study on compositionality in compound nouns. In *Proceedings of the 5th International Conference on Natural Language Processing*, 210–218. All data for the paper is available from the following site: http://sivareddy.in/papers/files/ijcnlp_compositionality_data.tgz. Chiang Mai, Thailand.

Ruge, Gerda. 1992. Experiments on linguistically-based term associations. *Information Processing & Management* 28(3). 317–332.

Rumelhart, David E. & James L. McClelland. 1986. On learning the past tense of English verbs. In David E. Rumelhart, James L. McClelland & the PDP Research Group (eds.), *Parallel distributed processing: Vol. 2 psychological and biological models*, 216–271. Cambridge, Massachusetts: MIT Press.

Sahlgren, Magnus. 2006. *The word-space model: Using distributional analysis to represent syntagmatic and paradigmatic relations between words in high-dimensional vector spaces*. Stockholm: Department of Linguistics, Stockholm University dissertation.

Sahlgren, Magnus. 2008. The distributional hypothesis. *Rivista di Linguistica (Italian Journal of Linguistics)* 20(1). 33–53.

Salton, Gerard & C. S. Yang. 1973. On the specification of term values in automatic indexing. *Journal of Documentation* 29(4). 351–372.

Sandra, Dominiek. 1990. On the representation and processing of compound words: Automatic access to constituent morphemes does not occur. *The Quarterly Journal of Experimental Psychology Section A* 42(3). 529–567.

Schäfer, Martin. 2013. Semantic transparency and anaphoric islands. In Pius ten Hacken & Claire Thomas (eds.), *The semantics of word formation and lexicalization*, 140–160. Edinburgh: Edinburgh University Press.

Schone, Patrick & Daniel Jurafsky. 2001. Is knowledge-free induction of multi-word unit dictionary headwords a solved problem? In *Proceedings of Empirical Methods in Natural Language Processing*. Pittsburgh, PA.

Schreuder, Robert & R. Harald Baayen. 1995. Modeling morphological processing. In L. B. Feldman (ed.), *Morphological aspects of language processing*, 131–154. Hillsdale, New Jersey: Lawrence Erlbaum.

Schreuder, Robert & R. Harald Baayen. 1997. How complex simplex words can be. *Journal of Memory and Language* 37(1). 118–139.

Schütze, Hinrich. 1993. Word space. In *Advances in neural information processing systems 5*, 895–902. Morgan Kaufmann.

Selkirk, Elisabeth O. 1982. *The syntax of words*. Cambridge, Massachusetts: MIT Press.

Shannon, Claude Elwood. 1948. A mathematical theory of communication. *Bell System Technical Journal* 27. 379–423, 623–656.

Shaoul, Cyrus & Chris Westbury. 2013. *A reduced redundancy USENET corpus (2005-2011)*. Edmonton, AB: University of Alberta. http://www.psych.ualberta.ca/~westburylab/downloads/usenetcorpus.download.html.

Shaw, J. Howard. 1978. *Motivierte Komposita in der deutschen und englischen Gegenwartssprache*. Tübingen: Narr.

Shoben, Edward J. 1991. Predicating and nonpredicating combinations. In Paula J. Schwanenflugel (ed.), *The psychology of word meanings*, 117–135. Hillsdale, NJ, England: Lawrence Erlbaum Associates.

Smith, Edward E., Daniel N. Osherson, Lance J. Rips & Margaret Keane. 1988. Combining prototypes: A selective modification model. *Cognitive Science* 12(4). 485–527.

Spalding, Thomas L. & Christina L. Gagné. 2008. Commentary: CARIN theory reanalysis reanalyzed: A comment on Maguire, Devereux, Costello, and Cater (2007). *Journal of Experimental Psychology. Learning, Memory & Cognition* 34(6). 1573–1578.

Spalding, Thomas L., Christina L. Gagné, Allison Mullaly & Hongbo Ji. 2010. Relation-based interpretation of noun-noun phrases: A new theoretical approach. In Susan Olsen (ed.), *New impulses in word-formation* (Linguistische Berichte, Sonderheft 17), 283–315. Hamburg: Buske.

Sporleder, Caroline & Linlin Li. 2009. Unsupervised recognition of literal and non-literal use of idiomatic expressions. In *Proceedings of the 12th Conference of the European Chapter of the Association for Computational Linguistics* (EACL '09), 754–762. Athens, Greece: Association for Computational Linguistics.

Stanners, Robert F., James J. Neiser, William P. Hernon & Roger Hall. 1979. Memory representation for morphologically related words. *Journal of Verbal Learning and Verbal Behavior* 18(4). 399–412.

Storms, Gert & Edward J. Wisniewski. 2005. Does the order of head noun and modifier explain response times in conceptual combination? *Memory & Cognition* 33(5). 852–861.

Sweet, Henry. 1891. *A new English grammar. Logical and historical. Part I: Introduction, phonology, and accidence.* Oxford: Oxford University Press.

Taft, Marcus & Kenneth I. Forster. 1975. Lexical storage and retrieval of prefixed words. *Journal of Verbal Learning and Verbal Behavior* 14(6). 638–647.

ten Hacken, Pius. 1994. *Defining morphology: A principled approach to determining the boundaries of compounding, derivation, and inflection.* Hildesheim: Olms.

Tic Douloureux, P. 1971. A note on one's privates. In Arnold M. Zwicky, Peter H. Salus, Robert I. Binnick & Anthony L. Vanek (eds.), *Studies out in left field: Defamatory essays presented to James D. McCawley on the occasion of his 33rd or 34th birthday*, 45–51.

Titone, Debra A. & Cynthia M. Connine. 1999. On the compositional and noncompositional nature of idiomatic expressions. *Journal of Pragmatics* 31(12). 1655–1674.

Travis, Charles. 2000. *Unshadowed thought.* Cambridge, Massachusetts: Harvard University Press.

Trips, Carola & Jaklin Kornfilt. 2017. *Further investigations into the nature of phrasal compounding.* Berlin: Language Science Press.

Turney, Peter D. & Patrick Pantel. 2010. From frequency to meaning: Vector space models of semantics. *Journal of artificial intelligence research* 37. 141–188.

Vendler, Zeno. 1963. The grammar of goodness. *The Philosophical Review* 72(4). 446–465.

Wagner, Anton R. & Robert A. Rescorla. 1972. A theory of Pavlovian conditioning: Variations in the effectiveness of reinforcement and nonreinforcement. In Abraham H. Black & William Frederick Prokasy (eds.), *Classical conditioning II: Current research and theory*, 64–99. New York, NY: Appleton-Century-Crofts.

Walter, Liz. 2014. *A bit up and down– describing emotion with metaphors of height.* Cambridge dictionaries online. From the blog "About Words", available at http://dictionaryblog.cambridge.org/2014/09/17/a-bit-up-and-down-describing-emotion-with-metaphors-of-height/, accessed 2015-09-14.

Ward, Gregory, Richard Sproat & Gail McKoon. 1991. A pragmatic analysis of so-called anaphoric islands. *Language* 67(3). 439–474.

References

Warren, Beatrice. 1978. *Semantic patterns of noun-noun compounds* (Gothenburg Studies in English 41). Gothenburg: Acta Universitatis Gothoburgensis.

Watt, William C. 1975. The indiscreteness with which impenetrables are penetrated. *Lingua* 37. 95–128.

Wickelgren, Wayne A. 1969. Context-sensitive coding, associative memory, and serial order in (speech) behavior. *Psychological Review* 76(1). 1–15.

Wisniewski, Edward J. & Gregory L. Murphy. 2005. Frequency of relation type as a determinant of conceptual combination: A reanalysis. *Journal of Experimental Psychology: Learning, Memory, and Cognition* 31(1). 169–174.

Wong, Mungchen & Caren Rotello. 2010. Conjunction errors and semantic transparency. *Memory and Cognition* 38. 47–56.

Zwitserlood, Pienie. 1994. The role of semantic transparency in the processing and representation of Dutch compounds. *Language and cognitive processes* 9(3). 341–368.

Name index

Language index

Subject index

adjective
  color, 83–85
  intersective modification, 78–79, 83
  lexical blocking, 85
  non-predicating, 96
  non-subsective modification, 81–82
  pragmatic anomaly, 86
  predicative, 79
  privative, 82, 83
  subsective modification, 79–81
  technical and scientific, 79
    see also adjective noun constructions
adjective noun constructions
  Pustejovsky's examples, 117–119
  distributional semantics model, 140
  formal semantic analysis, 78–86
  in the Reddy et al. dataset, 163–164
  qualia structure, 121
ambiguity, 164
  habitual vs. instantaneous readings, 111
  in Fanselow's system, 115
  vs. analytic indeterminacy, 93
  vs. promiscuity, 163, 164
analytic indeterminacy, 92–93, 163

  experiment on, 99
anaphoric island, 59–60

basic relations
  Fanselow's system, 107–110, 112–115
BiasC, *see* compound measures
BNC, 21, 219, 220, 222, 223, 226–229, 231, 232, 263
  characterization of, 226

CARIN model, 24–28, 142, 217, 219
CELEX, 21, 31, 34, 50, 149, 157, 222, 223, 226–229, 236, 263, 264
  and lexicalized compounds, 35–36, 222
  characterization of, 227
centering, 47, 240
  effect on collinearity measures, 240
choice rule, 26
collinearity, 178, 240
  centering and, 240
common noun, 103
complex nominals
  case relations, 88–89
  conjunction behavior, 88
  nondegreeness, 88
compositionality, 66–68, 157
  Fanselow on, 107
  Lahav on, 84
  conventionality vs., 71–72

www.ingramcontent.com/pod-product-compliance
Lightning Source LLC
Chambersburg PA
CBHW081112160426
42814CB00035B/289